DEEPENING LOCAL DEMOCRACY IN LATIN AMERICA

Benjamin Goldfrank

DEEPENING LOCAL DEMOCRACY IN LATIN AMERICA

Participation, Decentralization, and the Left

The Pennsylvania State University Press
University Park, Pennsylvania

Library of Congress Cataloging-in-Publication Data

Goldfrank, Benjamin.
Deepening local democracy in Latin America : participation,
decentralization, and the left / Benjamin Goldfrank.
p.   cm.
Includes bibliographical references and index.
Summary: "Addresses the question of why institutions meant
to attract citizen participation succeed in strengthening civil
society and improving state responsiveness and transparency in
some places, but fail in others. Focuses on urban politics in
Porto Alegre (Brazil), Montevideo (Uruguay), and Caracas
(Venezuela)"—Provided by publisher.
ISBN 978-0-271-03794-3 (cloth : alk. paper)
1. Political participation—Latin America—Case studies.
2. Municipal government—Latin America—Case studies.
3. Porto Alegre (Rio Grande do Sul, Brazil))—Politics and government.
4. Montevideo (Uruguay)—Politics and government.
5. Caracas (Venezuela)—Politics and government.
6. Comparative government—Case studies.
I. Title.

JS2300.G65 2011
320.8098—dc22
2010041995

Contents

LIST OF FIGURES   vii

LIST OF TABLES   viii

ACKNOWLEDGMENTS   ix

LIST OF ACRONYMS   xi

Overview   1

1
Democracy, Participation, and Decentralization   11

2
A Tale of Three Cities   34

3
Caracas: Scarce Resources, Fierce Opposition, and Restrictive Design   84

4
Montevideo: From Rousing to Regulating Participation   121

5
Porto Alegre: Making Participatory Democracy Work   165

6
Stronger Citizens, Stronger State?   219

Conclusion:
The Diffusion of Participatory Democracy and the Rise of the Left   247

BIBLIOGRAPHY   267

INDEX   292

Figures

2.1 Scope of jurisdiction over urban services 71

2.2 Municipal budget per capita (first term in office) 73

2.3 Decentralization indicators 74

3.1 Parish government structure 99

3.2 Level of need and investments, by parish (1993) 104

3.3 Level of need and investments, by parish (1994) 105

3.4 Level of need and vote for LCR, by parish 119

4.1 Redesigning structures of participation 143

4.2 Degree of possibility to influence decisions in different spheres 149

4.3 What should be done to improve decentralization? 150

4.4 Poverty and spending 159

5.1 Structure of participatory budgeting 195

5.2 How could the PB be improved? 199

5.3 Underserved population and budget assembly participation (1993) 205

5.4 Underserved population and budget assembly participation, by district (1995) 206

5.5 Why do you participate in PB assemblies? 207

5.6 Investments and budget assembly participation, 1989–2000 211

5.7 Investments planned and budget assembly participation, by district (1991–1994) 212

5.8 Investments planned and budget assembly participation (1995–2000) 213

5.9 Population size and budget assembly participation (1993) 214

5.10 Population size and budget assembly participation (1998) 215

6.1 Principal problems of the neighborhood 228

Tables

2.1 Vote share for the PT in Porto Alegre   39
2.2 Municipal and metropolitan population size in 1990   47
2.3 Municipal land area   48
2.4 Basic service provision   53
2.5 Socioeconomic indicators (circa 1990)   54
2.6 Number of registered neighborhood associations   56
2.7 Size of municipal bureaucracy   63
4.1 Poverty, vote share, and spending   161
4.2 Poverty, spending, and participation   162
4.3 Age and education distributions   164
5.1 Opinion of participatory budgeting   198
5.2 Need, spending, population size, and participation
     (district-years)   216
5.3 Distributional formula   217
6.1 Summary   221
6.2 Favorable ratings of city services (in percentages)   229
6.3 Increased street paving   233
6.4 Municipal government housing construction from 1950 to 2000   233
6.5 Participation in civic organizations   240
6.6 Quality of local democracy   246

Acknowledgments

Over the course of several years of researching and writing this book in several different locations, I have accumulated far too many debts to acknowledge them all individually here. What follows is my best attempt to recognize all those who have helped me in some way or another to make the book possible.

Most of all, I want to thank the dozens of people who allowed me into their homes and offices for often lengthy and always interesting interviews in Caracas, Montevideo, and Porto Alegre. Many of them are named in the course of the book; I have changed the names of those who were not public officials to protect their identities (and of one city employee who preferred anonymity). While all translations of interviews (and of passages from written work) are my own, I owe thanks to Ivette Goldfrank and Nicole Caso for their help translating some particularly tricky *dichos*.

In each of the three research sites, some individuals went beyond what I expected to provide me with extra help, facilitating access to libraries and data and assisting me in arranging important interviews, and to them I am particularly grateful: Rosangel Alvarez, Carlos Contreras, Ana Maria Sanjuán, and Edgardo Lander in Caracas; Rita Grisolia, Alicia Veneziano, Javier Vidal, Maria Elena Laurnaga, Luis Eduardo González, and María José Doyenart in Montevideo; and, in Porto Alegre, Marcello Baquero and Manuel Passos at the Universidade Federal do Rio Grande do Sul, Regina Pozzobon and Sérgio Baierle at CIDADE, and Luciano Brunet, Marlene Steffen, and Assis Brasil at City Hall. I also benefited from frequent conversations and pooled resources with fellow researchers to whom I remain grateful: Gianpaolo Baiocchi in Porto Alegre and Daniel Chavez in Montevideo.

In Berkeley, my two chief advisors, Ruth Berins Collier and David Collier, encouraged me to pursue the study of what had originally been a little-known subject—participatory budgeting—and then consistently pushed me to clarify my concepts and arguments in countless conversations and email exchanges over a number of years. Chris Ansell and Peter Evans likewise provided excellent advice at crucial periods of the research and writing, particularly for the Montevideo case. Michael Watts offered sage advice in the early stages of designing the research project. I also owe thanks to several fellow students at Berkeley for their comments on different aspects of the project: Aaron Schneider, Laura Henry, Loren Landau, Zach Elkins, and Ken Foster. I am also grateful for the generous financial support for the fieldwork and writeup that I received from a number of sources, including the US Fulbright Commission and several institutions at UC Berkeley: the Department of Political Science, the Institute for International Studies, the Graduate Division, and the Center for Latin American Studies.

In Albuquerque, I am grateful to Kenneth Roberts and Andrew Schrank, who provided encouragement and advice, and to Mark Peceny, who read an early draft of the manuscript and offered excellent suggestions. I am also thankful for the Eugene Gallegos Lectureship from the University of New Mexico. In South Orange, I would like to thank Martin Edwards for his advice and support. Several colleagues also provided valuable feedback at conferences where parts of this book were presented, including Brian Wampler, Stephanie McNulty, Yanina Welp, Egon Montecinos, Carlos Mascareño, Alberto Ford, Eliza Willis, and Alfred Montero.

In various places, friends and family both old and new gave me immeasurable *apoyo moral*. In Caracas, the Flores Lugos brought me into their home and made me part of the family. In wintry Montevideo, Magdalena and Mario offered a warm welcome, as did Rita, Fernando, and Carlitos. And in Porto Alegre, Aaron, Gianpaolo, Jorge, and Jane were constant companions.

My parents, Lois and Wally Goldfrank, provided encouragement, an occasional writing refuge, and eventually, babysitting. Thanks especially to my father for reading and commenting on more than one draft.

Finally, I thank Ivette and Diego for their inspiration and their endless patience.

Acronyms

AD	Acción Democrática (Democratic Action)
ADEOM	Asociación de Empleados y Obreros Municipales (Association of Municipal Employees and Workers)
APRA	Alianza Popular Revolucionaria Americana (American Popular Revolutionary Alliance, Peru)
CAMP	Centro Assessoria Multi Profissional (Multiprofessional Consulting Center)
CANTV	Compañía Anónima Nacional Teléfonos de Venezuela (Venezuelan National Telephone Company)
CAR	Centro Administrativo Regional (Regional Administrative Center)
CCZ	Centro Comunal Zonal (Zonal Community Center)
CEB	Comunidade Eclesial de Base (Ecclesial Base Community)
CESAP	Centro al Servicio de la Acción Popular (Center in Service of Popular Action)
CIDC	Centro de Investigaciones y Desarrollo Cultural (Center for Research and Cultural Development)
CIESU	Centro de Informaciones y Estudios del Uruguay (Center for Information and Study of Uruguay)
COPEI	Comité de Organización Política Electoral Independiente (Independent Organizational Committee for Electoral Politics; Christian Democratic Party)
DS	Democracia Socialista (Socialist Democracy)
FA	Frente Amplio (Broad Front)
FACUR	Federación de Asociaciones de Comunidades Urbanas (Federation of Urban Community Associations)
FASE	Federação de Orgãos para Assistência Social e Educacional (Federation of Social and Educational Assistance Organizations)
FRACAB	Federação Riograndense de Associações Comunitárias e de Amigos de Bairros (Federation of Community and Neighborhood Associations of Rio Grande do Sul)

FUCVAM   Federación Uruguaya de Cooperativas de Viviendas por Ayuda Mutua (Uruguayan Federation of Mutual Aid Housing Cooperatives)

GAPLAN   Gabinete de Planejamento (Planning Cabinet)

HIPC   Highly Indebted Poor Countries

IADB   Inter-American Development Bank

LCR   La Causa Я, or La Causa Radical (the Radical Cause)

MDB   Movimento Democrático Brasileiro (Brazilian Democratic Movement)

MINDUR   Ministerio de Desarrollo Urbano (Ministry of Urban Development)

MOVEMO   Movimiento de Vecinos de Montevideo (Montevideo Neighborhood Movement)

MOVIDE   Movimiento Pro-Vivienda Decorosa (Movement for Decent Housing)

MPP   Movimiento de Participación Popular (Popular Participation Movement)

PB   Participatory Budgeting

PC do B   Partido Comunista do Brasil (Communist Party of Brazil)

PDT   Partido Democrático Trabalhista (Democratic Labor Party)

PFL   Partido da Frente Liberal (Liberal Front Party)

PLEMUU   Plenario de Mujeres del Uruguay (Uruguayan Women's Assembly)

PMDB   Partido do Movimento Democrático Brasileiro (Party of the Brazilian Democratic Movement)

PPB   Partido Progressista Brasileiro (Brazilian Progressive Party)

PPT   Patria Para Todos (Homeland for All)

PSDB   Partido da Social Democracia Brasileira (Brazilian Social Democratic Party)

PT   Partido dos Trabalhadores (Workers' Party)

PTB   Partido Trabalhista Brasileiro (Brazilian Labor Party)

SIMPA   Sindicato dos Municipários de Porto Alegre (Union of Municipal Workers of Porto Alegre)

UAMPA   União de Associações de Moradores de Porto Alegre (Union of Residents Associations of Porto Alegre)

UAPE   Unidad Asesora de Proyectos Especiales (Advisory Unit for Special Projects)

Overview

Ever since Latin America began a phase of democratic renewal toward the end of the twentieth century, pessimistic voices about the quality of the new democracies have dominated. Political leaders, citizens, and scholars alike lament the clientelism, corruption, and ineffective and unaccountable governments that, among other ills, have plagued the region. At the same time that national democratic regimes are criticized as "shallow," however, there is growing optimism about the potential of experiments in participatory government to deepen democracy at the local level. Such experiments became increasingly common in the 1990s, as voters in an ever-larger number of cities chose political parties on the Left that advocated giving citizens a more direct role in deciding public policy. By the year 2000, Left-leaning mayors had governed dozens of important cities, including the capitals of Brazil, Colombia, El Salvador, Mexico, Peru, Uruguay, and Venezuela. The new officeholders implemented a wide array of novel forms of citizen participation, which met with varying degrees of success. Many of them proved unsustainable, but a few endured and even went on to become models of how to deepen democracy for activists, scholars, and international development organizations.

This book examines the Left's participatory innovations, asking why only some experiments succeeded in enhancing the quality of local democracy.[1] I compare three initially similar participation programs that eventually yielded

1. There is a rich and growing literature on municipal government in Latin America (see, inter alia, Ziccardi 1991; Reilly 1995; Borja and Castells 1997; Dietz and Shidlo 1998; Myers and Dietz 2002), and particularly on the Left's experiments in participatory democracy (see, inter alia, Alvarez 1993; Rodriguez 1993; Jacobi 1994; Bava 1995; Fox 1995; Winn 1995; Abers 1996, 2000; Stolowicz 1999; Baierle 1998; Santos 1998; Schönwälder 1998, 2002; Nylen 2003; Baiocchi 2003, 2005; Wampler 2007a).

widely different results. Heading each experiment was a party that had won the mayor's seat for the first time with the explicit promise of participatory reforms in order to deepen democracy: the Workers' Party (Partido dos Trabalhadores, PT) in Porto Alegre, Brazil (1989–2004); the Broad Front (Frente Amplio, FA) in Montevideo, Uruguay (1990–present); and the Radical Cause (La Causa Radical, LCR) in Libertador, the largest municipality of the metropolitan area of Caracas,[2] Venezuela (1993–95). The core of their reform efforts focused on creating new institutions to give citizens influence over government spending, whereas prior administrations made budget decisions behind closed doors.

How successful were the new institutions in actually attracting and sustaining a large number of citizen participants and in stimulating new civic associations? What were the effects of the participatory mechanisms on improving local government transparency and responsiveness? The answers to these questions varied in each case, as will be shown in more detail in the following chapters. In brief, Porto Alegre's participatory budget process met each of these goals, becoming an international reference. In Montevideo, the participation program was less capable of sustaining a large number of participants or stimulating civic associations, but government transparency and responsiveness improved considerably, earning the program widespread public approval. Finally, the experiment in Caracas essentially failed. These outcomes lead to the central puzzle examined in this book: why do participatory experiments aid in deepening democracy in some cities but not in others?

The recent boom of studies on participatory local democracy in Latin America has yet to produce compelling cross-national comparative analyses to provide an answer. Much of the literature on participation programs is limited to individual success stories that ignore the politics of participation, that is, the motivations and strategies of the key actors advocating and resisting participatory institutions. And the new scholarly attention to the region's contemporary wave of presidential victories for the Left has all but ignored that the tide shifted locally first. Before addressing the central puzzle, then, we should examine two prior questions: why parties on the Left rose to local power in so many major cities in the 1980s and 1990s and why they chose to emphasize participatory democracy.

Three roughly simultaneous trends abetted the Left's local rise and participatory turn. While *political decentralization* provided Left parties with

---

2. Except where noted, the references to Caracas indicate the municipality of Libertador, which contains the city's historical center and whose government is known as Caracas City Hall (Alcaldía de Caracas).

the opportunity to run for local office, *urban economic crises* gave citizens reason to consider voting for alternatives to the populist or centrist parties holding national power, and *the Left's own ideological transformation*—with a new commitment to democracy—made it more appealing to the electorate. Until the late 1970s, when democratic transitions began in Latin America, many countries were politically centralized; they had either suspended or never held elections for all local government officials. Since that time, nearly every country in the region has implemented decentralization reforms (Campbell 2003, 3–4), including the introduction (or reintroduction) of direct elections for mayors in major cities. For example, Peru, Uruguay, and Brazil reintroduced elections for mayors of all cities in 1980, 1984, and 1985, respectively, while Colombia in 1988 and Venezuela in 1989 allowed voters to directly elect mayors (and governors, in Venezuela) for the first time in history. By 2000, Mexico, Chile, and Argentina had instituted unprecedented mayoral elections in their national capitals.

Region-wide moves toward democratic elections, in most cases both nationally and locally, overlapped with the combustible combination of rapid urbanization and impoverishment of the so-called lost decade of the 1980s and continuing economic stagnation of the next decade. The eruption of urban crises can be traced to the collapse of the import-substitution industrialization (ISI) model under the weight of the debt crisis and its replacement with a neoliberal export-oriented model. During the peak performance years of ISI, from roughly the late 1940s to the late 1960s, the major cities grew at tremendous rates (Portes and Roberts 2005, 44), making Latin America the world region with the most urbanized population by the end of the period. By the early 1990s, it led the world at a rate of 71 percent urban (Dillinger 1994, 5), with nearly a third of the population living in cities with over a million inhabitants (Angotti 1996, 13). With urban growth came increased poverty, even before the abandonment of ISI. As the rural poor moved to the cities, lured by subsidies for food and utilities and labor rights for unionized workers (Eckstein 2006, 10, 35), shantytowns mushroomed in the peripheral areas of major cities, and mansions in many formerly wealthy neighborhoods in city centers became overcrowded tenements.

Whatever problems the region's cities faced in the ISI era paled in comparison to those of the neoliberal era inaugurated in the 1980s with the debt crisis and the worst recession since the Great Depression. During that decade, while some rural areas benefited, the major cities saw falling incomes, rising inflation, unemployment, and inequality, and the reduction or elimination of subsidies and welfare programs (Villa and Rodríguez 1996; Burki and Edwards 1996; Portes and Roberts 2005). The cutbacks of food and utilities subsidies were often accompanied by currency devaluations, making cost of living increases in urban areas even more acute (Eckstein 2006, 27). Throughout the region, urban poverty grew in the eighties and nineties (Burki and Edwards 1996, 18; Rodriguez and Winchester 1996, 78–79), and by 1986 55 percent of the poor already lived in urban areas (Reilly 1995, 5). In Brazil, over two-thirds of the poor live in urban areas, and nearly one-third of the poor and one-third of all Brazilians live in the nine metropolitan regions with over a million inhabitants (Valladares and Coelho 1995). Urban service provision, including water, sanitation, solid waste collection, education, health care, and transportation, also suffered (Dillinger 1994, 5; McCarney 1996, 7), leading scholars to speak of Latin America's "urban crisis" during the 1980s (Castells, Belil, and Borja 1989, 32–36).

One response to the decline of urban living conditions was popular pressure, in both organized and unorganized forms: popular movement organizations for urban reform and more or less spontaneous riots against government austerity programs, perhaps most famously the "Caracazo" in Venezuela in 1989 (see, inter alia, Eckstein 1989; Escobar and Alvarez 1992; Walton 1989; López Maya 1999a). Voting Left parties and/or mayors into office has been another response, especially in cities with relatively high union membership, relatively large middle-class populations, and organized popular movements. The urban lower and middle classes were hit hardest by the urban crisis, and in several of the largest, most industrialized cities, they coalesced in support of new Left parties, at least temporarily. These constituencies have shared interests in defending a stronger role for the state, which had provided employment as well as subsidies and services, and in finding a more democratic interlocutor than had been available under the previous authoritarian and/or clientelist local governments.

For frustrated urban voters in the 1980s and 1990s, new or "renovated" parties on the Left offered a potential substitute as they renounced violence, embraced democracy, and proposed more collaborative state-society relations. During the preceding years of brutal military dictatorships and mostly failed guerrilla warfare, major portions of the Latin American Left underwent a significant ideological transformation.[3] The chief element was the change from

3. A fairly extensive literature has analyzed this transformation (see especially Angell 1996; Roberts 1998; Robinson 1992; Castañeda 1994; and, for a critical view, Petras 1997 and Petras and Veltmeyer 2005). The major catalysts of the ideological changes included the failure of most Latin American guerrilla movements to win or hold power, the installation of authoritarian regimes throughout much of the region, and, to a lesser extent, a reevaluation of Eastern European Communism before and after the fall of the Berlin Wall.

seeing democracy as bourgeois formalism or, at best, as an instrument to achieve power, to adopting democracy as a fundamental value and to deepening democracy as a permanent goal.[4] Deepening democracy became the "master frame" for both social movements and political parties on the Left and suggested "both procedural and substantive connotations, ranging from popular participation in the policymaking process to redistributive socioeconomic reforms" (Roberts 1998, 3). Parallel to its valorization of democracy, the renovated Left abandoned the "fetishism of armed struggle" (Robinson 1992, 5) to focus on elections and nonviolent social movement organizing and protest. The Workers' Party, the Broad Front, and the Radical Cause have all been seen as representative of this transformation of the Left. Indeed, several analysts have lumped the three parties together as embodiments of what they see as a positive trend: Angell (1996, 11–18) labels them the social democratic Left, Castañeda (1994, 136–55, 171–74) calls them the reformist Left, and Robinson (1992) sees them—as members of the São Paulo Forum[5]—as part of a new Left.

Importantly, while this new Left retained its classic positions such as anti-imperialism, redistribution, social justice, and a strong, interventionist state, the conceptualization of the state changed. The notion of an all-knowing and powerful centralized state gave way to calls for a permeable, transparent, decentralized state that would cogovern with civil society. This reconceptualization of the state, based partly on a rejection of the Soviet model, was connected to the revalorization of democracy. The radical, socialist, or deep democracy that the new Left parties aspired to signified consolidating and moving beyond periodic elections and individual liberties to the creation of more regular mechanisms by which citizens could collectively and directly influence state policy and monitor state performance. Decentralization would be a stepping-stone on the path to opening the state to citizen control. Formulating the public interest within the new participatory mechanisms would leave the state "less subordinated to the private appropriation of its resources" and result in public policy oriented toward generating social equality (Dagnino, Olvera, and Panfichi 2006, 48).

These ideological changes involved reconceiving other past practices and positions of the Left that prevented it from appealing to a broader electorate. Several parties moved away from Leninist, top-down, vanguardist

---

4. One of the classic statements on this change was written by Francisco Weffort (1989), one of the leading theorists for the Workers' Party in the 1980s.

5. The São Paulo Forum is a collection of dozens of parties and movements on the Left that hold occasional conferences, with its first hosted by the PT at the start of the 1990s.

organizations and toward creating democratic processes for selecting candidates and deciding party policy. Many Left leaders also vowed respect for the autonomy of social movements, which militants had previously often viewed as party vehicles. The focus on the working class as the sole bearers of "the revolution" has also been redirected. While organized labor remains a, if not the, central constituency of the democratic Left, a variety of social movements advancing claims based on issues of gender and racial equality, and consumption, services, and the environment have also gained significance. Likewise, the new Left parties began speaking less of *the* working class and more of working classes in the plural. Given the small size of unionized labor in Latin America, organizing along strict class lines has always produced relatively small voting blocs for Left parties, especially where facing competition from populists. In order to build and consolidate long-term power, the renovated Left realized it had to move beyond the core of union activists to gain the support of middle- and lower-class voters so as to create a broad, multiclass majority. The Left's proposed participatory mechanisms could contribute in this regard by helping to aggregate the diverse interests of the urban popular sector and to develop a common identity based on active citizenship. In other words, though party leaders never stated such aims publicly, some hoped that their participatory endeavors would help attract new adherents and win future elections.

It is perhaps not surprising, given the confluence of novel local elections, urban crises, and progressive ideological transformations, that the new democratic Left swept into office in many of Latin America's major cities starting in the 1980s. More interesting are the innovative participatory institutions that Left parties subsequently implemented and their differing effects on the quality of local democracy. When the PT, the FA, and LCR won power in Porto Alegre, Montevideo, and Caracas, each promised to deepen democracy through new channels of citizen participation. Their reforms bore a striking resemblance. Specifically, there was a focus on holding public assemblies to encourage debate over community priorities for investments in public works projects and social programs, investments that represented between 10 and 20 percent of the budget in all three cities. Each administration included measures to decentralize administrative functions as well. To facilitate widespread citizen involvement, each city was divided into a roughly equal number of districts: sixteen in Porto Alegre, eighteen in Montevideo, and nineteen in Caracas. The new institutions eventually included both open public assemblies involving direct volunteer participation and also smaller district-level forums for which participants were selected through some established procedure as representatives.

In the first year, hundreds and sometimes thousands of citizens in each city showed up to identify and prioritize projects for inclusion in the budget. However, within a few years, participation rates in Porto Alegre's participatory budget process had jumped, foretelling its future success, while the number of participants had stagnated in Montevideo and declined drastically in Caracas. Existing studies cannot explain why only Porto Alegre's participation program achieved each of the Left's goals of promoting an active citizenry, opening the local administration to public scrutiny, and responding effectively to a backlog of demands for government services, while initially similar programs fell short in Montevideo and especially Caracas.

The main argument I advance in this book is that two factors best explain these contrasting outcomes: the degree of national decentralization of authority and resources to municipal government, and the level of institutionalization of local opposition parties. These factors strongly shaped the ability of the progressive incumbents to design meaningful participatory institutions that could attract sustained citizen involvement. Only in Porto Alegre and Montevideo did the city governments have this capacity, because only in Brazil and Uruguay had the central state devolved sufficient jurisdiction and resources to the local level. The differing levels of institutionalization of local opposition parties had two important consequences for the design of the new participation programs. One was that while in Montevideo and Caracas the so-called traditional parties that had dominated politics for decades and developed strong organizations and societal roots had the motivation and the resources to resist the FA's and LCR's participatory channels, in Porto Alegre the PT faced feeble opposition from divided, weakly institutionalized rival parties that had few resources to act against the participation program or to try to shape its design to their advantage. The other consequence was that community organizations in Caracas and Montevideo were linked to either the opposition or incumbent parties, and they did not push for power in the new participation programs. In Porto Alegre, however, community organizations did not have strong party loyalties. Although many such groups engaged in clientelist relations, most were relatively autonomous and even mercenary, cultivating and breaking ties with different parties and constantly pressing for material improvements and for greater leverage in municipal politics. Porto Alegre's community organizations thus played a major role in shaping the ultimate design of the PT's participation program.

Thus, while the participation programs originally looked quite similar and the PT, FA, and LCR shared the same goals, the eventual design of the new institutions as well as the effects on the quality of democracy differed dramatically. In Caracas, nationally centralized authority and strongly institutionalized local opposition parties led to a *restrictive* design, in which the range of issues debated was narrow, the participants lacked decision-making power, and the structure privileged district boards, controlled by political parties, over the arenas for volunteer participation. This restrictive design contributed to a vicious cycle, in which the citizens' lack of influence over important issues and the continued dominance of party representatives discouraged participation as well as formation of new civic associations. In turn, the limited jurisdictional scope of the local government, paucity of municipal funds, and sabotage by the opposition impeded the government's ability to respond capably to citizen demands, thereby diminishing the incentive to participate. Overall, democracy remained shallow in Caracas.

Montevideo's pattern of significantly decentralized authority in the context of a strongly institutionalized opposition yielded a *regulated* design. I give it that label because, after beginning with a more informal structure without designated seats for political parties, the FA was essentially forced by the opposition to regulate participation. As in Caracas, seats on district boards were set aside for party members, some to represent the incumbents and others reserved for the opposition. While the range of issues was fairly broad, the role of citizens in decision making was limited. With this regulated design, participants saw little connection between their attendance at meetings and actual policy outcomes. Without a direct link between participation and the advances in service provision that were realized, residents had little incentive to become involved in the program, either individually or collectively. Uruguay's high degree of national decentralization thus allowed for the FA's partial success in Montevideo. Establishing effective local government represents a clear improvement over the past, even if incomplete.

Last, the weakly institutionalized parties in Porto Alegre, combined with Brazil's high degree of decentralization, allowed the development of an *open* design, which let participants engage in genuine deliberation, debating and voting on the most important city services and the most needed public works projects in their neighborhoods. Their votes determine how the government allocates its investment resources and in which neighborhoods. Their votes thus represent the exercise of real political authority. The range of issues open to debate was also widest, and in contrast to Caracas and Montevideo, there was no formal arena for party representatives. The open design of Porto

Alegre's participatory budgeting produced a virtuous cycle of deepening democracy. Participants saw the extension of the services they had prioritized, participated again, and revitalized old civic associations or formed new ones. Further, the participants demanded greater transparency and more decision-making power, supported higher tax rates, obtained greater service provision, and intensified their involvement, thus continuing the cycle.

Not surprisingly, the comparative study of Caracas, Montevideo, and Porto Alegre suggests that designing meaningful local participatory institutions is facilitated where decentralization brings both resources and responsibilities to local government. But one of the key discoveries of this study is the potential for strongly institutionalized parties to undermine the democracy-enhancing benefits of decentralization. This study also may provide insight into the rise of the Left in the region, the spread of participatory experiments under the Left's national governments, and the international diffusion of participatory budgeting under governments of varying ideological tendencies. Significantly, the participatory experiences in all three cities eventually affected the national politics of Brazil, Uruguay, and Venezuela, showing that even those institutions that do not entirely succeed can have important repercussions. The FA's only moderately successful program in Montevideo helped the party not only to hold on to local power but ultimately to win the presidency under its first mayor, Tabaré Vázquez, and to spread participation programs throughout Uruguay. And LCR's mostly failed program in Caracas would serve later as a reference for the Bolivarian Revolution of President Hugo Chávez, as its mayor, Aristóbulo Istúriz, played prominent roles in the Constituent Assembly and the Chávez administration. Under Chávez, Venezuela is now host to the most extensive and controversial experiment in participatory democracy in Latin America, if not the world. Of course, Porto Alegre, the PT, and participatory budgeting have garnered the most attention, even though the PT eventually lost the mayor's office. Porto Alegre became host to the World Social Forum, the gathering of anti-neoliberal globalization and pro–participatory democracy activists on the Left. The PT's first mayor, Olívio Dutra, went on to become governor of the state of Rio Grande do Sul (of which Porto Alegre is the capital), where he implemented participatory budgeting as well; he then served as minister of cities for President Luiz Inácio Lula da Silva. And participatory budgeting in some form or another has been adopted by hundreds of Brazilian cities and over two thousand cities in Latin America as a whole (Goldfrank 2007, 91), as well as in more than sixteen thousand cities worldwide (Sintomer, Herzberg, and Röcke 2008, 164). This book should help understand why.

In chapter 1 I outline the theoretical debates over whether participation and decentralization help or hurt democracy and present hypotheses about the likelihood of success of participatory experiments. I suggest that while scholars of development tend to focus on the state bureaucracy, sociologists on civil society, and political scientists on the mayor and party in power, opposition parties have largely been ignored. Furthermore, scholars have shown little concern for providing a complete explanation that integrates political actors' intentions, local and national sociopolitical conditions, and the design and development of new institutions. In chapter 2 I briefly describe the research design, rationale for selecting cases, and data-collection methods before demonstrating substantial similarities among the three cases with regard to the major explanatory elements emphasized by previous research: the ideology and constituency of the incumbent party, the extent of prior civil society organization, the quality of the municipal bureaucracy, and the city's size and level of development. I also lay out the crucial differences across the cases in terms of national decentralization and local opposition institutionalization.

In chapters 3, 4, and 5 I analyze Caracas, Montevideo, and Porto Alegre individually. I take a dynamic perspective, explaining how the design of the participatory programs evolved as community organizations and opposition parties responded to the incumbents' initial plans, and, in turn, how the resulting changes in the institutional design affected the level of participation. After examining why some experiments succeed in attracting and sustaining participants while others fail, I turn to the last link in the causal chain in chapter 6, comparing the effects of the experiments on broader citizen activism and on state transparency and responsiveness. Finally, in the conclusion, I analyze whether the argument for the three principal cases helps explain the success and failure of participatory budgeting as it spreads across Latin America and becomes a more mainstream policy tool, and I speculate about the future of participatory democracy in the region with the rise of the Left to national power in several countries.

1

Democracy, Participation, and Decentralization

While the spread of local-level participatory democratic experiments across Latin America described in the previous chapter generated excitement in many corners, it also encountered considerable controversy. Especially when under the auspices of Left-leaning governments, a rapid increase in popular participation can raise fears of threats to democracy, including tyranny of the majority and tyranny of the active minority. As a result, long-standing debates over the appropriate types and levels of participation and decentralization have resurfaced vigorously in recent years. For some analysts, increasing decentralization and expanding citizen participation are the keys to ensuring democratic stability or deepening democracy, while for others they represent dangers to democratic stability or even the end of democracy. In this chapter, after reviewing the often heated debates over these concepts and the connections among them and clarifying my own use of the terms, I argue that the path to deepening democracy through decentralization and participation is not so straightforward as protagonists hope but also not the impossibility that skeptics imply. Some experiments succeed in deepening democracy, others fail completely and wither away, and most fall somewhere in between. Toward the latter part of the chapter, then, I propose several hypotheses about what makes participatory experiments more likely to succeed and what makes them more likely to fall short.

"Deepening" Democracy and Citizen Participation

The most recent wave of debates on democracy's possible shortcomings and ways to address them is not limited to concerns about Latin America.

A growing academic literature questions the quality of democracy in the United States, focusing on the issue of civic engagement and pointing to the lack of equal voice in American politics (see, among others, Skocpol 2004; Elkin and Soltan 1999; Fullinwider 1999; Skocpol and Fiorina 1999). Sparked mostly by Robert Putnam's oft-cited article—and later book—on the decline of participation in voluntary associations, "Bowling Alone" (1995), much of this literature grapples with questions concerning the relationship between civic engagement and democratic government. The authors of these works disagree about whether there has been a decline in participation, and if so, whether this has had a negative or positive impact on democracy. For Putnam (2000, 403), the decline has definitely occurred, and he recommends increasing the "*supply* of opportunities for civic engagement" to reinvigorate our democracy. Others, like Barber (1984, chap. 10; 1998, 62, 67), Fishkin (1992), and Nylen (2003), explicitly advocate that the government itself should take on the task of expanding deliberative, face-to-face forms of citizen participation directly in public decision making. Such arguments have provoked strong rebuttals from those who counter that unequal levels of participation are not a serious problem in the United States (Weissberg 2006), that elsewhere high levels of civic engagement were not necessarily beneficial for democracy (Berman 1997), or that deliberative participation processes cannot overcome unequal citizen power but may instead reinforce it (Sanders 1997).

Within these (still unresolved) debates over civic engagement one clearly finds differing conceptions of participation and democracy.[1] Some scholars focus on the low or unequal levels of participation with regard to electoral turnout and membership in voluntary associations; they argue that increased and/or more egalitarian participation in these areas would make traditional representative democracy more responsive. For others, as noted, traditional representative democracy needs to be complemented by more direct forms of participation. Both views have merit. In Latin America, inequality is even greater than in the United States, and creating equal voice in politics is crucial. Yet although voting has been mandatory in several countries, including Brazil, Uruguay, and until recently, Venezuela, and turnout thus quite high, representative institutions generally have not proven satisfactory in providing transparent, responsive government. Thus, participatory institutions may be

---

1. For an excellent analysis of competing conceptions of democracy and the proper role and type of participation within it, see Fung (2007).

required to complement existing representative institutions in order to deepen democracy. But what exactly would deepening democracy mean?

At its core, democracy means that citizens participate in government and that government treats citizens equally. Holding periodic elections is the established form of realizing each of these ideals. Deepening democracy, then, requires moving beyond regular elections to take further steps toward strengthening citizenship and democratizing the state. Strengthening citizenship means transforming residents from passive subjects in dependent relationships with particular politicians or parties into active citizens who know that they have political rights, that they can legitimately make demands on the government for public services, and that they can make their voices heard in political debates. One way to discern strengthened citizenship in practice is to see if the number of citizens who regularly and directly participate in government decision making increases, which was the major goal of the experiments in this study. A second way is to look for changes in the strength of collective social actors, or civil society, to see if existing associations grow and become more politicized and if new associations begin to form.

Democratizing the state also involves two elements: transparency and responsiveness. Improving transparency entails that the state's deliberations and actions are more public and that corruption and clientelism are reduced if not eliminated. Responsiveness may be conceived in terms of how well the state delivers on the demands emanating from the new programs of citizen participation. That is, given the desperate need and desire for basic services in the poor neighborhoods of Latin American cities, and that the opening of participatory channels unleashes demands for these very services, one can ask whether the state delivers. This could certainly count as evidence of state responsiveness, and thus, democratizing the state. Though my definition of deepening democracy implies that greater citizen participation and enhanced state responsiveness should move in tandem, the analysis in the following chapters treats this as an empirical question.

Of course, there are myriad ways in which one might imagine improving or deepening democracy. The preceding definition builds on Roberts's (1998, 3) notion that deepening democracy involves efforts to "expand participation in the making of collective decisions and enhance governmental responsiveness to popular concerns."[2] Deep democracy finds similarities with Barber's

---

2. Roberts (1998, 30–31) provides an interesting discussion of the difference between deepening and "extending" democracy. The latter signifies the extension of "democratic

(1984, 133) concept of "strong democracy," in which "politics is something done by, not to, citizens." And it shares with Dahl's (1989, 322–24) conception of advanced democracy—or "Polyarchy III"—the notions that citizens would participate as equals and that the government "would actively seek to reduce great inequalities in the capacities and opportunities for citizens to participate effectively." In a deep democracy, citizens would participate in more frequent institutionalized ways in addition to voting in elections, and each citizen's voice would be granted equal status by the government.

To be clear, deepening democracy is not the impractical idea that all citizens participate in all public decisions at all levels of government, and it does not mean replacing representative democracy; it merely implies creating mechanisms of more direct forms of participation to complement the occasional casting of ballots and at least partially offset the myriad ways elites find to make their voices louder and more persuasive. While such mechanisms might take on various forms, this book focuses on a specific type of participatory program. Prior studies have produced numerous typologies in order to capture the range of dimensions along which participation may vary.[3] Participation may be active or passive (Zimmerman 1986, 7); may be voluntary/autonomous or obligatory/mobilized (Huntington and Nelson 1976, 7–10; Langton 1978, 210); may pertain to a certain level of government, policy, or agency (Langton 1978, 18); may allow more or less decision-making power (Arnstein 1971); and may take on a variety of forms that include voting, campaigning, donating funds or labor, personal contacting, and providing information and/or opinions. The programs in Caracas, Montevideo, and Porto Alegre each may be characterized as involving the active participation of volunteers who are invited (rather than obligated) by the municipal government to participate, particularly with regard to budget decisions. While collective discussion and voting in public assemblies and meetings of community representatives comprise the predominant forms of participation in each program, the amount of power the government grants to participants, the way the program is structured, and the range of issues debated vary. Because both citizens and municipal officials take

---

norms and procedures of collective self-determination" to socioeconomic spheres as well as the political arena. He notes that in Latin America the focus has been more on deepening than extending democracy.

   3. See, for example, Huntington and Nelson (1976); Langton (1978); Kweit and Kweit (1981); Zimmerman (1986); Berry, Portney, and Thomson (1993); Burns, Hambleton, and Hoggett (1994); Pretty and Chambers (1993); and Crook and Manor (1998).

part, I refer to these participatory programs as "state-society forums."[4] To facilitate widespread face-to-face participatory programs intended to deepen democracy such as these, several scholars in both the United States and Latin America suggest that some degree of decentralization is required.

Decentralization

But what kind of decentralization? As is true of the terms "democracy" and "participation," understandings of decentralization diverge remarkably, leading to a confusing array of typologies.[5] The variety of meanings attached to decentralization—from privatization all the way to popular empowerment—helps explain why it has been praised by authors favoring quite different ideologies, from Hernando de Soto of the "new Latin American Right" to Jordi Borja, representing the "new post-Marxist Left" (Coraggio 1991, 155). Two commonly used typologies depict privatization (erroneously in my view) as a type of decentralization. That used by many development scholars (Rondinelli, McCullough, and Johnson 1989; Dillinger 1994) names four types of decentralization based upon who receives responsibility for services from the central state. Decentralization to the private sector is *privatization;* to state administrative offices or agencies is *deconcentration;* to parastatals is *delegation;* and to the state, regional, or municipal levels of government is *devolution.* A somewhat overlapping typology advanced by several Latin American urbanists (Coraggio 1991; Felicissimo 1994) contemplates both what is transferred and to whom: *administrative* decentralization occurs when functions are transferred to lower levels of government or state agencies; *economic* decentralization occurs when resources or state-owned businesses are privatized; and *political* decentralization occurs when some quotient of public authority is devolved to society such that citizens are allowed to participate in decision-making processes, particularly in elections of state and local officials. In both typologies, a crucial element is missing—fiscal decentralization, or how much subnational governments raise and spend resources.

---

4. Other terms, such as "non-state public sphere" (Genro 1997) and "participatory publics" (Avritzer 2002), seem to hide the fact that government officials play significant roles in the participatory institutions.

5. Given the plethora of understandings of the concept, Leonard (1982, 28–29) suggests that a single, universally applicable typology of decentralization is not possible (cf. Schneider 2003).

These distinctions suggest the importance of specifying both one's definition of decentralization and the exact mix of resources, responsibilities, and authority that is being transferred, as well as who is on the receiving end. In my view, decentralization means the transfer of some combination of resources, responsibilities, and authority over public services or policy from one level of government to either lower levels of government, dispersed state agencies or parastatals, or state-society forums.[6] In particular, this study assesses two stages of decentralization. First, in the next chapter, it assesses the national decentralization processes that took place in Brazil, Uruguay, and Venezuela in the 1980s. These national processes involved primarily the devolution of responsibilities and authority from the central governments to state and municipal governments, accompanied by transfers of some financial resources. These processes took place largely prior to and helped open the way for further decentralization processes at the local level undertaken by municipal administrations in Porto Alegre, Montevideo, and Caracas. The local processes entailed a combination of the deconcentration of certain functions from city governments to submunicipal administrative offices with the devolution of some authority to submunicipal governments and state-society forums. Both the national and local processes vary across these countries and cities with regard to (A) the amounts and balance of resources, responsibilities, and authority devolved, and (B) who receives these new competencies.

While the national decentralization projects form a crucial part of the context, the local decentralization projects are intertwined with the participatory programs that are at the heart of this study. That is, the municipal administrations examined here each implemented programs that linked decentralization and participation, with the hope that in so doing they would help deepen democracy. Are such expectations warranted?

Decentralization and Participation: Expecting Pears from Elm Trees?

Both pragmatic and radical advocates of decentralization and participation would say yes, yet they disagree on definitions and ultimate goals. Adversaries and skeptics argue that decentralization and participation either

---

6. Because public services and policy remain under the state's ultimate jurisdiction, under this definition decentralization differs from privatization—the transfer of state-owned

harm democratic government or have no significant effects. That is, they believe that the advocates' hopes for democratic dividends from decentralization and participation are akin to expecting pears from elm trees.[7]

The advocates of decentralized government and participation have a long pedigree. Thomas Jefferson supported the division of counties into wards so that every citizen could participate directly in government. Rousseau, and later Mill, argued that civic participation educates people to become full citizens, reduces conflict by helping people accept government decisions, and integrates the community (see Pateman 1970). Tocqueville went beyond Mill in advocating citizen participation and emphasizing the virtues of local government, arguing that it provided a school in democracy for citizens (1988 [1848], 70). Decentralization was crucial for Tocqueville, since independent townships lead to active and public-spirited citizens, while centralization diminishes "civic spirit" (1988 [1848], 68–70, 88). More contemporary scholars focusing on everything from bureaucracy (Hagedorn 1995; Handler 1996), development (Rondinelli, McCullough, and Johnson 1989; Dillinger 1994; Campbell 2003), and state reform (Burki and Edwards 1996; Bradford 1994) to urban planning (Borja 1996; Borja and Castells 1997) and urban politics (Dowbor 1998) have argued in favor of decentralizing government and increasing citizen participation in public policy making in some form. Pragmatic and radical advocates share the views that decentralization projects open the way for increased participation at the local level, that when local governments expand citizen participation they are better able to meet local needs, and that this process benefits democracy. The two camps differ with regard to the precise meanings of decentralization and participation and exactly how democracy gains.

The pragmatic advocates, including Rondinelli and his colleagues (1989) and most international development donors (such as the United Nations Development Program, Inter-American Development Bank, and USAID), promote national decentralization on the basis of "subsidiarity," the notion that the lowest possible level of government should provide services because they are "closer to the people" and can thus allocate resources more efficiently. Pragmatists value decentralization not only for improving "the intrinsic

---

companies or state-provided services to private for-profit businesses—and from tertiarization—their transfer to nongovernment organizations (also known as the third sector).

7. I originally heard this phrase during an interview with a city employee in Montevideo, "Malena" (6/8/99), who suggested that expecting results from decentralized city offices without transferring adequate resources was like "esperando peras del olmo." It turns out to be a fairly common expression.

efficacy of the State," but even more because it "favors citizen participation" (BID/PNUD 1993, 43–44). Some development donor organizations have gone so far as tying funds to requirements for local participation (Blair 2000, 21; Chambers 1998, xiii). Indeed, as Cornwall (2006, 49) suggests, "participation has gained the status of development orthodoxy." For the pragmatist camp, however, participation can take on several meanings. The most common vision of participation among mainstream development thinkers is one that depicts citizens as information providers so that experts may improve public policy design.[8] Participation can also mean voting in local elections (this is still a relatively new phenomenon in much of the developing world; see Blair 2000), denouncing corruption and inefficiency through citizen watch groups, and voluntarily donating funds, materials, or labor (Campbell 2003, 81–92). A few development donors conceive of participation as private citizens organizing commercial ventures or volunteering in nonprofit organizations to take charge of providing public services (BID/PNUD 1993, 43). On the whole, pragmatists view decentralization and participation as part of a general reform of the state that would make it more accountable, responsive, and effective. This, in turn, would help reduce poverty and inequality, thus creating the conditions necessary for stable democracy.

In contrast to the pragmatic approach, which concentrates on national decentralization, consultative participation, and democratic stability, the radical advocates urge local decentralization, deliberative participation, and democratic deepening. The radical advocates criticize the pragmatic approach to decentralization as a "neoliberal" model that strips the state of its responsibility to provide public services through privatization. Scholars in this group, such as Coraggio (1991; 1999) and Bava (1996, 54), have been unimpressed with decentralization's record in Latin America, where responsibilities for services were often transferred to the regional or local level, but not financial support or democratic representation.[9] In fact, the radical critique emerged

8. For example, the World Bank introduced a new element for analyzing poverty called "participatory poverty assessment," in which the poor report their needs and resources (Salmen 1994). Some authors describe this as the "mainstream" or "pragmatic" view of participation (Martinussen 1997, 234–35; Schönwalder 1997, 756).

9. Icochea (1996) argues that in Chile responsibilities were transferred to local governments, but not representation, while in Colombia there was local democracy, but few responsibilities. This kind of observation has been made in other parts of the world as well. In a discussion of decentralization in West Africa, Ribot shows that "when local structures have an iota of representativity, no powers are devolved to them, and when local structures have powers, they are not representative but rather centrally controlled." He argues that in some cases decentralization has thus maintained and even furthered "ongoing legislative apartheid" by reinforcing the power of unrepresentative local chiefs (1998, 4, 1).

mostly from Latin Americans (and from Catalán observers of the region), beginning in the late 1980s, after initial rounds of decentralization. Radical advocates argue that decentralization should occur both at the national level and within large cities (Castells, Belil, and Borja 1989, 48–51; Borja 1992, 139), and that resources, responsibilities, and authority should be transferred to lower levels of government and state-society forums rather than to the private sector (Coraggio 1991, 164).

Radical advocates also criticize the pragmatic view of participation as "mere consultation" (Cunill 1991, 186). In the radical vision, participation involves deliberation within new "mechanisms of articulation between the State and civil society" (Cunill 1991, 38; Cunill Grau 1997, 96), but where the ultimate authority still lies with the state (Castells, Belil, and Borja 1989, 53–54; Borja 1992, 140). Their message is that the state should share power with society but should not relinquish it, either to nongovernmental organizations—as per the pragmatic approach—or to "popular councils"—as per the "dual power" revolutionary strategy that the Left encouraged in parts of Latin America in the 1970s and 1980s.[10] In Azevedo's (1988, 46–49) critique of the dual power strategy, he argues that popular participation is not a magic wand with which to create revolution but a way to build a more democratic society. For the radical advocates in general, local decentralization and participation deepen democracy through their effects on citizens and on the state. These effects include making the state more transparent, accessible, and open to change, thus helping the state to avoid particularism and insensitivity to social needs (Borja 1989, 263) and instead become more responsive. For citizens, not only is participation a democratic end in itself, but it also educates citizens in civic life, reinforces ties of solidarity, and facilitates citizens' acceptance of government decisions (Borja 1989, 264).

The adversaries of decentralization and participation, beginning with Plato and moving on through Mosca and Schumpeter, and later including Moynihan and Huntington, argue that too much participation leads to inefficiency, ungovernability, and citizen frustration, and that centrally organized

10. Certain parties in the Izquierda Unida coalition in Peru espoused this classic Leninist strategy (Schönwälder 2002), for example, as did a few factions of the Workers' Party in Brazil. In Fortaleza, where the PT had its first experience governing a major city (1985–88), the mayor was from one of the party's orthodox Marxist factions (the PCO, Partido Comunista Operário), and she envisioned the PT local government as the beginning of a "revolutionary situation." From City Hall, she and the popular councils that were supposed to emerge spontaneously would confront the state and national governments. The strategy proved unsuccessful when the popular councils failed to materialize, the higher levels of government cut off funding, the municipal workers went on strike, and the mayor and her faction were expelled from the PT (interview with Maria Luisa Fontanelle, 7/97, former mayor of Fortaleza)

government is a better locus of decision making. Huntington warns that an "excess of democracy" (1968, 430; 1975, 113), meaning rapid increases in participation, weakens government by overloading the system with demands and making it impossible to handle problems effectively, in both developed (1975, 103) and developing nations (1968, 430–31). Those who participate end up alienated because their demands cannot be met (Huntington 1975; Moynihan 1969). Moynihan concludes his review of community participation programs in the United States with pessimistic flair: "We may discover to our sorrow that 'participatory democracy' can mean the end of both participation and democracy" (1969, 164). More recent voices echo these concerns, arguing that too much direct participation by everyday citizens may undermine both elected representatives and specialists with technical knowledge as well as privilege the voice of an active extremist minority (Zakaria 2003, 245–55; Fiorina 1999). For Zakaria (2003, 248), "what we need in politics today is not more democracy but less." Even some scholars who are more sympathetic to the goals of increased participation warn about the risks to representative democracy (Souza 2007) and to "integrated, long-term, polity-wide planning" (Schönleitner 2006, 57).

Cooke and Kothari (2001, 7–8, 4) go so far as to claim that the discourse and practice of participatory development represents a "new tyranny" rather than a tool for enhancing democracy. They find three types of tyranny that are facilitated by the recent wave of participation programs in developing countries: one in which existing legitimate decision-making processes are overridden, a second involving the "reinforcement of the interests of the already powerful," and a third in which other potentially more beneficial methods of decision making are pushed aside. While their focus is on participation programs implemented by international development donors, they argue that "participatory development's tyrannical potential is systemic, and not merely a matter of how the practitioner operates or the specificities of the techniques and tools employed."

The adversaries also include those who argue not against participation but rather in favor of centralized government. They criticize the notion that lower levels of government are closer to the people and therefore more appropriate spheres for encouraging participation. Rather, decentralization presents a number of "dangers" (Prud'homme 1995, 201–20). Centralists argue that decentralization transfers social conflicts as well as resources and responsibilities to the local level, where there is greater political inequality, thus reinforcing relationships of subordination and "pulverizing the relative strength of subaltern actors" (Nunes 1996, 37). They insist that centralized government is necessary to protect the rights of minority interests that lack power at the local level (McConnell 1966, 107). And they claim that corruption and clientelism are more prevalent at the local level, making participation unattractive to many citizens and making participation itself not democratic (Melo 1996, 14–15; Prud'homme 1995). In addition to the dangers to participation, decentralization hinders development because local governments are less technically capable than the central government, because the state loses regulatory capacity and fiscal control, and because local elites will tend to benefit more than the poor (Melo 1996, 14–15; Prud'homme 1995; Manor 2006, 287).

Finally, the skeptics propose that, without more fundamental economic changes, decentralization and participation by themselves will be insignificant. The skeptics criticize both pragmatic and radical advocates. They accuse the mainstream developmentalists in the pragmatic camp of using a decentralizing discourse as a smoke screen for the advance of privatization, massive concentration of economic power, the weakening of the state's regulatory power, and the strengthening of the state's ability to monitor and control the population (Felicissimo 1994, 50; Slater 1989, 516–24). Skeptics imply that the radical advocates overestimate the potential of local-level processes to deepen democracy. Martins (1998, 47) argues that local participatory projects will not make a difference because city governments are limited by the "capitalist character of state structures." This means that the primary task of government is "the reproduction of capital," rather than encouraging citizenship or democratizing the state. Likewise, for Mattos (1989, 71), decentralization will not prove a panacea for Latin America's economic woes and democratic instability because a territorial reorganization of power will not change the underlying economic inequalities that plague the region's democracies. Last, Angotti (1996, 24–25) criticizes the strategy of relying "mainly on strengthening local government" because local governments in Latin America have "traditionally been a means for legitimizing elite power."

Much research supports skepticism. Two leading scholars on participatory democracy and town meetings in the United States, Mansbridge (1999, 291) and Bryan (1999, 215), both admit that though they believe local participation makes people better citizens, they cannot prove it. Mansbridge adds, "Neither, at this point, can anyone else" (1999, 291). Research on decentralization shows similarly limited results. For example, O'Dwyer and

Ziblatt's (2006) study of sixty-eight countries from across the globe shows virtually no effect of decentralization on the quality of governance, and Treisman's (2007, 5–6) review finds that "decentralization's consequences are complex and obscure. Many effects pull in different directions, leaving the net result indeterminate." And contemporary cross-national studies on decentralization *and* participation in peripheral countries show that, with a few exceptions (notably the state of Karnataka in India), they generally have not led to improvements in service delivery, especially with regard to government responsiveness to the poor (Blair 2000, 24–25; Crook and Manor 1998, 301). The authors agree that a particular problem with the decentralization efforts they studied was that local elites often dominated the process and directed resources to benefit themselves (Blair 2000, 25; Crook and Manor 1998, 280), which shows that the adversaries of decentralization have grounds for concern. However, these works should not be seen as the final word on decentralized participation.

What Blair calls "democratic local governance" and Crook and Manor call "democratic decentralization" is basically classic representative local government, where mayors and city councils are elected and have control over a certain amount of resources. By contrast, my concern here is with cities that have tried to complement and thus go beyond representative government by implementing policies of direct citizen participation at levels below the municipality. Thus, while available evidence largely supports skeptical thinking, the debate among the pragmatic advocates, radical advocates, adversaries, and skeptics remains open.

While many of the individual arguments made by the different authors presented here are valuable, there is at least one major drawback to all of these schools: with few exceptions, they all expect uniform outcomes. Decentralization and participation are always positive, always negative, or always insignificant. This is a slight oversimplification, but the general point remains that these schools look for uniformity rather than difference. To move the debate forward, we need to recognize that variation exists and find ways of explaining it. It seems clear that in some cases, national decentralization processes may help entrench local oligarchs with little desire to expand participation. Yet in other cases, these same processes seem to open political space for newcomers with participatory agendas. Furthermore, even where novices with an ideological commitment to participation win local office, the results of their attempts to implement decentralized participation programs vary, as the diverse outcomes in Caracas, Montevideo, and Porto Alegre show. In Caracas, for example, early citizen enthusiasm for the program gradually eroded, leaving the new spaces for participation empty. The opposite occurred in Porto Alegre, where each year more and more citizens became active in the administration's main participatory program, which in turn motivated the creation of new civic associations and contributed to enhanced government transparency and responsiveness. A more complete theory is necessary to explain this variation; that is, a theory that explains why participatory programs sometimes lead to citizen frustration, à la Huntington and Moynihan, and other times lead to deepening democracy.

When Does Participation Deepen Democracy?

Recent debates over state-society relations contain several possible avenues for advancing our understanding of divergent outcomes across cities. In the evolution of this literature, many analysts have moved beyond the notion of zero-sum relations between the state and society that was prevalent in previous decades. O'Donnell (1997, 15), for example, argues that the task for those seeking further democratization in Latin America is to direct the reform of the state toward the "extension of civil citizenship. . . . It is wrong to think of the legal state as in a zero-sum position in relation to society; quite the contrary, the more the former extends itself as rule of law, the more it usually facilitates and supports the independence of and the strength of the latter." Putnam's (1993, 98, 176) research on why Italy's northern regional governments performed better than those in the South following a major decentralization reform makes O'Donnell's argument in reverse: "The more civic a region, the more effective its government." Or, as he puts it later, "strong society, strong state." Putnam describes "civicness" as a combination of active citizen participation in politics and social organizations, political equality, solidarity, and trust, many of which are lacking in Latin American societies. For those hopeful that decentralization will "make democracy work" in Latin America, Putnam (1993, 183) makes the "depressing observation" that the "civic community has deep historical roots." In fact, he traces the civic-ness of the northern Italian regions back to the twelfth century and argues that physical and "social" capital (networks and norms of reciprocity) developed in a virtuous circle over hundreds of years. Putnam thus suggests that building civic communities and making democracy work takes decades, if not centuries.

Other scholars, however, have taken the more optimistic perspective that new forms of collaboration between the state and society may be mutually reinforcing,[11] and Putnam's (2000) own work on civic engagement and social capital in the United States implies a similar view. Evans (1996a; 1996b; 1997; 2001) has been a leading proponent of the notion of "state-society synergy," which occurs when state agencies and civic organizations possess cooperative, trusting ties with one another. When such synergistic relations occur, they produce more responsive and better-informed public agencies and more civic engagement. Evans asks, under what conditions will synergy emerge? He answers that "egalitarian societies with robust public bureaucracies provide the most fertile ground for synergistic state-society relations" (1996b, 1128). These preconditions make the prospects for synergy bleak, especially in developing countries. However, Evans also argues that synergy is "constructable" if reformers in the state find innovative ways (or "soft technologies") of organizing cooperative institutions and of presenting problems and interests as common to all involved (1996b, 1129).

The decentralized participatory programs in Porto Alegre, Montevideo, and Caracas represent one of the attempts to bridge the public-private divide that Evans suggests researchers should study. And synergy has a clear affinity with deeper democracy, as both involve the mutual strengthening of state and society. Indeed, recent research on participation programs mostly in Latin America have taken up this research agenda, developing similar concepts to analyze the effects of such programs on strengthening citizens and civil society, improving state responsiveness and accountability, or both. Thus, Nylen (2003), Avritzer (2002), and Baiocchi (2002) offer "empowerment," "participatory publics," and "synergizing civil society," respectively; Ackerman (2004), Santos (1998), and Evans (2004) contribute "co-governance for accountability," "redistributive democracy," and "deliberative development," respectively; and Fung and Wright (2003) suggest "empowered participatory governance." Despite the wealth of interesting concepts and the salutary recognition by recent advocates that participatory experiments do not always succeed, however, causal analysis of why some fail while others succeed remains underdeveloped.

With some exceptions, scholars have either provided long lists of potentially relevant variables or attempted to extract lessons from one or more successful

---

11. Migdal, Kohli, and Shue (1994); Ostrom (1996); McCarney (1996); Rodríguez and Winchester (1996); Woolcock (1998); Fung and Wright (2001); Ackerman (2004).

cases, making general conclusions difficult. These lessons often point to one or another key to success: a specific state, party, or civil society actor; a particularly clever institutional design (or soft technology); or certain propitious social or economic conditions. The list of features that purportedly affect program success begins (and, for some scholars, ends) with the existence of an incumbent party or mayor committed to participation and the presence of a vigorous civil society (Wampler 2007a); an alliance between the two may be helpful (Ackerman 2004, 459; Wampler and Avritzer 2004). Others point to certain "enabling conditions": some degree of political or social equality among participants that encourages deliberation rather than other strategies (Fung and Wright 2001, 24–25; Evans 1996b, 1128); a sufficient level of government resources to ensure concrete results (Schönwälder 1998; Peterson 1997, 16), sometimes linked to prior decentralization (Wampler and Avritzer 2004, 291; Abers 2000, 28, 105); and an effective bureaucracy to inspire participants' trust (Kliksberg 2000, 169; Evans 1996b, 1128).

Yet the importance of these variables, and their relation to institutional design features, is not always clear. For several authors, actors and preconditions drop out of the analysis once attention is turned to institutional engineering. One study of participatory budgeting concludes that crucial to its success in Porto Alegre were its focus on "localized, immediate needs" and its central placement within the city administration as its "hallmark" (Abers 2000, 220–21). Another directs attention to the institution's open format, which invites individual as well as group participation but does not privilege already organized groups nor allow leadership encrustation (Baiocchi 2004, 57, 54). And a comparative review of successful participation programs found three common design features—devolution of power to local units, supervision and coordination by the center, and a basis in formal state institutions, not society—as well as three general principles: oriented toward practical needs, grassroots participation, and "deliberative solution generation" (Fung and Wright 2001, 17–24).

The great variety of agential, contextual, and design requirements posited for successful participation programs may explain why so few existed until recently. Before the late 1990s, at least, participatory experiments occurred only in "exceptional circumstances" and were often "transitory" in Latin America (Herzer and Pirez 1991, 95). Recent research offers some clues as to why such experiments are increasingly successful, yet a compelling framework that integrates actors, preconditions, and institutional design remains elusive.

Implementing and Sustaining Participation

An effective theory of participation should integrate perspectives from three levels. At the macro level, one should examine the conditions from above that encourage or discourage the capacity of local governments to implement participatory programs. At the micro level, one can study the citizens themselves and their prior involvement in civic organizations. Finally, at the meso level, one must analyze how local governments design the institutions for participation and how political parties in and out of government react to the new institutions.

Macro Level: Decentralization and Local Government Capacity

Many scholars have pointed out that a general problem with local-level participation programs is limited resources. Schönwalder's (1998) study of two such programs in Lima shows that the inadequate funding available to them prevented the attainment of significant concrete results, which in turn convinced citizens that their participation was not worthwhile. Peterson (1997, 16) affirms that this is a common failing in many Latin American efforts to expand participation, and Evans (1996b, 1126) concurs that scarcity of resources impedes state-society cooperation. While the magnitude of resources is clearly crucial to the sustainability of participation programs, resources are only important in relation to the problems and responsibilities to which they are applied. We need to view the issue of resources as one of three crucial aspects that make up local government capacity. The other important elements are the extent of municipal jurisdiction for public services and the quality of local infrastructure. As a general rule, what matters is the sphere of authority for whatever level of government, state agency, or NGO sponsors the participation program. For the participation programs in this study, the municipal government's jurisdiction is what counts. In cities with ample infrastructure and efficient services, new participation programs will likely have difficulty attracting citizens regardless of municipal resources and responsibilities. In cities with serious deficiencies, citizen interest in such programs may be sparked, but to maintain that interest, the municipal government needs both sufficient resources and jurisdictional authority to address the problems. Without equivalent responsibilities, resources may be squandered on issues unrelated to citizens' needs. And without adequate funding, jurisdiction over serious problems undermines government capacity. In either case, participant enthusiasm will quickly fade.

A high degree of local government capacity—where resources and responsibilities at least come close to matching needs—largely depends on the degree of national fiscal and administrative decentralization. National laws determine which competencies pertain to the local level, which taxes local governments may levy, and how revenues are distributed between the different levels of government. In more decentralized countries, municipal governments have jurisdiction over a wide range of services, have greater powers to tax, and/or receive significant federal government transfers; they therefore administer budgets that are relatively large compared to municipal governments in less decentralized arrangements. In this sense, just as the advocates argued above, decentralization facilitates participation. Yet local government capacity is not shaped solely by the national degree of decentralization. The quality of local infrastructure is mostly endogenous to each city. And city size and level of economic development have a substantial impact on the size of the municipal budget.

Two related hypotheses emerge from this look at the macro level. First, participatory experiments are more likely to maintain citizen enthusiasm where the extent of municipal authority and the size of the local budget correspond to the city's needs. Second, a high degree of local government capacity is more likely to exist in countries where significant national decentralization has already occurred. In other words, where more resources, responsibilities, and authority have been transferred to the local level—and this has been done in a balanced way such that they can address citizen demands—city governments have a better chance of deepening democracy.

Micro Level: Social Capital and Social Movements

Scholars of both synergy and participation emphasize the importance of social ties at the local level. While Putnam and Evans may differ about the difficulty of creating especially civic communities, they agree that some measure of social capital—trust and solidarity built in local associations—aids good government and synergy. And there is consensus among participation scholars that the existence of community organizations is not only helpful but a requirement of participation programs (Cunill 1991, 127; Herzer and Pirez 1991, 91; Borja 1989, 266), with some recent researchers suggesting that for successful programs, the local civil society organizations be especially vigorous, autonomous, and capable of contentious collective action (Avritzer 2006a; Baiocchi, Heller, and Silva 2008; Wampler 2007a). Civic associations may first demand that city governments adopt participatory state-society forums and then help design, implement, and sustain them in a variety of ways. Associations may recruit potential participants, pressure the government to make participation worthwhile, and help defend and legitimize the decisions made in participatory processes to the media, for example, or to the city council.

Some scholars who analyze community associations more as social movements than as carriers or manifestations of social capital provide more critical perspectives. In this view, the social movements of Latin America may actually provide yet another challenge for local governments attempting participatory programs. The basic argument is that social movements would have difficulty cooperating with the state in the 1990s after opposing and making radical demands on it during the military dictatorships of the 1970s and 1980s. Several authors have made this case with regard to Brazil. Doimo (1995, 69), for example, argues that two conflicting ethics emerged in Brazilian social movements during authoritarian rule, one "expressive-disruptive" and the other "integrative-corporatist." Assies (1997, 113) agrees with Doimo that the PT municipal administrations' difficulties in constructing participatory popular councils were at least partly due to these conflicting ethics. The expressive-disruptive ethic, with its "logic of direct action," confronted the integrative-corporatist ethic, which was necessary for following the "rules of procedure" in the popular councils, making cooperation difficult both between state representatives and social organizations and among these organizations themselves.[12] Schönwalder (1997) presents a different take on the issue of social movements, arguing from their perspective rather than from that of government actors. Seeing the potential for co-optation of the movements in the Left's new participatory programs, Schönwalder proposes that in order for these movements to avoid co-optation yet still benefit from the new programs, they should attempt to build ties not only with the party in local power, but with other parties and NGOs, and with state agencies at other levels of government. The importance of such horizontal and vertical linkages

---

12. Assies (1997, 113); and see Doimo (1995, 182–84), Jacobi (1994, 13) and Abers (1996, 43). Stepan (1997) suggests that this is a general problem for consolidating democracies. He contrasts the type of society needed for a transition away from authoritarian rule with that needed for a consolidated democracy. The values and language of "ethical civil society," which is a contributor and sometime leader of transitions, often conflict with those of "political society," which is a requisite of consolidation. While ethical civil society in opposition claims "truth," perceives itself as the nation, rejects internal differences and represses conflicts, dismisses compromise and routinized institutions, and operates outside the state, political society in a consolidated democracy operates around interests, contains many different groups, attempts to organize and represent differences and conflicts, and accepts compromise and working with state institutions.

for organizational success has been highlighted by theorists of social capital and synergy as well (Woolcock 1998; Evans 1996b, 1124–25).

As this look at the micro level shows, analysts of participatory programs need to take into account both the positive and negative roles community organizations can play in their development and the relationships between such organizations and political parties. This latter theme is complicated, and it has only begun to receive attention in the literature on participation programs (Wampler 2007a; Baiocchi, Heller, and Silva 2008). Obviously, participatory proposals do not emerge from thin air. They are almost always either demanded by community associations, promoted by political parties, or the result of negotiation between the two. In all cases, associations have some kind of prior history not only with the parties that eventually implement participation programs at the local level, but with opposing parties as well.

Community organizations that helped develop participatory proposals and that are closely tied to the party in power can be expected to aid the implementation of the proposals, but since they might not welcome the involvement of other organizations or previously inactive citizens, they might endanger the sustainability of new programs. Organizations with strong links to rival parties are unlikely to serve as providers or recruiters of participants for new programs. The leaders of these types of associations may in fact look at participatory programs as threats to their position as conduits of neighborhood demands. On the other hand, some local organizations have a strong spirit of community autonomy and either explicitly reject connections with political parties or strive for balanced party representation in leadership positions and refuse to accept party-made decisions. These last two types of organizations have the most promise for helping to sustain participatory programs because they will probably welcome such potentially empowering programs, yet at the same time they are unlikely to view themselves as the programs' sole owners and thus attempt to exclude others from participating.

My hypothesis from the micro level, then, is that participatory experiments are more likely to engage citizens on an enduring basis where community organizations have forged strong ties to one another beyond their own neighborhoods and where they have not forfeited their autonomy in relationships with either incumbent or opposition political parties.

Meso Level: Political Parties and Organizational Strategies

An obvious prerequisite for the creation of participatory state-society forums is a politically powerful proponent within the municipal administration (Herzer

and Pirez 1991, 91; Cunill 1991, 127; Wampler 2007a), and such propo-
nents are most often on the Left (Nylen 2003; Chavez and Goldfrank 2004;
Avritzer 2006a). When local governments, and the political parties that head
them, are committed to adopting such participation proposals, they encounter
two fundamental challenges. One involves designing programs that encourage a large and representative group of participants. The other challenge
concerns overcoming resistance from opposition parties and from within
the incumbent party and the municipal bureaucracy. I will start with the
first challenge—the number and composition of participants.

If the number of participants is too small or if only certain types of people
participate, such as incumbent party supporters or members of specific well-
organized interest groups, the democracy-enhancing rewards of participation supposed by its advocates will be minimal or, at best, narrowly focused.
Furthermore, with a small or unrepresentative group of participants, the
potential problems with local-level participation pointed out by its adversaries
are more likely to materialize. Smaller numbers of participants may be more
easily manipulated by the incumbent party or by already powerful groups,
lending credence to charges of clientelism or of the reinforcement of existing
power arrangements. Even if the number of participants is large enough to
avoid the appearance of tyranny of the active minority, if the participants
are not representative of the wider community, the opposite problem may
emerge—tyranny of the majority, where voices of minority interests may be
excluded, ignored, or drowned out. Encouraging a substantial and diverse
number of participants is therefore crucial, yet remarkably difficult.

As scholars of both participatory democracy and collective action recognize, most people will participate voluntarily only so long as they believe
that their personal involvement benefits themselves (Dahl 1990, 30–39)
or their community (Mansbridge 1983, 72–75) and that without their participation, these benefits would be lost (Olson 1971). The mere creation of
opportunities for participation does not automatically transform a group of
passive city residents into active citizens (Cunill Grau 1997, 119). Even
when avenues for participation arise, people have a variety of reasons for
not showing up, including fear of public speaking, lack of time, and doubts
about the usefulness of their input, either because they think the authorities
will ignore them or manipulate them or because they consider themselves
unable to contribute constructively. City mayors undertaking participatory
experiments lack complete control over some of these issues, but with cre-
ative soft technologies, they can design new programs in such a way as to
minimize their effects. For example, they might reduce the length of public

meetings or schedule them at convenient hours and in multiple locations, limit the duration of volunteer commitment, and generally create open, welcoming environments for participants (especially first-timers). Most importantly, city officials can show that they value citizen input by inviting it on a wide range of issues, by not privileging representatives of political parties or of specific community associations, and by implementing participant proposals whenever they can (and when they cannot, explaining clearly why).

In the case-study chapters that follow, I therefore analyze the design of the new participatory institutions along three axes: range, structure, and decision-making power. Program *range* concerns the number of significant issues presented for debate. The wider the range, the larger and more diverse the number of participants should be. Program *structure* includes the method of choosing representatives, the length of their terms, and the periodicity and accessibility of meetings. More accessible, informally structured institutions—in which political parties are not formally represented, terms are short, and meetings are frequent, public, and well advertised—should lead to higher levels of participation and may also help prevent tyranny of the active minority. Last, *decision-making power* varies according to how the government perceives the importance of the citizens' role. From least to greatest importance, citizens may be expected to receive information from the government, provide information, provide opinions, provide proposals, make nonbinding decisions, and/or make binding decisions. The first three roles may be considered consultative and the last three deliberative, with the further along the scale toward deliberation, the greater the likelihood of attracting participants.

The first hypothesis from the meso level, then, has to do with the design of the new institutions for participation themselves. Participatory experiments are more likely to encourage and sustain widespread, diverse citizen interest where the new institutions allow input on a wide range of issues, structure participation informally such that it is accessible for volunteer participants, and entail more deliberative than consultative participation such that participants have greater decision-making power. Encompassing and reconciling these three key features requires creativity and commitment.

Yet even the most dedicated mayors armed with cleverly designed participation programs face the second challenge of overcoming resistance when trying to put the programs into practice. In the cases Evans (1996b, 126–28) reviews, public sector workers (see Tendler 1997) and political competition in general play mostly helpful roles in bringing about successful state-society cooperation. Yet he recognizes that this is not always the case, especially in nondemocratic contexts and where bureaucrats are paid and trained poorly. Other authors grant more importance to the potential for negative reactions from within the state. Borja (1989, 265), for example, cautions that members of both the bureaucratic apparatus and the incumbent party hierarchy frequently object to the introduction of new channels of societal participation and may try to prevent such channels. This objection stems both from the fear of stimulating new actors who might encroach on their power and from a belief that greater participation would inject too much unpredictability into local politics.[13]

In a different vein, both Nylen's (1996) study of PT administrations in small Brazilian cities and Schönwalder's (1998) study of United Left administrations in Lima suggest that the often intense competition among party factions in Left parties can undermine efforts to encourage citizen activism. The intrusion of internal party wrangling into public forums can drive away potential participants who recoil from party politics and from being pressured publicly to take sides in political debates. This is particularly significant in Latin America, where social organizations frequently criticize political parties for trying to use them to advance party goals rather than respecting their autonomy. Thus, maintaining internal party discipline may be vital.

All of these are excellent points. Yet something is missing from this meso-level view: the reaction to new participatory programs from the political parties out of office.[14] Given that such programs may lure important constituencies to the incumbents, we cannot assume that opposition parties will passively accept their arrival. Unlike in many other developing regions, in Latin America party competition in large cities is frequently fierce. Competition may be particularly intense in the cases studied here. The newly incumbent parties (PT, FA, and LCR) were all union-based parties looking to expand their social bases by increasing their presence among the traditionally dominant parties' voters and neighborhood association allies. Because these formerly dominant parties now in opposition fear losing their constituents and their power, we should expect that they will resist the introduction of participatory programs and, if that fails, do everything possible to impede their success. The ferocity of their

13. I would add that another reason for resistance to participation from these camps is that the new programs represent extra, and sometimes unpleasant, work, given that public meetings usually take place at night and the participants often make harsh critiques of municipal employees and political leaders.

14. Abers (1996, 50) refers to opposition parties but in a different kind of argument from the one I make here. She hypothesizes that one reason many PT administrations were reluctant to devolve decision-making power to citizens is that they feared that their conservative opponents might capture the new public spaces.

opposition should increase in accordance with how much they have to lose and the organizational resources at their disposal. Those parties with a long history of local power, strong ties to civil society, and robust organizations— and thus more institutionalized (see chapter 2)—should react more forcefully than lesser rivals.

The preceding discussion suggests three final hypotheses. Likelihood of success in implementing and sustaining participatory experiments should *decrease* where (1) public workers receive low pay and poor training; (2) incumbent parties lack internal discipline; and (3) incumbent parties replace strongly institutionalized parties. Overall, we are left with several individual hypotheses concerning actors, preconditions, and institutional design features, but not yet an integrated framework. Toward that end, I propose that the ability of committed, progressive incumbents to design effective participatory programs is linked to the extent of national decentralization and to the level of institutionalization of their political rivals at the local level. The design features that encourage participation and ultimately aid the deepening of democracy are contingent upon a decentralized national state that affords resources and responsibilities to the municipal government and a weakly institutionalized opposition that fails to resist the new participatory programs. The next chapter begins to examine these arguments in Caracas, Montevideo, and Porto Alegre.

2

A Tale of Three Cities

Why did Porto Alegre's participation program succeed most compared to similar programs tried in Caracas and Montevideo? As the second part of this chapter illustrates, many of the keys to success and the stumbling blocks preventing it described by scholars seem unpersuasive answers. The three cities were fundamentally similar with regard to most of the elements emphasized in the literature: type of incumbent party and civil society organizations, city size and level of development, and the quality of municipal bureaucracies. Initially, even the participation programs themselves were remarkably alike. Yet two crucial differences changed the trajectory of the participation programs in the three cities, as the third part of this chapter shows. One was the greater degree of national decentralization in Brazil and Uruguay than in Venezuela. The other was the existence of strongly institutionalized opposition parties in Montevideo and Caracas compared to the weakly institutionalized opposition in Porto Alegre. These two factors best explain the differences in the eventual design of the participation programs and, in turn, Porto Alegre's greater success in deepening democracy.

The tale of these three cities, however, cannot be told without first explaining why I chose them and what I did to learn the tale. That is, a few words on case selection and data collection are in order. My initial reason for selecting the participation programs in Caracas, Montevideo, and Porto Alegre as cases for comparison was that, of the many cities in which such programs were attempted in the 1980s and 1990s, the programs in these cities stood out in existing studies as the most comprehensive, city-wide initiatives.[1] For the most part, major participation programs in other cities

---

1. See, especially, the special issue on local government in *NACLA* (1995) and the series by Harnecker (1995a, 1995b, 1995c).

during this time period were either concentrated and compartmentalized in certain sectors, such as health care and housing in São Paulo, and milk distribution in Lima, or were in cities with much smaller populations, like Ciudad Guayana or Cuenca. The parties in charge of implementing these programs—PT in Porto Alegre, FA in Montevideo, and LCR in Caracas—were also prominent advocates of increasing citizen participation in local government. Porto Alegre, Montevideo, and Caracas thus represented the most appropriate sites for testing whether the benefits of participatory democracy claimed by its promoters were actually produced. At the same time, choosing cases in several countries allowed me to assess the independent impact of different national settings, particularly in terms of the prevailing types of political parties and the degree of national decentralization. Venezuela and Uruguay represent countries with histories of strongly institutionalized political parties, while Brazil's parties are notoriously weak. On measures of decentralization, Brazil usually scores very high (along with Argentina and Colombia), while Venezuela and Uruguay rank as moderate decentralizers compared to other countries in Latin America. Most importantly, though, Venezuela's municipalities have historically provided fewer services, had less political autonomy, and spent a smaller share of government revenues than their counterparts in either Brazil or Uruguay.

The three cases also made a good set for comparison because they were independent of one another. The programs were implemented in separate countries by parties without strong preexisting connections, and they began roughly concurrently (1989, 1990, and 1993). Thus, political learning processes in one case would not have affected outcomes in the others.[2] Finally, because it was difficult to determine exactly how the programs had affected

---

2. Indeed, although a few national party leaders had met at meetings of the São Paulo Forum, they did not learn of their similar municipal government programs until Marta Harnecker began conducting interviews with party leaders in each of the cities in the early 1990s. According to Maria Cristina Iglesias, the former substitute mayor of Caracas and one of LCR's leaders, even then the exchange of ideas between the parties was minimal (inteview, 2/9/99). Only in the mid-1990s, after the programs had been in place for several years in Porto Alegre and Montevideo, did communication between the PT and FA municipal administrations become more regular, beginning with the convocation of a seminar in Montevideo in which several Latin American and Spanish municipal officials described their local experiences with participation and decentralization (see IMM, AECI, and CAM 1994). This seminar did not include members of LCR's administration in Caracas. It does seem that, in the late 1990s at least, the FA administration may have borrowed from the Porto Alegre PT to some degree. Montevideo city officials began to call part of their decentralized participation program "participatory budgeting," adopting the name used in Porto Alegre, though not much more than the name. For a methodological discussion of independence of cases and historical learning (or "Galton's problem"), see Lijphart (1975, 171).

the quality of local democracy prior to conducting field research, I could not choose cases according to these outcomes.[3]

Once I had chosen the cities, I began collecting data from several sources. Foremost among these were the 145 in-depth interviews I conducted with current and former government and party officials, opposition party leaders, members of community organizations, and, in fewer numbers, with social scientists and journalists.[4] In addition to the personal interviews, my colleagues and I employed a series of original surveys in Porto Alegre and Montevideo, where the participation programs were ongoing.[5] I also observed more than one hundred meetings, including public assemblies of the participation programs, political party meetings, neighborhood association meetings, and City Council meetings. Of course, government documents, media reports, and academic articles proved to be invaluable sources of data as well. After a collective sixteen months living in these three cities, I discovered many remarkable similarities.[6]

Shared Traits

The previous chapter suggested several factors at the macro, micro, and meso levels that may aid or hinder the success of participation programs.

3. It was clear, of course, that the PT and FA had each won reelection while LCR had not, and that Porto Alegre's participatory budget process had been prized as one of the world's "best practices" in urban management by the United Nations' 1996 Habitat II Conference. Yet other than the general notions that the participation program was working in Porto Alegre and that it had not helped LCR win reelection in Caracas, I did not know what the results of the programs were in terms of democratizing the state and strengthening citizenship. The conclusions drawn from this study, therefore, are not biased due to "selecting on the dependent variable" (see King, Keohane, and Verba 1994, 129–32; and Geddes 1990; or, for an earlier admonition against choosing cases based on the outcomes, Lijphart 1975, 164).

4. Between October 1998 and December 1999, approximately seventy such interviews were conducted in Porto Alegre, fifty in Montevideo, and twenty-five in Caracas.

5. In Montevideo, one survey (with 219 respondents) was of the universe of local council members and was self-administered. Another (with 444 respondents) was of a random sample of city residents in three districts and was carried out by a team of university students. These surveys were designed and conducted in collaboration with Daniel Chavez. For more details on the Montevideo surveys, see chapter 4, particularly Appendix 4A. The surveys in Porto Alegre were of budget councilors from each district (31 respondents) and of district and thematic coordinators (15 respondents). The latter survey was self-administered, and was designed in collaboration with Gianpaolo Baiocchi.

6. One obvious difference between Porto Alegre on one hand and Caracas and Montevideo on the other is that Porto Alegre is a state capital but not a national capital. In the course of this study, this difference did not figure as highly relevant. In terms of legally mandated responsibilities for public services, the distinction does not seem to matter much. For the

For many scholars, two prerequisites of such programs are office holders motivated to implement participation and a preexisting community move- ment. A particularly egalitarian society and a disciplined, organized bureau- cracy are also seen as potentially beneficial. The obstacles to successful implementation of participation programs that analysts highlight include excessive factionalism within the incumbent parties and resistance from local bureaucrats. On these six traits (and others), the three cases line up similarly. The newly elected incumbent parties were all staunch advocates of participatory decentralization, yet each faced internal divisions. Each city housed a large number of neighborhood associations and other community- based organizations that had been especially active in the early 1980s but had declined in subsequent years. And none of these cities could boast of an especially egalitarian society or a robust bureaucracy. In fact, similar patterns of development left each city marked by social and spatial segrega- tion, and many municipal employees had been hired under patron-client norms by previous administrations. In no case did city workers welcome the participation programs being implemented by the new political challengers.

From Radical Opposition to Responsible Incumbents:
The PT, the FA, and LCR

The Partido dos Trabalhadores, the Frente Amplio, and the Causa Radical are exemplars of the Latin American Left's ideological transformation as described in the Overview. This is not to say that the parties responsible for implementing the participation programs in Porto Alegre, Montevideo, and Caracas were identical. The claim here is that the differences among the PT, the FA, and LCR were outweighed by a number of fundamental paral- lels. The most important commonalities among the three parties included: an ideological commitment to deepening democracy through opening new channels of participation and decentralizing power; a number of internal factions of various political tendencies including former guerrilla leaders; a membership base in unions and other social movements; a middle- and working-class constituency that did not originally include the very poor; a

---

most part, the mayors of Caracas, Montevideo, and Porto Alegre are mandated to provide the same services as the mayors of other Venezuelan, Uruguayan, and Brazilian cities. And, as related in the third part of this chapter, the fiercer opposition reaction to the participatory programs in Montevideo and Caracas compared to Porto Alegre stemmed more from the fact that the opposition parties were more institutionalized in the former cities than from their status as national capitals. The opposition's reaction to the PT government in Brasília was comparatively weak, given their weaker levels of institutionalization

lack of government experience; and a long path to local power that culminated in victory by a bare plurality due more to protest votes against national political leaders than to voters endorsing a platform of increased citizen participation. None of the parties had any *inherent* advantages, therefore, with regard to implementing a participation program. For instance, in no case could the new mayors rely on a completely cohesive party organization or on majoritarian support. A synopsis of each party's local history brings out the parallels cited above.

Partido dos Trabalhadores

Confident from a wave of massive strikes in the late 1970s, a group of Brazilian labor leaders identified with the "new unionism" joined together to found the Workers' Party in 1979, the year military rulers abandoned the two-party system they had created and allowed multiple parties to form.[7] Several small Marxist parties, which were illegal at the time and had engaged in guerrilla activities in the past, also entered the PT, along with hundreds of activists from urban and rural social movements, including health care and housing movements, progressive Catholic community groups, the women's movement, student organizations, and the landless peasant movement. In the state of Rio Grande do Sul, of which Porto Alegre is the capital, all of these components were present, with a leading role taken by Olívio Dutra, the head of the local bank workers union.

Although avowedly socialist and revolutionary in its early years, the PT has always contained diverse ideological currents, ranging from Trotskyism to social democracy. These differences are expressed in the party's many factions, called *tendencias,* some of which maintained separate existences as parties in their own right (until that practice was abolished in 1991).[8] The factions united around pursuing the party's goals nonviolently, preferring elections and grassroots mobilization over arms. Throughout the 1980s, the PT played a significant role in the opposition to the military dictatorship (1964–85). For example, it led the ultimately unsuccessful campaign for direct presidential elections in 1984. Yet the PT remained electorally insignificant until the 1988 municipal races. At the national level, the PT only won 2 percent of the vote for congressional elections in 1982 and 3 percent in 1986, which nonetheless earned the party eight and then sixteen congressional deputies. In local races, the PT won just two mayor's races in 1982,

---

7. For the definitive history of the PT (in English), see Keck (1992).
8. At that time, one of these parties-within-the-party, Convergencia Socialista, was expelled.

Table 2.1   Vote share for the PT in Porto Alegre

Year (type of race)	1982 (governor)	1985 (mayor)	1986 (governor)	1988 (mayor)
Percentage voting PT	3.9%	11.4%	12.6%	34.4%

SOURCES: Passos and Noll (1996, 49, errata), Prodasen (1982), and Tribunal Regional Eleitoral.

earning less than 3 percent of the vote nationwide. In the 1985 special state capital elections, the party won only in Fortaleza, capital of the northeastern state of Ceará, but increased its vote share to 11 percent. In Porto Alegre, the PT had just one city councilor from 1982 to 1988, and earned one national deputy, Olívio Dutra, in 1986. The party gradually gained ground in other local races until winning the mayor's office with Dutra as its candidate in 1988 (see table 2.1).

The 1988 elections brought the PT to power in thirty-six municipalities, including two other state capitals, São Paulo and Vitória, as well as other important cities in the state of São Paulo like Santos and Diadema. Though Brazil has over five thousand municipal governments, these thirty-six cities represented 40 percent of the national economy.[9] The PT's impressive showing in the 1988 elections stemmed in large part from its capture of the protest vote.[10] At the time, inflation had reached quadruple digits and the Center-Right government alliance between the PMDB (Partido do Movimento Democrático Brasileiro—Party of the Brazilian Democratic Movement) and the PFL (Partido da Frente Liberal—Party of the Liberal Front) had crumbled, leaving both parties discredited with voters. After the PMDB had won nineteen of the twenty-five state capital races in 1985, it won just five in 1988 (Shidlo 1998, 73).

Across Brazil, in Porto Alegre and elsewhere, the PT's slogans for the 1988 municipal elections were transparent administration, popular participation, and inverting priorities in order to favor the poor rather than the rich.[11] The PT's leaders in Porto Alegre wanted to "radically democratize democracy," in the words of Tarso Genro, who was Dutra's vice-mayor (Genro and Souza 1997, 18). Doing so at the municipal level required democratization in four

9. See Fox (1995, 15). For the PT's electoral evolution, see Branford and Kucinski (1995, 74) and Nylen (2000).

10. For the PT's victory in Porto Alegre, see Abers (2000, 57–59) and Schabbach (1995, 80). For the national repudiation of the status quo in the 1988 elections, see Shidlo (1998, 75–76).

11. In Porto Alegre, these slogans could be found in the PT's campaign platform and party pamphlets (see Schmidt 1994, 71–72).

senses: political-institutional, through the creation of new channels of direct citizen participation in municipal policy making; substantive, through a constant increase in "the number of residents benefited by urban infrastructure and by municipal public services"; economic, through changes in taxation policy and aid to those living in "extralegal" areas of the city (squatter settlements and shantytowns); and cultural, through expanding access to cultural events and promoting a new political culture that would "elevate individuals from mere inhabitants to citizens, conscious of their rights and duties" (Dutra 1990, 3–5). The PT considered that those who lived in areas without infrastructure were being deprived of their citizenship, and that true citizenship required both dignified living conditions and the ability to participate with an equal voice in public decision making.

The other guiding principles for the PT administration in Porto Alegre were the related ideas of "deprivatizing" the state and decentralization. Deprivatizing the state meant reducing the influence of individual interests and opening avenues for collective pressure on and oversight of the state. Decentralization was seen as an instrument for achieving this goal, and was conceived in both administrative and political terms, with the emphasis on decentralizing decision-making processes to the organized citizenry. According to one official government document (GAPLAN 1991), "Decentralization, understood as one of the paths to democratization, should be considered an essential part of the construction of popular sovereignty, stimulating and encouraging the people to direct their own destiny as active subjects. The guiding objective of this proposal is in the direction of altering the relations between the executive and the community in order to make them closer by implementing effective channels of communication, access, and participation, which will promote a competent and organized response to the people's demands."[12] Overall, the ultimate "strategic objectives" of the PT administration in Porto Alegre were the "democratization of the State and the strengthening of a civil society able to control the State" (Dutra 1990, 2).

Frente Amplio

The FA is an unusual mixture of electoral coalition, political party, and political movement that was established in 1971 to unite parties on the Left and Center-Left in order to compete in elections with the two traditionally

---

12. For further details on the Porto Alegre PT's conception of decentralization and deprivatization of the state, see also Fialho Alonso (1994), Dutra (1994), and Genro (1997, 15).

dominant parties, the Colorado Party and the National Party (Blancos).[13] A wide range of parties and factions coexists within the FA's structure, which also includes dozens of "base committees," consisting of political activists who are not necessarily members of the constituent parties or factions. When the FA was founded to support the presidential candidacy of a retired general, Líber Seregni, its components included the Communist and Socialist parties, the Christian Democrats, and important dissident factions from the Colorados and Blancos, as well as several smaller parties on the far Left. The ideologically eclectic FA also had the "critical support" of the Tupamaros, an urban guerrilla movement.[14] In the 1971 elections, the FA received 18 percent of the total vote and 30 percent of the vote in Montevideo, earning the party three senators.

The next elections would not take place for thirteen years, after a military dictatorship (1973–84) that imprisoned Seregni and exiled or imprisoned many other FA leaders, forcing party members into clandestine opposition movements based in labor unions, student groups, and new community organizations (such as housing cooperatives and soup kitchens). The 1984 elections would see the FA receive exactly the same vote share at the national level (18 percent) as it had in 1971, and a few percentage points higher than its earlier level in Montevideo (34 percent), but not enough to win the mayoral race. From 1984 to 1989, the composition of the FA changed, with the two largest Center-Left parties breaking away to form a new alliance and the Tupamaros formally joining the Frente after renouncing armed struggle.[15] Yet the FA remained ideologically diverse, with two new more centrist factions forming in the interim.[16]

In 1989, the FA's mayoral candidate for Montevideo, Tabaré Vázquez (an oncologist), won with 35 percent, and the party's national total rose to 21 percent, which gave Seregni his third defeat in presidential elections.

13. For a detailed history of the Frente Amplio, see the interviews with party leaders in Harnecker (1995a).

14. See Serna (2000, 224), who cites Costa Bonino (1995).

15. The Christian Democrats and the Party for the Government of the People (PGP) split from the FA to form Nuevo Espacio for the 1989 elections, while, in order to join the FA, the Tupamaros created a specifically political organization called the Movement for Popular Participation (MPP). The FA required that the Tupamaros give up violent tactics. Later, in 1993, the FA expelled one of its constituent parties, the Movimiento Revolucionario Oriental, because it "refused to eschew recourse to armed struggle" (Latin American Weekly Review, 2/22/96, 74).

16. The new factions were Asamblea Uruguay and Vertiente Artiguista. In addition, the Christian Democrats and one faction of the PGP reestablished an alliance with the Frente Amplio in 1994 called the Encuentro Progresista (see Luna 2007, 5, 18). From 1994, this alliance has governed Montevideo together and run joint slates in all elections as the EP-FA. For the sake of simplicity, this study uses the FA label throughout.

Because national and local elections occurred simultaneously in Uruguay until 1999 and voters had to choose the same party for all races (executive and legislative, national and local), it is difficult to determine whether local or national concerns governed the electorate's decision to support the FA in Montevideo.[17] In general, most analysts agree that in Uruguayan elections, national issues take precedence (Nickson 1995, 253; Rankin 1998, 234). For the 1989 elections, the evidence suggests that the tendency was to punish the governing Colorado Party for not living up to expectations after the return to democracy. All other parties increased their vote shares, with the neoliberal wing of the National Party winning the presidency, while the Colorados dropped to just 30 percent, their lowest proportion of the electorate ever.

Regardless of the electoral system's incentives, the Frente Amplio emphasized its municipal campaign in Montevideo, pushing Vázquez's candidacy at least as much as Seregni's and creating a separate thirty-page party platform for Montevideo.[18] The platform, known as "Document 6," reflected the FA's ideological evolution during the decade of military rule. As Document 6 made clear, deepening democracy had become the party's fundamental goal. For the FA, democracy has "a substantial and not merely instrumental significance." Deepening democracy meant creating conditions—equal access to municipal services and equal rights to formulate demands—that allowed for an organized and active community, such that city residents became true citizens. The tools to achieve deeper democracy were decentralization and participation: "Citizen participation is the irreplaceable road to impel the process of deepening democracy, and . . . decentralization in turn is the privileged path to implement participation" (Frente 1989, 3–7, 10). The FA's campaign stressed that while the traditional—Colorado and National—parties advocated only "deconcentration," or shifting municipal workers from the central office to neighborhood agencies, the Frente's proposal went further, advocating the decentralization of power.[19] As two local scholars put it, the FA's official equation held that "decentralization = participation = democratization" (Sierra and Charbonnier 1993, 17).

---

17. It is certain that at least 4 percent of Montevideo's electorate cast their ballots specifically and only for the municipal elections. Some thirty thousand voters for the Colorado, Blanco, and Nuevo Espacio national candidates withheld their support for their parties' municipal candidates—leaving the space blank—while nearly fifteen thousand voters chose Vázquez at the municipal level but did not endorse Seregni for president (see Klein and Lazovski 1993, 37; Mieres 1994, 137).

18. See Harnecker (1991, 66).

19. See Frente (1989, 10); Centro (1989, 47); and Harnecker 1995b, 61–62).

La Causa Radical

Alfredo Maneiro and ten other dissidents from the Venezuelan Communist Party founded the LCR in 1971.[20] During the prior decade, LCR's founders had taken part in a failed guerrilla movement led by the Communist Party, which had been excluded from the power-sharing agreements between the other major parties toward the end of the dictatorship of Marcos Pérez Jiménez (1948–58). Maneiro criticized both the top-down, exclusionary form of representative democracy installed by the major parties (Acción Democrática and Copei) and the authoritarian internal structure of the Communists. Instead, LCR proposed "radical democracy," in which citizens would participate in governing, not only in elections once every five years. The party itself would embody this notion; it would be a "bottom-up party, organically linked to the popular movement; a party in permanent construction and an ideology perpetually in motion" (López Maya 1995, 231). In fact, the party did not have statutes, formal membership rolls, or party ID cards, preferring public assemblies open to all who were interested. During the 1970s, LCR did not even post candidates for elections.

To build up the party, the founders dispersed in the early 1970s to create four organizations: a student movement at the central university (Prag), a community movement in Caracas (Pro-Catia), a group of intellectuals (La Casa del Agua Mansa), and a union movement in the state of Bolívar (Matancero).[21] The last was the strongest of the four, and its leader, Andrés Velázquez, eventually won the presidency of a major steelworkers union in 1979. Following the death of Maneiro in 1982 and the departure of Prag and Pro-Catia, Matancero became LCR's centerpiece, and its brand of "new unionism" began gaining adherents in other regions of the country, including

20. This summary of LCR's early history is based primarily on López Maya (1995) and Buxton (2001, chap. 6). The party was originally called Venezuela 83, and the name was not changed to La Causa Radical until 1979 (Buxton 2001, 136–49).

21. In 1999, after Hugo Chávez had become president of Venezuela, one of LCR's founders, Pablo Medina, published memoirs in which he claimed that LCR's strategy included a fifth site of operations in addition to the student, *barrio*, intellectual, and union sites. According to Medina, the fifth site was the military. From the late 1970s forward, Medina and other LCR members met with Chávez and his Bolivarian Movement 200 to discuss coordinating a "civic-military rebellion of a democratic nature" (Medina 1999, 93, 40). Other than Medina and a few others, LCR decided not to take part in the two eventual coup attempts in 1992, and the party nearly expelled Medina and his associates for their actions (Medina 1999, 108–15, 127–31, 43). In various interviews, Chávez has confirmed he had contacts with LCR, including a meeting with Maneiro (see, for example, Muñoz 1998, 273–75), but he and others suggest that the role of individual party members was quite limited in both coup attempts (Gott 2000, 63–65, 77; Buxton 2001, 159–63). Aristóbulo Istúriz, LCR's eventual mayor of Caracas, had no contact with Chávez (Muñoz 1998, 592) and evidently played no role in either coup attempt.

Caracas and Zulia (Hellinger 1996; Magallanes 1995, 249; Buxton 2001, 148). The only significant additions to LCR in the mid-1980s were another faction of ex-guerrilla members and a group of leaders from the Caracas teachers' union led by Aristóbulo Istúriz. Until 1988, LCR had little political presence, having won just over 35,000 votes (not even 1 percent of the electorate) in the 1983 legislative elections. In 1988, Istúriz ran for Congress along with Velázquez and one of the party's founders, Pablo Medina. After the party earned just 2 percent of the national vote, these three leaders became LCR's first national deputies. Each was associated with a somewhat different ideological position, with Medina seen as the most radical, Velázquez as closer to the Center, and Istúriz as somewhere in between.[22]

In 1989, Venezuela held elections for the positions of governor and mayor for the first time in its history. Previously, the president had appointed governors, and municipal governments had been run by city councils. LCR scored its biggest electoral prize yet when Velázquez won the governor's race in Bolívar, but at the same time the party won just two mayor's races.[23] That year also witnessed the Caracazo, the two-day riots against structural adjustment that delegitimated the government of President Carlos Andrés Pérez and accelerated the planning efforts of Hugo Chávez and his coup conspirators (Medina 1999, 108).

Chávez's coup attempt of February 4, 1992, in fact helped launch Istúriz to prominence. The day after the coup attempt, the AD government called on Congress to sign a statement condemning the rebel officers' actions. Deputy Istúriz gave a speech denouncing President Pérez instead. With the notoriety from this speech, Istúriz eventually became LCR's candidate for mayor of Caracas in the December election. On November 27, 1992, another group of military officers staged a second coup attempt, which also failed, just one week prior to the state and municipal elections. With 63 percent of the electors abstaining, Istúriz won by 10,576 votes, taking 35 percent of the valid vote. The only other important victories were in the state of Bolívar, where LCR earned reelection to the governorship and the mayoralty in the three largest of the state's ten municipalities (López Maya 1995, 229–30). In Bolívar, LCR may have won because of its strong position in the union movement and its

22. When LCR divided in 1997, Velázquez had been moving toward acceptance of privatization and foreign investment, while Medina and Istúriz remained avowed anti-neoliberals. Velázquez and his followers retained the Causa Radical name; the rest of LCR formed a new party, Patria Para Todos (Homeland for All).

23. One of these was in Ciudad Guayana (Municipio Caroní), where LCR started a participation program somewhat similar to the one it eventually implemented in Caracas.

management of the state and local governments, but in Caracas, Istúriz himself admitted that his unexpected victory was due to voters protesting against the national political crisis (Harnecker 1995c, 26–27).

Once in office, the Causa Radical had the opportunity to implement its ideas about deepening democracy, which until then had consisted mostly of a series of slogans rather than a coherent program. From the earliest writings of Maneiro until the 1990s, LCR had advocated radicalizing or deepening democracy, which meant "bringing government closer to the people, understanding that it is the people that will solve problems, not the party." LCR called for political decentralization under the slogan of "municipalizing democracy and democratizing the municipality"; that is, giving municipalities greater power within the federal system and giving citizens greater power within the municipalities (Istúriz 1996, 11). Like the FA and the PT, the Causa Radical promoted moving beyond administrative decentralization to political decentralization or the decentralization of power.[24] This conception of decentralization entailed the active participation of the community in government affairs, which was seen as "an indispensable condition" for resolving Venezuela's political crisis (Alcaldía 1994b, 2).

Istúriz, in particular, argued that Venezuela eventually needed to move from representative democracy, in which a small group "governs for the people," to a participatory democracy, in which "the people govern themselves." He viewed LCR's position of power in Caracas as a transition phase, in which his administration would "govern with the people." The ultimate goal of LCR's participation program in Caracas was to "transfer real power to the organized citizens" such that "participatory democracy replaces representative democracy" (see Harnecker 1995c, 280; Comisión 1994, 4; Alcaldía 1995b, 17). The Causa's administration in Caracas affirmed that while democracy was the only admissible form of political organization and that some degree of representation was necessary, direct participation was preferable because it gave democracy greater legitimacy (Alcaldía 1994b, 1–2). At the end of Istúriz's term, he described his administration's main strategic goals as deepening the city's democracy by "transforming city residents into citizens," by "being transparent, honest, and efficient with municipal public money," and through urban renovation by "building urgent public works projects, improving urban services, and rethinking and planning the city of the future" (Alcaldía 1995a, 4).

24. According to LCR's leaders, their concept of decentralization in political terms was what distinguished the Causa Radical from the other parties in Venezuela (see Harnecker 1995c, 313–16).

Patterns of Growth in Large Cities: Caracas, Montevideo, and Porto Alegre

For anyone who has visited these cities at the beginning of the twenty-first century, the notion that they are somehow similar might seem unreasonable, especially when comparing the relative order in Montevideo and Porto Alegre to the urban chaos and nearly constant sense of tension in Caracas during the era of Hugo Chávez. At the end of the 1980s and beginning of the 1990s, however, the cities did resemble one another in important ways. Among the most relevant of these were the similar size of their populations, the evolution of population growth and of city services, and key economic indicators such as the unemployment rate. When the FA, PT, and LCR came to office in Montevideo, Porto Alegre, and Caracas, respectively, the cities each had a population of between one and two million inhabitants, a well-served urban center that was losing population to peripheral areas without adequate city services, and modest levels of unemployment and poverty compared to Latin American standards.

In other studies of local politics in Latin America and in the United States, population size has been shown to be a significant factor in determining the rate of participation in civic activities. Montalvo (2008) reports AmericasBarometer individual-level data showing that citizens throughout Latin America are more likely to participate in municipal meetings if they live in small cities. Likewise, Schneider and Goldfrank's (2002) comparison of attendance at public budget assemblies using municipal-level data from the 497 municipalities of the state of Rio Grande do Sul showed that participation rates were higher in smaller municipalities. Bryan's (1999) study of participation in town meetings in New England shows similar results. In a more sophisticated analysis combining municipal contextual data with individual-level data concerning local voting, contacting locally elected officials, and attendance at meetings of community boards and voluntary associations in U.S. cities, Oliver (2000, 336–37) finds that as population size increases, the likelihood of participation in these activities decreases. For example, the probability of attending a community board meeting is 18 percentage points higher for a resident of a town of fewer than 2,500 inhabitants than for a resident of a city of one million or more (2000, 366, 372). Oliver's analysis does not test for differences in cities with populations above one million, but the results suggest that as city size approached one million, the effect of the size variable decreases (2000, 366n10).[25] One

25. Likewise, the data examined by Schneider and Goldfrank (2002) do not allow for testing differences in cities with more than one million inhabitants, given that of Rio Grande do Sul's

Table 2.2   Municipal and metropolitan population size in 1990

	Caracas	Montevideo	Porto Alegre
Population of municipality	1,823,222	1,323,926	1,263,043
Population of metropolitan area	2,731,722	1,712,843	3,059,087

SOURCES: For Caracas, OCEI (1993, 67) and Mitchell (1998, 7, table 1). For Montevideo, my calculations from Unidad (2002, 12). For Porto Alegre, Pozzobon (1998, 3).

of Oliver's most novel findings is that the importance of city population size is the same for municipalities located in both small and large metropolitan areas as well as for those in rural areas. The results of these studies suggest that controlling for population size by selecting cities with relatively similar numbers of inhabitants is worthwhile.

At the beginning of the 1990s, Caracas, Montevideo, and Porto Alegre each had a population of roughly 1.5 million and formed the main part of a larger metropolitan area (see table 2.2).[26] Thus, while none of these cities is a "mega-city" like São Paulo, Mexico City, Buenos Aires, or New York, they are all large, important cities at the hub of regional economic activity. They were three of thirty-eight cities in Latin America with a population over one million in 1990, and three of the top fifteen consumer markets in that decade, with annual consumer spending of over ten billion dollars in each city (CEPAL 2000, 90; InfoAmericas 1999, 6).

In addition to their similar size, Caracas, Montevideo, and Porto Alegre share common trajectories of population growth and public service expansion. Each city experienced accelerated population growth from the early part of the twentieth century until around the 1960s and 1970s and a declining rate of growth in the following decades. The population of metropolitan Caracas doubled between 1941 and 1950, and again between 1961 and 1971, while the

---

497 municipalities, the population of only one—Porto Alegre—reached over a million. Nonetheless, our data also suggest that the magnitude of the city size effect on participation rates decreases at the upper bounds.

26. The metropolitan area population reported in table 2.2 for Caracas refers to the five municipalities—Libertador, Chacao, Sucre, Baruta, and El Hatillo—closest to the city center. They are usually referred to as the metropolitan area and currently form part of the Metropolitan District (created in 2000 under Venezuela's new constitution). Higher population estimates, reaching a little over four million, have been made for what is known as the greater metropolitan area of Caracas (Mitchell 1998, 3; Alvarez 1998, 245). This area includes La Guaira (a newly created municipality in the old municipality of Vargas, which formed part of the old Federal District alongside Libertador), Los Teques, Guatire, Guarenas, and smaller bedroom communities in the Tuy valleys. The population estimates for Montevideo in table 2.2 were made using census data from 1985 and 1996, when the numbers of inhabitants in the municipality were 1,311,976 and 1,344,839, respectively. Metropolitan government did not exist in any of the three metropolitan areas.

Table 2.3   Municipal land area

Caracas	Montevideo	Porto Alegre
434 km²	530 km²	470 km²

SOURCES: For Caracas, http://revistacandidus.com/VisEst/distritocapital/
DFinfo.htm; for Montevideo, my calculation from INE (1996, 9); and
for Porto Alegre, Pozzobon (1998, 3).

population of Porto Alegre more than doubled between 1950 and 1970 (Marcano 1993, 58; DEMHAB 1999, 31). Montevideo's population nearly quadrupled between 1908 and 1963 (Canzani 1989, 3). In line with Latin American regional trends, the rate of population growth in each city slowed considerably in the 1980s and 1990s, while outlying cities of their metropolitan regions saw continued high growth rates.[27] In no case, then, did the incoming municipal administration face a sudden population explosion that might have made meeting new demands for infrastructure exceptionally difficult.

A particularly important common feature across the cities was the population decline in the established urban core and the continued population growth in the less developed peripheral areas, a centrifugal pattern noted by urbanists in many Latin American cities (see Portes 1989, 8). The municipal boundaries of Caracas, Montevideo, and Porto Alegre contain extensive land-masses (see table 2.3), including small agricultural zones in the rural parts of Montevideo and Porto Alegre and in one mostly rural district of Caracas, El Junquito. In fact, at the start of the twenty-first century one can still find horse-drawn carts on the streets of each city (at night, one can even find them in the city centers of Montevideo and Porto Alegre, where they collect refuse for recycling). Each city also includes large zones of protected parklands and other ecologically sensitive areas where construction is illegal. Ecologically sensitive areas refer to steep hillsides and the banks of rivers and creeks, all of which often serve as locations for squatter settlements.

Despite the legal issues, housing construction and population growth in the city peripheries soared in the 1980s and 1990s. In Venezuela's (now defunct) Federal District, of which Caracas is the largest part, the amount of land as protected green areas fell 35 percent between 1985 and 1992, from over 100,000 hectares to 65,000. This "vegetation massacre" was due

27. Growth in Montevideo had already slowed by the 1960s; see Unidad (2002, 12) and Facultad (1994, 16–17). For Caracas, see Marcano (1993, 58–59) and Mitchell (1998, 1–2). For Porto Alegre, see Martins and Loureiro (1997, 155–56) and Pozzobon (1998, 3). For the regional trend, see CEPAL (2000, 10–11).

to the construction of approximately seventeen *ranchos* (squatter homes) per day in the metropolitan area of Caracas in the early 1990s (*El Globo* 1/2/96, 10). In Montevideo, neighborhoods at the outer ring of the city, like Colón, Toledo Chico, and Villa García, grew tremendously in the 1970s and 1980s (up to 44 percent in a ten-year span), while the older central neighborhoods like Ciudad Vieja, Centro, and Barrio Sur all lost population in those decades. Ciudad Vieja, for example, lost nearly 25 percent of its inhabitants between 1985 and 1996.[28] Porto Alegre's central areas lost, on average, almost 1 percent of their population per year between 1980 and 1991, while its peripheral areas gained an average of 3 percent per year. Thus, 42 percent of Porto Alegre's residents lived in the city periphery by 1991 (Martins and Loureiro 1997, 165, table 8).

The simultaneous population loss in the urban core and growth in peripheral areas created serious, and expensive, difficulties for the municipal governments. Public services and infrastructure were satisfactory in the central urban areas by the 1960s, but were deficient in the periphery. Therefore, population growth in the periphery meant inefficient use of existing city services and extra costs for expanding such services beyond the urban core. In effect, although none of the incoming administrations faced a population boom, they each faced a population dispersion that produced similar results: increasing demand for public services.

This demand was especially acute given the prior pattern of service provision. In each of these cities, at one point or another before the 1970s, municipal and sometimes national officials had made concerted and relatively successful efforts to provide services to those living in the "formal" (legal) urban areas. At the same time, they either benignly ignored (and sometimes encouraged) the growing illegal squatter settlements in the periphery or, occasionally, engaged in repression through forced removal, especially during periods of dictatorship when military rulers attempted shantytown eradication programs. In Uruguay, the military regime quickly enacted a housing law to end rent control in Montevideo, causing a wave of homelessness, and then began evicting tenants in the old central parts of the city, particularly Barrio Sur, a traditionally Afro-Uruguayan neighborhood (Benton 1986, 40–46). Likewise, in the 1960s the military-appointed mayor of Porto Alegre ordered the eviction of an entire Afro-Brazilian neighborhood and relocated the residents from the downtown area to the periphery, creating a new neighborhood,

28. For the 1985 to 1996 census periods, see CLAEH (1996, 28–29). For the 1975 to 1985 period, see Canzani (1989, 5–7). See also Bluth (1988, 9–10) and Portes (1989, 19).

Restinga, a forty-five-minute bus ride from the city center.[29] In Caracas, the bulldozing of squatter settlements under the Pérez Jiménez dictatorship of the 1950s does not seem to have been related to race, though it did occur simultaneously with a state-sponsored wave of European immigration.[30] Later plans under democratic governments to eliminate *ranchos* in the predominantly Afro-Venezuelan neighborhood of San Agustín del Sur sparked the formation of the Committee Against Displacement, which had links to a black cultural organization, Grupo Madera (Fernandes 2007, 104–5).

Repression of informal housing arrangements was never widespread or long-lasting. Yet rather than attempting to urbanize the growing squatter settlements—by granting land titles and installing infrastructure—governments sometimes encouraged residence in the formal parts of the city by building public housing projects or enacting rent control. Over time, each city developed a similar binary categorization of neighborhoods—as either regular or irregular, formal or informal, or legal or illegal—that became strongly ingrained, marking an important social division reflected in the local language. In Caracas, one lives in either an *urbanización* (legal) or a *barrio* (illegal); in Montevideo, one lives in a *barrio* (legal) or a *cantegril* (illegal); and in Porto Alegre, one lives in a *bairro* (legal) or in a *vila* (illegal). The more widely known term for squatter settlement in Brazil, *favela*, is used only rarely in Porto Alegre.

In general, after the earlier success in providing infrastructure, government spending on public services began to decline in the late 1960s and 1970s in Montevideo and in the 1980s in Porto Alegre and Caracas, when state funds had dried up. By the late 1980s, after nearly a decade of the region-wide debt crisis, the patterns of population growth and public service provision had combined to produce a sizable contingent of residents living in the "informal" areas and demanding improvements in local infrastructure. Added to this mix were trends of deindustrialization, rising unemployment, and increasing informality in the labor force. The basic pattern of expansion and then stagnation of public services showed minor variations across the three cities.

29. Interview with Tális Rosa, Restinga district coordinator, 11/10/98; see also Baierle (1992, 41).
30. An unprecedented expansion of public housing also accompanied slum eradication in Caracas. Between 1954 and 1958, 180,000 residents relocated to the new government-built "super-blocks" in Caracas and La Guaira, the neighboring city on the coast (Barinas 1999). Some of the super-blocks were invaded before completion just as Pérez Jiménez was toppled, such as those in the neighborhood of 23 de Enero, which takes its name from the day the dictator fled the country.

The expansion occurred earliest in Montevideo, which in 1856 was the first city in South America with a sewer system.[31] Under *Batllista* welfare-state policies from the 1910s to the 1960s, Uruguay enjoyed a relatively high standard of living and was sometimes referred to as the Switzerland of South America. During this period, Montevideo's public services compared favorably to those in the rest of urban Latin America. However, in the 1970s a process of "urban involution" (Facultad 1994, 16) began, with the deterioration of infrastructure and housing stock, migration from the city center to the periphery and cities in the outlying metropolitan area, and emigration (or escape) out of Uruguay altogether. This involution, or atrophy, was due to the decline of the economy, to the lack of public and private investment in the city, and to the military dictatorship's repressive policies. One particularly noticeable sign of Montevideo's decay was the process known as *tugurización* (which might be translated as "slumification"), in which large, old, deteriorated houses in the city center were illegally occupied or parceled and rented out to poor families, despite their infrastructural inadequacy. By the end of the 1980s, the crisis in public services—as well as the rise of poverty, inequality, social segregation, and informalization of the labor force—led scholars to write of the "Latin Americanization" of Montevideo.[32]

Porto Alegre also has a long history of urban planning, dating back to the early 1900s, when much of Brazil, and especially Rio Grande do Sul, was under the influence of positivism. The Partido Republicano Riograndense (PRR) governed Rio Grande do Sul for forty years (1892–1930) with positivism as its guiding ideology. During this period, the party oversaw what has been called the "gaúcho model"[33] of economic development, which included the "socialization of public services" and rising government investment in infrastructure (Schmidt and Herrlein 2002, 3–6). Porto Alegre was one of the first cities in Brazil with a system of trolley cars, for example, which provided public transportation for workers in its growing industrial sector. Populist governments continued the relatively progressive policies in the state and its capital in the period of the *Estado Novo* under Getúlio Vargas (a former PRR national deputy for Rio Grande do Sul), and during Brazil's Second Republic, when Leonel Brizola was mayor of Porto Alegre and then state governor until a year before the 1964 military coup. During

---

31. See Bluth (1988, 42). For Montevideo's evolution, see also Canzani (1989), Facultad (1994), Portillo (1996, 25–25; 51–52), and Arana and Giordano (1992).

32. For the specific phrase, see Veiga (1989, 299). See also Canzani (1989), Aguirre (1993, 92), and Portes (1989, 30).

33. Residents of the state of Rio Grande do Sul are known as *gaúchos*.

the dictatorship that followed, however, Porto Alegre's appointed mayors emphasized large-scale projects to improve private transportation—bridges, tunnels, and viaducts—rather than expansion of infrastructure in basic sanitation or housing (Ferretti 1984, 143–44). From the late 1970s forward, municipal government spending on infrastructure fell dramatically, such that in 1986, such spending represented just 26 percent of that spent in 1977 (Horn et al. 1988, 8–9). In their comparative study of four Brazilian cities, Horn et al. lament the unfinished projects, deficiency of infrastructure and basic services, and the general decline of quality of life in Porto Alegre during the 1970s and 1980s, while noting certain advances in the other cities in the same period (Campinas, Curitiba, and Belo Horizonte).

The burst of population growth in Caracas came a few decades later than in the other cities, as did the attempts at urban planning. While Montevideo already had over half a million residents by 1940, Caracas had just half that many. The rapid urban growth in Venezuela in the following decades coincided with the expansion of oil revenues for the Venezuelan state. Oil wealth led to state largesse, especially after the establishment of democracy in 1958, and the avowedly social and Christian democratic governments provided the middle and working classes in Caracas with "subsidized housing, upgraded public education, improved collective transportation, cheap electricity, and ample water" (Myers 1978, 256). As in Porto Alegre, however, much of the public investment in infrastructure went to large-scale projects, especially to building a public office and housing complex with two skyscraping towers (Parque Central) and a network of highways across the city, complete with aerodynamic overpasses rivaling those of Los Angeles. According to David Myers (1978, 256), an urbanist writing during the period of Venezuela's oil boom, "Barring an unforseen [sic] drop in world petroleum prices, or a faster than expected depletion of Venezuelan oil reserves, services in Caracas will continue to be provided at a comparatively high level for the majority of the population." But oil prices did drop, and the quality of service provision fell in the 1980s. Already by 1978, problems of rapid urban growth like traffic congestion and environmental degradation had earned Caracas the ignominious distinction as the "most badly polluted city on the South American continent" (Violich 1987, 167). New problems of insufficient housing, unmaintained roads and sewage systems, and water shortages began to plague Caracas in the 1980s.[34]

34. Similar to what occurred in Montevideo, in some sections of Caracas, like El Paraíso, the old mansions of the upper classes gradually were converted into tenement slums (Marcano 1993, 59–60).

Table 2.4   Basic service provision

Percentage of domiciles . . .	Caracas (1990)*	Montevideo (1996)	Porto Alegre (1991)
with water supplied internally	92%	93%	96%
with electricity	96%	99%	99%
connected to sewage system	93%	77%	81%**

*Figures for Caracas are from the Federal District (which also includes Vargas).

**Includes domiciles connected to sewage or pluvial system.

Sources: For Caracas, OCEI (1993, 649); for Montevideo, INE (1996, 26, 97, 81); for Porto Alegre, IBGE (1991, 526, 538, 550).

Overall, then, Caracas, Montevideo, and Porto Alegre showed roughly similar patterns of growth, with each experiencing periods of rapid expansion of population and services prior to a period of deterioration in the 1970s and 1980s. As tables 2.4 and 2.5 show, by the early 1990s the level of service provision and the socioeconomic profile in the three cities were rather more alike than different. The large majority of residents in each city had access to essential services like water and electricity, yet in many cases such access was "informal" (that is, stolen) and the supply of water was not reliable in all parts of the cities, particularly in Porto Alegre and Caracas. Hidrocapital, the agency for water provision in metropolitan Caracas, was often referred to by residents as "Hidrocriminal."[35] Other basic services, such as paved streets, trash collection, public transportation, and public lighting, showed clear deficiencies.[36] At the same time, a considerable minority of the inhabitants in each city lived in poverty, and unemployment rates had grown higher than in the past.

The only substantial variation across the cities concerns the higher degree of income inequality in Porto Alegre (as seen in its Gini index) and the lower percentage of the population living in irregular housing areas in Montevideo. These differences seem less relevant than the overall similarities,

35. The water system in Caracas is notoriously inefficient. When this inefficiency combined with a drought in Caracas in the summer of 1992, neighborhood associations closed down streets, erected barricades, and even took over the offices of Hidrocapital to protest the water shortage (López Maya 1997, 120).

36. Comparable statistics for these services are not available for each city. However, scholars (and city residents) describing local conditions agree that services in these areas were inadequate. For Caracas, for example, see Vallmitjana et al. (1993); for Montevideo, Portillo (1996); and for Porto Alegre, Horn et al. (1988).

Table 2.5   Socioeconomic indicators (circa 1990)

	Caracas	Montevideo	Porto Alegre
Percentage of households below the poverty line	28% (1990)	27% (1991)	24% (1991)
Percentage of labor force unemployed	10% (1990)	9% (1991)	11% (1993)
Percentage of adults illiterate*	3% (1990)	3% (1985)	6% (1991)
Gini index	.40 (1990)**	.39 (1990)	.59 (1990)
Infant mortality, per thousand live births	21.4 (1990)**	20.3 (1990)	18.7 (1992)
Percentage of residents living in areas of irregular housing	41% (1993)	12% (1996)	34% (1991)

*For Caracas, over ten years old; for Montevideo, over eighteen years old; for Porto Alegre, heads of households.

**Figures are for the Federal District.

SOURCES: For Caracas, Ministerio (Cuadro 7), OCEI (1993, 579), Wikander (1994, table 8), UNDP (1996, Cuadros 4–8), OCEI et al. (1997, 313), and Fundacomún (1993, 1); for Montevideo, Unidad (2002, 120, 48, 124), INE (1996, 16), Bucheli and Rossi (2001, table 1), and Lombardi et al. (n.d., 4); for Porto Alegre, Mamarrella (1998, 6), PMPA (1998, 17, 37), Pozzobon (1998, 32), Balarine (1995, table 12), and Martins and Loureiro (1997, 164).

especially given that most housing units have electricity and basic sanitation services, even in the irregular housing areas in Caracas and Porto Alegre, and that the figure for irregular housing in Montevideo does not include those residing in the rundown tenements, or *tugúrios*, where an estimated seventy thousand residents lived in 1985.[37]

Cycles of Protest: Community Organizing and Neighborhood Associations

The history of community-based organizations in Caracas, Montevideo, and Porto Alegre largely mirrors the general Latin American pattern of a rise of such organizations in the 1970s and early 1980s followed by a decline in their numbers and influence by the end of that decade.[38] In addition to the

37. See Portes (1989, 20). In addition, according to the National Institute of Statistics, 44 percent of Montevideans were living in "inadequate housing" in 1991, defined as presenting one or more of the following characteristics: a residence that is neither an apartment nor a house, not built to be lived in, built with precarious materials, needs major reparations, or in which there are more than two occupants per bedroom (Unidad 2002, 134).

38. See, among others, Nickson (1995, 90).

participatory rhetoric and practices emanating from Catholic activists inspired by liberation theology and from women's organizations (some inspired by feminism), the impetus of community movements, particularly the neighborhood associations, reflects the deterioration of urban services across the region in the 1970s, while the movements' subsequent decline corresponds to the weakening of the state's ability to respond to demands during the debt crisis. At the same time, in countries under authoritarian rule in the 1970s— like Brazil and Uruguay—community organizations often served as an outlet for opposition to dictatorship. Once democracy was restored in the mid-1980s, this motivation disappeared. Thus, both achievement of movement goals (restoring democracy) and failure to do so (improvements in living conditions) contributed to diminished interest in neighborhood activism in the late 1980s. Though obviously in a different political context, Venezuela's neighborhood associations experienced a similar pattern, with their success coming in the form of the creation of local rather than national democracy (the direct elections of state and municipal executives in 1989) and their failure epitomized by the unplanned and undirected riots collectively known as the Caracazo. The Catholic Church's turn away from liberation theology, the entrance of women into institutional politics, and the transformation of many women's organizations into NGO-like service providers in the 1980s and early 1990s also diminished community activism.[39] A final source of decline for neighborhood movements across the region—and particularly in Caracas, Montevideo, and Porto Alegre—was the attempt by political parties and state officials to use neighborhood associations to distribute benefits, especially subsidized milk for children and nursing mothers. This kind of domestication of community groups frequently resulted in residents seeing them as appendages of the state rather than as vehicles of protest.

---

39. The literatures on the Catholic Church and on women's movements in Latin America are too vast to summarize here. For the rise and fall of liberation theology activism, see Daudelin and Hewitt (1995); for women's activism in the democratic transitions, see Waylen (1994); and for the NGO-ization of feminism, see Alvarez (1999). Notably, scholars of Brazil and Venezuela observe that the rise of women's organizations in the 1970s was closely linked to progressive Catholic organizing (Alvarez 1990; Fernandes 2007). The life history of one of Uruguay's most prominent feminists, Senator Margarita Percovich, suggests that a similar process may have occurred there as well. Percovich started her activist career with the Catholic Church during the time of the Vatican II Council. She later worked with Archbishop Carlos Parteli and became influenced by liberation theology, particularly that produced by Uruguay's own Juan Luis Segundo. In the 1980s and 1990s, she helped create several feminist organizations such as PLEMUU before becoming a city councilor and president of the city council in Montevideo for the FA. See Percovich's biography on the Mujeres en el Parlamento Web page at http://www.parlamento.gub.uy/externos/parlamenta/m_margarita.html.

Table 2.6   Number of registered neighborhood associations

Caracas (1994)	Montevideo (1988)	Porto Alegre (1988)
427	626*	300

*Of these, 436 were functioning. For the other cities, the number of functioning associations is not certain.

Sources: For Caracas, Wikander (1994, 82); for Montevideo, González (1995, 39); for Porto Alegre, Baierle (1992, 68, table 1).

Recognizing the pattern of rising and falling fortunes of community movements, scholars of Brazil, Uruguay, and Venezuela have separately analyzed such movements in terms of "cycles of protest."[40] Consistent with this pattern, by the end of the 1980s, the once-vibrant community organizations in Montevideo and Porto Alegre had entered a phase of decline or disenchantment, which would be reached in Caracas by the early 1990s (following two coup attempts and the impeachment of sitting president Carlos Andrés Pérez). Despite this period's downward trajectory for local community movements—in terms of creation of new groups, expanding membership, level of activity, and political weight—several hundred neighborhood associations remained in existence in each city, as did dozens of other types of organizations such as housing cooperatives, soup kitchens, mothers' clubs, and collective health clinics. Table 2.6 displays the number of neighborhood associations registered with the municipal government at about the time the participation programs began. Figures for the other types of community groups are not available in all cases, but the evolution of territorially based organizing within each city shows interesting parallels.

Caracas

The rich and extensive literature on the Venezuelan neighborhood association movement flags 1971 as a key moment.[41] That year marked the founding of FACUR (Federación de Asociaciones de Comunidades Urbanas). Though FACUR originally represented just fourteen neighborhood associations

40. Most of these analysts make reference to the work on protest cycles by Tarrow (1994). For Brazil, see Hochstetler (2000); for Uruguay, see Canel (1992); and for Venezuela, see Levine (1998). López Maya (1997) describes a different cycle of protest in Venezuela, one from 1989 to 1993, when President Carlos Andrés Pérez was impeached. This may be seen as a second cycle, coming after that from the early 1970s to the late 1980s in which the repertoire of protest was less violent.

41. The discussion below is based primarily on Ramos (1995), Ellner (1999), Gómez (1990; 1998), García-Guadilla (1994), Silberberg (1992), and an interview with Elías Santana (12/23/99).

located in middle-class zones of the southeastern part of the Caracas metropolitan area, it grew to become a significant political actor. Prior to the creation of FACUR, neighborhood associations had played only minor roles in politics, forming first toward the end of Vicente Gómez's dictatorship in the 1930s, disappearing under Pérez Jiménez, and emerging again when mobilized by the state in the late 1950s and 1960s.[42] It was only in the following decade, however, that neighborhood associations began to gain political importance. FACUR and its allies pushed for reforms to give citizens greater input into local decision making and demanded greater government control over the chaotic urban sprawl that was threatening the environment. They quickly won significant victories on both fronts, including legislation in 1979 that recognized neighborhood associations as entities with legal rights vis-à-vis local government and separated municipal from national elections, and the creation of a large public park in the eastern part of metropolitan Caracas, the Parque del Este.

The legal recognition and other successes, in addition to the ongoing urban problems, sparked a city- and nationwide explosion of associations in the 1980s as local leaders reformed preexisting organizations into neighborhood associations or founded new ones in both middle-class *urbanizaciones* and lower-class *barrios*. With FACUR and a new NGO—the Escuela de Vecinos (School for Neighbors)[43]—leading, the neighborhood association movement continued pressing for political reforms, including creation of—and direct elections for—city mayors, recall of elected officials, autonomy for municipalities, direct citizen participation through such measures as referenda and town hall meetings, local elections every three years, direct elections for governors, and single-member districts in legislative elections rather than closed-list proportional representation. In 1987, FACUR, now representing 120 associations from all parts of Caracas, gathered one hundred and forty thousand signatures in support of the first five of these proposals. The national government's decentralization program incorporated many of the movement's proposals in 1989, including mayoral and gubernatorial elections (Ramos 1995, 98, 161, 151–56; Gómez 1990, 281–88). Furthermore, the number of neighborhood associations in Venezuela had grown from 25 in 1971 to 5,036 by 1989, with between 400 and 650 in Caracas alone (Hanes 1993, 185–86; Vallmitjana 1993, 183). In sum, the rapidly growing

---

42. Neighborhood associations were originally known as *juntas pro fomento* or *juntas pro mejoras de la comunidad.*

43. The Escuela de Vecinos was formed in 1980 to serve as a resource and training center for leaders of neighborhood associations.

neighborhood association movement was at the forefront of the social movements' "demands for participatory democracy and decentralization of the state" (García 1992, 167, 157).

In addition to FACUR and the Escuela de Vecinos, a host of other new organizations arose, including environmental groups, women's movements (headed by the Coordinator of Women's NGOs, CONG, and including the Circulos Femininos Populares based in the *barrios*), progressive Catholic organizations (including the CESAP Social Group and the Jesuit-led Centro Gumilla), cooperatives of various types, and other community organizations not legally registered as neighborhood associations. The most important of these nonregistered community groups in Caracas was Pro-Catia, which had been started by members of LCR in the early 1970s.[44] Pro-Catia was based in the *barrios* of the largest parish in Caracas, Sucre (also known as Catia). One of its earliest fights was for the creation of a Park of the West, in response to the park built in the richer eastern part of the metropolitan area. Though Pro-Catia won this battle, it failed in its other major quest, to reform the Caracas City Council. In 1976, Pro-Catia gathered twenty-four thousand signatures in favor of its proposal to change council elections, such that each councilor would be tied to a local district (one per parish) and citizens could recall councilors who failed to represent them.[45]

Pro-Catia had gradually lost force as a movement at the end of the 1980s, as had the more middle-class-oriented FACUR. The early 1990s saw other attempts to coordinate *barrio* organizations, such as the Regional Neighborhood Coordinator and the Assembly of Barrios (named after the one in Mexico City), but these were short-lived (Francke 1997, 50–52). In general, after the proliferation of community organizations and especially neighborhood associations in the 1980s, the movement "lost momentum" in the following decade, failing to live up to the "lofty expectations" of many analysts (Ellner 1999, 76–77; see also Gómez 1998, 180–81). Despite the neighborhood association movement's inability to consolidate itself as a unified force or to achieve major victories in the 1990s, thousands of community members—organized or not—actively demonstrated against President Pérez's structural adjustment program alongside student groups, street vendors,

---

44. Pro-Catia is generally overlooked in the literature on the neighborhood association movement. This discussion is based on an interview with Rafael Uzcátegui (1/21/99) and on López Maya (1995, 217–18).

45. A mixed electoral system was eventually adopted more than ten years later (in 1989), with roughly half the councilors elected to represent districts and half according to proportional representation but biased so that the party that won the mayor's race would have a majority on the council.

and unions in a country-wide wave of protest that lasted from the Caracazo in February 1989 until the December 1993 elections (see López Maya 1997).

Montevideo

Although less storied and studied than the neighborhood associations of Caracas, those in Montevideo were more numerous at their height and, along with other community-based organizations, played an important role during the economic hardships and political persecution in Uruguay's decade of military rule (1973–84).[46] Neighborhood organizing began in the early twentieth century in Montevideo, and even by 1991, many associations[47] that had been founded in the 1930s still existed (González 1995, 39). Until the late 1970s, however, the tradition of neighborhood associations was only strong in specific parts of the city (for example, La Unión, El Cerro, La Teja, Colón). At that point, Montevideo experienced an explosion of community organizing, including not only neighborhood associations but soup kitchens, food cooperatives, groups of housewives, health clinics, and housing cooperatives. Coordinating committees emerged for each type of group, and they received financial and technical support from unions, international NGOs, and the Catholic Church, which also supported Christian "base communities" (CEBs) under the progressive archbishop of Montevideo, Carlos Parteli. Local research centers and NGOs like CIDC, CIESU, and the School of Architecture at the University of the Republic also assisted the new community movements. Human rights groups, anchored by the mothers of those jailed and disappeared, also emerged at this time.

According to Canel (1992, 279), by 1985, there were 740 neighborhood associations registered with the municipal government, of which approximately 600 were active. Around 100 of these associations belonged to the coordinating committee, called MOVEMO (Movimiento de Vecinos de Montevideo), while another twenty-odd shantytown organizations united under MOVIDE (Movimiento Pro-Vivienda Decorosa). The federation of housing cooperatives, FUCVAM (Federación Uruguaya de Cooperativas de Vivienda de Ayuda Mútua), which had been founded in 1971, also had dozens of affiliates in Montevideo, reaching over 119 by the end of the decade (CLAEH

---

46. This section is based primarily on Canel (1992), González (1992; 1995), and Aguirre (1993). Aguirre (1993, 93) writes that in Uruguay, urban organizations with a territorial base (such as neighborhood associations) historically "had a lesser presence than in other Latin American countries."

47. In Uruguay, the terms *comisión de fomento* and *comisión vecinal* are used rather than *asociación*.

1996, 154). The various organizations simultaneously provided cover for opposition to military rule and tools for coping with Uruguay's economic crisis.

After the return to democracy in 1985, these community-based movements began to decline. For example, the number of soup kitchens and food cooperatives declined by half over a two-year period, and by 1988, MOVEMO had only a dozen members participating in meetings (Canel 1992, 280). The health clinic coordinating committee and MOVIDE maintained their prior levels of organization, however, as did women's groups like PLEMUU. Nonetheless, FUCVAM, described as Uruguay's "most significant urban social movement," also entered a period of decline in the late 1980s (Sierra and Charbonnier 1993, 27n3). Despite the gradual loss of momentum, hundreds of community organizations of various types remained active and had sufficient presence at the end of the decade that Mariano Arana, a prominent urbanist (and future mayor of Montevideo for the FA), proclaimed them to be a "substantial resource with which to initiate a policy of change to a participatory and pluralist basis at the city level" (Arana and Giordano 1992, 159).

Porto Alegre

Like many of Brazil's major cities, Porto Alegre has a long history of neighborhood organizing, dating back to the 1930s.[48] A federation of community associations for the state of Rio Grande do Sul (FRACAB) was founded in Porto Alegre in 1959.[49] It survived the initial years of the military dictatorship by maintaining a cooperative relationship with local authorities. By the mid-1970s, however, community-based social movements of several kinds had begun mobilizing opposition to the authoritarian regime under diverse banners in Porto Alegre and throughout urban Brazil, including movements for health, housing, and transportation, and against unemployment and inflation (Doimo 1995, 95–122). As in Caracas and Montevideo, women played important roles in these wider community movements as well as in mothers' clubs and in explicitly feminist organizations, like Porto Alegre's S.O.S. Mulher. And despite the conservatism of the local archdiocese, Catholic base communities also became important voices for democracy in many neighborhoods. Silva (2001, 110–14) emphasizes the strong influence of liberation theology on Porto Alegre's "combative camp"

---

48. This section is based primarily on Ferretti (1984) and Baierle (1992).

49. FRACAB stands for Federação Riograndense de Associações Comunitárias e de Amigos de Bairro. The terms for neighborhood association in Porto Alegre are *associação de moradores* and *sociedade de amigos de bairro*.

of community activists in the 1970s. FRACAB assumed a pronounced antiregime stance in these years, provoking the municipal and state governments (which had been appointed by the military rulers) to "declare war on FRACAB" by cutting off its financial subsidy (Ferretti 1984, 163). After the local governments failed to close down FRACAB, they tried to create parallel organizations—the Conselhão and the Movimento Comunitário Gaúcho—but these groups did not attract many followers.

With the democratic opening that followed in the early 1980s (with state-level elections in 1982), a separate organization was founded to coordinate the neighborhood associations in Porto Alegre alone (UAMPA, the União de Associações de Moradores de Porto Alegre). UAMPA united fifty-one associations at its founding in 1983, and over two hundred by the end of the decade (Baierle 1992, 68). In several individual city districts, territorially based "popular councils" and "unions of associations" began to organize as well. Local NGOs, or centers for popular education, like FASE, CAMP, and CIDADE, provided support to the new community movements, facilitating seminars, helping to write pamphlets, and aiding in the formulation of public policy proposals. In 1984, the local movements in Porto Alegre coalesced around the call for direct presidential elections, organizing large street demonstrations.

After the end of military rule in 1985 (with an indirect presidential election), the organizing momentum began to slow down or reverse in Porto Alegre, as in the rest of Brazil.[50] Nonetheless, although the numbers of participants had fallen off, many neighborhood associations remained active, though often through their presidents (a pattern seen in Caracas and Montevideo as well). In addition, UAMPA and individual community associations took part in the discussions for the new municipal organic law in the late 1980s and, together with FRACAB and local NGOs, formed a Popular Forum for Urban Reform that had some links to similar organizations in São Paulo and Rio de Janeiro. Indeed, the goal of urban reform had been a constant since the 1970s, and included both specific policy recommendations and more general calls for democracy, decentralization, and popular participation.

In summary, the community organizations in Caracas, Montevideo, and Porto Alegre had reached a kind of developmental peak and entered a downswing prior to the election of LCR, FA, and PT, respectively. Indeed, these parties may have contributed to this decline because they each recruited

50. For Porto Alegre, see Pereira and Moura (1988, 7, 13), Baierle (1992, 10, 67–72, 106), and Abers (2000, 43). For Brazil, see Mainwaring (1989, 198–99) and Doimo (1995, chap. 8), among others.

many community leaders to work in municipal election campaigns and in government. Yet hundreds of associations remained. And the cycle of rise and decline had bequeathed a legacy of activism, as thousands of women and men had either belonged to some kind of community organization or had participated in the recent past. To different degrees across neighborhoods and across cities, local activists had been influenced by ideas about citizen participation emanating not just from political parties, but from feminist and progressive Catholic organizations as well. Nonetheless, community-based groups held heterogeneous political views, particularly regarding relationships to political parties. Some had strong clientelist or ideological ties to individual parties, and some sought balanced party representation in leadership positions, while others rejected party involvement altogether. As argued below (in the section on opposition parties), the specific mix of more or less autonomous community organizations differed across cities, but in ways closely related to the type of local parties that had historically predominated.

Municipal Bureaucracies: Overstaffed, Underworked, and Underpaid

In many Latin American countries, city jobs—like government jobs in general—have frequently been distributed as favors in exchange for political loyalty. According to local government expert Andrew Nickson, "Overstaffing is a major consequence of clientelism in local government" (1995, 77). For many cities, the results of overstaffing and clientelist hiring practices include a municipal workforce that is poorly motivated and underqualified. Not surprisingly, the reigning stereotype of municipal employees across the region is one of lazy, inefficient, rude, and occasionally corrupt workers (Nickson 1995, 18). In the late 1980s, the municipal bureaucracies in Caracas, Montevideo, and Porto Alegre did not escape such characterizations.

    When the LCR, FA, and PT arrived in office, each faced a bloated payroll. Table 2.7 shows the absolute and relative numbers of employees for each city. The higher number of employees in Porto Alegre is largely due to the large number of teachers and other workers in the city government's primary schools (a service provided by other levels of government in Caracas and Montevideo; see below). In each city, the payroll included hundreds if not thousands of "ghost" workers, meaning those who only showed up to receive a paycheck. In Porto Alegre, for example, newly installed PT officials complained of the existence of four thousand employees who did not work (Schabbach 1995, 86n59). LCR in Caracas and the FA in Montevideo made similar accusations (Harnecker 1995d, 58–61; 1995b, 41).

Table 2.7   Size of municipal bureaucracy

	Caracas (1992)	Montevideo (1989)	Porto Alegre (1988)
Number of active employees	15,000 (est.)	12,541	17,494
Number of employees per 1,000 residents (estimated)	8.2	9.5	13.8

SOURCES: For Caracas, Harnecker (1995d, 10); for Montevideo, Varela (1996, 96, Cuadro 1); for Porto Alegre, PMPA (1997, 106).

Indeed, in their first year in office, each of these parties retired hundreds of city workers. The PT administration in Porto Alegre reduced its payroll by not quite one thousand workers in its first year. Subsequently, the administration made several thousand new hires, with the payroll reaching over twenty thousand active employees by 1994 (PMPA 1997, 106). A large proportion of the hiring was of teachers for the growing number of city schools and students.[51] LCR's administration in Caracas paid for the retirement of several hundred workers (Dirección 1993). In Montevideo, the FA's policy of reducing personnel continued throughout the 1990s, such that by the end of the decade fewer than ten thousand workers remained (Unidad 2002, 57).

Combined with the initial overstaffing were problems of inefficiency, petty corruption, lack of discipline, and failure to maintain the municipal government's equipment, installations, and machinery. The deterioration of the municipal bureaucracy in Montevideo occurred concomitantly with the general process of urban "involution" that the city experienced during the military regime. Portillo (1996, 51–52) provides an evocative description of the decline of Montevideo's municipal apparatus prior to 1990:

Political clientelism inundated the already inflated payroll with unneeded personnel, salaries were progressively reduced, the repairs and maintenance of equipment necessary for responsible government were not carried out, and so on, consecutively contributing to the general process of decay through action or omission. Within the municipal government, worker discipline progressively deteriorated, the corruption of the rest of the public administration became institutionalized,

51. The number of students in city schools jumped from 18,200 in 1988 to 30,518 in 1994, an increase of 68 percent (see PMPA 1997, 141).

the average age grew older, and administrative personnel continued increasing, to the detriment of technically qualified workers or laborers, all together forming a scenario of growing inefficiency with clearly negative effects on urban administration.[52]

The conditions of the city bureaucracies in Porto Alegre and Caracas were much the same. Fedozzi (1997, 65–111) sees the municipal government in Porto Alegre as representative of traditional Brazilian patrimonialism. Its traits include private appropriation of public resources, clientelism and particularism in the allocation of public resources, and lack of transparency. Baierle (1992, 37–43; 46n105) gives examples of Porto Alegre's local patrimonial state in action, from apartments for vote gathering in the precoup period to filling municipal jobs with supporters toward the end of military rule.[53] The bureaucracy grew worse under the first elected mayor after the return to democracy, Alceu Collares. Collares allowed real wages for municipal workers to fall dramatically during his term (provoking long strikes in 1987 and 1988), and his administration left supplies unstocked and city machinery in complete disrepair.[54] According to "Lidio" (interview 5/11/99), who worked for over thirty years as a driver for the municipal department of public works and roads, when Collares left office, "The municipal administration had two concrete mixers: one hadn't been used in about four months, the other for a month and a half, because they had broken parts, and the administration didn't have the money to replace the parts. None of the forklifts were working. There were no more tractors, they were all broken. The Collares administration made a total debacle, it was a disaster."

Finally, municipal governments in Venezuela, including that in Caracas, traditionally served as "paradises of clientelism" for the country's two major parties, Acción Democrática and Copei (Timmons 1995, 18). In describing the general situation in Venezuelan municipal governments, Nickson (1995,

---

52. Other analysts provide similar accounts of Montevideo's municipal bureaucracy (see Filgueira 1991, 46; Martínez and Ubila 1989, 129–31).

53. In order to avoid the legal requirement of public contests for city jobs, Porto Alegre's military-appointed mayors created a number of municipal "foundations," which were city agencies by another name. "Lidio" (interview 5/11/99), a veteran municipal insider who has worked for the city government since 1964, also gave me dozens of examples of personalism and of corruption schemes, large and small, over the years, mostly involving kickback arrangements between city officials and contractors (including some in his own family).

54. Interview with Pedro Chaves (12/7/98), press secretary for the municipal government from 1975 to 1984; see also Schabbach (1995, 86) and Abers (2000, 68).

263, 264) writes that the dominant parties imposed "clientelist practices in the selection, promotion, and dismissal of staff at all levels." Furthermore, "job stability in local government was heavily enforced as a result of pressure from powerful trade unions that forged strong links to clientelist political parties. This combination of job stability and weak human resource management has led to a degree of overstaffing and inefficiency in local government that is unparalleled in Latin America." Nickson's account of Venezuelan municipal governments in general seems to portray conditions in Caracas fairly accurately as well. Caracas administration officials from LCR described incidents of corruption, theft, disobedience, and even outright sabotage by city workers who had won their jobs through political connections (Harnecker 1995d, 10–12, 58–62).

Clearly, then, the bureaucracies in Porto Alegre, Caracas, and Montevideo, represented obstacles to the new incumbents. In fact, rather than welcoming the participatory, decentralizing proposals of these parties, the majority of municipal workers in each city viewed the proposals with suspicion, and some actively resisted. In Porto Alegre, municipal employees were skeptical about increasing citizen participation and opposed to decentralizing city services, and many "tried to put the brakes on the new administration" by deliberately slowing down administrative procedures (Schabbach 1995, 86–87). In Caracas and Montevideo, numerous city workers refused to perform certain tasks, arguing that they could only carry out a limited set of specific functions. For example, in the Caracas department of conservation and maintenance, there were workers who only washed floors and those who only washed windows. In Montevideo, job classifications were similarly rigid, and municipal employees opposed the idea of multifunctional positions, something that was required for the FA's decentralization program to work (Harnecker 1995d, 59; 1995b, 79). Of course, the classic form of worker resistance, the strike, was also used in each city. It was a tool both for demanding wage increases and for expressing rejection of the new administrations' reforms.

Differences

On one hand, the broad parallels across the three cases are striking. Indeed, in a number of ways, the cases conform to the general pattern of urban development in Latin America, especially in the middle-income countries.

None of these cities represents an anomaly. Even Montevideo's exceptional prosperity in the first half of the twentieth century did not last into the 1980s. On the other hand, after controlling for several potentially important sources of variation, two key factors stand out: the degree of national decentralization in each country and the level of institutionalization of the opposition parties in each city. The national governments in Brazil and Uruguay had transferred more resources, responsibilities, and authority to the municipal level by the 1980s than had Venezuela's government. And the opposition parties in Montevideo and Caracas were much more institutionalized than those in Porto Alegre. These differences had important consequences for the ability of the participation programs to improve the quality of local democracy.

Degree of National Decentralization

As in many other Latin American countries, the national governments in Venezuela, Uruguay, and Brazil undertook decentralization reforms during the 1980s, increasing the powers of local governments to some degree. However, both the extent of the reforms and the previous status of local governments differed substantially. Local governments in Uruguay and Brazil historically had more resources and responsibilities than those in Venezuela, and the decentralizing reforms of the 1980s went further in Brazil than in the other countries. In fact, since the redrafting of its constitution in 1988, Brazil has become one of the most decentralized countries in Latin America in terms of resources raised and spent by subnational government (Souza 1996, 103; Abers 2000, 28). The varying degrees of decentralization meant that when the Left came to power in Caracas, Montevideo, and Porto Alegre, the municipal governments offered unequal capacities. While LCR inherited a municipal administration with a poor revenue base and limited jurisdictional scope, the FA and PT took over administrations with more ample budgets and greater authority over service provision. The latter parties could therefore design participation programs that offered citizens decision-making opportunities over a wide range of issues. LCR faced constraints on its ability to do the same.

The historical patterns of decentralization and local government power in the federal republics of Venezuela and Brazil contrast with one another as well as with that of Uruguay, which is organized as a unitary republic. Venezuela's legal reforms in 1988 and 1989 introduced dramatic changes in the country's political-institutional framework.[55] Before then, stretching back to the era of the Gómez dictatorship (1908–35), Venezuelan government had been extremely centralized on all dimensions. Through the first thirty years of stable democracy (1958–88), the national administration controlled the vast majority of revenues, provided nearly all public services, and the president appointed the governors of all twenty-two states. City councilors were elected to run the municipal governments, but voters could only choose party slates, not individual candidates, and voting for different parties at the municipal and national levels was not permitted until 1984.

A series of laws aimed at decentralizing power was finally passed in 1989. In addition to creating the position of a directly elected mayor for each municipality and allowing elections for state governors (except in the case of the Federal District), the legal changes established greater transfers of central government resources and assigned new (but shared) responsibilities to subnational governments. The reforms also legitimated new forms of citizen participation at the local level. They created submunicipal districts (or parishes) with elected boards to serve as interlocutors between the mayor and community organizations and authorized municipal referenda to contest the public record of the mayor. On paper, the legal changes seem remarkable, yet in practice, the decentralization process has been characterized as "gradual, unequal, flexible, and negotiated" (Guerón and Manchisi 1996, 384). The revenue transfers were implemented slowly and to the benefit of smaller municipalities, and the reassignment of responsibilities occurred either by individual agreements signed by national and local governments or when the national government simply discontinued a particular public service.

Two aspects of Venezuela's decentralization process merit particular attention. On one hand, after the reforms and especially the direct election of mayors, citizens began to expect much more from municipal government, but municipal revenues only increased slightly. The municipal share of total government revenues rose from 4.19 percent in 1989 to 5.68 percent in 1993 (Mascareño 2000, 66, Cuadro 8). The proportion of revenues for the Caracas municipal government has been minimal. Of the five municipalities in the metropolitan area, Caracas City Hall had the lowest per capita

---

55. This section is based primarily on González (1998), Guerón and Manchisi (1996), Mascareño (2000), and Vallmitjana (1993).

budget in the 1990s (Guerón and Manchisi 1996, 392). On the other hand, centralism was not completely reformed. The national government still intervened in the provision of major public services in most cities, as municipal governments took on few of the shared responsibilities (Mascareño 2000, 62–63; Dillinger 1994, 21). Caracas represents a particularly dramatic case of overlapping jurisdictions. In the early 1990s, urban services were provided by the Caracas municipal government, the government of the federal district, two national ministries (Urban Development and Transportation and Communication), and several nationally funded agencies (including Centro Simón Bolívar, Fundacomun, CANTV) and metropolitan entities (the Metro and Hidrocapital). Decentralization in Venezuela, such as it is, did little, if anything, to benefit Caracas.

Compared to those in Venezuela, Brazil's subnational governments have played more important roles dating back to the First Republic (1889–1930), when federalism was established. Even as central government powers increased during the *Estado Novo* (1937–45) and the Second Republic (1946–64), state and local governments continued to provide important services and maintained some political autonomy, with regular elections for subnational offices. While autonomy would be curtailed during the following two decades of military dictatorship, local service provision remained significant, and local spending actually began to grow considerably toward the end of authoritarian rule (Kugelmas and Sola 2000, 64, 68; Eaton 2004, 141). The authoritarian rulers allowed state and local legislative elections, as well as direct elections for mayor in cities other than state capitals and several dozen other "strategic" cities.[56] And, in the course of the long democratization process, direct elections for all mayors would take place in Brazil before a direct election for president.[57]

Even prior to the 1988 constitution, then, Brazil already had a long history of greater administrative, fiscal, and political decentralization than Venezuela. With the new constitution, Brazilian municipalities gained a higher share of direct transfers, more sources of own revenues, more responsibilities for service provision (although many of them were shared with the state and/or national levels of government), and autonomy guaranteed in the

---

56. In all, 201 of the more than three thousand municipalities were prohibited from holding elections (Eaton 2004, 140). Of course, in all elections during the authoritarian period, only two political parties were allowed to participate, the official government party (ARENA) and the official opposition (MDB—Movimento Democrático Brasileiro).

57. Mayors of most cities were elected in 1982, for state capitals in 1985, and again for all cities in 1988. The first postdictatorship direct election for president took place in 1989.

constitution itself.[58] According to Montero (2000, 65), municipalities nearly doubled their share of total government revenues after the 1988 constitution. The autonomy clause meant that municipal governments could pass their own organic laws (similar to a city constitution) not subject to state or federal approval (Samuels 2000, 82). Indeed, one comprehensive study of decentralization in Latin America noted Brazil's "uncommon degree of decentralization: substantial automatic transfers, weak conditionality over the use of funds, increased subnational taxing powers, and a weak delineation of responsibilities" (Willis, Garman, and Haggard 1999, 24). Porto Alegre saw substantial gains, with municipal government revenues increasing 14 percent from 1988 to 1989, and 82 percent from 1988 to 1992, with much of the growth coming from transfers.[59] Compared to other state capitals, Porto Alegre's per capita revenues were just below the average each year from 1989 to 1991, and slightly above the median (see Rosenblatt and Shidlo 1996, 105, table 2).

Uruguay is unique in Latin America in that it has only two levels of government: the national government and nineteen provincial governments, known as departments (*departamentos*) and headed by mayors (*intendentes*).[60] Montevideo is the sole department with the title of "municipal government," given that all other departments comprise a number of urban settlements as well as rural areas. Despite Uruguay's unitary history,[61] the departments have a long record of raising revenues, providing services, and operating as outlets for political opposition to the national government. In fact, two civil wars broke out at the turn of the twentieth century (1897 and 1903–4) over the opposition's right to hold local office. The ruling Colorado Party, which defeated the opposition Blancos on the battlefield as well as in national elections, appointed the provincial mayors until the constitution of 1918 (Eaton 2004, 146–48). In addition to allowing elections for local offices, the 1918 constitution gave the provincial governments new powers of taxation and new responsibilities, and allowed for the creation of local boards (*juntas locales*) in the rural areas of the departments that could perform certain administrative tasks and advise the mayor. From that time until the

58. See Abers (2000, 28), Montero (2000), and Samuels (2000) for a description of the new taxes and transfers given to municipalities and other changes made in the 1988 constitution.

59. My calculations from Verle and Müzell (1994, 16, table 2) and from PMPA (1997, 121).

60. To be exact, Uruguay is unique in Spanish-speaking Latin America: Suriname, Guyana, and Jamaica each have only two levels of government as well.

61. The 1967 constitution defines the country as a centralized state with partially autonomous political administrations at the local level (Filgueira et al. 1999, 7). For the early history of decentralization in Uruguay, see Eaton (2004, 146–50).

1973 coup, Uruguayan mayors were elected simultaneously with national political leaders (except for the 1934–37 period of autocratic rule). As in the later Venezuelan municipal contests, the provincial elections were fused with national elections, such that voters could not choose different parties at different levels of government. In contrast to Venezuela, however, voters could select from among several candidates for mayor within the same party.[62]

During military rule, mayors were appointed and the departments' taxation powers were reduced. Since the return to democracy in 1985, however, Uruguay "has witnessed the rising visibility, power, and appeal" of the provincial governments, reverting to elected mayors, transferring responsibilities downward, and enhancing local revenues and spending. Indeed, real per capita spending by the provincial governments grew by 100 percent between 1985 and 1997, spurred by growth in central government transfers and in own revenues (Filgueira et al. 1999, 7, 15). Montevideo, however, has received much less from the central government—in per capita terms—than have the other eighteen departments. At the same time, the central government retained the powers to override provincial taxation measures and to prevent the departments from taking on external debt (this latter rule also applies to Venezuelan municipalities but not to Brazilian municipalities). Overall, Uruguay has a longer history of stronger decentralized government than Venezuela, but does not reach Brazil's degree of decentralization. Uruguay's central government has preserved more tools to control the subnational level than has the central government in Brazil. Most importantly, because Uruguay is unitary, not federal, its departments lack the autonomy granted to Brazilian municipalities.

The important point here is that the different processes of decentralization in the three countries led to varying capabilities of the municipal governments in Porto Alegre, Montevideo, and Caracas. Jurisdictional authority and budgetary resources were greater in the latter cities than in the former. Figure 2.1 compares the responsibilities of the three municipal governments when the participation programs began in the early 1990s. It lists public services provided at least partially by at least one city government from least prominent to most. The scoring of the different services takes into

---

62. This peculiarity of the Uruguayan system, known as the "double simultaneous vote," essentially links the internal party primaries to the standard elections, and was used for both the provincial and the national elections. The 1996 constitutional reform eliminated this practice from national contests, instituting separate primaries instead, but allowed a modified form of it in the provincial elections of 2000 (each party could have two mayoral candidates), with the proviso that it would be ended in 2005. The reform also separated the national and provincial elections.

	Porto Alegre[*]	Montevideo	Caracas
Overall scope (score)	67	63	46

Specific services:

	Porto Alegre[*]	Montevideo	Caracas
Police department (crime)	0	0	1
Hospitals	2*	0	0
Primary education	2	0	1
Tourism	2	2	0
Basic welfare (children/handicap)	2	2	0
Industrial and commercial licensing	2	0	2
Local economic development	2	0	2
Primary health care (clinics)	2	2	1
Sewage system	3	2	0
Water	3	2	0
Public housing (provision)	3	2	0
Food hygiene	0	4	2
Public lighting	3	4	0
Storm drains	3	3	2
Recreation, sports, parks	3	3	3
Culture	3	3	3
Local road construction	3	4	2
Squatter settlement upgrading	3	4	2
Public housing (maintenance)	3	2	4
Public transportation	4	4	2
Building inspection	3	4	4
Garbage collection	4	4	3
Preschool	4	4	4
Public markets	4	4	4
Land use zoning	4	4	4

Code:
0 = No municipal role
1 = Municipality plays supplemental role
2 = Responsibility shared with other levels of government
3 = Mainly municipal role in practice
4 = Municipal responsibility

*In Brazil, all functions are shared, in principle, with higher levels of govenment except public transportation, solid waste management, and preschool education. Porto Alegre assumed complete responsibility of hospitals in 1998.

Fig. 2.1 Scope of jurisdiction over urban services

account both the constitutionally defined roles of the municipal governments as well as which level of government had assumed the responsibility
in practice.[63] The scoring does not distinguish between the more essential,
expensive services and those of lesser importance.

Two important findings are evident in the figure. First, the municipal
governments in Porto Alegre and Montevideo provide more public services
than their counterpart in Caracas. Second, in the former cities, the municipal
governments have jurisdiction over more of the services considered essential
by residents. Most importantly, the Caracas municipal government lacked
authority over the agencies responsible for the two most urgent problems for
Caraqueños: water shortages and crime. The municipal governments in the
other cities, however, did have the jurisdiction to address their most significant
problems, respectively: trash collection and public lighting in Montevideo,
and road construction and sewage systems in Porto Alegre.

A comparison of local government budgets shows that the PT and FA
also had the benefit of larger revenue streams than LCR in Caracas. Figure
2.2 demonstrates that not only were municipal government receipts greater
in Porto Alegre and Montevideo, but that they grew impressively during the
first few years of the term, while shrinking in Caracas.[64]

A final figure (figure 2.3) combines the previous two to bring out the stark
contrasts across the cities in terms of both jurisdictional scope and revenues.
The budget bars demonstrate that on average, compared to the municipal government in Caracas, the Porto Alegre and Montevideo administrations could
spend twice as much per person per year. The measure of jurisdictional scope
from figure 2.1 underscores the greater responsibilities for urban services for
the municipal governments in Porto Alegre and Montevideo.

In Caracas, the municipal administration lacked the jurisdiction and the
budget necessary to address the most important needs of local residents.
LCR attempted to overcome these limits by inviting service providers from
other levels of government to take part in their participation program. However, since these other entities were not committed to LCR's participatory
project, the program's participants usually could not convince them to pay
attention to their requests (see chapter 3). Thus, the design of the participation

63. Several sources were consulted to construct this figure. In addition to the budgets of
each municipality, I consulted Nickson (1995, 122, 253–57, 262–63), Harnecker (1995a),
World Bank (1997, Annex 1, 4), and Inter-American Development Bank (2001, 7).

64. The data for figure 2.2 are my calculations from IESA (1998, 271–75, and converted
to dollars from *Coyuntura,* January 1999, table 9) for Caracas; IMM Budget and Planning
Division (N.D.) for Montevideo; and Verle and Müzell (1994, 16) for Porto Alegre.

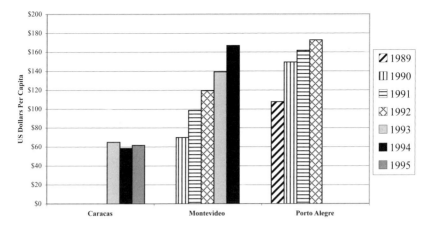

Fig 2.2   Municipal budget per capita (first term in office)

program in Caracas was constrained to include only a limited range of issues that citizens could meaningfully debate. Furthermore, the municipal government's nearly empty coffers made it difficult to respond to citizen demands, thus reducing the power of participation.

In Porto Alegre and Montevideo, by contrast, the incumbents benefited from an encompassing jurisdictional scope and a relatively large budget. This combination was crucial. It meant that the design of the participation programs could theoretically allow participants input over a wide range of issues and that the municipal governments had the resources to carry out these decisions, which would give participants a taste of real power. This is indeed what eventually occurred in Porto Alegre, but not in Montevideo. Decentralization thus helps explain the outcomes in the three cases, but it does not account for the differences between Montevideo and Porto Alegre. It is here that the role of opposition party institutionalization becomes important.

Opposition Party Institutionalization

The concept of party institutionalization employed here borrows from Huntington's (1968) original formulation and others' adaptations.[65] Generally, parties are considered more institutionalized the more they create ties of loyalty with members, voters, and interest groups and the greater their

---

65. More recent refinements of the concept include Kreuzer and Pettai (2004) and Randall and Svåsand (2002).

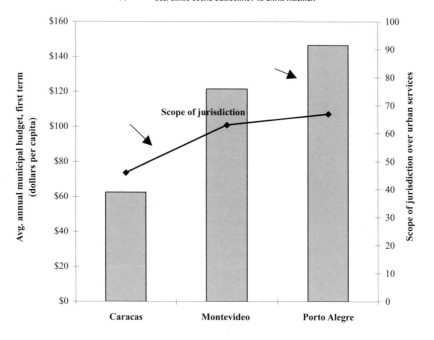

Fig. 2.3   Decentralization indicators

organizational complexity (with multiple territorial or functional subunits and regular interactions, and not dependent on a single charismatic leader). Party longevity reflects and reinforces institutionalization. Most studies of party institutionalization focus on individual incumbent parties (Levitsky 2003) or entire national party systems (Mainwaring and Scully 1995); this study concerns local-level opposition parties for empirical and theoretical reasons. Empirically, the type of incumbent party that introduces participation programs is generally the same, an unseasoned challenger seeking innovations to expand constituencies; it is in the opposition that one finds differences. Theoretically, the level of institutionalization of individual parties can vary both within a party system and within a single party across cities or states. Though national party systems were largely mirrored in Caracas, Montevideo, and Porto Alegre, with two strongly institutionalized parties in each of the former cities and several inchoate parties in the latter, the local incumbents did not fit the patterns. At the time they won local office, the LCR, FA, and PT were all relatively weakly institutionalized, though the former two were less institutionalized than their rivals and the PT arguably more.[66]

66. Compared to one another, though none of these parties was dependent on a single leader, the FA and PT were more strongly institutionalized than LCR, and the FA perhaps

Most importantly, the new incumbents in Montevideo and Caracas faced two historically dominant parties with roots in the early nineteenth and twentieth century, respectively, that had long-established patron-client networks, deep partisan identification among members and voters (creating distinct party cultures), and a custom of power sharing to exclude challengers. The historic parties had lost the mayor's seat, but maintained several city councilors with strong ties to municipal bureaucrats, community organizations, and powerful national leaders. In Porto Alegre, by contrast, the newly incumbent PT represented just one more party within an array of weakly institutionalized parties. There were no historically dominant parties with robust party organizations, but rather several parties founded within the past decade, displaying little internal coherence or discipline despite one or more popular leaders. The parties had not yet established stable alliances with each other or durable links to voters, community groups, and city workers.

The differences in opposition party institutionalization meant that when the FA and LCR attempted to introduce participation programs, their opponents had more to lose than did the PT's rivals, and many more weapons at their disposal. The opposition parties' resistance was thus much stronger in Montevideo and Caracas, and it prevented the FA and LCR from designing their participation programs as they originally intended. The opposition's reaction against the PT's participation program in Porto Alegre was comparatively insubstantial, giving the PT more freedom to pursue its original goals.

One especially important aspect of these differing levels of opposition party institutionalization was that they affected how community organizations responded to the new participation programs. Porto Alegre's weakly institutionalized opposition parties had developed strong ties to community groups in only a few neighborhoods, and thus territorially based organizations there generally enjoyed greater autonomy than those in Caracas and Montevideo. From Porto Alegre's most organized, autonomous city districts, neighborhood activists joined together to push the PT administration for an effective participation program, with greater decision-making power over an ever-expanding range of issues. The traditionally dominant parties in Caracas, on the other hand, had penetrated many if not most of the city's

slightly more institutionalized than the PT, as several of the FA's constituent parties had participated in Uruguayan politics for decades. Nonetheless, the PT also had incorporated older parties and their members and had participated in more elections than the FA at the time the parties reached local office. Overall, the differences in level of institutionalization among the three parties were not nearly as consequential as the difference among the opposition parties they faced.

community organizations, leaving only a handful of neighborhoods with more autonomous organizations. Rather than support LCR's participation program, then, neighborhood activists often followed partisan orders to sabotage it. In Montevideo, many neighborhood associations had party ties as well, though their loyalties were split between the FA and the opposition. While opposition-aligned neighborhood associations mostly ignored the FA's participation program, those associations aligned with the FA supported participation but rarely pushed for greater power.

Caracas

In Caracas, as in Venezuela more generally, the two main political parties were not merely institutionalized. From shortly after the dictatorship of Marcos Pérez Jiménez in the 1950s until the early 1990s, Acción Democrática and Copei completely dominated the political and social arenas: "For decades, the parties have practically monopolized collective life, exercising their control and influence over everything from the explicitly political to union and labor organizations and even a wide variety of economic, scientific, and cultural activities" (Lander 1995, 165). Both parties had strong multiclass support, a robust apparatus organized territorially and functionally, and a dominant role in civil society organizations (Levine 1989, 264; Molina 1999, 29). Acción Democrática, in particular, had very strong ties to the labor movement and an enormous party membership, with over two million affiliates in 1985, according to Coppedge (1994, 29, 31–35). Indeed, Coppedge goes so far as to label the Venezuelan political system a "partyarchy" to indicate the degree of power wielded by the two dominant parties and especially by top party bosses. Their influence stretched from the national to the local level, such that the National Executive Committee of AD, for example, even interfered in the selection of city council candidates in local elections (Coppedge 1994, 21). When Venezuela's first mayoral elections were held in 1989, the candidates from AD and Copei won 254 of the 269 races (Alvarez 1998, 260, table 10). AD alone won 57 percent of the municipal races.

AD's domination extended to Caracas, where it won with Claudio Fermín as its candidate. During his term, Fermín helped solidify AD's ties with the municipal workers' unions and with neighborhood associations. He was helped in the latter by President Pérez's policy of distributing subsidized powdered milk through the associations.[67] In fact, since the late 1970s, both

---

67. Interview with Elías Santana, former president of FACUR (1988–89) and leader of the Escuela de Vecinos (12/23/99). See also Silberberg (1992, 137n43) and Ellner (1999, 82). The proliferation of neighborhood associations around the time of the milk program led to the

AD and Copei had attempted to co-opt the neighborhood association move-ment. The parties sponsored new associations and formed federations of associations to compete with each other and with FACUR.[68] In addition to providing powdered milk as an incentive for neighborhood leaders to seek out the parties, AD gave association presidents automatic voting rights in the party's internal conventions, which prompted party bosses to seek out the associations. As a former president of FACUR told me, "The parties were accustomed to penetrating and controlling the unions, and they began to make themselves present [in the neighborhood associations]. . . . At the beginning of the 80s, the party that invested most in this was Copei, because it held the presidency. At the end of the eighties, it was AD, which created a huge national structure to control the neighborhood associations."[69]

By the early 1990s, AD had significant clout in the neighborhood asso-ciations of Caracas. The municipal federation of neighborhood associa-tions (Favemli), for example, had an AD-affiliated president and over three hundred member associations (*El Universal* 9/25/93). When LCR barely defeated Acción Democrática in the Caracas municipal election in 1992, AD had many resources at its disposal, from neighborhood associations to unions to its extensive membership. Furthermore, as Coppedge (1994, 23–35) shows, AD members were extremely loyal in following the party line. In fact, before the 1992 election results were announced in Caracas, rumors circulated that AD would try to steal the election from LCR, and supporters of both parties clashed in the streets (López Maya 1995, 229; Alvarez 1998, 250–51). This confrontation was a preview of AD's battle to retake Caracas during the next three years. That battle, which was ulti-mately successful, placed further constraints on the Causa Radical's ability to design and implement its participation program.

Montevideo

Uruguay's strongly institutionalized traditional parties stretch back further into the past than Venezuela's; they are the oldest successful political parties in Latin America (Sotelo Rico 1999, 140). Both the Colorado and the National parties were founded in 1836 and spent much of the nineteenth century

---

coining of the derogatory term *asociaciones lecheras* (milk associations) by independent com-munity activists.

68. The acronyms of the federations suggest the political affiliation. For example, Copei created Confafev and Convecinos (which represented rival factions within the party), and AD created federations like Avinco at the national level and Freindeco at the district level (mem-bers of AD are known as *adecos*).

69. Interview with Elías Santana (12/23/99).

fighting one another for political control, including a major civil war that lasted a dozen years. As part of their peace agreements in the early twentieth century, the Colorados and the Blancos devised a system of "coparticipation" in which they distributed political and administrative positions proportionally according to their vote shares in national elections (Gillespie and González 1989, 211). The two parties jointly received over 80 percent of the vote until the 1973 coup, and thus could staff the national and provincial bureaucracies with their supporters with impunity. Panizza (1990, 67) notes that this "colonization of the State" reached its peak in the 1950s and 1960s.

It was in Montevideo that the Colorado Party had its stronghold (while the Blancos performed better in rural areas), and where it used its control of the bureaucracy to cultivate and maintain political support. With two brief exceptions (1958–62 and 1983–84), the Colorado Party ruled Montevideo consecutively from the founding of democracy in 1918 until 1989. The Colorados—and to a lesser extent, the Blancos—set up hundreds of "political clubs" across Montevideo, each with a neighborhood *caudillo* who was both a public employee and a political activist.[70] Through the political clubs, residents of poor and working-class neighborhoods sought out personal favors such as jobs and payment of hospital bills, and sometimes public services like water or electricity. According to Panizza (1990, 70), while in other Latin American countries clientelism frequently functioned through unions, "in Uruguay clientelism operated fundamentally as a relationship among parties (in fact, factions), the state bureaucracy, and the popular sectors."

Even military rule did not interrupt the Colorado Party's political control, given that the military rulers allowed the elected Colorado mayor to continue in his post until the last year of the dictatorship. In the first election following military rule (1984), the Colorados won again in Montevideo—as well as nationally—and attempted to resume their previous style of patronage politics. On one hand, the party's "most conservative faction (Pachequismo) reestablished an important network of 'clubs' in an appeal to its traditional pre-dictatorship clientele" (Aguirre 1990, 6). The renewed political clubs operated with the support of the city councilors. On the other hand, the Colorado mayor created a new office (the special projects unit, or UAPE) to establish direct and formal relations with neighborhood associations for the first time. Through UAPE, the Colorado administration encouraged the formation of neighborhood associations with its Neighborhood Action

---

70. See Panizza (1990, 69–77), Benton (1986, 46), Biles (1978, 93–95), and, for a series of in-depth interviews with local *caudillos*, Rama (1971).

Program and its Emergency Solidarity Plan, which distributed food stamps to registered associations (Canel 1992, 285–86; Aguirre 1990, 6). Indeed, over half of the existing neighborhood associations in 1988 had been founded between 1985 and 1988, and 26 percent started the year UAPE was created, 1985 (Bruera 1993, 49).

The cycle of neighborhood associations appearing when the municipal government offers new programs repeated in the 1989 to 1991 period, when the Frente Amplio proposed and then implemented its decentralized participation program. Of the 371 existing associations in 1991, only 10 percent had been founded in the 1985 to 1988 period, while 37 percent were founded in 1989 or after. Twenty-two percent of the associations were founded in 1990, the year the FA took office (Bruera 1993, 49). These figures suggest that the neighborhood associations of Montevideo are strongly influenced by municipal politics. At the time the FA was elected, the neighborhood associations were characterized as having a "weak degree of coordination" amongst themselves, while their relationship with the municipal government was "bilateral, dependent, and lacking in negotiating power" (Mirza 1996, 91). Yet if the Colorados had a strong presence in the associations at the end of the 1980s, the Frente Amplio was gaining ground. And the strongest community-based organization in Montevideo, FUCVAM, had long-standing ties to the FA, and especially to the Socialist Party.[71] When the FA began implementing its participation program in 1990, those associations aligned with the Colorados and Blancos largely ignored it. Those aligned with the FA did not make coordinated efforts to change the design even when they believed it to be flawed. At the same time, the opposition city councilors reacted strongly against the Frente Amplio's program, and used their national connections to prevent the FA from designing a program that transferred real power to citizens.

Porto Alegre

Brazil's parties are much newer than those in Uruguay or Venezuela. In 1979, the military regime abandoned its earlier attempt to create a two-party system. The only legal opposition party up until that point—the MDB—had been performing well in elections, and the authoritarian rulers allowed new parties to form in an attempt to dilute the growing threat posed by the MDB. From then on, dozens of parties were created, and no single party or even

71. Interview with Javier Vidal, advisor to FUCVAM (6/11/99). The Socialist Party was the party of Tabaré Vázquez, who was elected mayor in 1989.

pair of parties gained hegemony.[72] By 1987, eleven parties held congressional seats, and three years later this figure reached nineteen parties (Power 2000, 29). Most of these parties were not only small, but fleeting. Most parties lacked complex organizational structures and many were mere labels for politicians, such as President Fernando Collor's (1990–92) personal vehicle, the Partido da Reconstrução Nacional (Party of National Reconstruction). Furthermore, parties often changed labels, and politicians changed parties even more frequently. Brazil is notorious for its weakly institutionalized political parties, which are often blamed for inhibiting democracy, accountability, and strong political leadership (Mainwaring 1999).

The national situation was reproduced in Porto Alegre. No single party or pair of parties created strong organizations or gained durable majoritarian support. Eight parties gained seats on the city council in the 1988 municipal election, and eight again in 1992. Electoral alliances among the parties encompassed strange bedfellows and changed frequently, but most often the individual parties ran alone.[73] Thus, five candidates competed in the mayor's race of 1985, and eight in 1988. Three different parties were elected to the governorship in the three elections from 1982 to 1990, and two different parties won the mayor's office in 1985 and 1988. Failure to win reelection in Porto Alegre represented continuation of the predictatorship pattern.

Despite the general fragmentation and weakness of local parties, there were at least two in Porto Alegre that potentially could have developed strong connections to society: the PMDB and the PDT (Partido Democrático Trabalhista—Democratic Labor Party). The PMDB was the party formed out of the official opposition during the dictatorship. Thus, it had had a relatively long history compared to other parties. However, the PMDB did not have a municipal-level party organization in Porto Alegre. The state and national leadership in Brasília decided which candidates the party would run in municipal races, for example.[74] Furthermore, the creation of new parties in the 1980s weakened the PMDB nationally, and hit especially hard in Porto Alegre and Rio Grande do Sul. Many leaders of the local PMDB left to join other parties, particularly the PDT. The PDT was founded by Leonel Brizola, the former mayor of Porto Alegre and governor of Rio Grande do Sul, who

72. The PMDB did dominate the elections of 1986, winning nearly all the governorships and a majority of the congressional seats.

73. In 1985, for example, the PMDB allied with both of the communist parties, on one hand, and with the conservative PFL, on the other hand. For election results in Porto Alegre, see Passos and Noll (1996).

74. Interview with Sebastião Mello, president of the Porto Alegre PMDB, (5/4/99).

enjoyed immense local popularity. Brizola had initially wanted to refound the historic PTB of the Vargas era, yet Vargas's daughter claimed the name for the party she created. Thus, competing labor parties were founded in the early 1980s, but Brizola's PDT received the most support in Porto Alegre. In the first mayoral election in 1985, the PDT candidate, Alceu Collares, won easily. When Brizola ran for president in 1989, Porto Alegrenses voted for him overwhelmingly, granting him 69 percent of the vote (Noll and Trindade 1996, 143).

Yet the PDT was mostly that: Brizola, Collares, and a few other historic populist leaders. As a party, it failed to establish a strong organization despite its attempt to create a network of neighborhood leaders during the Collares administration in Porto Alegre. Collares had promised to create popular councils for citizen participation linked to each of the administration's divisions, but this proposal was never implemented.[75] Instead, "'neighborhood inspectors' who were in fact nothing more than the PDT's neighborhood political brokers" were used by one city department "to 'represent' neighborhoods vis-à-vis the government" (Baierle 1998, 127). The failure of the Collares administration to deliver on its promise of effective participation tarnished his image with the neighborhood associations. The leaders of UAMPA had been proposing not just sectoral popular councils for the municipal government's different administrative departments, but direct input into the entire municipal budget (Schmidt 1994, 71).

By the late 1980s, then, none of the political parties in Porto Alegre can be said to have established strong social connections with voters or social organizations. Unlike in Caracas, the municipal workers' union in Porto Alegre always had a plurality of parties in its leadership.[76] And unlike in both Caracas and Montevideo, few neighborhood associations were subordinated to a single political party. It is not that clientelist associations did not exist; they did. Indeed, in the early 1980s, especially, the neighborhood associations were arenas of party competition and conflict (Ferretti 1984, 172, 182, 199). And both the PDT municipal government and the PMDB state government made efforts to cultivate relations with the associations,

---

75. The proposal was discussed in a series of meetings with community organizations and sent to the city council. After languishing for a year, it was finally rejected. Collares never lobbied for the bill, and several PDT councilors voted against it, in both cases outraging the neighborhood leaders who had participated in the original meetings (see Abers 2000, 40–42).

76. During the Collares administration, the municipal workers' union (SIMPA) was still an association rather than a union, but its leaders came from diverse parties on the Left. From 1989 to 1991, the leadership was multiparty but the president was from a party on the Right. Interview with Cesar Pureza, president of SIMPA, 1995–99 (5/20/99).

the latter through "milk tickets" (Baierle 1992, 80–81). What was different in Porto Alegre was that many of the more clientelist-style associations were mercenary. They developed only transitory relationships with politicians and parties, or, more often, allowed multiple parties in so that none could dominate. Throughout the 1980s and 1990s, the leaders of UAMPA and FRACAB, for example, came from multiple parties (Baierle 1992, 62, 90; *Zero Hora: Caderno* 12/18/88, 1–2). The less formal, district-level coordinating groups also had multiparty leadership, like the "union of *vilas*" in Cruzeiro, the popular councils in Partenon and in the North district, and the "coordination of the popular movement" in the Leste district.

When the PT won the 1988 mayor's race in Porto Alegre and began to implement its participatory budget process, the opposition parties had little to lose compared to AD in Caracas or the Colorados in Montevideo. Porto Alegre's opposition parties also lacked the kinds of organizational resources that would have enabled them to challenge the PT's participation program effectively. At the same time, the PT did face constant and coordinated pressure from dozens of community organizations, especially from those linked to the district-level popular councils. These community groups pushed the PT administration to design a participation program that gave citizens an opportunity to make decisions over important issues. And the high degree of jurisdictional authority and the expanding municipal budget allowed the administration to carry out these decisions.

Conclusion

This chapter has argued that, after a series of important similarities across the cases is taken into account, two factors—national decentralization and local opposition party institutionalization—best explain the eventual differences in the design of what were originally similar participation programs in Caracas, Montevideo, and Porto Alegre. In terms of the hypotheses laid out at the end of chapter 1, the macro-level conditions of greater degrees of national decentralization in Brazil and Uruguay compared to Venezuela led to superior local government capacity in Porto Alegre and Montevideo and to the corresponding potential for the PT and the FA to design effective participation programs. Further, while the meso-level conditions of underperforming bureaucracies and internally divided incumbents were omnipresent but not crucial, the strongly institutionalized and traditionally dominant parties in Montevideo and Caracas that now found themselves in the opposition did significantly impede the FA and LCR as they designed and implemented their participatory experiments. Finally, at the micro level, though community organizations proliferated in each city despite a cyclical downswing in activism, given Porto Alegre's history of weakly institution-alized political parties that had failed to develop robust social ties, community groups there enjoyed the most horizontal links with local organizations beyond their own neighborhoods as well as vertical links with multiple polit-ical parties. These links helped preserve their autonomy and thus facilitated their vigorous involvement in the new participation program. The next trio of chapters fleshes out these arguments, telling the story of how LCR, the FA, and the PT tried to design effective participatory institutions in each city and how their efforts were thwarted or rewarded, ultimately leading to different institutional designs in each city: restrictive in Caracas, regulated in Montevideo, and open in Porto Alegre. The chapters also provide evi-dence for the other meso-level hypothesis—that an informally structured, wide-ranging, and deliberative institutional design is more likely to sustain citizen interest than are more formal, narrow institutions that limit partici-pant decision-making power.

3

Caracas: Scarce Resources, Fierce Opposition, and Restrictive Design

Of the three cities in this study, only in Caracas did the incumbents fail to consolidate their participation program. The initial enthusiasm with which city residents greeted the program in 1993 quickly gave way to disillusionment throughout most of the city's nineteen parishes. By the end of the Causa Radical's administration in 1995, popular participation within the program had fallen dramatically in all but three parishes. In the administration that followed, the mayor from Acción Democrática completely dismantled LCR's participation program. This chapter describes the participation program in detail and explains its inability to sustain large numbers of participants. After outlining the program's origins and general functioning, the chapter presents evidence for a two-step explanation, evidence which shows that Caracas had the benefit of exactly none of the factors at the macro, meso, or micro levels hypothesized to favor successful participation programs.

First, the lack of resources and responsibilities afforded the municipal government by the still relatively centralized federal government combined with the fierce opposition from the previously dominant but still strongly institutionalized traditional political parties constrained the design of the program. The municipal government consulted with participants about their preferences over the narrow range of issues under municipal jurisdiction, and city officials aggregated these preferences as they wished, but, given their small budget, still failed to implement many of the citizens' demands. Participants thus lacked decision-making power over the issues most important to them. Further, the program's formal structure included boards in each parish that were reserved for members of the incumbent and opposition parties. The opposition parties insisted that the arenas for direct citizen participation be subordinated to these party-controlled boards. The opposition also instructed their community and municipal employee allies to obstruct the LCR's program.

The second step is that the program's restrictive design undermined its ability to attract participants. When city residents saw that real decision-making power over the issues they cared about lay elsewhere, and that party representatives remained in control in the program's overly formal structure, participation sharply declined. Nonetheless, the decline did not occur evenly across the city's parishes, and this variation is used in the last sections to further test the chapter's two main arguments.

The Beginning: Massive Assemblies, Enormous Demands, and Organizational Problems

When Aristóbulo Istúriz became mayor of Caracas for the Causa Radical in January 1993, he did not know exactly how he would promote the ideas he had campaigned on: turning the city's inhabitants into active citizens and bringing urban services to the *barrios*. Since Istúriz had not expected to win, he had no concrete program of government, only general ideas about expanding citizen participation and decentralizing services to the parish level. Immediately upon taking office, he and his team of city officials held public assemblies in the nineteen parishes in order to find out the residents' priorities and create a plan of government for the next three years. They held hundreds of multitudinous assemblies at the neighborhood level and convened more than nineteen parish-wide assemblies, known as *cabildos abiertos*.[1] Thousands of residents attended these forums throughout the city. But rather than receiving organized plans from each neighborhood and parish, city officials were faced with enormous lists of demands of a wildly diverse nature, which "overwhelmed the municipality's capacity to respond," according to Istúriz (Harnecker 1995d, 17).

Two general problems needed immediate solutions. The first involved finding a way to organize participation such that the administration could make sense of the demands and respond effectively. LCR's goal of radical transformation of inhabitants into citizens would be neither easy nor reachable in the short run. Rather, in Istúriz's words, a transition phase would be

1. The exact numbers of assemblies and participants remain uncertain. According to *El Diario de Caracas* (7/7/93), two hundred meetings took place, while Istúriz claims between three hundred and four hundred (Harnecker 1995d, 17). Numerous newspaper articles from January to April of 1993 report on the assemblies. The director of CESAP (one of Venezuela's most

needed: "After the first experiences, we saw that although the strategic objective we were pursuing was that the people governed themselves, since our people did not have a culture of participation, they do not have real experience governing themselves. And at the same time, we, who are part of the people, did not have experience governing, so a transition phase was necessary between governing for the people and them governing themselves. . . . We needed to govern with the people" (Harnecker 1995d, 18–19). Governing with the people would require a greater commitment of the city government's personnel to the parish level and an attempt to train community leaders in democratic governance.

The second problem involved the administration itself. The initial public assemblies made it clear that many of the issues raised by the participants—such as crime, water provision, health care, and education—lay outside the municipal government's jurisdiction, and that attending even to those issues within its purview would require far more resources than the government enjoyed. As a first step toward solving these problems, Istúriz's team decided to create a program of parish governments. Istúriz thought of parish governments as public arenas where community members and government organs from different levels could convene to solve local problems collectively. Mayor Istúriz promoted the parish government idea, which remained somewhat vague,[2] in another round of well-attended *cabildos abiertos* held throughout the city. During the next three years, Istúriz and LCR tried to shape the parish governments into effective channels of participation. The municipal government's lack of capacity and the implacable opposition from rival political parties, however, would prevent LCR's success.

Designing, and Opposing, Participation: La Causa Я Confronts Acción Democrática

The Parish Government Program

As envisioned by Istúriz, the parish governments would consist of the already existing parish boards (*juntas parroquiales*), the newly instituted parish technical

---

important NGOs), Father Armando Jansen, confirmed that he had attended many of these assemblies where hundreds of city residents gathered (interview, 10/7/99). Francke (1997, 94, 72) reports that two thousand people attended one such assembly in El Valle and that hundreds attended dozens of other assemblies.

2. A pamphlet produced by City Hall, *What Is the Parish Government?* states that "it is nothing more than the bringing together of the Municipal Government and the people."

cabinets, and all citizens who wanted to participate. The parish boards, each with between seven and nine members (depending on the size of the parish), were created in most of Venezuela's municipalities in 1989 as auxiliary bodies for the municipal government.[3] In 1989, the parish boards had been appointed by the City Council; in 1992, they were elected alongside the mayor and City Council on party slates. In Caracas, LCR had won pluralities on nearly all the parish boards, but the opposition parties together could form majority voting blocs. The technical cabinets consisted of workers assigned to the parishes from various municipal departments, and included both professionals and a team of skilled manual laborers that could perform repairs and carry out small-scale projects. The government hoped that local community groups, especially neighborhood associations, would mobilize residents to participate alongside the parish boards and the new technical cabinets.

In theory, the parish governments would operate through public meetings convoked by the parish boards where those gathered would prioritize the community's problems and collectively decide how to resolve them. The engineers, architects, and social workers in the technical cabinet would provide the information necessary to determine which level of government should intervene: the technical cabinet itself, a municipal-level department, or, if the issue lay outside municipal jurisdiction, one of the many other public organs involved in providing urban infrastructure and services. If necessary, the parish board would invite representatives from these other organs to address the parish government and to work with the community to solve its problems.

One of the most important functions of the parish governments would be to deliberate over the parish budget for public works and services (Situado Parroquial de Obras y Servicios), another novel concept initiated by LCR's administration. City officials would provide each parish government with information concerning how much money was available in the budget for local investments. The parish governments would then decide on a list of projects. The administration thought that providing information about the city's financial resources would help citizens make more realistic demands and encourage them to prioritize the most important issues. The parish

---

3. The 1988 regulation of the Organic Law of the Municipal Regime, which created the parish boards, produced ambiguity regarding their functions. One article describes the parish boards as auxiliaries of the City Council, a legislative body, while another states that they should fulfill administrative functions and provide services, which suggests that the parish boards would be more like executive bodies. This contradiction in the regulation provided the grounds for future battles between LCR and the opposition over the nature of the parish boards.

public works budget was subject to the approval of the mayor and his cabinet, and ultimately to that of the City Council as well.[4]

The realization of LCR's parish government proposal was not uniform throughout the parishes and only matched Istúriz's original formulation in a few cases. The administration did, however, implement parts of the proposal universally. In every parish, city officials established technical cabinets and discussed the parish public works budget in public assemblies (at least in the first year) with the cooperation of the parish boards and/or the technical cabinets. A separate parish budget for culture was discussed in most of the parishes, and in several cases not only the decisions but the administration of the cultural budget was turned over to parish-level community organizations.[5] Another common mechanism created in many parishes were service committees (*mesas técnicas* and *comités de usuarios*), where residents affected by problems with a certain public service could meet to find solutions and then monitor the work of the corresponding government organ. The Catholic NGO, CESAP, provided training workshops for these committees in several parishes (Armando Jansen, interview 10/7/99). In addition, many of the parishes held public assemblies to debate transportation prices with the bus owners' union.[6]

In order to fortify participation in the parish governments, Istúriz promoted the activation of existing community organizations and the creation of new ones. Finding that the neighborhood associations were often empty organizations headed by life-term presidents, Istúriz sent social workers from the technical cabinets to "democratize" the associations by helping organize new elections.[7] His administration also gave technical and financial

---

4. The parish budgets represented between 80 and 90 percent of the administration's investments. City officials retained control over large-scale investment projects that affected the city generally or more than one parish. A separate city agency, Fundacaracas, also implemented small-scale investment projects that do not seem to have been under the parish governments' purview.

5. In eight of the sixteen parishes in which local groups discussed the cultural budget, a local cultural coordinating committee also received responsibility for administering the budget (Alcaldía 1995a, 19). The first five committees were established in 1993 in the parishes of Caricuao, La Pastora, La Vega, Macarao, and Antímano (*El Diario de Caracas*, 10/20/93, 39).

6. In all other municipalities, the mayor and the bus owners agreed on a uniform city-wide price. In Caracas, the negotiations took place at the parish level, resulting in numerous delays, a strike by the owners, and different prices across the parishes, which caused confusion and which bus owners frequently ignored. Most bus routes cross parish lines, and many of them cross municipal boundaries as well, which complicated the price negotiations (see Concejo 1994, 16–17).

7. Indeed, one study found that only 14 percent of Libertador's 427 neighborhood associations held regular elections (Wikander 1994, 82).

assistance to innovative groups already in existence, such as La Calle es de los Niños (The Street Is for the Children) in the parish of San Agustín and the Catuche Consortium in La Pastora.[8] In many cases, the social workers also attempted to help form parish-wide coordinating organizations for neighborhood groups involved in culture, sports, and environmental protection, depending on the parish. Finally, city officials turned several municipally owned buildings into open houses (*casas de la gente*) for local groups to meet in and for the municipal department of culture to offer classes and workshops.

LCR's Administrative Reforms: Challenging Absurdity, Collecting Taxes

Alongside the measures aimed at encouraging participation directly, Istúriz launched a series of reforms focused on modernizing the municipal government and improving its capacity to provide services and respond to local demands. These reforms included a complete reorganization of the bureaucracy and attempts to increase municipal revenues. One of the first steps Istúriz took to modernize the bureaucracy was to create a new personnel policy, revising labor contracts from previous governments that allowed for four-hour work days, permanent sick leave, and "preretired" workers.[9] Alirio Martínez, the budget director under Istúriz in charge of restructuring personnel, told me, "We found unusual job titles on the payroll— cooks, hairdressers—that we had no idea what they were doing there. . . . It was absurd."[10]

After reassigning city workers to productive jobs and attempting to clean up the payroll, Istúriz took more drastic steps toward increasing the bureaucracy's agility. He reorganized the administration's seventeen departments into four—internal affairs, urban management, citizen affairs, and economic management—and instituted new autonomous agencies that would attempt

8. La Calle es de los Niños united parents, children, and liquor store owners in the fight against violent crime in the parish *barrios*. Its frequent protest marches succeeded in lowering the crime rate, according to the president of the parish board, Rafael Uzcátegui (interview, 1/21/99). Jesuit priests began the Catuche Consortium in the areas surrounding the polluted Catuche creek; in 1996 the project won an award as one of the one hundred "best practices" at the Habitat meeting in Istanbul (as did Porto Alegre's participatory budget program).

9. A "preretired" worker is one who had reached legal retirement age but remained on the payroll without working because the government lacked the funds to pay retirement benefits.

10. Interview (1/18/99). Martínez, a professor of urban policy who had worked with Clemente Scotto in the municipality of Almacaroní in the previous term, took on several roles in the Istúriz administration, including Budget and Planning Director, Director of the Administrative Police, and finally General Director in 1995.

to provide services outside the municipality's normal jurisdictional scope. The Corporation for Municipal Services was created at the end of 1994, for example, to help provide services that were the province of higher levels of government but that had been demanded in the public assembles (such as water, sewerage, and electricity). The Corporation was intended to take over these services eventually. In the meantime, it provided emergency assistance for these and a variety of other services on a twenty-four-hour basis. Because the Corporation was an autonomous entity contracted by the municipal government, it could avoid the rigid labor laws that regulated public employees. According to the former director, Julio Montes, the Corporation's autonomy meant that he could hire qualified personnel rather than the employees contracted by the previous clientelist governments, and that he could fire incompetent workers.[11] In response to overwhelming demands in the public assemblies for solutions to the rising crime rate, Istúriz also created a municipal "administrative" police force.[12] Because of concerns about overstepping jurisdictional boundaries, however, the new police force had only two tasks—checking business licenses and acting as security guards at schools, parks, and other public spaces—and remained something of a pilot project, with only 250 administrative police officers in total (Alcaldía 1995a, 62).

A major fiscal reform complemented the organizational changes. When Istúriz took office, the municipal cadastre had registered only about twenty thousand of the approximately seven hundred thousand real estate properties in Caracas, and property tax collection was minimal (Harnecker 1995d, 10; Martínez, interview 1/18/99). In general, Venezuelan municipal governments had been unable or unwilling to maintain cadastres with which to ascertain correct values for property tax collection. Vast numbers of citizens therefore did not pay property taxes at all because their property was not registered, and the "immense majority" of those who did pay paid much less than their property was worth.[13] The lack of a taxpaying culture afflicts all

11. See Harnecker (1995d, 78). For more on the Corporation for Municipal Services, one of the Istúriz administration's most successful endeavors, see Harnecker (1995d, 75–79) and Alcaldía (1995a, 38–41).

12. The number of homicides per 100,000 inhabitants tripled in the federal district between 1986 and 1991, then doubled from 1991 to 1993 (my calculations from OCEI, PNUD, and FNUAP 1997, 101). By 1995, a major newspaper reported an average of thirty violent deaths per weekend in Caracas (*El Universal* 10/14/95, 1–7).

13. Vallmitjana et al. (1993, 141). A study by IESA of sixty-six Venezuelan municipalities in 1993 reveals that only two-thirds collected any property taxes at all (my calculations from IESA 1998, 271–72).

of Venezuela, according to Karl (1997, 172), who cites ex-president Jaime Lusinchi as saying, "In Venezuela only the stupid pay taxes." The Istúriz administration began to update the cadastre in Caracas and then raised property taxes in many parts of the city. City officials also made greater efforts at enforcing collection of all types of municipal taxes, such as on businesses and vehicles, but property tax collections increased the most. Indeed, after the reform, property tax revenues more than tripled in nominal terms and more than doubled in real (dollar) terms, which meant an extra six million dollars for the municipal government in 1995.[14]

No other major municipality in Venezuela attempted this kind of dramatic tax reform during the 1993 to 1995 period.[15] Of the seven largest municipalities in terms of government revenues, only two—Caracas and, to a lesser degree, Valencia—increased property tax receipts in real terms, by 65 percent and 27 percent, respectively. In both municipalities, however, the rise in property tax receipts did not offset losses in commercial tax receipts. In fact, only one municipality, Maracaibo, increased commercial tax receipts in real terms (by 4 percent), but this was not enough to compensate for a drop in property tax receipts (44 percent). Overall, each of the major municipalities experienced declining real revenues during the 1993 to 1995 period, but Caracas and Valencia experienced the smallest losses. Thus, while the Istúriz administration's tax policy did not achieve its goal of providing for a major increase in spending on investment projects, it did prevent the city from suffering drastic budget cuts.

Many in the Causa Radical now view the property tax increase as a mistake that cost the party votes in the following election. As one LCR parish board member told me, "Aristóbulo made a political error with the property taxes when he increased them and made them obligatory" (Debora van Berkel, interview 10/21/99). Martínez, the budget director (interview 1/18/99), shared the idea that citizens had not considered paying taxes obligatory: "Caracas is a city without a tax culture. Caracas does not pay taxes. And our tax policy

14. Based on my calculations from municipal revenue data in IESA (1998, 271) and exchange rates in *Coyuntura* (January 1999, 40), property tax receipts increased from $4.9 million in 1994 to $11 million in 1995, while real commercial tax receipts fell. In current dollars, the change in property tax receipts amounted to a 124 percent increase from 1994 to 1995, and a 65 percent increase from 1993 to 1995. However, since commercial taxes represented a much larger portion of municipal revenues, the increase in property tax receipts did not offset the drop in commercial tax receipts; total revenues thus decreased five percent in current dollar value from 1993 to 1995.

15. The following paragraph is based on my calculations from municipal revenue data in IESA (1998, 271–76) for Libertador (Caracas), Caroní, Valencia, Baruta, Chacao, Sucre (Miranda), and Maracaibo, and on exchange rates in *Coyuntura* (January 1999, 40).

was very radical, something like going from situation A to situation Z. We wanted to obligate the people to pay their taxes." He also agreed that the policy contained several errors and "brought a terrible questioning of our administration."[16] Whatever their drawbacks, the organizational and fiscal reforms undertaken by the Istúriz administration represented ambitious attempts to overcome the municipal government's lack of capacity, which was a legacy of Venezuela's incomplete national decentralization plan and of thirty years of clientelism and mismanagement under the AD-Copei dynasty.

With these reforms ongoing, and after a year of a wide array of experiences with the parish government program in different parts of Caracas, LCR's administration called a city-wide public conference in mid-1994 to evaluate the program. Community activists, members of the parish boards and technical cabinets, and city councilors debated the merits of the parish governments and discussed creating a municipal ordinance to regulate them. Although Istúriz and other LCR members recognized several limitations with their participatory experiment, they advocated strengthening the parish governments by providing them with explicit legal recognition, assigning them specific functions and resources, and granting decision-making authority to the volunteer participants within them. On the other hand, city councilors from opposition parties, and particularly from Acción Democrática, argued against legal reforms that would reinforce direct participation. Instead, AD called for strengthening the parish boards, where all political parties had representatives. While the Causa Radical struggled to design a functioning participation program and to build a capable municipal government, AD was attempting to disrupt, destabilize, and incapacitate the Istúriz administration. Fighting against the parish government ordinance was just one battle among many.

Acción Democrática's "Three-Year War"

After dominating political life in Caracas (and Venezuela as a whole) for three decades, Acción Democrática intended to immobilize the Istúriz administration in order to improve its own chances of winning back City Hall in

---

16. According to Martínez, the administration committed two principal errors in designing the tax increases. First, though the increases varied in different areas of the city, depending on general property values, some of the middle-class areas with high property values also included sections with very poor residents, and because the tax rates were based on relatively large areas, the poor often faced high rates. Second, city officials did not take into consideration that while property values in Caracas rose dramatically in the 1990s, the real value of wages had dropped.

1995. Using all of the party's connections—to labor unions, courts, government officials, neighborhood associations, and even street vendors—AD's municipal leaders attacked LCR and its participation program from many directions. Indeed, although all of the opposition parties in Caracas worked to undermine the Causa Radical, limiting its ability to design the parish governments program freely, AD started earliest and fought hardest, making it party policy to prevent the success of LCR and its participatory proposal. As a former parish board president from Santa Teresa told me, AD launched a "three-year war" against LCR's administration (José Gregorio Muñoz, interview 12/9/99).

The municipal workers' unions linked to AD went on strike constantly, motivated partially by political reasons and partially by Istúriz's attempts to restructure the bureaucracy.[17] Union protests started at the very beginning of Istúriz's administration with a month-long strike of the Auditor's Office workers, which delayed all public works contracts (*El Diario de Caracas* 7/7/93). Overall, there were seven strikes by workers in different municipal departments and one general strike by all municipal employees in Istúriz's first year in office. Workers also sabotaged the administration by destroying computers and city records and by stealing municipal property, such as tools, car parts, and tires from city buses. But given AD's control of the unions and labor courts, the mayor found himself largely unable to fire workers. It even took Istúriz over a year to fire an armed municipal employee who had assaulted him, and the worker still preserved his job as union representative. City workers and street vendors took Istúriz to court forty-eight times in a single year, especially hot dog salesmen operating without permits, who argued that Istúriz had violated their constitutional right to work.

Elías Santana (interview 12/23/99), a veteran leader of the neighborhood association movement, explained why the Istúriz administration faced such trouble from municipal workers:

> The bureaucracy, don't forget, was built by the governments of the big parties. It was a party structure where the unions had a lot of weight, a structure in which Aristóbulo could send an order from the top of the

---

Home owners thus might see their nominal taxes jump from three thousand bolívares to sixty thousand, and they "would go nuts complaining" (interview, 1/18/99).

17. This paragraph is based on interviews with Martínez (1/18/99), Maria Cristina Iglesias, the Director of Citizen Affairs under Istúriz (2/9/99), and Carlos Contreras, who worked in La Candelaria's technical cabinet (1/11/99); and on Harnecker (1995d, 12, 29–31, 58–62) and Istúriz (1997, 144–46).

pyramid and it would not pass through the middle. It might not get to the bottom and get carried out. He had a lot of serious problems the first year. . . . They made his life impossible politically. It's part of the game, of course, but it's a terrible game because, sure, the union in Acción Democrática's hands succeeds in sabotaging Istúriz's administration, but what it's doing is permanently sabotaging the city. That's the bad part of the dynamic, the perverse part.

According to a technical cabinet worker in La Candelaria, Carlos Contreras (interview 1/11/99), "All of those union activities were supported by the existing laws. There was no way to mess with them. That is, there was no way to fire someone who wasn't working because the law supported them. . . . And the union supported them, too. If you fired anyone, they paralyzed everything." The frequent confrontations between the municipal workers' union and Istúriz weakened the administration's ability to respond effectively to the demands for public services from the parish governments and city residents in general.

Acción Democrática's other main ally, the neighborhood associations in the *barrios*, also joined the attack on LCR's administration, often impeding rather than aiding the implementation of the parish governments. Santana (interview 12/23/99) told me that the actions of the neighborhood associations corresponded to AD's stance against participating: "There are some neighborhood leaders from parties, party members, who might be very pro-Aristóbulo and open and everything, but if the man is from AD and he received a party line that says that he has to be against this government, what he did was fire lead at the government." A neighborhood association vice president and AD member in La Pastora reported that the party line was to boycott the Catuche Consortium, an LCR-supported participation program in her area (Francke 1997, 177–78), which provides some support for the claims by Santana and by LCR members concerning AD. According to my interviewees from the parish boards and technical cabinets, the neighborhood associations generally did not support the parish government proposal except in a limited fashion in a few of the more middle-class areas in El Recreo, Coche, and Santa Rosalía. Most often the board and cabinet members had to look for the collaboration of other types of community groups involved in culture, sports, or the environment. In nearly all parishes besides Macarao, the technical cabinets' attempts to democratize the neighborhood associations failed, backfiring by turning dozens of long-enthroned association presidents against the administration and any of its programs. In more than one parish the neighborhood associations openly confronted the mayor.

For instance, an unofficially AD-affiliated organization representing fifty-six neighborhood associations in La Vega, Freindeco, convened a "popular referendum" against Istúriz in 1994 (2001 3/3/94). But La Vega, a parish with over one hundred and fifty thousand inhabitants, also has a tradition of independent, Left-leaning community organizations,[18] and these may have helped sustain citizen interest in the parish government there. Several radical community organizations existed in Macarao, 23 de Enero, and Antímano as well, and offered some support for the parish government proposal.[19] In all cases, however, they were a minority among the AD-dominated neighborhood associations. Only in Macarao did an autonomous, broad alliance of community organizations exist (Macarao y Su Gente, or Macarao and Its People).[20] In general, AD succeeded in preventing the neighborhood association movement from offering strong backing for the parish governments, and no other community groups were numerous or coordinated enough to play a supportive role in most parishes.

AD's battle against the Istúriz administration also had direct effects on the parish governments. Representatives from Acción Democrática on the parish boards and on the City Council conspired against the parish government idea. The board members avoided or tried to obstruct the public assemblies in the parishes. For example, a former member of the Coche parish board told me, "If AD knew that the parish board was going to have an assembly with the bus owners, they would give distorted information to people in order to disturb the assembly. AD fought hard against the parish governments because they were taking power away from their party members on the parish boards."[21] Carlos Contreras (interview 1/11/99) agreed: "There was opposition to everything that meant participation. And that was a party

18. Interview with Jesús Jiménez, former technical cabinet social worker in La Vega (2/4/99). See also Francke (1997, 84–87).

19. In 23 de Enero, many of these organizations were semiclandestine armed groups with revolutionary aims, including several that had aligned with Hugo Chávez and taken part in the coup attempts of 1992 (Juan Contreras, interview 1/25/99).

20. Macarao y Su Gente eventually split apart after some of its members joined LCR in 1993, rupturing the tradition of autonomy (interviews with Raúl Pinto, 10/28/99, and Rafael Fernández, 11/17/99, members of Macarao y Su Gente who later worked in the parish technical cabinet).

21. Interview with Berkel (10/21/99). Berkel and other LCR parish board members noted that in general the board members from the opposition parties did not attend the public assemblies, but Berkel attributed this decision partly to LCR's exclusionary rhetoric: "In Coche there were leaders from the traditional parties who wanted to be social agents [gestores].

line that existed throughout Caracas. It was a decision taken in Acción Democrática's Sectional Executive Committee, and all the members of AD knew that they had to oppose all those [participation programs]. It was a political decision."

When the parish governments accomplished anything, AD's board members or city councilors tried to take individual credit rather than granting that the citizens had made a collective achievement by participating, an idea that LCR tried to promote (see Harnecker 1995d, 51). Another common complaint charged that once the parish public works budgets arrived to the City Council for approval, AD's representatives would change the priorities emanating from the parishes. And though LCR had received an automatic majority on the City Council by virtue of winning the mayor's race, Istúriz could not always count on LCR councilors to vote unanimously, especially after one of them became an independent a year into his term.

Opposition to Istúriz's administration from all rival parties intensified after LCR's unprecedented and unexpected success in the national elections of December 1993. LCR's presidential candidate received 22 percent of the vote in a tight four-way race, and led in the federal district with 35 percent, after receiving only 1 percent five years earlier. The party also experienced a dramatic increase in its congressional delegation, from three deputies in the previous term to forty deputies and nine senators.[22] Suddenly, the Causa Radical was transformed from a minor regional party into Venezuela's third-largest party, with approximately 20 percent of the seats in each house of congress. AD and Copei had maintained their combined congressional majority, but, for the first time since the Pact of Punto Fijo, they lost the executive branch. A new party, Convergencia, now held the presidency in alliance with several small parties. The declining electoral fortunes of AD and Copei only made them fight harder to regain their former strength, while the Convergencia governing alliance attempted to consolidate its position as the alternative to *adecopeyano* dominance. Thus, the pressure on LCR's administration in Caracas would increase after 1993. The offensive against Istúriz began immediately, with the opposition city councilors refusing to approve his administration's accounting report (*memoria y cuenta*) of its first year (*El Nacional* 2/10/94, 3).

They never attended the assemblies. But the very attitude of LCR excluded the other parties, because LCR members called the others corrupt, et cetera."

22. For the election results, see López Maya (1995, 225–26, 230, tables 3 and 4). The municipality of Libertador has about 85 percent of the federal district's population, thus the figure for the federal district probably reflects LCR's electoral support in Libertador fairly faithfully.

Most importantly, in mid-1994, when Istúriz tried to consolidate the parish governments by creating a legal ordinance for them, the opposition parties fought the ordinance for nearly eighteen months. LCR's main rivals at the local level (AD and Copei) based their arguments against the parish government ordinance partly on the notion that it was unconstitutional to have something called "government" below the level of the municipality (Arconada 1995, 348). In the conference to discuss the ordinance, a clear division between LCR and its rivals was evident. LCR supported strengthening the parish governments' power. As LCR city councilor, Reinaldo Morales, stated, "My proposal is that in the Council we move toward converting these parish boards, instead of auxiliaries of the Legislature that exist legally, converting them legally into parish governments that can make decisions on administrative issues, and on issues that are important for the parishes, like the public works projects" (Comisión 1994, 91). The opposition, however, advocated maintaining representative democracy, embodied by the parish boards.

The leader of AD's city councilors, Carlos Blanco, argued in favor of strengthening the parish boards because "they enjoy the legitimacy and the representativeness that come from the fact that they were elected by the people" (Comisión 1994, 81). Josefina Nieto, a city councilor from Copei, agreed: "That government [the parish government] and everything that they plan there should be through the parish boards, because in some way or another, in the past elections they were legitimated as the representatives of those communities" (Comisión 1994, 87). When asked directly by the audience, Blanco stated, "In terms of whether or not to consolidate the parish government, I am in favor of consolidating the parish board, which is the only authority that is truly recognized by law" (Comisión 1994, 93). Blanco maintained that the parish boards might be allowed to decide on the parish public works budget, but only if the "decisions on the budget are unanimous, that there is no type of influence on the development of the boards' work" (Comisión 1994, 85). It seems clear that the traditional parties had no desire to concede power to volunteer participants, nor to allow even the parish boards much authority, given that LCR held a plurality in most parishes.

Overall, AD's war to retake Caracas from the Causa Radical crippled Istúriz's ability to design the parish government program as he wished, both directly, by sabotaging the practical functioning of (and legal framework for) the parish governments, and indirectly, by impeding the municipal administration from operating effectively in general.

The Restrictive Design of the Parish
Governments and the Decline of Participation

In practice, LCR's original idea of an agile, effective, and bottom-up participation program did not survive the fierce opposition from a still-powerful Acción Democrática and the limited capacity of municipal government in Venezuela's still-centralized system. Instead, for the most part the design of the parish government program that emerged on the ground was restrictive. The design included (1) a formal structure of participation that often excluded volunteer participants while privileging political party leaders and municipal technocrats who competed for power at the top, (2) a constricted range of subjects that participants could meaningfully discuss, and (3) an almost complete absence of decision-making power. This restrictive design, in turn, discouraged many residents from participating in the parish governments. Caraqueños did not see a direct link between their involvement in parish government meetings and benefits for themselves or their communities. Without that link, participation dissipated.

Structure

As envisioned by Istúriz, the structure of participation would entail public assemblies of community volunteers at the top of the chain of command, with the elected parish boards and the appointed technical cabinets facilitating the assemblies and implementing the collective decisions made there. In a speech at the city-wide conference on the parish governments, Istúriz reiterated his vision of how they should function: "The ideal is that at least once a week the people are convoked alongside the technical workers and the board members. . . . Everyone together for the discussion. And what is agreed upon there is what the board and the cabinet will do" (Comisión 1994, 37). In practice, the structure of participation was more top-down than bottom-up, privileging formal officials over participants from the community. The structure varied somewhat across the parishes, but generally either the parish boards or technical cabinets served as the locus of decision making, while volunteer participants in public meetings and in the service committees played minimal roles in making individual demands and providing information or suggestions. And state agencies of the national and federal district government essentially ignored the parishes altogether (see figure 3.1).

In spite of the mayor's instructions to abide by collective decisions made by local residents, members of the boards and cabinets frequently clashed

Parish government structure in theory

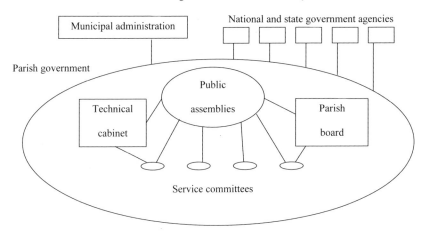

Parish government structure in practice

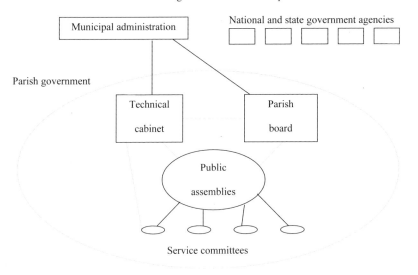

*Rectangular shapes indicate that the structure is for government officials or employees only; circular shapes indicate that the structure is for civil society as well. Dashed lines indicate less consistent interaction than whole lines.

Fig 3.1 Parish government strucure

over which of the two held ultimate authority at the parish level. This conflict had at least three sources: the lack of clearly defined roles for each entity, the diversity of political party loyalties, and the ability of each side to claim legitimacy. The members of the parish boards had been popularly elected on party slates using proportional representation. They served three-year terms, during which they would receive a small stipend as long as they regularly attended the board's official weekly meetings. The boards were supposed to serve as the link between the municipal government and the local community. Parish board members could claim legitimacy based on the elections, but this legitimacy was tied to their respective parties, since voters had not chosen individual names. The workers in the technical cabinets came from different municipal departments and received regular salaries. Their legitimacy stemmed from their position as permanent municipal employees and from their knowledge of a particular field, especially for the engineers, architects, and social workers. Though the technical cabinets were supposed to be apolitical, in practice many of their workers supported LCR and its parish government proposal.

In a few parishes, the boards and cabinets worked together, but in most they competed.[23] Rather than holding open public assemblies in which both entities were present, the boards and cabinets usually met separately, and only on occasion opened their meetings to city residents. The service committees set up in some parishes, on the other hand, did provide a more regular arena for volunteer participants, and the assemblies held in the first year to discuss the budget and to debate bus prices also offered a forum for residents. Generally, though, the options for citizen participation were limited. In the city-wide conference to evaluate the parish governments, Istúriz criticized the parish boards for meeting behind closed doors and complained, "Not all the parishes have permanent, regular assemblies. The board is functioning alone as a board, in many cases separately from the cabinet, and the cabinet, in some cases, is meeting by itself somewhere else. That is what has been occurring, and the people are left without a space" (Comisión 1994, 37, 6–8).

At the same conference, the conclusions of the roundtable discussion groups suggest that one result of the closed meetings is that on the parish boards "the interests of the party predominate over the interests, needs, and demands of the communities" (Comisión 1994, tables 1 and 3; and see Harnecker 1995d, 51). The discussion groups suggested several changes in the structure of the parish government program in order to increase the power of volunteer participants and to create a direct link with the central

---

23. Conflicts between the boards and cabinets were described to me by members of each in different parishes (interviews with Raúl Pinto 10/28/99; Aida Henriquez 11/18/99; José Contreras 10/29/99; Ana Alvarez 12/13/99).

municipal administration. These proposed changes included a provision to allow for the recall of parish board members and the creation of a permanent city-wide forum, with representatives from each parish government, that would negotiate directly with the mayor and his cabinet (Comisión 1994, tables 1, 2, and 4). Yet the city councilors from AD especially made it clear that they opposed any changes to the structure of participation that might weaken the parish boards' authority. It is telling that both the recall mechanism and the permanent city-wide forum were also absent in Montevideo's participation program but present in the program in Porto Alegre.

Range

Given the minimal scope of jurisdiction granted municipal governments in Venezuela and the frequent refusal of national- and state-level organs to collaborate with the parish governments in Caracas, the range of significant issues that participants could effectively debate in fact proved quite narrow. Most of the urban services provided solely by the municipal government—such as maintenance of parks, cemeteries, and public markets—did not coincide with the priorities of most residents. Critical issues, like water provision and crime, remained under the control of either national- or state-funded entities: Hidrocapital, in the case of water and sewerage, and the federal district government, in the case of police. Different levels of government shared responsibility for many other services, yet the municipality usually played a minor, supplementary role, as in the case of health care and education.

When the parish boards or technical cabinets asked representatives from other levels of government to attend to localized demands or to meet with parish residents, they usually received negative responses. As Francke (1997, 76) argues, "The relations of the parish entities with other state organs, like the federal district government, MINDUR, CANTV, Hidrocapital, was weak: those organs paid little attention to the communications from the parishes and only rarely attended the meetings to which they were invited." This was a common complaint at the parish government conference. The conference discussion group on interinstitutional relations blamed the lack of attention from other levels of government on the recentness of the parish governments—which meant that they were relatively unknown—and on the "partyization" of government institutions in general (Comisión 1994, table 3). A hallmark of the inability of the different levels of government to work together is that neither the federal district governor nor the national minister of decentralization, both of whom belonged to Convergencia, accepted Istúriz's invitation to participate in the conference on parish governments (Concejo 1994, 7).

Martínez (interview 1/18/99), the former Budget Director, offered an example of the degree to which the parish governments were ignored by other entities and restricted in their capabilities:

> The neighbors would go to the president of the parish board and complain that an entire avenue was dark, the streetlights had burned out. And the president of the parish board would call La Electricidad de Caracas, but no one listened to him. So he had to go to the mayor, or talk to me or one of the other directors, so that we could help him. . . . The people realized that there was no reason to go to the president of the parish board when he doesn't even have the ability to get a street light fixed.

When asked why the other institutions would not collaborate with the parish authorities, Martínez continued:

> It has to do with our political culture. Many of our presidents of institutions or private businesses do not speak with the mayors nor with the governors. Now some are talking to the governors. But our government has been so centralist that everybody took their problems to the president or a national minister. And much of the time, these enterprises, like Electricidad de Caracas, which is a big, important corporation in the city, spoke with the president, or with the minister of transportation and energy. But from there down, nothing. They would not even talk to the mayors.

Decision-Making Power

With few exceptions, the degree of decision-making power granted volunteer participants in the parish governments was negligible. City residents offered opinions and suggestions, received and provided information, and made demands, but they did not, by and large, make decisions. The parish boards and technical cabinets competed for decision-making authority and generally viewed volunteer participants as actors to be consulted but not necessarily respected. With regard to the most important decisions, the boards and cabinets could be overruled by the central municipal administration (the mayor and department directors) and by the City Council. The only occasion on which volunteer participants throughout the parishes seem to have had genuine decision-making power was during the negotiations over local transportation prices, and even that experience was limited, as bus drivers sometimes set their own prices. An analysis of the decision-making process around the parish public works budget will illustrate the lack of power for participants that characterized the parish government experiment in general.

During the first year of the parish government program, 1993, Istúriz convoked public assemblies in which he informed residents of the size of the municipal budget and opened discussion on what investments were needed. The parish boards and technical cabinets made lists of projects based on these discussions, and then decided which of the projects should be prioritized. Members of the technical cabinets provided estimates on the cost of the various projects and determined which of the projects were technically feasible as well as under municipal jurisdiction. Using this information, the parish boards decided on a final list for delivery to the mayor. The mayor, in turn, discussed the budget with his team of department directors and with the budget director. This group decided on the allocation of investments across the parishes and among the different departments, and then, in some cases, would meet with parish boards to renegotiate the final list of projects. Finally, the City Council could adjust the parish budget before approving the mayor's version. In some instances, the parish boards would learn of a city councilor's attempt to alter a project, and residents would come to City Council to protest. The second and third years of the parish government program followed the pattern of the first year, with the important exception that only some parishes held parish-wide assemblies. More often, either the parish board or the technical cabinet would hold neighborhood-level meetings or meetings with specific community organizations to gather lists of demands.

For the most part, then, volunteer participants had little influence over which individual projects were prioritized for their parish, and they played no role in deciding the larger issues of which city services in general needed greater attention and how to distribute investments across parishes. In fact, although members of LCR's administration claim to have redirected investments to the lower-class *barrios*, the distribution across the parishes does not reflect this claim. On average, poorer parishes did receive a very slightly higher percentage of the municipality's investments than did richer

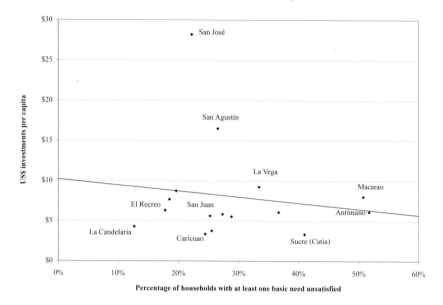

Fig. 3.2   Level of need and investments, by parish (1993)

parishes.[24] However, when one analyzes per capita investment figures, the lack of redistribution becomes clear, because more populous parishes were also poorer. Figures 3.2 and 3.3 demonstrate that the less-developed parishes with numerous large *barrios,* like Antímano and Sucre, received about the same per capita investments as did centrally located parishes with more developed urban services and few *barrios,* such as La Candelaria and El Recreo.[25]

24. The Pearson correlation coefficients measuring the correlation between percentage of households with basic needs unsatisfied and percentage of municipal investment spending are small (.16 for 1993 and .32 for 1994) and statistically insignificant (p = .27 and p = .11).

25. A correlational analysis of the data presented in figures 3.2 and 3.3 confirms that poverty levels and per capita spending show virtually no association. The Pearson correlation coefficients for both 1993 and 1994 are very small (−.14 and .01, respectively) and do not come close to statistical significance (p = .31 and p = .49). The data for the figures and the analysis are for sixteen of the nineteen parishes. They exclude Coche and El Junquito, parishes for which the percentage of households with basic needs unsatisfied was unavailable, as well as Catedral, the smallest parish at the heart of Caracas, which was an outlier in terms of investments per capita. The basic needs indicator comes from the Central Office of Statistics and Information (OCEI), as reported in *El Globo* (1/2/96, 10); it is calculated using five measures: households in which school-age children (ages seven to twelve) do not attend school; overcrowded households (more than three people per bedroom); households with inadequately constructed homes; households without basic urban services (water and sewerage); and households with high degrees of economic dependence. Investment statistics come from the municipal administration's annual accounting reports and include spending for both new projects and repairs or

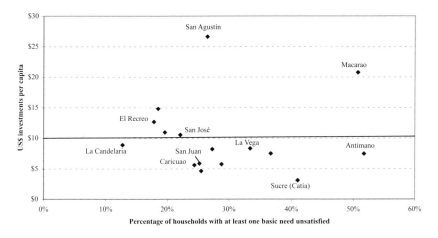

Fig. 3.3   Level of need and investments, by parish (1994)

The municipal government's funding of the Catuche Consortium in La Pastora figured as the one major exception to the paucity of investment projects for the poorer parishes. However, city officials made this decision, not participants in La Pastora's parish government, and the funds did not appear in the parish public works section of the budget but in the transfers section. The top-down process in the Catuche decision reflected the power-lessness of the parish governments in general. And it is clear that this lack of decision-making authority was not lost on those who participated. One of the main conclusions at the 1994 parish government conference was that the existing design did not provide opportunities for participants to establish local priorities, make decisions, or formulate policy (Comisión 1994, table 1). Indeed, as the director of CESAP told me, "It was more the dynamic of partici-pation but without decision and implementation" (Jansen, interview 10/7/99).

The Fall of Participation: Many Meetings, Few Projects

By all accounts, the parish government program failed to sustain participants after the first year. Despite some variation across the parishes, on the whole, the original eagerness to participate shown by the thousands of people

upgrades of existing infrastructure (Alcaldía 1994a, 220, 286; 1995b, *Gestión Parroquial*). The conversion to dollar figures is based on rates published in *Coyuntura* (January 1999, 40). The accounting report for 1995 did not specify investments for each parish.

who attended the assemblies in the beginning of 1993 went unmatched in the next two years. Responsibility for the fall of participation lies with the restrictive design of the parish government program and with the municipal government's jurisdictional and fiscal impotence. When participants realized that they could not effectively decide on the issues they most cared about—because of the narrow range of issues open for discussion and because of the still-powerful presence of party representatives above them—they gradually stopped attending parish assemblies.

In interviews, parish board members, technical cabinet workers, city officials, and observers all agreed that the number of residents involved in the parish governments and the frequency of their activities declined after the first year. Already by the mid-1994 city conference, attendees described participation in the parish governments as limited, episodic, and temporary.[26] The major reason interviewees offered for the fall of participation was that residents did not see concrete results stemming from their involvement:

> When we arrived there were a lot of people that really did want to participate but then it cooled down when they didn't see a rapid solution. (Gisela Aybar, parish board member in San José, interview 12/13/99)

> In El Recreo participation also dropped off after the first year. There was a disappointment because of the lack of solutions. The people said, "Why should I go there if they're just going to say the same things?" (Henríquez, interview 11/18/99)

> The people in the *barrios* did not feel the projects with Aristóbulo. The participation processes promoted slowness in decision making, which is normal, but the people felt that it wasn't working. . . . There was greater response to the participation proposal at the start, but it did not last over time. It was participation to see if one's community could obtain some benefit. (Jansen, interview 10/7/99)

> At one point the people thought that problems were going to be solved, and when they saw that they weren't being solved, that the same old mistakes were being made, that it was looking like more of the same,

---

26. See Comisión (1994, table 1). In describing the conference's conclusions, a magazine published by the City Council reported that "massive participation in the activities of the parish governments" had not been achieved (Concejo 1994, 6).

they withdrew to their houses. (Juan Contreras, cultural coordinating committee member in 23 de Enero, interview 1/25/99)

The lists [of demands] from the barrios were books, definitely. It wasn't a page of problems, it was a book of problems. And they saw that it was only possible to satisfy a very small quota, because the resources were not enough to satisfy all the demands and there were projects that required a lot of investment. When the projects finally started being built, the people saw that there were a lot of meetings and only a few projects. (Martínez, interview 1/18/99)

The vast majority of the people in the barrios and lower-class urbanizaciones did not seem to share LCR's participatory ideology. They did not want more generic opportunities for participation; they wanted immediate solutions to their needs. Though some were willing to participate in the parish governments in the beginning, they abandoned them when the results were slow or unforthcoming. As Martínez (interview 1/18/99) told me, "It was not that the people did not commit themselves. In the beginning the people came, they attended the convocation, but they attended the assemblies under the 'give and give' idea: you give to me and I give to you." In the end, the residents could "give" their participation, but the municipal government, lacking funds and authority, could not deliver the expected results.

Instead of concrete improvements in their parishes, participants saw immobility because of conflicts between political parties and the refusal of different government entities to cooperate. The discussion group on intra- and interinstitutional relations at the city conference concluded that the parish government's "current structure limits the participation that was expected. The interinstitutional 'passing the buck' discourages citizens and generates criticisms and confrontations. The tendency of the members of the parish board to respond to party interests limits community participation" (Comisión 1994, table 3). The former director of the Corporation of Municipal Services, Julio Montes, agreed that while city officials had been unable to respond effectively to demands from the parishes, "the reign of the political parties" on the parish boards and the internal struggles played out there within and among the parties prevented the development of the parish government proposal (Comisión 1994, 64–65). Istúriz argued similarly that "we have problems between the members of some of the boards that have a party war, and they create such an environment on the board that many neighbors don't feel like going" (Comisión 1994, 6). And according to a technical cabinet worker in Macarao, Raúl Pinto (interview 10/28/99), "We couldn't give immediate solutions because of the difficulties created by the opposition. Our solutions were not quick because they cut our projects from the budget in the City Council, they slowed down the projects."

Nonetheless, party conflicts did not reach the local level in a few parishes, such as in San José, where the board members from different parties worked together. According to the former board president there, the fact that the board members were all educated professionals may have facilitated such cooperative relations (Aybar, interview 12/13/99). Without information on the class status of board members in other parishes, it is impossible to evaluate this explanation, but it does seem that while party loyalties were privileged in many parishes, such loyalties were not universally absolute.

In a few parishes, interviewees complained not just about the sabotage from the opposition parties (especially AD), but about "traditional party" behavior from the Causa Radical. For example, in 23 de Enero, Juan Contreras (interview 1/25/99) told me that the traditional clientelist attitude of certain LCR parish board members and administration officials disappointed independent community activists: "At the beginning the people were taken into account, but by the end they were not because the political disputes started. Some individuals in the technical cabinet began doing the very things for which we had all criticized Acción Democrática and the other parties. They began doing political proselytizing, putting their own people first. In order to get something done you had to be in the party or agree with the party, and if you didn't, it wouldn't happen."

Patterns of Participation Across the Parishes

While the parish governments clearly did not sustain a large number of participants over time, it is difficult to assess how well the participants represented the wider community in terms of class, gender, race, party identification, or organizational affiliation because neither the city nor external researchers recorded data on individual participants (unlike in Montevideo and Porto Alegre). Nonetheless, from the responses of interviewees, some patterns, variations, and exceptions emerge within the larger trend of declining participation. For one thing, it appears that, on the whole, more people participated on a slightly more regular basis in the poorer parishes than in the better-off parishes, a pattern that characterizes Montevideo and Porto Alegre as well. Though class differences may have mattered, interview respondents did not note gender and ethnic disparities in participation. Given the large number of women in positions of power on the parish boards and the fact that Istúriz is one of the country's most prominent Afro-Venezuelan politicians, this is not surprising.[27] With regard to partisan loyalties, despite the complaints in 23 de Enero about LCR proselytizing, it does not appear in general that only members of LCR-affiliated community organizations participated or even that they predominated. The problem with the parish governments experiment was not so much that it failed to encourage a diverse, representative group of participants but that it failed to sustain many participants at all.

In addition to the falling rates of participation, one other clear pattern emerged nearly throughout the city. Those residents who did continue to participate tended to direct their involvement toward the technical cabinets rather than the parish boards because the engineers, architects, social workers, and manual laborers in the former entity could actually provide solutions for at least some local problems. More often than not, this kind of participation lapsed from regular, ongoing collective decision making into sporadic individualized complaints or demands. The major exceptions to the widespread decline of participation were the experiences of the water committee, sewage repair, and the budget process in the parish of Antímano, and, in smaller measure, the more limited experiences in Macarao and La Vega. An examination of the variation in participation across the parishes can serve as a check on the institutional design explanation for its general decline presented in the previous section.

In a simple categorization, one finds four basic types of participatory experiences in the parishes: (1) *weak participation:* where the parish government assemblies and activities never achieved substantial numbers of participants (La Candelaria; La Pastora; El Junquito); (2) *vanishing participation:* where the initial response from citizens was positive, but their participation quickly declined, leaving only a small number of people participating regularly (San Juan; San José; Santa Teresa), or slightly larger numbers participating on an infrequent basis (El Recreo; Altagracia; Santa Rosalía); (3) *diminishing participation:* where the initially high numbers of participants dropped continually over the period, though a consistent group of activists participated in relation to two or three particular concerns (Caricuao; Sucre; El Valle; San Agustín; 23 de Enero); (4) *strong participation:* where a larger number of people mobilized around a number of issues and continued participating

27. In my own sample of LCR parish board member interviewees, women comprised roughly half, and the one Afro-Venezuelan was elected president of the parish board in San Agustín, which has a large black population. Women and Afro-Venezuelans also figured prominently in Istúriz's administration.

regularly throughout the term (Antímano; and to a lesser extent, Macarao and La Vega).[28] The following paragraphs take an example from each category to provide a detailed picture of the functioning of the parish governments and to verify whether or not the variation in participation corresponded to local-level differences in the design of the parish governments.

Weak participation: La Candelaria

Carlos Contreras (interview 1/11/99), coordinator of special programs for La Candelaria's technical cabinet, explained to me that local residents did not have a "culture of participation" and never became much involved with the parish government. La Candelaria is a solidly middle-class parish close to the city center with adequate infrastructure except in the few small *barrios* located along the banks of creek beds in the northern part of the parish. It housed approximately 62,000 residents in 1990.[29] Of those, at most 40 attended La Candelaria's largest assembly, convoked to discuss the parish budget. The technical cabinet and parish board created the budget proposal prior to the assembly and invited the residents to suggest changes. Given that the parish mostly enjoyed decent public services, the high crime rate figured as the residents' most common complaint, yet this problem did not fall under municipal jurisdiction and could not be addressed in the parish budget assemblies. The technical cabinet and parish board also held joint meetings open to the public on Tuesday afternoons, but only fifteen people usually showed up during the first year, and half that number afterwards. Parish board members from the opposition parties generally did not attend the public meetings and would constantly question the validity of the technical cabinets and the parish government proposal overall.

Not one of the four neighborhood associations in the parish had held an election in the previous five years, and, partially because the AD leaders presiding over them resisted new elections, the technical cabinet's social worker failed to democratize a single one. His attempt to work with residents to arrange elections in one association provoked fistfights when the incumbent president attempted to bus in outsiders to vote. This caused tensions in the

28. My placement of parishes in different categories is based on interviews with members of the parish boards and/or technical cabinets in fourteen of the parishes, on Francke (1997) for La Pastora and El Valle, on Arconada (1996) for Antímano, and Figuera (1996) for Sucre. I did not obtain information on the smallest parish, Catedral, with a population of approximately four thousand people.

29. See census figures in OCEI (1993, 67). In 1994, La Candelaria was divided, allowing for the creation of a new parish, San Bernardino. La Candelaria's board and cabinet continued serving the entire area until the election of a separate board for San Bernardino in 1995.

parish board as well, because the association president (an AD member) served on the board. The technical cabinet also tried to start a parish newspaper, but no one joined the staff, so only two editions were ever published. Contreras told me, "It didn't make sense for the technical cabinet to publish a paper in the name of the community when the community didn't participate." No service committees or sports or cultural coordinating organizations formed either. Contreras concluded that the parish government was "reduced to a space to receive complaints and resolve occasional problems. It did not achieve the objective of community participation."

Vanishing participation: San Juan

Located in the middle of Caracas, San Juan is a large parish, with nearly 140,000 residents in the 1990 census, and very diverse in terms of social class, with a few middle- and upper-class neighborhoods, many lower-middle-class areas with public housing projects, and dozens of poor *barrios*.[30] During the Pérez Jiménez dictatorship, San Juan earned a reputation for combativeness, one that continued in the 1960s when several Leftist groups operating in the housing projects and *barrios* made parts of the parish known as "red zones." With the fading out of the guerrilla movements in the following decade, other forms of participation also declined, although some *barrio* residents did participate in the Caracazo and the 1992 coup attempts. In general, however, by the 1990s San Juan had become an AD stronghold, with several neighborhood associations allied to the party.

In 1993, around 200 residents came to the initial public assembly called by the new administration, yet in the following year, participation declined precipitously. Only a few residents attended the meetings held infrequently and separately by either the parish board or the technical cabinet, which fought each other for authority. After Istúriz proclaimed that the cabinet should obey the board, most cabinet workers returned to their municipal departments, leaving only an architect and an engineer. In 1995, the discussion of the parish budget was reduced to the remnants of the cabinet deciding "which projects were most important based on petitions from the residents and from their own tour of the parish" (José Contreras, interview

---

30. The description of San Juan is based on interviews with José Contreras (10/29/99) and Jesús Covarrubia (11/16/99), both former members of the parish board, and on two reports of parish activities (Junta Parroquial 1994, and Comisión 3/12/94). Contreras and Covarrubia contradicted one another occasionally, and when they did, I relied on the written record. San Juan ceded some of its territory in 1994 for the creation of a new parish, El Paraíso, which also received territory from La Vega.

10/29/99). The parish board attempted to create service committees, but none of them worked except for the short-lived transportation committee, which dissolved shortly after its one public assembly to discuss the bus price increase. As in La Candelaria, conflicts erupted between LCR board members and those from opposition parties. In San Juan, the opposition board members often refused to attend public meetings and withheld or delayed approval of the parish public works budget. In general, neither the board nor the cabinet could respond to the demands of parish residents. A report by the board in mid-1994 states that it tried to help residents find solutions with the federal district government, the national government, and the municipal government without success, and that by itself, the board had "not been able to resolve or provide solutions to practically any of the community's problems" (Junta Parroquial 1994).

Diminishing Participation: Caricuao

Like San Juan, the parish of Caricuao is large (141,000 inhabitants), but it is located in the southern periphery of Caracas and has somewhat less social diversity, consisting mostly of 1960s-era large public housing projects surrounded by *barrios* of a more recent period.[31] In the first year of the Istúriz administration, members of the parish board and the technical cabinet in Caricuao started to implement the parish government idea by holding meetings first with the neighborhood associations and then open meetings by apartment block and by *barrio*. The level of involvement in the parish government activities was relatively high, with numerous well-attended assemblies around specific issues such as the parish budget, the bus prices, school improvements, cleaning public areas around the housing projects, and the creation of a cultural coordinating committee. Discussion of the latter two issues produced immediate and enduring results: regular volunteer clean-up days convoked by a garbage committee and held in conjunction with Cotécnica (a private waste management company contracted by the municipal government), and a new parish-wide cultural organization, the Toromaina Coordinator, that included theater groups, a community press, and an incipient local television station.[32] A number of neighborhood-level environmental groups arose from the garbage service committee, and through

31. This account of Caricuao's experience with the parish government program is based mostly on an interview with the ex-administrator of the parish board, Ana Alvarez (12/13/99), with supplemental information from Comisión (1994, 35, 43–45, 64) and Harnecker (1995d).
32. Toromaina is the name of the tribe that inhabited the valley of Caracas at the time of the conquest; the chief was the famous Guaicaipuro (Comisión 1994, 43).

Toromaina's meetings to discuss the parish cultural budget, the television station (TV Caricuao) received funding from the municipal government to purchase an antenna.

Despite these minor initial successes, however, participation in most parish government activities began to decline after the first year, when the expectations raised about more significant public works projects went unmet. According to Ana Alvarez (interview 12/13/99), the former administrator of the parish board, the national decentralization plan had transferred some responsibilities to the municipal government, but no resources, which reduced the ability of city officials to provide solutions. Alvarez told me that the result, for most community organizations, "was a long and sweet wait for things that never came." The municipal government's lack of resources was compounded by the constant, "fierce" opposition of parish board members from rival parties AD and Copei. They refused to approve any proposals from LCR's delegation, leading to complaints from residents about the board's inaction and incessant hostility. For example, a partici-pant at the 1994 conference asked, "What can we do about the parish board in Caricuao? They are always fighting" (Comisión 1994, 35). The board and technical cabinet in Caricuao did not have serious confronta-tions as in many other parishes, but conflict reigned among members of the board itself. LCR's lack of a majority on the board prevented it from implementing ideas emanating from the public assemblies. Overall, although the Toromaina Coordinator and a few environmental groups continued meeting throughout the period, participation concerning broader issues mostly faded away.

Strong participation: Antímano

In nearly all respects, Antímano is the antithesis of La Candelaria.[33] Whereas only 13 percent of La Candelaria's households lack basic needs, this is true of 52 percent of the households in Antímano, making it the city's poorest parish (*El Globo* 1/2/96, 10). Located in the western edge of the valley of Caracas, Antímano consists almost entirely of *barrios* precariously situated on hillsides. Despite its large population (between 117,000 and 250,000),[34] only twenty policemen patrol the parish's eighty *barrios* (*El Universal* 2/7/95). The problem of violence that plagued the parish was paralleled in intensity

33. By all accounts, Antímano's experience with the parish government was the most important in Caracas (Arconada 1996; Alvarez 1997; Contreras and Martínez 1997; López Maya 1999b). Except where noted, the following summary is based on those sources.

34. These figures come from the 1990 census (OCEI 1993, 67) and *El Universal* (2/7/95).

only by the issue of water, which was not available in many *barrios* for up to two months in a row. By the mid-1970s, Antímano residents had become so frustrated by government inattention that they began blockading the main freeway heading west out of Caracas in protest.

The water shortages remained the most significant problem years later when Istúriz held a parish-wide assembly in early 1993 and proposed that the community organize a parish government and service committees to address specific issues. More than a hundred people showed up four days later for the first meeting of the new water committee. A parish board member, an engineer from the technical cabinet, and a representative from Hidrocapital also attended. During the next months, the water committee helped Hidrocapital's engineers design a plan to build aqueducts to service Antímano, and formed dozens of neighborhood water groups to organize the distribution of water from the water trucks. The distribution rate went from once every two months to once every two weeks. (Eventually, two separate aqueducts and a new water plant would also be built, but not until the end of Istúriz's tenure in December 1995.) The regular Wednesday meetings of the water committee—with between 35 and 120 participants, depending on the meeting—eventually became known as the parish government.

At one of these water committee meetings city officials read aloud the list of public works contemplated for the parish for 1993. The participants complained that several of the most critical issues had not made the list, including the five-year-old problem of a damaged sewage pipe. The leaking pipe had created an enormous crater overflowing with raw sewage at the main intersection of the largest *barrio*, Santa Ana, with approximately fifty thousand inhabitants. Even though the proposed repair fell outside the jurisdiction of the municipality, the assembly insisted upon a solution. With the coordination of the technical cabinet, financial support from the municipal administration, and the collaboration of volunteers from the community, the parish government decided to form a microenterprise to carry out the project.

The concrete successes in improving water provision and replacing the sewer main spurred interest in the parish budget process, and in 1994 there were regular Saturday meetings to deliberate over the next year's parish budget and decide which projects should take precedence. Other service committees also formed, such as transportation committees to address the unregulated service of the jeeps that charged exorbitant prices to take people up the hillsides where buses could not pass. A new organization emerged to coordinate the parish's cultural associations around the discussion of the parish culture budget. Finally, a number of neighborhood associations held elections to replace the leaders who had presided over them for years. Unlike in most of the other parishes, participation in the various activities of Antímano's parish government continued throughout the entire LCR administration.

In comparison to the other parishes, Antímano represented an outlier in terms of the level of participation achieved and sustained by the parish government proposal. The crucial difference in Antímano was that the design of the parish government program in practice more clearly resembled the ideal design originally envisioned by Istúriz and LCR. That is, the participants moved beyond the formal, party-dominated structure of the parish board, the range of discussion extended past the municipality's narrow jurisdictional boundaries to include important issues such as access to water, and the participants attained at least some measure of real decision-making power. Because of these differences, participants achieved significant, concrete results relatively quickly, which encouraged continuing involvement in parish government activities. The other two parishes where considerable participation continued throughout the three-year period also experienced somewhat more open participatory processes that produced important, tangible results: most notably, property titles for *barrio* residents in La Vega and health care improvements in Macarao.[35]

The question that remains is why these three parishes had more open designs. Most likely, the reason has to do with the fact that Antímano, La Vega, and Macarao all had significant histories of autonomous community organizations that had avoided or escaped penetration by AD and Copei.[36] Residents of Antímano fought for thirty years for access to regular water supply, and a variety of community groups were organized after the Caracazo, with particular activism from La Yaguara factory workers and local Jesuit priests influenced by liberation theology. In parts of La Vega, "worker priests" had supported long struggles over property rights, protection from land-slides, and pollution from the local cement factory. Last, in the late 1980s the parish-wide organization Macarao y Su Gente united more than sixteen

35. Specifically, a new pediatric health care cooperative was established in Macarao with partial funding from the municipal government, and the parish health committee coordinated a polio vaccination campaign with the help of the newly democratized neighborhood associations (Raúl Pinto, interview 10/28/99; Harnecker 1995d, 25).

36. The only other parish with notable community movements was 23 de Enero, yet many of these groups wanted more large-scale, revolutionary changes than a municipal government might be expected to initiate. My sources for the history of organizing in the three parishes are as follows: for Antímano, Contreras and Martínez (1997, 105–13); for La Vega, Jiménez, interview (2/4/99) and Fernandes (2007); and for Macarao, Grohmann (1996) and Fernández, interview (11/17/99).

community groups to create a health center, a business cooperative, and a newspaper. In addition to the history of independent local movements in each of these parishes, Antímano also seems to have received more attention from higher-level government agencies—particularly from Hidrocapital—than did other parishes in general. It may be that Hidrocapital collaborated with the residents of Antímano more than it did elsewhere because the agency's recently appointed president, José de Viana, had classified the parish as receiving the worst water service in the metropolitan area (Arconada 1996, 158). Alvarez (1997, 212–13) reports that de Viana met personally with Antímano's water committee on a weekly basis to discuss solutions to the water shortage. It also happens that de Viana was raised in Antímano.

Ultimately, however, La Vega, Macarao, and especially Antímano represented the only cases in which the parish government proposal sustained relatively large numbers of participants. Elsewhere, by LCR's final year in office in 1995, the parish governments—in fact the parish boards and especially the technical cabinets—generally had become ineffective receptors of community demands from a few dozen activists at most.

Legislating Participation

In August 1995, at the beginning of the municipal election campaign, the City Council finally opened discussion of LCR's proposed ordinance to regulate the parish governments. Four months later, with Istúriz trailing in the polls, the city councilors passed the ordinance just days before the December municipal elections that would sweep the Causa Radical out of office. The ordinance essentially ratified the parish governments as originally envisioned, but went further by granting volunteer participants the legal status that they had lacked in practice. According to the ordinance, volunteer participants, parish board members, and technical cabinet workers would enjoy equal privileges (to voice and vote) within the new parish government structure.[37] The ordinance also established that the parish governments had the power to elaborate a five-year development plan as well as the annual parish budget. While the ordinance did not make the decisions of the parish government binding on the municipal administration, it did offer some degree of power by including a provision allowing the parish governments to censure any municipal employee "whose negligence gives rise to the failure to carry out

---

37. All residents had the right to voice in the parish government, and those who had attended the previous three meetings had the right to vote. See Concejo (1995, article 3).

or the excessive delay of the plans and programs in the respective parish" (Concejo 1995, article 7). After three votes of censure in at least two parishes, the City Council would have to investigate the employee and vote within fifteen days on whether or not to dismiss the employee.[38]

Conclusion

One can only speculate as to whether the parish government ordinance would have stimulated greater participation, or if, in a more likely scenario, the municipal government's lack of capacity and Acción Democrática's powerful resistance would have continued to discourage participants in the long run. The victory of AD's António Ledezma over Istúriz in 1995, and the subsequent derogation of the last-minute ordinance, signified the definitive demise of the parish governments. In the 1995 mayor's race, Istúriz finished second with thirty thousand fewer votes than Ledezma (33 percent to 42 percent of the valid vote). As in 1992, however, most voters chose to stay at home. The abstention rate jumped from 63 percent to 70 percent in the Caracas mayor's race. LCR also lost the parish board elections in twenty of the twenty-two parishes, winning only in 23 de Enero and the newly created San Pedro. Overall, LCR's slate for the parish boards received less support than Istúriz (with 79 thousand votes compared to Istúriz's 109 thousand).[39]

The reasons behind LCR's defeat at the polls are undoubtedly numerous and include issues that extend beyond the party's performance in the municipal government of Caracas. These broader issues include, among others, LCR's inability to construct electoral alliances with other parties at any level of government;[40] Istúriz's ambiguous relationship with an unpopular national president;[41] LCR's internal divisions over which candidates to

---

38. To pass, the censure and dismissal votes required a two-thirds majority of the parish government public assembly and of the City Council, respectively (Concejo 1995, article 7).

39. All election results are from the now extinct Consejo Supremo Electoral.

40. In 1995, LCR unsuccessfully attempted a municipal-level alliance with Movimiento al Socialismo (MAS) (Jesús Covarrubia, interview 11/16/99). All other Venezuelan parties formed alliances that varied by state and municipality. It is telling that LCR's only gubernatorial victory in 1995 came in Zulia, where it supported a former leader of one of the 1992 coup attempts, Francisco Arias Cárdenas.

41. Istúriz had gained notoriety in 1992 when he and Rafael Caldera were the first congressional representatives to speak after the February coup attempt, and both had condemned Carlos Andrés Pérez's administration. Their speeches linked them, to some degree, in the eyes of voters. When Caldera became president of Venezuela and Istúriz mayor of Caracas, the "cordial relations" between them hurt Istúriz within LCR and ultimately hurt his reelection bid (Ellner and Myers 2002, 115).

select and support for the 1995 race;[42] and LCR's evolution from a small, unconventional party of outsiders to a more prominent party with a large congressional delegation at the same time that Hugo Chávez and his Movimiento Bolivariano Revolucionario 200 represented a more radical alternative and called for abstention in the 1995 elections.[43] It seems that many of the protest voters who brought LCR to office in 1992 simply abstained in 1995.

A complete listing of the issues contributing to LCR's defeat must also include those local-level factors that hurt the successful implementation of the participation program: the municipal government's lack of capacity and the unrelenting opposition from AD, which combined to prevent Istúriz's administration from producing major improvements in the quality of life of city residents. When asked, most survey respondents could not remember any "concrete projects" during Istúriz's administration, while most could recall the projects of the previous mayor, Claudio Fermín, from AD (*El Nacional* 10/30/95). In fact, the majority of those polled considered that Fermín had performed better as mayor than Istúriz, and favored a candidate who would continue Fermín's work (*El Nacional* 8/24/95). The major attempt to improve local government capacity, the property tax increase, was also unpopular with voters (Ellner and Myers 2002, 115). Overall, the electorate had a generally negative evaluation of Istúriz's performance. In opinion polls from 1995, between 40 and 50 percent of those surveyed held negative opinions of Istúriz, while around 30 percent held positive opinions (Guerón and Manchisi 1996, 393; *El Nacional* 8/24/95).

Interestingly, opinion polls showed Istúriz favored by the upper and middle classes and with less support among the lower classes (*El Nacional* 8/24/95). LCR's failure to expand its electorate in the poor areas is most likely due to greater support for Chávez in these areas, where abstention rates soared and where many voters expected more radical political and economic change than that offered by LCR. At the same time, the AD party

42. Although LCR unanimously chose Istúriz in Caracas, in its other stronghold of Bolívar state a conflict over who would succeed Andrés Velázquez erupted, dividing two of the party's top leaders, Velázquez and Pablo Medina. Their differences had already emerged in 1993, when Medina wanted Velázquez to contest the presidential election results, but the 1995 candidate selection dispute crystallized the division within the party, which would become formal in the 1997 split and the creation of Patria Para Todos. According to some former LCR members now in the PPT, the Velázquez faction did not wholeheartedly support Istúriz's campaign in 1995 and may have even sabotaged it (interviews with Carlos Castillo 2/10/99, Rubén Oropeza 1/27/99).

43. A survey by Canache (2002, 148–49) shows that in 1995 23 percent of those polled in Caracas and Maracaibo considered Chávez the most influential person in Venezuela, and 17 percent considered Chávez the most influential for themselves personally.

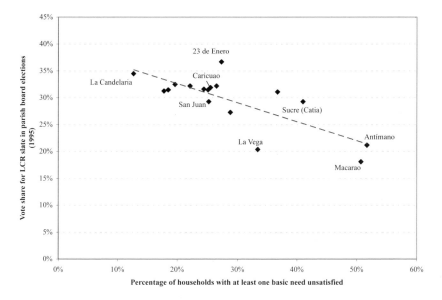

Fig. 3.4   Level of need and vote for LCR, by parish

machine remained strongest in poor districts. Analysis of the 1995 parish board elections strongly supports the notion that LCR fared better in the richer areas of the city.[44] Figure 3.4 shows that, on average, LCR received a lower share of the vote in parishes with higher percentages of households with unsatisfied basic needs. The Pearson correlation coefficient is -.76 and is highly statistically significant (p = .000).

The figure also reveals the striking fact that in the three parishes with the highest levels of ongoing participation—Antímano, La Vega, and Macarao—LCR earned lower vote shares than in other parishes where participation in the parish government program had been minimal, like La Candelaria and San Juan. This outcome probably indicates that voters did not evaluate Istúriz and LCR based on the performance of the parish governments. After all, even in the most successful parish governments only a small proportion of the local population participated.

The public's indifference toward the parish governments was confirmed when no resistance emerged against Ledezma's move to terminate them as soon as he began his term. Ledezma's administration immediately eliminated the technical cabinets and ended the parish-level discussions of the

44. Unfortunately, only data from the 1995 parish board elections were available broken down by parish; thus it was impossible to compare these data with the 1992 board elections or perform a similar analysis on the mayor's race for either year.

budget. The AD-led City Council also passed new ordinances restoring the parish board members to their preeminent position and reducing the role of residents in local policy making to not much more than that of spectators.[45]

The case of Caracas reveals the multiple obstacles that stand in the way of successful implementation of participation programs. Despite the presence of a progressive incumbent dedicated to participatory ideals, a relatively large number of community organizations, and a host of urgent problems with urban public services that might galvanize participation, the parish government experiment failed in the face of overwhelming hurdles. Because the macro-level national decentralization process had hardly advanced, the municipal government in Caracas lacked the resources and responsibilities necessary to facilitate the design of an effective participation program. Meso-level factors all presented stumbling blocks as well. Most importantly, because LCR replaced a strongly institutionalized rival—AD—in City Hall, it faced fierce resistance to its parish government experiment, further reducing LCR's ability to design an inviting and accessible participation program. AD used its meso- and micro-level allies in the municipal employees' unions and neighborhood associations to disrupt the participatory experiment. Ultimately, weak decentralization and strong opposition parties thwarted LCR's efforts to design a more informally structured, wide-ranging, and deliberative participation program. The resulting restrictive design of the parish governments disappointed those who participated and discouraged ongoing, sustained involvement, therefore frustrating LCR's objective of deepening democracy.

45. Article 14 of Ordinance 1608-A states that the parish boards should hold one public assembly per month. Articles 54 through 68 of Ordinance 1639-A provide strict regulations concerning these assemblies. They stipulate that no decisions should be made at the assemblies, but rather only in the board's ordinary (nonpublic) sessions. Several provisions limit the residents' right to speak, such as by restricting their use of speech to only once for fewer than five minutes and by requiring that questions and proposals be written and read aloud by the board's secretary and pertain to subjects selected by the board. The parish board also has the rights to restrict the public assembly to only those it invites, to block discussion of any subject that might cause "disturbances," and to suspend or cancel the assembly (see Concejo 1996a and 1996b).

4

Montevideo: From Rousing to Regulating Participation

The story of participatory decentralization in Montevideo presents some
parallels to that of the parish government program in Caracas. Montevideans
welcomed the new opportunity to participate opened by the Frente Amplio
in 1990 with massive attendance at budget assemblies throughout the city.
Powerful, well-institutionalized opposition parties, however, prevented the
incumbents from consolidating the original design of the participation
program. After the opposition impelled a change in the design, the number
of participants began to decline, and within a few years city officials and
residents worried about the "crisis of participation." Participation never
dwindled to the abysmally low levels seen in the parish governments in
Caracas, yet the participatory decentralization program in Montevideo failed
to sustain the high levels of participation that it initially encouraged and that
were reached in Porto Alegre. Nonetheless, unlike LCR, the FA continually
won reelection and kept its program in place, such that several thousand
citizens continue to participate each year.

Two other important differences with the Caracas case should be highlighted at the outset. Crucially, because Uruguay's national decentralization
efforts had advanced further than those in Venezuela, the municipal government in Montevideo enjoyed more resources and broader jurisdictional
scope than its counterpart in Caracas, and could thus more ably respond to
local demands. In fact, a significant increase in revenues over time allowed
the FA administration to expand spending on the public works projects
and social programs that residents wanted. The failure of Montevideo's
participation program to sustain large numbers of diverse participants
therefore cannot be traced to deficiencies in municipal finances or jurisdictional scope. Instead, the failure should be traced to the FA's yielding to

pressure from strongly institutionalized rival parties to abandon its original participatory decentralization program and to redesign it in 1993.

The other important difference with Caracas concerns institutional design. In Montevideo, the participation program's initial design, from 1990 to 1993, was relatively open. It offered a channel of participation that was more direct, inviting, and potent than that allowed either by the parish governments in Caracas or by the reformed program that followed in Montevideo from 1994 to the present. Rather than creating a new form of direct democracy and stimulating more citizens to participate, the reforms to the design at the end of 1993 added two layers of representation, which obscured the link between participation and results. The regulated design of the eventual program was characterized by a formal structure of participation, a moderate range of issues under discussion, and low decision-making power. While this regulated design proved somewhat less constricting than the restrictive design of the parish governments in Caracas, it still discouraged sustained participation.

This chapter compares the pre- and post-1993 designs, demonstrating the negative effects of the institutional redesign on the level of citizen participation. It also causally analyzes the change, arguing that without pressure from an autonomous, coordinated community movement, and faced with the rigidity of a centralist Uruguayan constitution that denied municipal autonomy, the Frente Amplio gave in to the opposition parties' demands for guaranteed seats at the local level and for the subordination of volunteer participants.

The Original Design of Participatory Decentralization (1990 to 1993)

At the start of his term, Tabaré Vázquez, the FA's first mayor of Montevideo, had at least one advantage over his counterparts in Caracas and Porto Alegre: a plan. In the months leading up to the 1989 elections, the Frente Amplio developed a fairly detailed proposal for how it would govern Montevideo in case of victory. The party printed a thirty-page booklet listing its general principles of government and presenting specific policies on everything from taxation and transportation to health care, housing, and day care centers. This booklet, often referred to as Document 6, describes a detailed plan for participatory decentralization. The FA proposed dividing the city into a number of zones and creating three new entities in each zone: a popularly elected board (*junta local*), an administrative office with municipal workers, and a volunteer Deliberative Assembly composed of "irrefutably representative" community organizations (Frente Amplio 1989, 11). Although the booklet did not specify the precise functions each entity should perform, it made clear that the Deliberative Assembly should be the "principal subject of decentralization" and that the ultimate goal was for city residents and community organizations to participate directly in public decision-making processes (11, 4–11).

First Steps to Participation: Trying to Implement Document 6

Upon entering office in February 1990, Vázquez began to implement the participatory decentralization plan laid out in Document 6. His first official act was to submit a resolution to the City Council dividing Montevideo into eighteen zones, establishing community centers (Centros Comunales Zonales, or CCZs) and Deliberative Assemblies in each zone, and designating a delegate of the municipal executive for each zone.[1] As its eventual goal, the resolution called for elections to an unnamed "political organ" to head each zone at an unspecified future date. In the meantime, the mayor's delegates began holding public meetings to diagnose each zone's problems and to establish contacts with and among community organizations. In these first meetings, participants agreed to set up monthly public assemblies as well as thematic commissions to discuss specific local issues.

Before the FA's program could take shape, its opponents in the City Council collected one thousand signatures to present their case against Vázquez's resolution before the national Congress.[2] Despite the opposition's legal maneuvering, the mayor's delegates continued meeting with local community organizations. In May 1990, Vázquez announced a new resolution to replace the earlier one. The new resolution modified the terms of the

---

1. See Resolution 133 BIS/90, February 28, 1990, in Junta (1994, 10–12). The zones comprise between three and five neighborhoods and range in population size from 34,000 to 134,000, with an average size of 75,000.

2. The Uruguayan constitution allows the contestation of any municipal government act when eleven city councilors present one thousand signatures to the Congress (Harnecker 1995b, 53). This provision impeded the Frente Amplio majority in the City Council from ensuring implementation of the party's program. The mayor's decentralization resolution included a number of items that could be construed as violations of national laws. For example, the eventual "political organ" could be thought of as the local boards (*juntas locales*) that Uruguayan law allows for in rural areas of each department. Only eleven of Montevideo's eighteen zones were considered rural. Furthermore, the local boards are subject to national regulations that prohibit them from being elective offices without approval from both chambers of Congress (Cabrera 1994, 31–33).

project, removing references to the mayor's delegates, deliberative assemblies, and political organs, but reaffirmed the executive's right to a direct relationship with community organizations and insisted on the establishment and functioning of the CCZs by identifying thirty municipal services and activities they would carry out (see Junta 1994, 12–15). As part of the direct relationship with the community, Vázquez began holding cabinet meetings in a different neighborhood each week, thus offering citizens a public opportunity to air requests and complaints and to learn more about municipal affairs. An even more important demonstration of the FA's intention to continue with the participatory decentralization program was the discussion of the five-year budget plan, for which the administration invited community organizations and individuals to attend public assemblies in each zone. Thousands of residents participated in the assemblies, listing hundreds of demands for municipal services and, in some cases, prioritizing the demands in terms of urgency. At the same time, the mayor's delegates—now titled "zone coordinators"—continued convening regular assemblies and working with the thematic commissions.

The zone coordinators also oversaw the CCZs, which began operating in October. By the end of the first year, sixteen CCZs were functioning as outposts of the municipal administration. Initially, each CCZ had a small group of municipal workers, including administrative personnel, a group of professionals (an architect, a social worker, and a teacher), and teams of skilled manual laborers who could provide a limited number of localized services such as repairing public lighting and maintaining public parks and plazas. Gradually, Vázquez transferred more administrative responsibilities to the CCZs. Ninety-seven different administrative procedures— ranging from denouncing the presence of rats or illegal pig raising to paying taxes and obtaining birth certificates—could be conducted through the CCZs by the end of 1991 (Cabrera 1994, 63–67). Previously citizens had needed to make the trip downtown to the municipal administration's central office to wait in long lines outside the infamous "palace of bricks." Now they could visit or call their local CCZ to complain that their trash had not been collected, for example, or that their streetlights had burned out, and CCZ workers could be dispatched more quickly to resolve the problem. One early success of the CCZs, in conjunction with environmental commissions set up in several zones, was the elimination of more than a thousand chronic, illegal garbage dumps that had plagued the city.

In the first few years of the participatory decentralization program, it benefitted from a fairly open institutional design. The structure of participation was very informal, with several arenas for volunteer participants and few fixed procedures. The range of issues discussed was fairly wide, and included important issues such as health care and housing. The degree of decision-making power, on the other hand, was not very high. Participants in the thematic commissions and deliberative assemblies had no guarantee that their proposals and demands would be carried out by the municipal administration. They did have a direct link to the mayor through the zone coordinator, though, and CCZ workers were oriented to meet their small-scale concerns. Surveys of community organizations in 1991 and 1992 indicate that although most did not perceive a high degree of decision-making power through the participatory decentralization program, the large majority had a positive evaluation of the program and could list concrete results stemming from their relationship with the local CCZ.[3]

The relative openness of the program's design seems to have attracted a fairly large number of residents, as the activities sponsored by the CCZs and the zone coordinators maintained a high level of participation in the initial years of the FA administration. Undoubtedly the most well-attended public assemblies were those to discuss the five-year budget plan in 1990. According to one of the city officials in charge of the process, between twenty thousand and twenty-five thousand residents participated, representing several hundred community organizations, including neighborhood associations, sports clubs, and Catholic groups.[4] More regular participation took place through the deliberative assemblies and thematic commissions in each

3. In a survey of 123 community organizations in four zones of the city, 33 percent of the respondents perceived that they had participated in some degree in the administration's decision-making process concerning local issues within the past year, while 43 percent stated that they had participated in preliminary discussions but not in final decisions. The same survey showed that 76 percent of the respondents could name a successful case of their relationship to the CCZ, such as the realization of public works projects, the collaboration with day care centers or health clinics, and the creation of recreational facilities. Finally, 72 percent believed that the presence of the zone coordinator and the opening of the CCZ had an important effect on the efficacy of their organization (Pérez and Charbonnier 1992, 31, 17–18). Results of a separate study of all 371 neighborhood associations in Montevideo showed that 71 percent of them believed that the CCZ was partially or completely fulfilling its principal role, which was perceived either as improving the administration's efficiency, setting priorities with local residents, or cogoverning with the residents. Similarly, 75 percent considered that the CCZ had contributed to the resolution of problems in their neighborhood, at least to some degree, and 76 percent of the neighborhood associations reported that the CCZ had facilitated their efforts (Bruera 1993, 62, 61, 59).

4. See Portillo (1996, 110; 1991). Other reports on the budget assemblies number the participants in the thousands as well (Cabrera 1994, 49; González 1995, 107; Harnecker 1995a, 294; Aguirre 1990, 11). These estimates seem convincing given that other sources indicate that several hundred community organizations took part in the budget discussions. Bruera's (1993, 59) study of the city's neighborhood associations shows that over two hundred

zone. By 1992, there were seventy-seven thematic commissions across the eighteen zones, with a maximum of twelve functioning in one zone and only one in other zones (González 1995, 109–10). In interviews, members of community organizations and CCZ workers described high levels of participation in the years before 1993. For example, a former social worker in Zone 8 told me, "At the beginning, we had assemblies with 150, 200 people. The number of participants and their commitment was high. There was an echo in the population, a tremendous solidarity" (Lucia Hornes, interview 8/18/99). A veteran neighborhood activist from the same zone agreed: "In the first period there was an excellent level of participation because you could feel that they were listening to you" ("Roberto," interview 8/22/99).[5]

While the thematic commissions thrived, they lacked institutionalization, forming and dissolving frequently with constant changes in the number of participants and in the organizations represented (González 1995, 108–11). The regular zonal assemblies also appeared somewhat disorderly. Julio Listre (1999, 4), a participant on the communications commission in Zone 14 during the first two years, writes of the initial assemblies, "I have a memory of a lot of effervescence and chaos from that time. . . . There were hundreds of people who, in a very organic form, discussed everything at the same time." In general, the pre-1993 period saw an enthusiastic response from residents to the Vázquez administration's new participation program. In evaluating those early years, a group of CCZ social workers conclude, "The breadth and depth that citizen participation had acquired created two problems to solve: the institutionalization of this participation and the rapid resolution of the problems and demands presented" (Calvetti et al. 1998, 3).

In order to increase the municipal government's ability to meet the flood of demands, the FA administration embarked on a series of tax reforms that it had proposed in Document 6. The measures included refusing to offer amnesties to taxpayers in arrears, decentralizing tax collection by allowing payment in several of the CCZs, and raising property taxes on empty lots. In keeping with Vázquez's campaign pledge—"who has more, will pay more, and who has less, will pay less"—the administration exonerated the elderly poor and members of housing cooperatives from paying property taxes.

---

of them participated, and another investigation reports that in Zone 9 alone, between ninety and one hundred community organizations of diverse types participated in the first budget plan (CIDC 1997, 25).

5. High levels of participation occurred in other zones as well (for Zone 9, see CIDC 1997, 25; for Zone 14, see Regent 1999, 25–27, 41–42).

The administration's most far-reaching proposal called for updating the city cadastre in order to allow the government to appraise the individual value of each property, something governments had ignored since 1964 (Bluth 1988, 212). Vázquez proposed increasing property taxes and basing rates on the newly established individual values, rather than on the property's general location. However, implementing this reform required cooperation from the entire City Council, which the FA could not obtain (Winn 1995, 22; IMM 1994, 5–9). Despite the failure to raise property rates, real municipal revenues (in constant pesos) increased by more than 35 percent during the 1990–94 term, almost entirely due to improvements in tax collection.[6]

Overall, the FA administration enjoyed success on several fronts in the early 1990s. Municipal revenues were up, services had improved, and Vázquez and especially his participatory decentralization program enjoyed high approval ratings.[7] The *Economist* (7/25/92, 46) had even written up Vázquez as the "marvelous mayor of Montevideo." However, although the FA's program was underway, it was also under attack. Uruguay's two strongly institutionalized traditional parties, the Colorado and the National, had determined to prevent the Frente Amplio from implementing its original program.

Defenders of the Two-Party System Strike Back

The opposition's struggle to impede the FA's success in Montevideo took many forms and found many avenues of expression. Although they eventually failed to prevent the FA's reelection, the Colorados and Blancos did achieve their goal of minimizing the changes in local governance that the Vázquez administration sought. Most importantly, their persistent obstructionism succeeded in compelling Vázquez to negotiate the design of his participatory decentralization program.

The first major conflict between the FA and its rivals occurred over the decentralization resolution signed by Vázquez upon taking office in February

6. In 1994, 83 percent of municipal government revenues came from four sources: property, vehicle, domicile, and commercial taxes. In dollar terms, municipal revenues more than doubled from 1990 to 1994. All calculations are based on the figures reported by the Budget and Planning Division and on Unidad (2002, 52–53).

7. In public opinion polls, Vázquez consistently had around a 50 percent approval rating and less than 30 percent disapproval; this rating was higher than his vote share and much higher than the ratings received by the previous mayors (see *El Observador* 9/29/2000 at http://www.equipos.com.uy). The participatory decentralization process earned even higher levels of public support, with most respondents of opinion polls agreeing that decentralization is necessary (64 percent) and that participating in CCZ activities is positive or very positive (85 percent). See Cabrera (1994, 55–56) and Sierra and Charbonnier (1993, 20).

1990. Eleven opposition city councilors collected a thousand signatures and appealed to the national congress to void the resolution, arguing that it violated the constitution, especially the provision granting powers to the mayor's delegates. The Colorado and National parties united to mount a public opinion campaign against the FA's participatory decentralization program using city councilors, party leaders in the congress, and even Uruguay's President, Luis Alberto Lacalle. Although President Lacalle called the confrontation open but "very à la Uruguayan," suggesting that it was civilized and peaceful, the FA administration did not perceive the conflict in those terms (Moreira 1993, 167, 171–72). According to Susana Regent (1999, 11), the former coordinator of Zone 14, "From February 17, 1990, to the end of May of the same year, we lived through a climate of strong tension and threats from the Right (including physical threats like bombs, beatings, etc.)."

Under pressure from the opposition, and on questionable legal grounds after the Congress ruled against him, Vázquez called for a city-wide debate in May 1990, inviting the opposition parties to discuss decentralization and citizen participation. The speeches by Colorado and Blanco city councilors reiterated the position of their parties during the 1989 municipal election campaign. For example, a representative of the Colorado Party, Lucio Caceres, stated, "We did not share this concept of political decentralization: we did propose executive or administrative decentralization" (IMM 1990, 5). This meant that municipal services might be transferred to a lower level, but not decision-making power (see IMM 1990, 8–9, 15–16, 44–45). Several representatives of the traditional parties argued implicitly against the idea of mayor's delegates and deliberative assemblies and explicitly insisted that the neighborhood associations should continue their customary role of demand making. Pascual Pernas described the Blancos' stance as follows: "We would not give the zonal community centers the character of permanent participation. Rather, the neighborhoods themselves would propose their needs, and it would be City Hall that made the decisions" (IMM 1990, 8–9). Some Colorado representatives argued for the reestablishment of the *juntas locales,* or local boards (IMM 1990, 9–10, 45), which had existed sporadically in parts of Montevideo in the 1920s and again from the 1940s to the 1960s, and which had long formed part of the political system of the departments outside the capital. Given that the constitution granted political parties the right to designate the members of the local boards according to vote share, the creation of such boards would provide the Colorados and Blancos with automatic positions of authority in each zone.

Opposition leaders clearly worried that the participatory decentralization program would undermine their hold on local constituencies. Colorado city councilman Ricardo Domínguez articulated this fear most dramatically and openly. Domínguez warned that the FA's proposal to decentralize power "generates an idea of catastrophe" (IMM 1990, 43). He predicted that the new participation mechanisms would endanger representative democracy and were aimed at strengthening the Frente Amplio's party organization. According to Domínguez, the FA's proposal was "apparently trying to create a new base organization (forgetting the independence of action of the neighborhood promotion commissions), delegitimate and reject the honorary and honorable work of the traditional parties' city councilors, and gradually implement a direct democracy against the representative democracy instilled in our constitution" (IMM 1990, 44). Domínguez insisted that any changes in municipal government should strictly adhere to the constitution and proclaimed that the Colorados would not accept political decentralization "under any circumstances" (IMM 1990, 44–45). His conclusion perfectly sums up the fears of the traditional parties: "If you create the zonal community centers legally, in a new version, what we demand is that they do not displace the legitimate representatives of the people, who are the city councilors" (IMM 1990, 45).

Mayor Vázquez appeared to recognize the opposition's suspicions and tried to allay them in his speech and in his invitation to play a part in designing the decentralization resolution. Using his typically florid language, Vázquez opened the debate by avowing that his program was "not trying to liquidate the important role of those magnificent instruments, the political parties" (IMM 1990, Apertura). Just days after the forum, the FA administration modified the language in the resolution such that it conformed much more to the opposition's insistence on administrative decentralization without legal transfer of power.

The opposition parties' attacks on the FA's program, however, continued unabated. Colorado and Blanco politicians constantly denounced the Vázquez administration in the media, accusing the Frente Amplio of using the CCZs as sites of recruitment and political manipulation. While exaggerated, these charges were not entirely without foundation. Though the FA did not explicitly engage in "poaching" through the CCZs, a pair of articles in the Uruguayan weekly *Búsqueda* documents an interesting exchange between Frente Amplio leaders in 1991 about the potential political usage of the CCZs. The FA's national political secretary, Carlos Baraibar, proposed using the meetings of the CCZs to "incorporate" non–Frente Amplio supporters in order to guarantee the party's success in the municipal government and thus in the 1994 elections (*Búsqueda* 3/21/91). Vázquez, however, affirmed that he would "not allow the CCZs to be used to capture citizens of other political parties [for the Frente Amplio]" (*Búsqueda* 4/4/91). From the beginning of his term, Vázquez had pledged to govern for all Montevideans, not just for FA supporters, and he publicly announced that he was "breaking the umbilical cord" with his party (Harnecker 1995b, 15). Nonetheless, opposition politicians went as far as charging the FA with copying the practices of the Cuban Committees for the Defense of the Revolution and the Soviet KGB. President Lacalle reinforced the opposition's message, labeling the Frente administration "totalitarian." Altogether the opposition attacked the FA's participatory decentralization program in the press more than 150 times during the first two and a half years of Vázquez's term.[8]

Yet the attempt to undermine the FA administration and its program was not limited to criticism in the press and the creation of obstacles in the City Council. The traditional parties also tried to impede the progress of participatory decentralization through neighborhood associations, the municipal bureaucracy, and the national government. Not all of these mechanisms provided the results that the opposition wanted. Neighborhood associations with links to the opposition were relatively few in number by the early 1990s.[9] Most importantly, they did not uniformly follow party lines; they took varying stances toward participating in CCZ activities, with some refusing invitations to assemblies and others accepting, depending on the zone and the association (see Charbonnier 1992, 13, 24). For example, the coordinator for Zone 14 maintains that neighborhood associations tied to the traditional parties continued to meet with her "despite the 'order' from the Colorado and Blanco leaders" (Regent 1999, 12–13).

The opposition had more success with municipal employees, particularly with higher-level bureaucrats who had received their jobs through

8. See Sierra and Charbonnier (1993, 18–19, 28nn9–10); see also Rebellato and Ubilla (1999, 2n2). The study of the press discussed by Sierra and Charbonnier analyzed only criticisms that related directly to the CCZs and did not include the dozens of charges of unconstitutionality against the first resolution. The most frequent criticisms included that the CCZs were "partyized," that they formed part of a Marxist-Leninist plot, and that they added to bureaucratization and inefficiency.

9. Only 7 of 371 neighborhood associations admitted to having a political affinity with either the Colorados or Blancos (my calculations from Bruera 1993, 48, 63). It seems unlikely that the true number was this small, given the descriptions of neighborhood associations by local activists and zone coordinators I interviewed, but this self-reporting does suggest that the true number was not very large either.

contacts in previous Colorado administrations. According to municipal division directors and the secretary general of the municipal employees union (ADEOM) during Vázquez's term, the traditional parties worked through the bureaucracy to sabotage the FA administration: "The traditional parties always bet on bipartisanship, they always agreed that we win today and you win tomorrow. The problem is produced when the Frente Amplio enters the government. It was then that they united to block our path."[10] Within the bureaucracy, officials with Colorado ties deliberately blocked or slowed down the processing of paperwork. Within ADEOM, those tied to traditional parties had often acted as strikebreakers during Colorado administrations, but with the FA in office, these same functionaries became active union members for the first time, and constantly pushed the union to strike (see Chasquetti 1995, 102; Harnecker 1995b, 43). Nonetheless, strike activity during the Vázquez administration was minimal, with only one twenty-four-hour general strike of municipal employees between 1990 and 1993 (Chasquetti 1995, 101). The reluctance to strike on the part of ADEOM stemmed from at least two sources: the wage increase granted by Vázquez at the start of his term and continually adjusted upwards, and the fact that the Communist Party (a FA founder) held the dominant political position in the union, having won every ADEOM election since the return to democracy in 1985 (see Chasquetti 101–6).

Though the traditional parties achieved only partial success with the neighborhood associations and the municipal bureaucracy, they fared better with the national government, where the two parties had a solid congressional majority as well as control of the courts and the presidency. Lacalle, in fact, came from the most conservative Blanco faction, Herrerismo, and he attempted to build a coalition with the Colorados (which would not be completely successful until the 1995–99 period, under a Colorado president). Each branch of the national government worked against the FA municipal administration. To begin with, the national executive completely cut government transfers to Montevideo, while increasing transfers to Uruguay's other departmental governments (Filgueira et al. 1999, 2, 15, 41). Lacalle also refused to adhere to contractual agreements made by the previous president to fund the larger part of a major sanitation project in Montevideo, despite the facts that the national government paid for all sewage projects

---

10. See interview with the former director of tourism, Washington Puchetta, and similar views by Eduardo Platero and Carlos Coitiño, the ADEOM general secretary and director of commercial and productive activities, respectively, in Harnecker (1995b, 45, 41–45).

in Uruguay's eighteen other departments and that the Montevideo project had also received financing from the International Development Bank. Only after long negotiations did the national and municipal government chiefs agree to a fifty-fifty arrangement (while in the previous period the national government had paid 90 percent).[11]

In another effort to block the flow of revenues to the FA administration, the national Accounts Tribunal rejected the municipal government's property tax proposal after an appeal to the court from opposition city councilors. Likewise, the central government blocked Vázquez's plan to guarantee financing for the renovation of the city's fleet of buses.[12] Even on eminently municipal issues with little fiscal impact on national government, such as regulating street vendors, the opposition challenged the FA administration. The lower house of Congress annulled Vázquez's street vendor resolution in 1991 with votes from the Colorado Party and the Herrerista faction of the Blancos, which used the issue as part of "their oppositional strategy against the Frente Amplio municipal government" (Moreira 1993, 176).

With their constant pressure on the FA administration, the traditional parties succeeded in forcing Vázquez to try to achieve some sort of truce in order to carry out his participatory decentralization program. In March 1991, Vázquez invited the opposition city councilors to form a joint committee (called the "Mixed Commission") of city councilors and administration officials to find a consensual formula for institutionalizing the new channels of citizen participation.

Negotiating Institutional Design: The FA Compromises on Its Original Program

Generating consensus around an institutional framework for participation took two years of negotiations in the Mixed Commission between the Frente Amplio and the opposition, but both sides eventually ceded on several issues after the FA administration convened individual residents and community organizations to a city-wide forum assembly called Montevideo in Forum.

---

11. In the period from 1985 to 1989, when the Colorado Party governed both Montevideo and Uruguay, the national government had agreed to pay 67 percent of the down payment and 100 percent of the loan for the sanitation project (Moreira 1993, 173–74). At each of the zonal public assemblies I attended in 1999, Mariano Arana, Vázquez's successor, repeated that the national government used to pay 90 percent of the sanitation project, then 50 percent, and, in the 1995–99 period, only 10 percent.

12. Two years later the national government decided to adopt the refinancing program itself and apply the program to the transportation system for the entire country (Portillo 1996, 68).

While the Forum itself seems to have stimulated the Mixed Commission to come to a final agreement on the design, the discussions at the Forum had little impact on the content of the Commission's ultimate accords. In analyzing the negotiations and the resulting design of participation, the most important issues concern why the Frente Amplio was willing to compromise so much of its original program—to the point of ignoring the appeals made by residents at the Forum for equal power with the party representatives—and why residents did not push harder for their demands to be met.

The primary reason behind the Frente Amplio's initial willingness to negotiate was clearly the relentless opposition from the Colorados and Blancos, and particularly their constitutionally granted ability to veto the FA's program by challenging it in the National Congress, which they had done once already. Yet at least two other concerns also pushed the FA to attempt to create a more solid legal basis for its participation program. Selva Braselli (1994), who had helped write Document 6 and had served on the Mixed Commission and later as Director of Decentralized Services, outlined these issues in her speech at a 1994 seminar. First, the party wanted to guarantee the program's sustainability beyond Vázquez's term. The party feared that if the municipal government changed hands before a new resolution could be passed, the program might disappear, and there might even be some form of repression from a future government with a different political stance (Braselli 1994, 61). Second, the existing participatory mechanisms—the thematic commissions and deliberative assemblies—had not yet developed routinized, standard procedures. The Frente administration wanted consistent and legitimate channels of participation. The continually evolving assemblies and commissions of delegates from community organizations and individual volunteers did not provide stability, while they did provoke questions about their legitimacy. As Braselli (1994, 62) put it, "From the point of view of the residents, there were the assemblies, the commissions, there were a lot of things, but what did not exist was something that, in an orderly fashion, laid down the functions, the norms, and that established precise relationships within the institution." In short, the participatory mechanisms lacked institutionalization.

The Frente Amplio viewed negotiating with the opposition in the Mixed Commission as a solution to these concerns. From March to December 1991, the Mixed Commission invited a number of specialists in constitutional law and urban planning to provide advice.[13] Their debates revolved

---

13. See the transcripts of the Mixed Commission's meetings, as well as its final resolutions, in Junta (1994).

around the type of political and social entities that could be created at the submunicipal level. In general, the opposition parties favored the creation of local boards whose members would be appointed by the political parties proportionate to their share of the City Council—as the constitution established—and they resisted the granting of functions to any new social entities (Portillo 1996, 37). The Frente, in contrast, favored new elective political organs and the conferring of delimited functions to deliberative assemblies, as Document 6 proposed. Miguel Fernandez, an FA city councilor, best sums up the party's original position on the creation of local boards: "A local board designated by political quota does not help the participation of the residents. It is more like putting something on top of the people's movement" (*La República* 4/3/92). In December, the FA presented its first proposal for the new entities, in which the party maintained its position on the political entity but compromised slightly on the social entity. The proposal called for the creation of "special commissions" (rather than local boards) and for local advisory (not "deliberative") commissions composed of delegates from community organizations (Cabrera 1994, 72–73; Rebellato and Ubilla 1999, 7–8). The opposition rejected this proposal outright, and the Mixed Commission continued meeting and inviting more experts through much of 1992, but without reaching agreements.

In order to break the impasse in the Mixed Commission, the FA proposed that the discussion of the program be carried out in each zone as well. To facilitate the discussion at the zonal level, the Mixed Commission agreed on a preliminary proposal to send to each CCZ. The proposal announced the Commission's agreement that the political entities to be installed would be local boards whose members would initially be appointed but might be elected in the future if the National Congress passed a law authorizing such elections.[14] It also named the new social entities "local advisory commissions," but presented their functions and their composition as suggestions open for debate (Junta 1994, 135–36). This proposal represented further compromises for the FA: accepting party-appointed local boards and subordinating the sphere for volunteer participants to these boards. In exchange, the opposition parties allowed the Mixed Commission to move closer to an

---

14. In fact, in order to adhere strictly to the constitution, the proposal called for the creation of local boards in the eleven rural zones of Montevideo and "special delegated commissions" in the seven urban zones. Once installed at the end of 1993, the special delegated commissions were identical to the local boards in all respects but the name. In the interest of concision, I refer only to local boards throughout the text.

agreement. They also allowed for the convocation of a city-wide forum to bring residents from each zone together to discuss the proposal.

In August 1992, after a series of preliminary meetings in each zone, between 560 and 1,300 residents participated in the event, called Montevideo in Forum.[15] The participants, most of whom came from community organizations that had been active in the CCZs, divided into fourteen working groups to draw up proposals for the new local institutions. The participants' disappointment with the suggested functions of the local "advisory commissions" was evident in the working groups' reports (see Junta 1994, 137–49). The municipal Director of Decentralization at the time, Alberto Roselli, told reporters, "There was a clear tendency to take away the word 'advisory' from these entities" (*La República* 8/13/92). In more than half the working groups, the participants explicitly demanded decision-making power for what they called local councils rather than "advisory commissions." As one newspaper article put it, "one could feel in the Forum the clear demand for greater power to the citizens in the spheres of decision" (*La República* 8/13/92). Several of the groups proposed that local councilors be granted seats on the local boards and argued that the two entities should have equal amounts of power. Some working groups went further toward direct democracy, calling for zonal assemblies to make decisions, especially in cases where the local board and council disagree. As in the similar assembly held in Caracas, a number of groups proposed creating a permanent city-wide forum in which entities from each zone could meet regularly, which forms part of the structure of Porto Alegre's participation program. Each of the working groups read its proposals aloud, and the Mixed Commission collected the proposals for its own future internal debates (Cabrera 1994, 89–90).

After the Forum, it took the Mixed Commission four months to agree on the wording of resolutions to create the new institutions. In exchange for the Frente Amplio's consenting to the creation of local boards with five appointed members (three selected by the incumbent party and two by the opposition), the Blancos and one faction of the Colorados agreed that the City Council would send a resolution to the National Congress requesting that it pass a law authorizing elections for the local boards. Although the City Council did eventually send a resolution of this nature, the Congress

15. Different newspapers reported different figures. *La Mañana* (8/9/92) and *Ultimas Noticias* (8/10/92), the more conservative papers, printed lower estimates; *Mate Amargo* (8/12/92) and *La Juventud* (8/9/92), papers linked to former Tupamaros and the FA, respectively, printed higher estimates.

never passed such a law, and it seems likely that the opposition parties (and possibly the FA as well) foresaw this outcome.[16] The Frente Amplio also conceded that the position of zonal coordinator—which the traditional parties had constantly criticized in the press—would be replaced. Instead each zone would have a "secretary" designated by the mayor as a political representative for the local board, and a director for the CCZ chosen according to seniority and competence and forming part of the municipal bureaucratic hierarchy (Harnecker 1995b, 77). The creation of appointed local boards and CCZ directors meant that the opposition would have guaranteed positions of authority in each zone, both in the local boards and the CCZs, given that nearly all senior-level career bureaucrats were Colorados.

The only major sticking point in the negotiations involved the new social entities. The majority on the Mixed Commission finally agreed to use the Forum participants' term for the new entities—"local council" rather than "advisory commission"—and that they would consist of from twenty-five to forty councilors elected through secret balloting. Yet the Mixed Commission granted the local councils neither decision-making power nor equal status with the local boards. Arguments over precise language figured prominently in the debates, and even spelling provoked contention. In Spanish, the local councils could have been spelled as *concejos* or *consejos,* with the latter word connoting a second meaning of "advice." According to Portillo (1996, 38), the decision to use the *concejo* spelling was an "explicit allusion to the tradition of councils coming from Hispanic local law, in which the council governs, it does not give advice." The subordination of the local councils to the local boards, however, belied the choice of labels and spelling. In other long debates over wording, the opposition city councilors also ensured that the local councils could not establish direct links with the central municipal administration without the presence and often the mediation of the local boards (Junta 1994, 196–99).

After the majority on the Mixed Commission had agreed on the resolutions, opposition city councilors delayed the voting for another seven months. In the end, the Blancos joined the Frente Amplio in supporting each of the resolutions, while the Colorados were split. One faction, List 15 with half the party's city councilors, supported the creation of the local boards. The other major faction continued to denounce the entire participatory decentralization program for creating excessive bureaucracy and for undermining

16. To declare the local boards in Montevideo elective bodies, the Congress would have to pass a law that essentially amended the constitution, which explicitly states in article 288 that the capital may not have elective local boards.

the role of city councilors (see Junta 1994, 167–73). Councilman Domínguez asked, "What will be the role of the city councilor? Will it be limited? For what reason will Montevideo's city councilors exist if you have created so many local boards and if you plan to create local councils in the neighborhoods?" (Junta 1994, 170). His colleague Zimarioff used more colorful language to deride the entire proposal as *una mamarracha,* or "a worthless mess" (Junta 1994, 173). The Colorado bench as a whole did not support the resolution on the local councils, with List 15 refusing to endorse the local councils because they were not labeled "advisory" (Junta 1994, 189–90). Though the Colorados did not vote for the resolution, however, they also did not collect signatures in order to challenge the resolution in the Congress, as they had done before.

The Frente Amplio's concessions on each resolution seem to have been driven by the need to achieve the support or at least acquiescence of the opposition for the program as a whole. Vázquez himself apparently opposed the idea of the local boards from the beginning, but he finally accepted them in order to assure that the constitutionality of the participatory decentralization program could no longer be questioned.[17] While FA leaders must have known that the subordination of the local councils to party-appointed boards would upset the community activists who had participated in the Forum, the immediate veto potential of the traditional parties far outweighed any possible risk of losing activist support in the future. Significantly, because of its history of party penetrated civil society, Montevideo lacked strong, autonomous district- and city-wide community movements like those in Porto Alegre. Such movements might have pressured the FA—and the opposition—to negotiate an institutional framework that granted more power to volunteer participants and less to party representatives.

After Montevideo in Forum, community activists did not push the Mixed Commission to implement their proposals. And though neighborhood leaders in a few zones complained that the City Council's ultimate resolutions had ignored the Forum—removing the best proposals and disregarding the demands for deliberative powers for the local councils—they did not take any action.[18] Their criticisms remained isolated and ineffective. Community activists did not react more strongly for diverse reasons. As mentioned, most were simply not integrated into the kinds of autonomous

---

17. Interview with Arlés Caruso, former coordinator of Zone 12 and informal advisor to both Vázquez and the subsequent FA mayor, Mariano Arana (7/22/99).

18. For criticisms in Zone 9, see CIDC (1997, 26, 34, 41); for Zone 14, see Listre (1999, 11–12).

networks through which they might find shared grievances and with which they might launch collective protests. Instead, the linkages that did exist for those community activists whose organizational connections extended beyond their particular associations were frequently political party linkages. Activists tied to opposition parties had little reason to protest, given that the FA had conceded on most points of the program's design. Activists linked to the Frente, on the other hand, did have cause, given that many of them shared a committment to the ideas in Document 6. Yet rather than push the party to preserve the program's original design, many FA-affiliated neighborhood leaders accepted the compromises as necessary and, in some cases, decided to work within the local boards to try to ensure that they respected the local councils and did not become obstacles to citizen participation.[19]

At least two factors likely contributed to their acceptance of the local boards. First, the FA had promised that instead of party leaders designating its local board members outright, it would choose board members through internal party elections in each zone. Thus, veteran party-affiliated neighborhood activists could become candidates for these positions as well as for the local councils. In some zones, the board and council elections became arenas of competition for the various factions within the Frente Amplio.[20] Second, from the beginning of the FA administration, the party had established local government groups (*agrupaciones del gobierno local*), which meet regularly to manage the relationship between party members outside of the administration and those inside the administration. According to Jorge Abellá, the president of the municipal FA, these groups serve to resolve conflicts among party factions and "analyze what political strategy is the most appropriate for the zone."[21] Any complaints from FA-affiliated neighborhood leaders about the Mixed Commission's resolutions would have been discussed first

---

19. Zone 14 is a prime example of this decision. See Listre (1999, 12) and Regent (1999, 62).

20. For example, *La República* (10/21/93) reported that in the 1993 local council elections in Zone 14, the Movimiento de Participación Popular's candidates received the most votes, with other sectors of the FA receiving fewer votes (and at least one councilor elected by the Blancos).

21. Interview (8/4/99); also see Harnecker (1995b, 23–24). The local government groups consisted of the zonal coordinator, FA-affiliated CCZ workers, a city councilor, a representative from the central municipal government, and representatives from the local party nuclei (and after 1993, FA-affiliated local councilors and board members). The FA also created a municipal government group, including the mayor, the national party president, and representatives of the party's deputies, senators, city councilors, municipal directors, the municipal party organization, and different factions. Of the three cities in this study, only in Montevideo did the incumbent party create permanent groups of this type. LCR established local electoral committees in Caracas, and in Porto Alegre the PT held occasional forums to resolve specific disputes between party members in and out of City Hall, but neither party established permanent groups at the district level.

in this setting, where party officials could explain their reasoning directly to local activists and try to persuade them that the legalistic compromises were necessary.[22] Finally, some interviewees suggested a cultural explanation for the acceptance of the convention-conforming compromises on the part of the FA and its supporters. One city official offered a pair of typical (and stereotypical) arguments: "In Uruguay, one has to have everything regulated. For every four Uruguayans there is generally a statute" (Rosario Revello, interview 7/14/99).

In the end, the FA administration recognized that the agreements in the Mixed Commission were "delayed, costly, and complex," but reasoned that the negotiations had allowed the administration "to arrive at a good conclusion" (Braselli 1994, 62). Indeed, with the establishment of the local boards and councils at the end of 1993, the FA administration had been able to maintain the participatory decentralization program as its centerpiece, and the public seemed to approve. Approximately seventy thousand voters participated in the first elections for the local councils (representing not quite 7 percent of eligible voters), and twenty thousand Frente Amplio members voted in the internal elections for the local boards, whereas the opposition Blancos and Colorados chose to appoint their board members. Perhaps more importantly, the 1994 municipal elections validated the FA administration, returning the party to office in Montevideo with 45 percent of the local vote for Mariano Arana, up 10 percentage points from 1989. Mayor Arana continued Vázquez's program, devolving a few more services and city procedures to the CCZs, though he ended the practice of rotating cabinet meetings. In May 2000, the FA once again won the mayoral elections. Arana earned reelection with 58 percent of the vote, 30 percentage points ahead of his closest rival (*La República* 5/16/2000). These electoral results suggest that the FA's participatory decentralization program did win popular support. Nonetheless, the change in the program's design in 1993 hampered its ability to attract and sustain participants.

The Regulated Design and the Crisis of Participation (1993–1999)

At the end of 1993, after four years of resolutions, attacks, negotiations, and more resolutions, the Frente Amplio's participatory decentralization program

---

22. How well these local government groups worked in maintaining party coherence varied considerably according to the zone and the individual party member. To take two contrasting

had become completely legal. The program's design was regulated in all its multiple aspects, from the local councils to the CCZs and their directors to the local boards and their secretaries. In its confusing intricacies and overlapping authorities, the regulated design of participation in Montevideo matched that of the parish governments in Caracas, or even went further. As Portillo (1996, 38) writes of the design, "With its baroque complexity, it is evidently a product of the Uruguayan institutional tradition at its best." Separating the design into component parts—structure, range, and decision-making power—will simplify the analysis of the program's regulated (and convoluted) design. It will also highlight the features that eventually undermined the program's attractiveness to potential participants. Most fundamentally, the regulated design does not provide a clear, inviting, and potent channel for participation. It is not clear because of multiple layers of representation; it is not inviting because of closed meetings and excessive attention to minutiae and formality; and, crucially, it is not potent because citizens lack the power to directly influence the most important issues—particularly in the budget—because City Hall retains control.

Structure

The structure of participation in Montevideo is highly formal. Not only do official political party representatives sit on the local boards, but formal elections determine who serves on the local councils. Furthermore, the councils, which are the realm of "civil society" and considered consultative, autonomous entities, are legally subordinated to the boards. After being selected by the parties, board members serve for five years, simultaneous with the mayor's term (though the first board served only two years, being replaced in 1995 after the previous year's elections). Local councilors face voters every two and a half years in zonal-level elections organized by the CCZs and community organizations, not by the national electoral institute. After the change in design in 1993, the social organizations that had previously sent delegates to the deliberative assemblies began presenting candidates

---

examples, the discussion at the local government group meeting that I attended (7/30/99) in Zone 7 suggested a high degree of consensus among party members and a confidence that the FA local councilors would vote as a bloc. In Zone 8, on the other hand, a veteran neighborhood leader and Socialist Party activist, "Alberto," told me (8/22/99), "I personally never accepted that the party gave me a line. I always worked for the neighbors first. The majority of the local councilors acted as independent neighbors. And I had problems with my party because of that. The majority of us did not accept the big party line that wanted us to applaud the mayor. We strongly castigated Tabaré many times, and the directors too."

for the local councils. Individuals can also nominate themselves with the signature of ten other residents. On average, the councils have thirty-five members, and each member has a substitute as well.

Generally, the boards and councils each hold separate meetings twice a month; regulations require the boards to do so. Local board meetings are not open to the public, though they schedule occasional meetings to receive the public in some zones, or residents may ask for an audience in others. Even the meetings of some of the local councils are only semiopen to the public in several zones, requiring that residents receive previous permission to attend.[23] The roles of the councils comprise consulting with the boards on the zone's budget and public service priorities, proposing projects and improvements for the zone, and acting as monitors over government implementation. The roles for the local boards are nearly identical to those of the local councils, with the differences that the boards are considered part of the municipal executive branch and thus have some degree of authority over a few zonal issues and responsibility for overseeing the CCZ's operations.[24]

Many of the councilors and a few of the board members also participate in the thematic commissions, which continued from the previous period. These commissions also meet regularly to discuss specific issues (road construction, the elderly, transportation, parks), providing residents outside the councils with an opportunity to participate in addition to the yearly discussions to modify the annual budget. According to Regent (1999, 65), in Zone 14 even the thematic commissions became increasingly formalized and "semi-closed" after 1993. A member of one such commission provides an example: "The work meetings became more and more like meetings between 'specialized' councilors and directors. The traditional neighborhood associations, which [in the prior period] had gone to the deliberative assemblies with concrete and urgent demands without accommodating to the order of the day at all, began to get upset. They were now told to go to the meeting of the corresponding thematic commission, where they ended up registering their demand as if before an office" (Listre 1999, 17).

Figure 4.1 illustrates the structure of the local institutions, which exist in each of the eighteen zones, showing how it changed from a relatively

23. This was the case, for example, in a Zone 8 council meeting that I succeeded in attending (6/28/99). City officials told me that the local councils in general tended to meet alone rather than encouraging residents to attend (interviews with Rosario Revello, from the Division of Decentralization, 7/14/99, and with António Carámbula, Secretary of the Local Board in Zone 1, 7/13/99).

24. For instance, according to article 57 of the Ley Orgánica Municipal (from 1935), the boards can impose fines on infractors of municipal laws.

simple structure in the pre-1993 period to the "baroque complexity" of the post-1993 period. This unfortunately but necessarily complicated figure reveals two important changes from the previous period. First, the arena for civil society lost its direct link to the central administration. Whereas previously demands from community leaders in the deliberative assemblies proceeded directly to City Hall through the zone coordinator, with the new structure, demands had to pass through two filters—the council and the board—first. And the local councils became essentially orphaned. The local board secretaries and the professionals in the CCZs, such as social workers and architects, focused attention on the boards. Second, the potential for competition and conflict among the local institutions multiplied. City offi-cials, board members, councilors, and observers all stressed that the different entities frequently clashed. For example, the Director of Social Welfare, Elisa Valea (7/2/99), told me, "There are conflicts of power among all four: the local council, the local board, the local board secretary, and the director of the CCZ."[25]

As occurred in Caracas's parish governments, each group could claim legitimacy from separate sources: the councilors from the zonal elections, the boards from their political parties (and the parties' corresponding munic-ipal vote shares), the secretary from the mayor, and the CCZ directors from their position in the bureaucratic hierarchy. The latter two positions gener-ally seem to win the internal power struggles, in part because they are both full-time paid positions, while board members and councilors are part-time volunteers. Yet the boards and councils typically do not act in concert to increase their leverage. In most zones, a common complaint is that inter-action between board members and councilors is scarce, and that the board frequently acts without consulting the council. The words of a councilor at a meeting I attended in Zone 14 (8/20/99) epitomize a criticism of the structure of participation heard frequently among councilors: "Political power is overriding popular power."

Range

The types of issues under discussion in the local councils, thematic commis-sions, and the annual budget assemblies range considerably, from important

---

25. Several interviewees reported the same idea, including Carámbula, the local board secre-tary in Zone 1 (7/13/99); "Eva," councilor from Zone 8 (8/20/99); and Lucia Hornes, CCZ worker in Zone 8 (8/18/99). See also Regent (1999, 59–65) and Rebellato and Ubilla (1999, 20).

1990–1993 structure

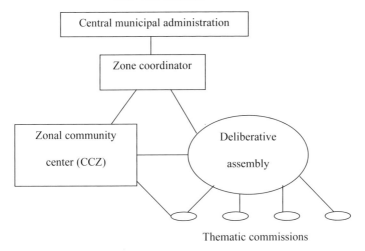

1993–1999 structure

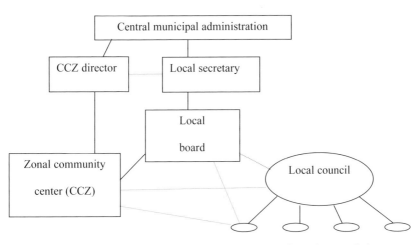

*Rectangular shapes indicate that the structure is part of the executive branch; circular shapes indicate that the structure is independent. Dashed lines indicate less consistent interaction than whole lines.

Fig. 4.1   Redesigning structures of participation

general matters to mundane individual complaints. Most of the major urban issues are addressed in the local arenas—sewage, street paving, transportation, housing, health care, trash collection, public lighting, and parks, among others—except education and crime, which do not come under municipal jurisdiction in Uruguay. Limitations also exist on the extent of municipal authority over certain areas, such as housing and health care, for which the national government has primary jurisdiction. Given the acrimonious relationship between the national and municipal governments, little cooperation on issues of shared competency has been achieved. Nevertheless, the range of issues is relatively extensive.

Despite the broad possibilities for discussion, however, much of the time in local council meetings is spent debating protocol or discussing *expedientes* (files), that is, small, often individual problems of little interest to the typical citizen. In the winter of 1999, for example, more than six months after the instatement of the third set of local councilors (following the October 1998 local council elections), many council meetings continued to revolve around how the meetings should be run. In Zone 8, the first half hour of a long meeting (from 7:30 until past 10:30 in the evening on 6/28/99) was spent reading the minutes of the prior meeting and debating whether to read the minutes of the meetings in such a detailed way in every meeting. My observations of a council meeting in Zone 14 (8/20/99) provide a sense of the inward focus that dominates many meetings:

This is the second week in a row that they haven't reached quorum—there are only twenty councilors present, and they need twenty-one (there are forty councilors in total). Last week there were only ten councilors. There's a long debate, that's been running for several meetings, about whether substitute councilors can come to the meetings and speak. So far they've agreed that they can come and listen, but not vote. A councilor says there's a permanent problem of reaching quorum. The council president says that the substitutes don't need to vote. A councilor disagrees and says they should vote, partially because the council never reaches quorum so they can never decide on anything. Another councilor, who has served in all three periods, says that the substitutes who want to be able to vote now never participated when they were titular councilors earlier. Now they're going to vote a motion to allow the substitutes to vote. They will add an article to their statutes. They continue to discuss the substitute problem, now lamenting that they didn't change the statutes earlier.

Perhaps local councilors focus on such minutiae because they lack much decision-making power over more important issues.

Decision-Making Power

Generally, for volunteer participants, including the local councilors, the type of participation allowed is more akin to providing proposals than to making decisions. A description of the annual budget process illustrates the limits on citizen involvement. The process starts with the mayor's cabinet determining the budget amounts destined to each zone and to each aspect of city government, both in terms of how much to allot for new investments versus how much for services and in terms of how much for transportation versus how much for public lighting, for example. The local boards and councils in each zone receive the resulting budget plan that details the amount of money each zone can expect with regard to several types of spending. In some instances, municipal authorities engage in a round of negotiating with the boards and councils if they complain about the amounts listed in the original budget. The boards and councils then agree on lists of priorities for each category. For example, for the 1997 budget, Zones 9 through 18, excluding Zones 15 and 16, could each send a list of thirty-five locations to install covered bus stops, and Zone 8 could choose sixteen.[26] The councils are expected to receive input on the budget priorities from residents, and councilors do this differently in each zone. Some councilors set up meetings in their neighborhoods to hear suggestions, and in some zones they place suggestion boxes in the CCZ and other public buildings. In other zones, the councilors simply draw up the lists on their own. As with all local issues, the board has the final word on the list of priorities that the zone returns to the central municipal administration. In the end, despite the title of *concejo* with a "c," the local council's role is advisory.

In addition to their input on the annual budget, the local councils provide proposals and advice and monitor nearly all the ongoing municipal services in each zone. The perception of many councilors, however, is that the municipal administration only occasionally acts on their advice. An important example of the administration's willingness to override the local councils regards the use of municipal properties. The resolution regulating the local

26. See Division (1997, 26). Zones 1 through 7 and 15 and 16 make up the urban core of Montevideo, and historically have had better infrastructure, including protected bus stops. They are also generally wealthier areas (except Zones 6 and 15). Zone 8 represents a mixture of extreme wealth and luxurious houses along the coast of the Río de la Plata, working-class housing cooperatives farther inland, and squatter settlements in dire poverty close to the border with the neighboring department of Canelones.

councils specifically grants them the right to advise the city government about municipal properties located within their zone.[27] When the local council exercised this right in Zone 14, proposing that an old building—the Hotel del Prado—be transformed into a cultural center, as had been agreed in the five-year budget plan, the municipal administration leased the building to a private company instead, and, in so doing, refused to negotiate with the local council (Rebellato and Ubilla 1999, 44–47). This incident took place in 1998, shortly after the City Council had issued a new decree reaffirming the autonomy of the local councils and stating for the first time that the municipal administration must seek the councils' advice on municipal properties.[28]

According to "Rosa," a CCZ worker in Zone 1 (interview 7/23/99), the 1998 decree helped clarify the advisory role of the local councils: "In 1993, when the local councils were created, there were big expectations about the degree of decision-making power they would have. There was confusion about the roles and responsibilities of the different entities. The new decree of the local councils in 1998 served so that the residents understood their true responsibilities and competencies better. They have assumed their role as advisors to the local board. The previous expectations are gone. The final decision is made by the local board."

The only sphere in which the local councils have a high degree of decision-making power is their own. That is, each local council writes its own statutes, which determine how it will function, including such aspects as the number of council seats (from twenty-five to forty) and how to organize elections. For example, some councils reserve seats for a representative of the elderly or the young, and some distribute seats proportionally across the different neighborhoods within the zone depending on population size, while others distribute seats equally.

Overall, other than writing their internal rules, the degree of decision-making power for councilors and for participants in the budget assemblies and thematic commissions is low. And many of these actors perceive their influence over local decision making as insufficient, as was apparent during Montevideo in Forum II. In 1996, the municipal administration held a second forum, similar to the first, with a series of meetings in each zone followed by a city-wide assembly in order to evaluate the decentralization

27. See Decree No. 26019 of the Junta Departamental, article 10 (Junta 1994, 214–15).
28. See Decree No. 28119 of the Junta Departamental, article 10, which superseded Decree 26019 (Junta 1999, Anexo).

process and urban policy issues in general. A study of the reports produced by each zone shows that nearly all of them objected to the local councils' lack of power, with dozens of complaints that "there is no real decision at the local level" and "there is no real transfer of power" (Rebellato and Ubilla 1999, 19–21). In addition to proposing greater faculties for the local councils (and in some cases for the local boards), the reports from the zones call for more training and capacity building for the local entities, more coordination among them at the local level and at the city level, and a better and greater flow of information from the municipal administration to the local entities (Rebellato and Ubilla 1999, 21–29). Interestingly, the administration's official summary of Forum II makes only slight mention of the demand for more power (IMM 1997, 23–24).

In 1999, the local councils' weakness remained an issue. A few participants at the 1999 budget assemblies praised the municipal administration. A participant in Zone 1 said, "We are lucky to have the mayor and the directors here and that we can say everything we want" (6/9/99). A resident of Zone 3 praised the annual meetings as "sensational" and as "the best thing City Hall has done in the last two administrations" (7/12/99). Yet most participants were critical. As my notes from several meetings attest, participants charged the municipal government with failing to respect the local councils and criticized the councils for their general ineffectiveness.

- In Zone 3, one councilor announces her official resignation from the council, saying that she does not want the council to meet just in order to discuss and cry over neighborhood problems without getting anything done, and she gets huge applause (7/12/99).
- In Zone 1, an ex-councilor says that she stopped going to the council meetings because the council doesn't do anything; it just has endless meetings. The next speaker says the local councils do not have decision-making power, they are just consulted, and about the installation of parking meters in her neighborhood they were not even consulted (6/9/99).
- In Zone 8, a neighborhood association member says, "The residents come here to complain, to make demands, but it doesn't seem to me that anyone is registering what we're proposing" (7/22/99).
- In a Zone 14 council meeting (8/20/99), a councilor says of the budget assembly a few weeks earlier that it was not useful: "It was obvious that the mayor wasn't paying attention to the councilors' reports and that the directors didn't pay attention either."

Evidence from survey data suggests that city residents in general seem to share the notion conveyed in the budget assemblies that citizen influence on municipal decision making is minimal. Figure 4.2 shows the responses to a similar question on four surveys, from 1989, 1992, 1999, and 2001. My colleague and I designed the 1999 survey and applied it to a random sample of residents in three representative zones of Montevideo.[29] We based it on a similar survey conducted in 1992. The 1989 and 2001 surveys drew random samples from Montevideo, not from the three zones used in the other two surveys. We asked, To what degree do you consider that people like you have the possibility to influence the decisions of the national government, of the municipal government, and of neighborhood organizations?

The key finding revealed by figure 4.2 appears in the municipal government column. From 1989 to 1992, corresponding to the period of the opening of the CCZs and the creation of the deliberative assemblies and thematic commissions, the perception that residents can influence municipal government decisions markedly increased. Yet after the change in the design in 1993, this trend reversed. By the late 1990s, high percentages of respondents reported little or no possibility to influence the municipal government, nearly reaching the levels prior to the implementation of the participatory decentralization program and not far from the perception of inefficacy with regard to the more distant national government. The survey results suggest that less than a third of Montevideans perceive that they can influence municipal decision making.[30]

One last piece of evidence that the degree of decision-making power is perceived as insufficient comes from a survey of local councilors we conducted in August 1999.[31] Figure 4.3 shows the answers to two open-ended questions: What do you think of the current form of decentralization? And, what should

29. I am indebted to Daniel Chavez for his collaboration in the funding, design, and implementation of the 1999 survey. We conducted the survey jointly with the help of Maria José Doyenart and a group of ten students from the Universidad de la República in August 1999. For a description of the survey, see Appendix 4A. For the results of the 1989 survey, see Canzani (1989, 37); for the 1992 survey, see Aguirre et al. (1992) and Aguirre, Sierra, and Iens (1993); and for the 2001 survey, see IDES (2001, 38, table 9).

30. Our survey results indicated that, in fact, only 25 percent of respondents considered that they participated in some degree in the municipal decisions affecting their neighborhood. The 1992 and 2001 surveys reported similar figures, while the 1989 survey did not use this question (Aguirre, Sierra, and Iens 1993, 126, table 12; IDES 2001, 43, table 21).

31. My colleague Daniel Chavez and I also designed and conducted this survey, though without extra help. Of the eighteen zones, sixteen returned the questionnaires that we distributed, for a total of 219 councilors participating in the survey. There were 617 councilors elected in 1998, but with an approximately 50 percent dropout rate, the universe of councilors was roughly 310 in late 1999. The response rate of 71 percent of 310 seems fairly high.

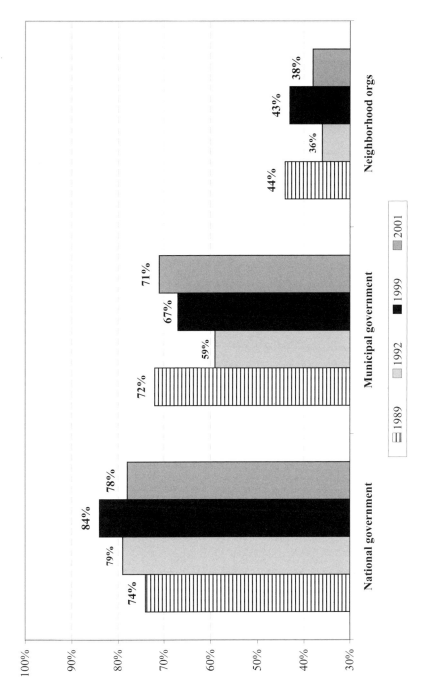

Fig. 4.2   Degree of possibility to influence decisions in different spheres

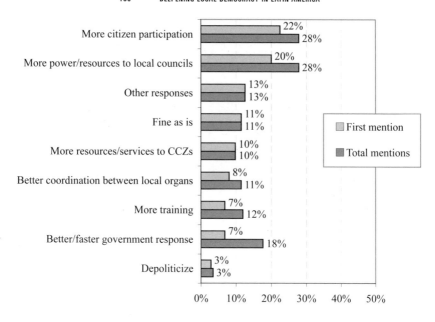

Fig. 4.3   What should be done to improve decentralization?

be done to improve decentralization? The answers to the questions have been added together because many respondents used the space provided following each question to suggest improvements or make complaints about the current decentralization system. The sum of "Total Mentions" adds up to more than 100 percent because all the responses were counted in the numerator while the denominator remained the same (the total number of councilors who responded to at least one of the two questions). As figure 4.3 reports, the local councilors considered that the two most important areas for improvement in the participatory decentralization program were the councils' inadequate power and the citizens' lack of participation.

The Crisis of Participation: From Ebullience to Lethargy

In contrast to the enthusiasm residents showed toward taking part in the participatory decentralization program in the early 1990s, by mid-decade a decline in participation was evident. While observers described participation in the earlier phase as "ebullient," by the mid-1990s participation was "languishing," and even the administration's official summary of Montevideo in Forum II decried a "crisis of participation" afflicting its program (Rebellato and Ubilla 1999, 53; IDES 2001, 61; IMM 1997, 9–10). In fact, one finds wide agreement that sometime after 1993, participation began to wane (Portillo 1999, 73; Canel 1998, 11; Zabalza 1998, 37). It is no coincidence that 1993 saw the implementation of the new regulated design of the FA's program. The redesigned program's formal structure and low degree of decision-making power combined to discourage ongoing participation.

Since the change in the program's design, several signs of the crisis of participation have become apparent. In interviews, many neighborhood activists and CCZ workers in different zones told me that the large numbers of participants in the deliberative assemblies and thematic commissions began to decrease after 1993. In Zone 1, for example, "Rosa" told me (interview 7/23/99), "In the beginning participation was very good. Decentralization was very attractive for the residents. . . . In this zone we held zonal assemblies in which 120 to 150 people participated, which is very relevant. That [level of] participation continued until 1993." Answers like these were most common, but one CCZ worker in Zone 8 told me that the participation level dropped before the local council elections in 1993 (Hornes, inteview 8/18/99). In other zones, organizing the council elections seemed to stimulate participation. Listre (1999, 11) reports that in Zone 14, the period between 1992 and 1993 was "perhaps the peak of participation" as the zonal deliberative assembly "began to acquire greater relevance with the upcoming Local Council elections."

In almost all zones, the thematic commissions functioned only with the presence of a few councilors and maybe a local board member, and in some zones even this muted existence was in question. At a local council meeting I attended in Zone 16 (7/21/99), after it was announced that the culture commission was no longer functioning, a councilor said, "We councilors work in the thematic commissions, but the residents don't. How can we get the residents to participate more?" In a Zone 8 council meeting, a councilor complained that the culture commission had not met for nearly two months and was at the point of disappearing (6/28/99). And according to "Rosa" (interview 7/23/99), there were no thematic commissions at all in Zone 1.

One of the most pronounced signs of the failure to sustain participation is the high proportion of councilors who stop participating before the end of their terms. In a study of the second cohort of local councilors in 1997, the dropout rate ranged from 7 percent in one zone up to 74 percent in another, with a total dropout rate of 45 percent (Calvetti et al. 1998, 13–14). The desertion problem seems to have plagued the local councils in the first and third cohorts as well. For example, "Alberto," a councilor who represented the elderly in Zone 8 during the 1993–95 term, told me that only fifteen of the thirty councilors continued meeting throughout the period, and that although the council created thematic commissions, "they didn't work because of a lack of people" (interview 8/22/99). Similarly, in the same period, only fifteen of the forty councilors in Zone 9 continued participating (CIDC 1997, 105). In the term beginning at the end of 1998, the dropout problem had already appeared by 1999. Councils in several zones reported difficulties in reaching quorum. The local boards have been plagued by the same problem, with the members from the opposition parties and even from the Frente Amplio frequently deserting their seats.[32]

Finally, participation in the budget process also declined. While more than twenty thousand residents participated in the assemblies to plan the five-year budget in 1990, only between three and five thousand residents participated in the same kind of assemblies in 1995 (*Brecha* 9/1/95). By the late 1990s, in the annual assemblies to assess budget implementation and make proposals for the future, my best—and generous—estimate is that approximately two hundred residents participated in each zone, or roughly thirty-six hundred for Montevideo as a whole. At the seven assemblies I attended in 1999, I estimated an attendance of between one hundred and three hundred, although administration officials and other municipal employees made up some proportion of those present. Rosario Revello, an official in the Division of Decentralization, told me that in the annual budget assemblies, "Normally about 200 people participate at a maximum, and that is a success for us" (interview 7/14/99). Neither the central municipal administration nor the individual CCZs count the participants or provide official estimates.

There is one sense in which participation increased. The number of voters participating in the local council elections expanded from 68,558 in 1993 to 82,496 in 1995, and then to 106,909 in 1998 (Unidad 2002, 137). In terms of the percentage of the Montevideo electorate turning out to vote, this represents an increase from 6.5 percent to about 10 percent. Nonetheless, in subsequent years the number of voters in local council elections decreased back down almost to the original number.[33] Moreover, even before this decline, participation in the local council elections was not deemed a success for a few reasons. For one, the opposition derided the turnout in

---

32. See Oholeguy (1999, 12). The local boards have been the site of dozens of conflicts between the FA's various factions, particularly after 1995, when Mayor Arana chose several secretaries for the boards who were rejected by board members. In several zones, many FA board members resigned, and in Zone 7 they all did (*Brecha* 1/26/96, 8).

33. There were 100,194 voters in 2001; 76,643 in 2004; and 74,319 in 2006 (*La República* 11/26/01, 6; *El País* 5/27/04, online; *La República* 10/24/06, online).

the local council elections as minimal, given that turnout in other elections is typically around 80 percent.[34] In addition, one might question the value of voting in local council elections, given that the councilors wield little power, that half of them (understandably) abandon office before completing the term, and that the vast majority of city residents have no idea what specific functions the councils serve.[35]

Most importantly, for the Frente Amplio, the goal had not been merely to add another kind of election and hold it more often than every five years. The party had specifically called for enhancing direct democracy and proposed participation in decision making in the formulation of government policy. As Document 6 stated, "'Local' power is not 'popular' power if the categorical division between representatives and represented is not broken, if there is not a more direct exercise of power by the popular majorities, if there are not effective mechanisms of control over the representatives" (Frente 1989, 10). It is probably because of this conception of participation that most FA officials and supporters still lament that a crisis exists and never mention the increase in voter turnout for the local council elections as a possible signal of the contrary.

Indeed, the FA's ultimate goals as laid out in Document 6 included the creation of a participatory arena in which the historically excluded sectors of society, particularly the poor, would have greater input into the decisions that affected their lives. Partially to compensate for their underrepresentation in other political and social arenas, the intention was that the "popular majorities" would be overrepresented at the zonal level. On the whole, the participatory decentralization program has not allowed for this, which likely adds to the sense that not just the level of participation is wanting, but the types of participants as well. It is true that participation rates in local council elections are generally higher in poorer zones of the city than in richer zones. Nonetheless, one can best assess how well the participatory decentralization program represents historically excluded sectors as well as the community in general by comparing the results of our surveys of local councilors with those of city residents. This comparison shows that the local councils neither overrepresent the excluded nor, in important respects, represent a broad cross-section of their communities.

34. Of course, for municipal and national elections, voting is obligatory, even if Uruguayan law does not specify the punishment for failing to vote.

35. In one survey, only 23 percent of respondents could name a single function of the councils, despite the fact that 72 percent of respondents considered that it was necessary to strengthen the councils (IDES 2001, 51, table 37).

Significantly, local councilors do not overrepresent but rather under-represent the poor. While 42 percent of residents' households earned less than 5,000 pesos per month (roughly $450 at the time of the survey, and approximately five times the national minimum wage), only 21 percent of local councilors' households earned that amount. Over half the local councilors' households earned more than 9,000 pesos per month, compared to about a third of residents' households. Similarly, 75 percent of local councilors have attained at least a high school degree compared to 45 percent of residents. In addition, our survey results showed that much lower percentages of the poor have used the CCZs. Only 44 percent of those from households earning up to 3,000 pesos per month had frequented a CCZ, and the rate of visiting a CCZ goes up steadily in each income bracket, reaching 82 percent of those from households earning 20,000 pesos or more.

On the other hand, women, historically absent from positions of political and social power in Uruguay, have gained a stronger voice through the FA's decentralization participation program, gaining nearly equal representation (though not over-representation). On the local boards of the 1995–99 period, 34 percent of the members were women, and 50 percent of the board presidents were women. In the following term, 50 percent of local board members were women (Celiberti and Quesada 2004, 11). On the local councils, the percentage of women councilors went from 38 percent in the 1995–98 period (Calvetti et al. 1998, 11–14) to approximately 44 percent in our survey during the subsequent period. In comparison, in the late 1990s, only 10 percent of national senators, 13 percent of national deputies, and 29 percent of city councilors were women.[36]

In terms of the different organizational expressions of the community, the local councilors do represent a wide gamut of groups. Specifically, 6 percent of local councilors belong to community day care centers or soup kitchens,

36. The figures for senators and deputies are my calculations from http://www.parlamento.gub.uy/palacio3/index1280.asp?e=0&w=1600. The figure for city councilors is my calculation from http://www.juntamvd.gub.uy/es/ediles/index.html. Afro-Uruguayans, arguably the most excluded sector of Uruguayan society, make up about 9 percent of the population in both Uruguay and Montevideo, yet did not hold a single seat in either house of parliament until the twenty-first century, when Edgardo Ortuño was elected national deputy in 2005. I was unable to obtain data on how many local councilors are Afro-Uruguayans. In 1999, they were not especially active in the meetings and assemblies I attended, yet without data, one can only speculate that the participatory institutions in Montevideo did not provide enhanced representation for Afro-Uruguayans. Later FA administrations have focused on the issue of reversing racial exclusion, compensating those forcibly removed from Barrio Sur during the dictatorship by rebuilding their houses and creating a Municipal Thematic Unit for the Rights of Afro-descendants in City Hall as well as a network of community agents working in the CCZs to promote the participation of Afro-Uruguayans (see http://www.montevideo.gub.uy/node/10370).

9 percent to religious organizations, 10 percent to women's organizations, 11 percent to parents' associations, 15 percent to neighborhood health clinics, 16 percent to social or sports clubs, and 57 percent to neighborhood associations. These percentages make them fairly representative of residents' community organizations in general (see chapter 6), with the exception of neighborhood associations, given that only 4 percent of residents belong to neighborhood associations. And strikingly, while only 3 percent of residents claimed membership in a political party or club, 44 percent of local councilors were party members. Of all local councilors, roughly 37 percent were FA party members. And of all local councilors who claimed party membership, 90 percent belonged to the FA. In addition, 33 percent of residents but 74 percent of local councilors indicated the FA as their party of preference. While given their specific interests it may be logical that neighborhood associations participate more than other groups in the local councils, the overrepresentation of Frente Amplio members suggests the possibility that the local councils may not represent their communities ideally. Although a majority of residents (54 percent) considered the local councils to be representative, in interviews, several current and former local councilors spontaneously volunteered that the councils had become, or were in danger of becoming, "party-ized." In our survey, when we asked local councilors to evaluate the statement "The Local Councils are very party-ized," not quite 50 percent responded that they either agreed or "more or less" agreed. Overall, the class, organizational, and partisan composition of the local councils did not alleviate the sense of participation in crisis.

Municipal officials usually explain the crisis of participation using two arguments: that a weakening economy made participation more difficult because of increasing time pressures; and that the competitive, individualistic, consumerist culture encourages shopping and working to pay for consumer items rather than participation in public affairs. The official report on Montevideo in Forum II, which presents some of the participants' views, includes these two arguments and adds three others. Specifically, the report suggests that the failure to sustain participation stemmed from the "overloaded" organizational scheme, discouragement over the administration's failure to provide prompt responses to the participants' proposals, and, in the case of local councilors, from the difficulties of belonging to both a community organization and the council itself given the growing time constraints (IMM 1997, 10).

The pattern of an initially high level of participation until 1993 followed by an immediate decline thereafter suggests that parts of the official explanation may be overdrawn. Neither time constraints nor popular culture usually change rapidly. In fact, a comparison of the 1992 and 1999 surveys referred to earlier indicates no such change in time pressures. In each year, respondents were asked why many residents did not participate in CCZ activities. The percentage of those surveyed that answered "Lack of time because of work or home constraints" actually decreased from 53 percent in 1992 to 37 percent in 1999.[37] Furthermore, the official explanation that double membership in community organizations and the local councils requires too much time and work is also not supported by our data from the survey of local councilors. When we asked how joining the council had affected their participation in other organizations, 77 percent of the councilors responded that they continued participating the same amount or began to participate more in other organizations after becoming a councilor, while only 23 percent participated less.

Explaining the Crisis

Although the crisis of participation in Montevideo surely has multiple sources, the evidence suggests that chief among these is the regulated design of the program, particularly the formal structure and low degree of decision-making power. The participatory decentralization program in Montevideo simply does not provide a direct channel through which residents can influence local policy and achieve concrete results. It was not the case that the administration failed to improve city services and expand urban infrastructure as in Caracas, but that the connection between these achievements and participation in the local level entities—the local council, thematic commissions, and budget assemblies—was ambiguous. Evidence from interviews, observations of the budget assemblies, public opinion surveys, and statistical analysis of participation data supports the argument that the program's failure to sustain large numbers of participants derives mostly from problems with the design itself.

The creation of boards with official party representatives and the introduction of a formal election process for the local councils have hindered ongoing participation by residents in a number of ways. In several interviews, city officials, local board members, and councilors told me that one cause of the lack of participation was that once residents thought they were "officially"

---

37. The other two most frequent answers in 1992 and 1999, respectively, were "They could be politically manipulated" (16 percent to 13 percent) and "They would waste their time in useless meetings" (8 percent to 10 percent). The 1992 survey results are from Aguirre, Sierra, and Iens (1993, 124, table 10).

represented by the local boards and councils, they did not feel the need to participate any longer because they had someone else to do it for them. The president of the local board in Zone 14, Juan Padros, told me another version of this idea: "Once you've been elected councilor, you're a king and you don't participate anymore with the residents" (interview 8/11/99). The statement by "Manuel," a councilor and neighborhood association president from Zone 8, suggests a combination of the previous ideas: "At this moment the people are not participating, but they stop you [councilors] on the street. It is not necessary for each resident to come to meetings, that's why there's no participation" (interview 8/21/99).[38] Whether residents feel as if they have been relieved of their duty to participate or councilors and board members have discouraged them from doing so by acting like typical politicians, which are not mutually exclusive possibilities, the formal structure seems to have reproduced traditional political hierarchies rather than encouraging more horizontal forms of participation.

A description of the annual budget assemblies also demonstrates that the permeation of hierarchy and formality throughout the program, as well as the lack of significance given to participant input, discourages ongoing participation. In the 1999 assemblies, the number of residents attending varied from approximately one hundred to three hundred per zone. Yet by the end of the normally three-hour assemblies, less than a third of the initial crowd remained, most having left after the first hour. The assemblies are generally organized so that the presidents of the local board and the local council speak first, welcoming the mayor, followed by a forty-five-minute speech by the mayor. The majority of those present often leave once the mayor finishes talking. If they have stayed patiently, they still must sit and listen as several members of the local council present their proposals and questions and the municipal cabinet members make their replies. By this time the mayor has often retired from the assembly because of other obligations, as has most of the rest of the public. Thus, by the time the average citizen has a chance to address the assembly, there is almost nobody left.

A particularly dramatic example of this occurred in Zone 18 (7/16/99). Before his speech, the mayor spent at least twenty minutes announcing the names of eighty-two squatter settlement residents who had just been granted land titles by the city government and handing over the titles one

---

38. Other interviewees expressed similar ideas as well, including Revello, city official (7/14/99); "Roberto," Zone 8 councilor (8/21/99); and "Malena," a CCZ worker in Zone 5 (6/8/99).

by one, with a handshake or a kiss on the cheek. Ten minutes after the mayor finished speaking, half the audience left the assembly.

The only exception to the general pattern occurred in Zone 5 (7/24/99), where there was very large attendance, the audience stayed until the very end, and the structure of the assembly was quite different. In Zone 5, the public first chose between attending one or another of a number of smaller meetings dedicated to particular themes, where they were allowed and encouraged to ask questions and make proposals, and then later convened in a single assembly. It is interesting to note that Zone 5 is one of the wealthiest zones of Montevideo and that the zone's problems hardly compare to those in poorer areas. For example, one of the most contentious issues in Zone 5's assembly was that of whether to enact and how to enforce an ordinance forcing people to clean up after their dogs.

No other assembly replicated the effervescent participation and ebullient mood in Zone 5. In fact, rather than constructively engaging with fellow citizens and city officials, several local councilors and former local councilors used the budget assemblies to denounce the local councils' lack of influence and to renounce their seats publicly. The connection between the local councils' inability to affect local policies and the desertion of the councilors seems to be generalized. In 1998, municipal social workers who had provided technical advice to the local councilors conducted a study of the councils' "crisis of immobilism." The social workers suggested that the high desertion rate resulted from the councilors' frustrations over their limited ability to influence policy, especially given the expectations of "co-government" initially raised by the municipal administration (Calvetti et al. 1998, 5–7). In a separate series of interviews and workshops carried out by a local NGO, Praxis, local councilors complained that neighborhood activists had stopped participating "because they feel that the Local Council has no power to make decisions" (Rebellato and Ubilla 1999, 32).[39] For several councilors, participating in council meetings seemed a "waste of time," given that the discussions rarely translated into results (Rebellato and Ubilla 1999, 37, 36–43). Even active members of the Frente Amplio recognize this problem. "Dinora," for example, a member of the local government group in Zone 7, told me, "What most empties the local entities of participation is that the people feel that in reality they are not deciding, that their demands are not being received, and that they're wasting their time" (interview 7/21/99).

---

39. Interestingly, in our own survey of the local councilors, Daniel Chavez and I found that of those who still remained active in the councils, over 62 percent of the respondents agreed with the statement "Decentralization is effectively transferring power to the grassroots."

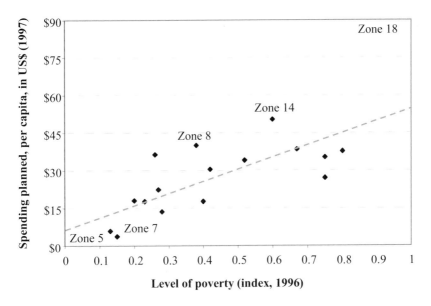

Fig. 4.4   Poverty and spending

Paradoxically, the FA administration consistently received high marks from residents for the provision of public services (see chapter 6). In fact, what is striking about the Montevideo case in comparative terms is that, unlike the Causa Radical administration in Caracas, the Frente Amplio government was able to improve services and invest heavily in public works projects. New roads, parks, plazas, sewer pipes and sewage treatment plants, and public lighting have transformed Montevideo since the FA gained power in 1990. Furthermore, and again unlike in Caracas, the largest share of municipal government spending in Montevideo went to the poorer zones of the city (Revello 1999, 9, 12–13, apps. 7, 8). In 1997, for example, taking individual zones as the units of analysis, the Pearson correlation coefficient between level of poverty and per capita municipal government spending was .75 and highly statistically significant (at p < .001).[40] Figure 4.4 presents this correlation graphically, showing that the richest zones, 5 and 7, received a far smaller share of government spending than did poorer zones, like 14 and 18.

40. I constructed a 0 to 1 poverty index for this analysis (and the others that follow) using six highly correlated indicators from the 1996 census and presented by zone in Unidad (2002, 16–29): percentage of homes constructed with deficient materials; percentage of homes with deficient sewage service; percentage of households not connected to the water system; percentage of households that are overcrowded (more than three people per bedroom); percentage of adults with less than six years of education; and percentage of residents without health insurance. For municipal government spending per capita, I combined spending amounts planned

The strong relationship between poverty and spending holds up in multiple regression analysis using spending as the dependent variable and adding vote share for the Frente Amplio in 1994 as a control variable. Table 4.1 presents the regression results.[41] It shows that, *ceteris paribus,* zones with higher levels of poverty received more per capita spending, by about four dollars per person for every .1 increase on the 0 to 1 poverty scale. The statistical insignificance of the vote share variable (given its high p-value) suggests that it is unlikely that the Frente Amplio administration deliberately directed resources to zones where it received a higher percentage of the vote.[42] In other words, the results do not suggest that the FA used the municipal budget as a tool to reward supporters along the lines of traditional clientelist parties.

---

for 1997 on the three most important areas of spending that are broken down by zone and dollar amounts in government accounts: street paving, health care (Division 1997, 4–5, 84–101), and amount spent on social programs such as soup kitchens, day care centers, and domestic abuse prevention (IMM 1998a, 148). The only other large shares of spending are taken up by sewage services and housing programs, but they are not broken down by zone. The figures for the population of each zone are taken from Unidad (2002, 22–26). I was unable to obtain multiyear budgetary data broken down by zone, and therefore I could not repeat this analysis for other years or carry out time series analysis. For these kinds of analyses, see chapter 5 on Porto Alegre.

41. Unless otherwise noted, all regression analyses in this book use the ordinary least squares (OLS) technique to estimate the relationship between the independent (predictor, or X) variables and the dependent variable (the outcome, or Y). (This note is intended for readers not familiar with statistical methods.) OLS models the relationship as linear, such that values of Y are a function of values of X, after taking into account a "constant" term. For each independent variable, OLS provides a coefficient (labeled B in the regression tables) that estimates the effect of the independent variable on the outcome holding other independent variables constant, a standard error term that expresses the precision of this estimate, and a "p-value" that expresses the probability that the true value of the coefficient is significantly different from zero, which would indicate no relationship (this is often referred to as "statistical significance"). The R-squared (or R^2) term in the regression tables varies from 0 to 1 and expresses how much of the total variation in the dependent variable is explained by all the independent variables in the model. Finally, the N in the regression tables refers to the number of cases. Because the number of cases is fairly small in all my analyses, I do not use more than a few explanatory variables and therefore do not report the "adjusted R-squared" term, which adjusts for models with many explanatory variables that artificially inflate the R-squared term. In the regression tables, a higher B indicates a stronger effect of the independent variable, while larger standard errors (relative to B) indicate less precision and low p-values (especially below 0.1, or even better, .05) indicate greater confidence that the relationship between an independent variable and the dependent variable is statistically different from zero. Finally, a higher R^2 term indicates that the model explains more of the variation in the outcome, such that .597, for example, suggests that the model presented in table 4.1 explains 59.7 percent of the variation in public spending.

42. The electoral data come from *Brecha* (12/8/94), which breaks the votes down into eighteen districts that correspond, but not perfectly, to the eighteen zones used by the municipal administration. For the four districts in which the overlap was not identical, I estimated the vote share using the map in Facultad (1994, 37) and the neighborhood population figures in IMM (1998a, 28).

Table 4.1   Poverty, vote share, and spending

Variable	B	Standard error	Significance (p-value)
Level of poverty (1996)	39.09	13.31	.010
Percentage of vote for Frente Amplio in 1994 elections	75.97	64.29	.256
Constant	-22.63	25.54	.390

$R^2 = .597; N = 18$.

The statistical analyses demonstrate that the FA administration did engage in redistributive spending, unlike the Causa Radical in Caracas. The next step is to test whether or not the higher levels of spending in the poorer areas stimulated participation, as occurred in Porto Alegre (see chapter 5). If a strong relationship between spending and participation existed, it could be taken as evidence against my argument that the program's failure to provide a potent channel for citizens to influence policy discouraged participation. If no relationship existed, then my argument would be strengthened.

To test for an association between spending and participation, the only participation data available is the number of residents voting in the local council elections (given that there is no official or unofficial count of participants in budget assemblies by zone). A correlational analysis of per capita spending in 1997 and the percentage of adult residents who voted in the 1998 local council elections, in fact, shows a statistically significant correlation (with a Pearson correlation coefficient of .63). However, if one introduces the level of poverty as a control variable, regression analysis suggests that the correlation between spending and participation is spurious. Table 4.2 presents the results of a regression analysis in which the rate of participation in local council elections is the dependent variable, and per capita spending and level of poverty are the independent variables. The table shows that, controlling for the level of poverty, municipal spending has no statistically significant effect on participation. The level of poverty, however, strongly affects the rate of participation. For each 0.1 increase on the 0 to 1 poverty scale, there was an increase in the rate of voting in local council elections of 1.7 percentage points on average.

Two comparative points can summarize the preceding statistical analyses. First, the FA administration in Montevideo pursued redistributive spending policies, unlike LCR in Caracas but similar to the PT in Porto Alegre. Second, these spending policies do not seem to have encouraged higher participation rates in Montevideo, whereas they did in Porto Alegre. Pro-poor spending alone, therefore, does not appear to stimulate participation.

Table 4.2   Poverty, spending, and participation

Variable	B	Standard error	Significance (p-value)
Level of poverty (1996)	.169	.042	.005
Municipal spending			
per capita (1997)	.00002	.001	.978
Constant	.05284	.001	.005

$R^2 = .710$; N = 18.

Taken together, the evidence suggests that Montevideo's crisis of participation—in the local councils, thematic commissions, and budget assemblies—stems largely from the program's regulated design. The participatory decentralization program as reintroduced in 1993, with its formal structure and weak decision-making power, gave city residents insufficient incentive to continue participating.

Conclusion

In the end, Montevideo represents an interesting case of partial success for the Frente Amplio. While the FA's participatory decentralization program failed to sustain a large number of diverse, representative participants, its municipal administrations did achieve substantial improvements in providing local infrastructure and services (see chapter 6), thus maintaining support for the program with voters. How can this mixed outcome be explained? On one hand, the facilitating macro-level conditions of Uruguay's relatively high degree of national decentralization and Montevideo's correspondingly robust local government capacity meant that the FA had the potential to design an effective participation program and to deliver concrete results. On the other hand, at the meso level, the program faced fierce resistance from the strongly institutionalized Colorados and Blancos, who prevented the FA from implementing the program as originally envisioned. Most importantly, this entrenched opposition used a crucial lacuna in Uruguay's otherwise fairly decentralized system—the lack of constitutional autonomy for the municipal government—in order to bring in their national government allies to help them force the FA to redesign its original program. Finally, while this new regulated design did not stimulate ongoing participation, it did help the FA take advantage of the municipal government's capacity to improve services.

FA candidates thus earned increasingly wide margins of victory in municipal elections. In 1999, the Frente Amplio came close to winning the presidential elections while holding up its administration in Montevideo as a model and running former mayor Tabaré Vázquez as its candidate. Of course, five years later, Vázquez won the presidency. The FA's recurring electoral victories in Montevideo provided the party with the opportunity to address the crisis of participation by modifying the design of its program. In fact, already in the late 1990s some advisors to Mayor Arana began to call for greater decision-making power for participants in the budget assemblies (IDES 2001, 87), and one faction within the Frente Amplio—the Movement for Popular Participation (MPP)—continued to advocate changes in the design of the program, including an increase in the power of the local councils and citizens.[43] Without a powerful community movement backing these calls, however, major changes took several years and the rise of the MPP to a dominant position within the party and eventually City Hall. As discussed in chapter 7, only in the late 2000s did Montevideo adopt a participatory process that began to match that of Porto Alegre in terms of the quality of participation and the quantity of participants.

Appendix: Survey of Montevideo Residents

The survey of Montevideo residents was carried out in person by ten university students from August 14 to August 22, 1999. We randomly selected city blocks in the three zones used in the 1992 survey, which had been chosen to represent the different types of areas in Montevideo: Zone 7 to represent the wealthier areas along the eastern coast; Zone 3 to represent the central urban areas in decline (where the level of poverty was higher); and Zone 9 to represent the peripheral areas of the city with significant numbers of poor households. We had hoped for 450 completed questionnaires, and the final sample size was 444. In terms of the distributions of gender, age, and education, the survey sample was quite close to the figures

43. See Zabalza (1998). Some members of the Socialist Party also favored strengthening the decision-making power of the councils and the boards, as well as making the boards elective bodies and providing more resources to the CCZs. The two other large factions within the FA—the Vertiente Artiguista (Arana's faction) and Asamblea Uruguay—apparently did not agree with these changes (interview with "Dinora," a Socialist Party activist and member of the local government group in Zone 7, 7/21/99).

Table 4.3   Age and education distributions

Age	20–29	30–39	40–49	50–59	60+
Population	21.3	18.1	17.0	14.6	29.0
Survey	18.8	17.8	16.3	16.8	30.3

Education	None	Primary*	Jr. High	Secondary**	Magisterial	University	Other
Population	1.0	32.6	21.7	26.1	2.7	15.2	0.6
Survey	2.0	28.6	24.8	26.6	3.0	14.3	0.7

*In the population, this includes those who did not complete primary school.

**This includes both general secondary education and technological schools.

for the population over nineteen years old taken from the *Anuario Estadístico* 1999 (from http://www.ine.gub.uy for the year 1998). While women (over fourteen years of age) make up 54.1 percent of the population (over fourteen years of age), they made up 56.5 percent of the survey. For age and education distributions, see table 4.3.

5

Porto Alegre: Making Participatory Democracy Work

Porto Alegre's now famous experiment with participatory budgeting initially gave little indication that it would endure, let alone become an international model. After planners at the United Nations Habitat meeting in 1996 selected the city's participatory budget process as one of the world's "best practices" in urban government, Porto Alegre began to host hundreds of visitors from across the globe to study and emulate its success in providing public services and revitalizing civic life. Yet judging from the first two years of the participatory budget process, when participation rates were anemic, the budget for public works was minuscule, and dissension within the Workers' Party was rife, no one could have predicted the eventual success of participatory budgeting. Nonetheless, unlike in Caracas and Montevideo, where the public's eagerness to participate declined and never recovered, in Porto Alegre participation rebounded in the third year after initial frustrations and then continued to grow throughout the 1990s. In examining how participatory budgeting evolved in Porto Alegre, this chapter completes the trilogy of case studies and explores why the PT's program ultimately achieved more success than its counterparts in the other cities.

The experience of Porto Alegre differs from that of Caracas and Montevideo because of macro-, meso-, and micro-level differences. At the meso level, in the latter two cases, strongly institutionalized opposition parties forced significant changes in the incumbents' new programs. In Porto Alegre, by contrast, the opposition was weak and divided, and it failed to resist the new participatory budgeting process or to influence its design. Rather than negotiating the design of its participation program with an uncompromising opposition, the PT negotiated with autonomous, coordinated community organizations. Indeed, at the micro level, unlike the party-penetrated neighborhood groups in Caracas and Montevideo—which played negative or minimal roles, respectively—community organizations in Porto Alegre became the key actors pushing for a more open design of the new participation program. Of course, the PT administration itself also played a central role in designing the program and helping it rebound, as many observers of Porto Alegre have pointed out. Most importantly, at the macro level, city officials took advantage of the capacity afforded municipal government by Brazil's high degree of decentralization compared to Uruguay and especially to Venezuela. Brazil's newly minted, decentralizing 1988 constitution granted powers to increase taxes and expand popular participation. Unlike most accounts of Porto Alegre, however, this chapter looks beyond the actions of the empowered local administration to emphasize the absence of a strongly institutionalized opposition and the corresponding important role of autonomous community groups in allowing participatory budgeting to evolve toward a more open design. When administration officials initially attempted a more regulated design of participation, community leaders pressed for a more direct, informal structure of participation, and continually called for ever-greater decision-making power over an expanding range of important issues. Once this more open institutional design was in place, participatory budgeting successfully sustained a larger and more diverse group of participants than did the more restrictive and regulated programs in Caracas and Montevideo.

The first two sections of this chapter examine the evolution of participatory budgeting, explaining how its open design came to fruition. The third section describes the budget process as it operated as of the late 1990s and early 2000s and explains how its open design attracted and sustained participation.

Failure in the First Two Years

The Workers' Party faced a series of difficulties in the first two years of Mayor Olívio Dutra's term (1989–92) that made the eventual success of participatory budgeting appear unlikely.[1] Dutra's administration inherited a disastrous financial situation from the previous mayor, whose fiscal planning left Dutra

---

1. This chapter draws from interviews with city officials, PT leaders, and budget participants, as well as from several published accounts of the PT's early experience in Porto Alegre (Abers 2000, 65–90; Andreatta 1995; Fedozzi 1997, 111–46; Harnecker 1993; Horn 1994; and Navarro 1997).

with only 2 percent of the budget available for badly needed public works projects in the first year. Party leaders could not agree on how to implement their proposals for greater citizen participation in city affairs—nor, more generally, on how and for whom the PT should govern. And the administration's first move, taking over many of the city's privately owned bus lines, sparked an immediate wave of condemnation from business leaders, the media, and opposition parties. By the end of Dutra's inaugural year, the PT administration faced criticism on all sides: from within the party itself, from frustrated community activists, from the business elite and its political allies, and from city workers.

Starting Out: Fiscal Chaos and Internal Dissent

The most immediate practical problems the administration faced were financial. Dutra's Finance Secretary, João Verle, describes his "memories of an awful day" when he first arrived in January 1989 to confront the city's chaotic fiscal conditions: the city had fallen several months behind in payments to suppliers, contractors, and city workers, January's revenue barely managed to cover municipal workers' salaries, and a large short-term loan would come due in a few weeks (Cassel and Verle 1994, 28–29). This financial disarray owed partly to Brazil's multiple economic crises during Sarney's presidency (1985–89), when triple-digit inflation was not uncommon, and partly to the fiscal policy of Alceu Collares, the previous mayor. Collares had held down city workers' wages throughout his term (1986–88), only to grant them an enormous raise in December 1988 after his party—the PDT—had lost the mayor's race. This last-minute action left the PT administration to pay for the wage increase.

In addition to the urgent financial situation, the PT was beset by internal battles over a fourfold quandary. For whom should the party govern: should the party focus on policies to benefit the working class only or look to satisfy the whole city? Who should decide government policy: the mayor, the party leadership, or popular movement organizations such as unions and community groups? Should the PT govern as had other parties and merely "administer the crisis of capitalism," should it start a socialist revolution, or should it find some middle path? And how exactly should the government encourage participation: by ceding power to autonomous "popular councils" or by creating a more institutionalized form of participation?

Debates over these questions took on great importance as the party's various factions jockeyed for power within and over the new administration.

Most cabinet posts had gone to the second- and third-largest factions, Articulação (Articulation) and Nova Esquerda (New Left), linked respectively to the mayor and his union ties and to the vice-mayor and other ex-Communist dissidents. The principal faction controlled the party's municipal organization, but had been almost completely excluded (and had excluded itself) from Dutra's cabinet after losing the primary election by only five votes. This faction, the Trotskyist Democracia Socialista (Socialist Democracy, DS), and several other more orthodox Left factions harshly criticized Dutra's administration in the early years. Party leaders eventually resolved their differences through a series of compromises. For instance, the party decided that it would govern for the whole city but from the workers' perspective and that the mayor and his cabinet (which represented leaders of different party factions) would have the final decision on policy.[2] Most sectors of the party realized quickly that it was impossible to start a revolution from City Hall. Still, the factions outside the administration mobilized against it several times and came close to declaring themselves in open opposition to the government they had helped elect.[3]

The PT's Participation Debate: All Power to the Soviets?

For the story of participatory budgeting, the most important of the PT's internal debates concerned popular participation. The party platform in the 1988 elections called for participation through the creation of "popular councils," yet PT leaders had formed no consensus over the form and purpose of such councils.[4] The more orthodox factions envisioned popular councils as a strategic instrument for taking power. According to the city planning coordinator at that time, the orthodox proposal "viewed popular councils as a parallel power, like soviets. The form they proposed, the PT program itself before the elections, was completely based on the idea that

---

2. At the national level, the PT leadership resolved that mayors should have the final decision on divisive issues (Couto 1995, 143).

3. Interviews with Tarson Nuñez (4/12/99), city official in GAPLAN in the first PT administration; Eduardo Mancuso (4/16/99), PT municipal secretary during much of the 1990s; and Iria Charão (5/12/99), city official in charge of community relations in the first PT administration. See also Harnecker (1993, 8–13).

4. Moura (1993, 282–83); and interview with Gildo Lima (4/15/99), PB coordinator in the first PT administration. It does not appear that the popular councils in the party platform referred directly or solely to the district-level popular councils composed of various community organizations that had been formed in some regions of the city during the 1980s under the name of popular councils, neighborhood unions (*união de vilas*), and movement coordinators or "articulations." In addition, the platform did not refer to participatory budgeting.

the popular councils should decide all policies. At base it was a classic Leninist vision of dual powers. The bourgeois state has to be destroyed, let's build a popular power. . . . That original proposal from some sectors of the PT was voluntarist, mistaken. It was almost 'All power to the popular councils. All power to the soviets'" (Luciano Fedozzi, interview 5/12/99). Others argued that the popular councils would serve to help democratize the state, bourgeois or not. For these more moderate sectors of the PT, the councils would not assume power, but at best would share power with the municipal government by contributing to the formulation of certain policies.

The first major participatory initiative taken by the administration started out adhering more to the vision of popular councils as "soviets" and involved transportation rather than the budget. It was largely considered a failure. In February 1989, Porto Alegre's major private bus companies, fearing government intrusion, refused to submit to an audit of their finances initiated by the Dutra administration and threatened to stop service if the audit continued. In response, Dutra ordered city officials to occupy several bus company offices and to take over the buses in order to maintain public access to transportation (Abers 2000, 68). To build support for the intervention, the administration held assemblies with union, community, and student activists. In the initial assemblies, city officials asked whether the government should continue with the intervention and heeded the assemblies' calls to go forward. However, the bus company owners reacted violently to the takeover, sending hired goons to shoot at the buses and sabotaging company computers and records. When the administration tried to move beyond assemblies to call on the activists to protect the buses, the community movement did not respond, the assemblies shrank, and the "self-defense" committees proposed by city officials never materialized. Ultimately, the pressures from sabotage and lawsuits, and the technical difficulty of operating a large bus fleet, forced the administration to return the bus companies to the owners (Harnecker 1993, 27).

Despite the failure of the popular council model during the bus intervention, many sectors of the PT clung to it when the administration started the *orçamento participativo* (participatory budget process, PB) several months later.[5] The more orthodox Marxist, Leninist, and Trotskyist factions— which made up slightly less than half of the PT membership—distanced themselves from Dutra's administration and viewed the initial budget

---

5. The name *orçamento participativo* was actually not used until the second year of the budget assemblies.

meetings with skepticism. As a member of the DS told me, "A big part of the PT did not believe much in participatory budgeting. . . . There are significant 'currents' within the PT itself that criticize PB because they think that it's just dividing the crumbs, you know, and that ultimately it ends up accommodating the people within the horizons of the bourgeois state."[6] Those orthodox Left segments of the party who did participate in the first meetings tried to push for radical consciousness raising rather than debating the nuts and bolts of the budget. One community leader and PB veteran described several participants who "thought that City Hall was going to have to launch the revolution that year" ("João," interview 4/2/99). PB began, then, without consensus within the party over how, or even whether, it should be implemented.[7] Nonetheless, Dutra and his inner circle were committed to encouraging popular participation, and the community movement seized the opportunity to shape the administration's initiative into a useful program.

Crafting PB: Tensions Between the Administration and Community Leaders

In September 1989, with city coffers nearly empty, the business class still enraged at the bus intervention, the PT divided, and the public skeptical, the administration made its first attempt to discuss the city budget openly with citizens. Using the city's Urban Development Plan (Plano Diretor de Desenvolvimento Urbano) as a guideline, planning officials divided the city into five districts and invited the public, and especially community organizations, to open assemblies. Fitting with the PT's origins, they held the first assembly at the local metalworkers' union hall. Approximately 720 community activists attended the initial five assemblies (Andreatta 1997, 25).

By all accounts, the assemblies proved disappointing to the participants. Leaders of the community movement complained that the five-part division of the city created districts too large to allow for adequate participation or representation. The large districts meant that participants would have to spend more time and money getting to meetings, presenting yet another obstacle for activists, who already faced problems of overcoming the skepticism of a

---

6. Interview with Nuñez (4/12/99). Several other interviewees confirmed that the extreme Left factions in the PT did not support participatory budgeting in the first few years.

7. According to Nuñez (interview, 4/12/99), though PB is now universally considered positive within the PT in Rio Grande do Sul, neither the radical nor moderate sectors of the party have "really been able to incorporate PB theoretically because PB is a reformist practice. It democratizes the actually existing state, whether or not that state eventually becomes socialist. It is not contradictory with capitalism."

large segment of the population that considered popular participation an empty campaign promise. Community leaders also protested that the discussions led by city officials were "confused and improvised" and pitched in overly technical language (FASE, 1989, 2). Furthermore, many activists argued that the administration tried to impose its own proposals and did not allow the community members much input. Administration officials concurred with some of these complaints (Andreatta 1997, 17; Fedozzi 1992, 4–5). They agreed to discuss a redivision of the city and a new method for continuing the budget discussions at a meeting with community leaders from neighborhood associations and the district-level popular councils at the office of the union of neighborhood associations, UAMPA.

Dividing the city into new districts occurred easily. With the already-existing districts within UAMPA (Pereira and Moura 1988, 2) and the presence of six district-level popular councils (either formed or in the process of forming), community leaders had relatively little trouble agreeing upon a division of the city into sixteen districts. The administration accepted this new districting proposed by the community leaders.[8]

However, the issue of how to organize the budget discussions remained divisive, both within the PT and within the community movement. The administration officials most closely involved with the budget process argued in favor of holding open public assemblies in each district and allowing those assembled to directly elect representatives to a municipal budget council. Yet the PT's more orthodox Marxist factions argued against this open formulation because it would "strengthen a bourgeois, individualized conception of citizenship," rather than promote community organization (Fedozzi, interview 5/12/99). The directorate of UAMPA, on the other hand, favored limiting participation in the budget assemblies to neighborhood association members and argued that the municipal budget council should be reserved for UAMPA itself. The majority of UAMPA's leaders worried that direct public access to municipal decision making would weaken neighborhood associations by making them less needed as mediating institutions. In fact, UAMPA initially proposed that the municipal budget council be composed of UAMPA's directors plus representatives of the city workers'

8. These districts remained in place until 1995, when two districts merged (eliminating the smallest district, Ilhas, the population of which reached barely over five thousand), and another district, Eixo da Baltazar, was split into two (creating the new district of Noroeste, which also encompassed several neighborhoods from the Centro district). Over the years, other more minor adjustments were made to the boundaries of the different districts, always after a vote of approval by the municipal budget council.

union (UAMPA, 1989, 3). Leaders of the district-level popular councils dis-agreed with this formulation. The popular councils included neighborhood associations but also squatters' movements and health care movements, day care centers, mothers' clubs, and other community-based organizations. Such groups opposed a policy that allowed only neighborhood associations to participate.

This division over how to organize the budget process coincided, albeit imperfectly, with political party positions. Most PT activists (other than the orthodox Marxists) in the administration and in the community move-ment—especially in the popular councils—favored the open method, while the dominant parties in UAMPA (the PDT and PC do B[9]) preferred the method focused on associations. The administration decided on a slightly revised version of the open formula, in which all municipal budget coun-cilors would be elected in public assemblies save one selected by UAMPA and one by the municipal workers' union. As a result, UAMPA refused to support participatory budgeting and urged its members to refrain from participating in the budget assemblies. According to Waldir Bohn Gass (interview 3/15/99), who served as UAMPA's president from 1984 to 1988, UAMPA did not send a representative to the budget council until 1992, when "the PC do B criticized its own former position, saying that UAMPA had made a mistake."

Round Two: More Dissension over PB's Design

With the city now divided into sixteen districts, the administration held a second round of open assemblies at the end of September to discuss the budget for 1990. Approximately nine hundred people attended the meetings across the city.[10] In addition to listening to the administration's explanation of the budget process, presenting large lists of their own demands, and voting on which government services should be prioritized, the partici-pants elected ninety delegates to a municipal budget council, one for each group of ten people present at the meeting. This council continued to meet with city officials to debate the finer points of the budget throughout the rest of the year.

9. The *Partido Comunista do Brasil* (Communist Party of Brazil) is one of several small communist parties in Brazil.

10. No definite number of participants exists for 1989. Andreatta (1997, 25) puts the figure at 790, FASE (1990, 5n2) suggests that approximately nine hundred people participated, and an internal mimeograph from City Hall also lists nine hundred.

The community movement had a mixed reaction to the budget assemblies. On one hand, participants were pleased with the opportunity to voice their demands. Long-time community activists argued that the administration had not understood that the public's need for basic infrastructure trumped its interest in improving public transportation until the budget meetings were held. As a leader of the Partenon district's Popular Council told me, "The administration came in wrong because it meddled with transportation first [the intervention in the bus companies] and the population had to correct the administration. We put our own priorities first" ("Edilson," interview 3/23/99). "Pedro" (interview 5/6/99), a delegate from the Leste district in PB's first year, concurred: "In that era [1989], the idea of the PT was to take over the public transportation system. When they realized what the people wanted, it was other things. It was improvement in the infrastructure of the neighborhoods. All these mobilizations started and, well, practically pressured a little the creation of PB itself." The city's finance secretary, Arno Augustin (1994, 52), presents a similar view from within the administration. Indeed, a survey of UAMPA members in 1988 showed that for most community activists, street paving, housing, and especially sewage were the principal local problems.[11] And in the budget assemblies, participants consistently prioritized these three issues.

On the other hand, many community leaders criticized the restrictions placed on the new demand-making channel by the administration, both in terms of which parts of the budget would be open for debate and in terms of how much decision-making power the participants would be given (FASE 1990, 1–2). Since the early 1980s, the community movement, and especially UAMPA, had called on city government to allow citizens input into local budget decisions. Some community activists thus attended PB assemblies thinking that they would be able to discuss and modify the entire budget, including revenues and all types of expenditures (UAMPA 1989, 3). In the assemblies, however, discussion was limited to expenditures on investments—primarily public works projects. During the first decade of PT administrations, investments usually represented between about 10 and 20 percent of city spending. In 1990, investments made up 11.2 percent of spending, or approximately 21.5 million dollars.[12] City officials provided

11. In a multiresponse question, 69 percent of the UAMPA members surveyed listed basic sanitation (sewage and water) as one of the main problems confronting their community; 35 percent listed both street paving and problems with housing; and transportation came in fourth, with 29 percent. See Pereira and Moura (1988, 11).

12. Dollar value estimated using figures from Augustin (1994, 53) and Verle and Müzell (1994, 16, table 2).

information about revenues (from taxes, fees, and government transfers) and about other types of spending (such as personnel, administrative expenses, and debt financing), yet did not raise these as items for debate but rather as fixed limitations on the amount available for investments.

The administration also invited participants to put pressure on the City Council to approve its new package of tax proposals (which many participants did), but not to provide input into the proposals themselves. Community leaders complained, "The first meetings created expectations. The community thought it was going to discuss a lot, in financial terms, you know, and it took us a while to adapt to the reality that what we could really discuss was just the money for investments. . . . That disappointed many of the leaders who had started to participate" ("Pedro," interview 5/6/99). Several of the district-level popular councils had even drawn up proposals with regard to revenues and the other expenditure items beyond investments (FASE 1990, 5n3).

City officials always responded to these complaints that budgetary laws and fixed spending items restricted the budget debates. It is true that municipal and federal laws set limits on city government spending. A minimum of 13 percent of total spending must be applied to health care, and a minimum of 30 percent of revenue from taxes and transfers must go to education; a maximum of 4 percent of current revenues can be allocated to the City Council, and a maximum of 65 percent of current revenue can be spent on personnel. In addition, the amount and kind of spending allocated to personnel and to administrative costs cannot vary too widely from year to year. Nonetheless, these limits on citizen input and the administration's defense of them have come under constant pressure from community leaders hoping to expand PB's influence over other areas of the budget. Critics of PB have also frequently pointed out that while the PT lauds participatory budgeting as a major achievement, in fact citizens make decisions over only that portion of the budget dedicated to investments.

The overwhelming number of demands and the question of who had the right to prioritize them posed a second set of problems for participants. Given that the city's poor neighborhoods lacked basic infrastructure but the local government could not resolve all the problems in a single budget year, the key dilemma concerned which neighborhood to help first. As former vice-mayor (and later mayor) Tarso Genro writes of those early meetings, "everyone wanted everything all at the same time" (Genro and Souza 1997, 24). Delegates to the municipal budget council reported that the discussions were poorly organized. For example, "Pedro" (interview 5/6/99) told me that the meetings "lacked a real structure, and there were no well-defined criteria because it was an experiment, you know? In the end you had no way of knowing whether you were right or wrong. Demands began raining down, and everyone wanted to be first. It created confusion." ·

The administration's initial proposal to solve the demand overload problem—concentrating municipal investments in just three *vilas* (poor neighborhoods)—did not gain the support of community leaders. According to "João" (interview 4/29/99), "The first year, City Hall itself, the people from the Planning Secretary, wanted to use all the money from PB to fix up three *vilas*, leaving them perfect . . . in the center of the city. And then we said, 'No.' During a long time after that our district was like the administration's enemy because we fought against it. We said, 'No, let's share the misery.'" Consequently, city officials backed down from their plan of focused investments and essentially allowed the participants to submit demands without any systematic prioritization or hierarchy. In some of the districts with popular councils, however, PB participants began to develop their own criteria for prioritizing their demands. In Leste, for example, the participants used the criteria of access to schools, degree of poverty, and level of community mobilization to determine which streets would be prioritized for paving.[13]

Yet the demands from the district assemblies bore little relation to the administration's initial budget proposal, which city planners had drawn up in meetings with municipal department heads without much consideration of PB assemblies. In their first meeting, the ninety budget delegates thus attempted to guarantee results for their participation by insisting on the creation of an "investment plan" (*plano de investimentos*) that would list the public works projects for each of the sixteen districts and the administration's "institutional" investments as well. The latter concern only projects that affect the entire city, that span more than one district, or that are determined to be necessary to expand or maintain services; they are proposed by the administration and voted on by the budget council.

The investment plan, conceived by community activists, not city officials, later became the centerpiece of PB, with thousands of copies printed each year so that citizens could check on the projects the administration has promised to carry out. Prior to this invention, municipal budgets did not

---

13. Interviews with "Pedro" (5/6/99), "João" (4/29/99), and Eunice Araujo (4/26/99), the district PB coordinator for Leste during the early 1990s.

specify exactly which projects the government would complete.[14] The first investment plan, though it may have represented a victory for the community movement, was in fact wildly unrealistic. It listed many more projects than City Hall had the financial or administrative ability to realize. Community leaders thought they had won the power to set their own budget priorities, but this power proved illusory the following year, leading to widespread disenchantment.

From Bad to Worse: The Insolvent
Administration and the Decline of Participation

In the beginning of 1990, the city's continuing financial difficulties and the unrealistic nature of the investment plan impeded the administration's ability to carry out the projects it had agreed to in PB. As a result, community activists felt deceived and disappointed, and participation declined in the district budget assemblies. Almost none of the public works projects listed in the 1990 investment plan were being implemented. For instance, one of the participants' most important demands had been street paving, but given its financial disarray, the administration failed to pour even one of the forty-two kilometers of pavement projected for the year (Augustin 1994, 53). Community leaders, particularly those who had participated in the budget meetings the year before, were furious. All the hours they had spent in budget meetings and all their efforts to convince their neighbors to participate appeared to have been wasted. Led by the district popular councils, community activists held protests in front of City Hall calling for the administration to carry out the investment plan, and later they demanded that the secretary of public works resign (Abers 2000, 74; Baierle 1992, 121). As a former budget delegate said, "We didn't defend City Hall, but we defended the process [PB]. When the public works projects didn't appear, we hit City Hall hard" ("João," interview 4/29/99).

Frustrated by the lack of results, only half as many city residents as had participated in the budget assemblies of 1989 attended the first round of budget assemblies in 1990. Twelve of the sixteen districts registered fewer than twenty-five participants, and nearly half registered fewer than ten.[15]

14. According to the Porto Alegre NGO, FASE (1990, 6n8), "Traditionally, the budget plan does not specify nor list the projects under the item investments. It does not come close to being a programming budget, but is rather a generic accounting document that generally tends to be merely formal."

15. The total number of participants in the first round of meetings was 348. From 1990 onward, the administration recorded the actual numbers of participants (rather than estimates

Even in Leste, the district with the second-highest number of participants, distrust of City Hall ran high. In a letter to city officials, Leste's Popular Council (in formation) wrote, "Although we know that Porto Alegre's problems are numerous and complex, until now very little has been done to improve people's lives even minimally. The failure to complete the Leste projects agreed to in the 1990 budget is also discouraging and leads to lack of faith in City Hall."[16] In addition to the waning of the community movement's support, residents of Porto Alegre in general disapproved of the PT administration. Throughout 1990, Dutra's government received a "bad" or "terrible" rating from over 40 percent of those polled, while fewer than 24 percent rated the government "good" or "excellent" (Fedozzi 1992, 8; PMPA 1991, 1). Furthermore, divisions remained over how to conduct the government both within the administration and between the administration and *petistas* outside it. However, rather than imploding, the administration rebounded, and PB along with it.

Regaining Credibility Through Administrative Reform and Community Pressure

Two central factors aided the revival and expansion of participatory budgeting. One was the administration's implementation of a set of financial and organizational reforms, to which several observers of Porto Alegre have rightly pointed when explaining PB's recovery after its rocky start (Abers 2000, 75–81; Fedozzi 1997, 135–38; Santos 1998, 476–78). These reforms achieved more than the FA and LCR's similar reforms in Montevideo and Caracas because the PT faced less resistance from strong opposition parties and because of Brazil's higher degree of decentralization. Specifically, the PT's reforms began to take effect concurrently with an increase in federal transfers to municipalities. A second, equally important cause of PB's revival was the community movement's continued demand for and assertion of decision-making power. After all, stimulating participation requires not only concrete results, but results that relate clearly and directly to the participants' deliberations. From the outset, it was the community movement that tried to force the administration to give participants real decision-making

---

as in 1989). For participation figures for PB assemblies from 1990 to 2000, see Pont (2000, 27, table IV).

16. "Região Leste," letter from the "Articulation of the Leste Region," photocopy, 1990 (provided to me by "Pedro").

power within PB by redrawing the city districts, rejecting the concentration of investments in government "showpieces," calling for the creation of a meaningful investment plan, and protesting the lack of government adherence to that plan. It was at least partly in response to this pressure from community groups that the administration embarked on the organizational reforms. And community leaders continued to fight for more influence over the budget even after the administration had gained organizational coherence and fiscal strength through its restructuring.

The importance of this restructuring, nonetheless, should not be minimized. The administration's primary reforms involved an overhaul of the local tax system and the creation of a new office to oversee participatory budgeting and coordinate PB's interaction with the various municipal departments. The tax reformulation had started in 1989, when Dutra launched a series of reforms to improve the city's finances. During the 1980s, Porto Alegre's population had increased by 10 percent while city revenues fell from an annual average of approximately 146 million dollars in the early part of the decade to about 121 million dollars per annum in the 1986–88 period (Verle and Müzell 1994, 25). City officials attempted to counteract this trend in several ways. While the previous administration had granted two amnesties to tax evaders in three years, which encouraged nonpayment, the PT administration published lists of tax evaders to convince them to pay and publicly declared the permanent end of amnesties. In addition, city residents received discounts if they paid taxes early. According to Augustin, the finance secretary, the percentage of households failing to pay property taxes declined from 20 percent toward the beginning of the PT administration to 13.5 percent in 1995 (cited in Schneider and Baquero 2006, 16). Finally, Dutra sent fifteen new tax laws to the City Council that established new fees for some services and recalibrated several other taxes, making the property tax more progressive, for example (Cassell and Verle 1994). Combined with the improvements in city revenues due to increased transfers from the federal government, the tax reforms enabled the administration to dedicate more of the city budget to investments, the spending category under PB's direct influence. Real total revenues expanded by more than 50 percent between 1989 and 1991, and investments as a percentage of spending increased from 3 percent to nearly 18 percent over the same period (Cassell and Verle 1994, 38; Augustin 1994, 52–54).

Before the tax overhaul began to become effective, toward the end of 1990, Dutra and his advisers already had devised a strategy for overcoming the paralysis characterizing their first year and a half in office. The strategic plan laid out a single set of objectives and guidelines for the administration and for each of the municipal departments in order to harmonize their activities. The objectives called for each municipal organ to focus on improving the quality of public services, especially in the poorest neighborhoods, and on creating more effective channels of citizen participation. To coordinate meeting these objectives, the strategy entailed setting up a new city budget and planning office, GAPLAN (Gabinete de Planejamento), to work directly under the mayor's supervision. GAPLAN replaced the planning secretary in managing the technical aspects of the budget process and began to serve as the link between PB and each municipal department. The administrative reorganization also included placing the mayor's Community Relations Office in charge of coordinating the district budget assemblies and the budget council meetings. The Community Relations Office appointed a coordinator for each of the sixteen PB districts to help organize meetings and encourage new participants.

Dutra also began an administrative decentralization process, creating three "regional administrative centers" (CARs) in the most peripheral areas of the city—in districts like Restinga, Norte, and Ilhas—so that residents could make demands or complaints to municipal officials more easily and could have regular contact with the district coordinators. In later years, the government created five other CARs in other city regions beyond the central district. Each CAR serves two or three districts. As the official in charge of the CAR redevelopment plan in 1998 told me, though a few CARs have small work units, the CARs, for the most part, were not intended to perform services (like the technical boards in Caracas or the CCZs in Montevideo), but to transmit information between local residents and relevant city agencies, as some agencies had already been decentralized (António Prado, interview 11/4/98). With these changes, the administration reinforced its commitment to implementing a workable participation program by positioning PB at the center of City Hall and by creating internal links with the municipal departments through GAPLAN and external links with community activists through the Community Relations Office and the CARs.

The fiscal and organizational reforms significantly enhanced the administration's capacity both to process and to meet the demands made in PB. The reforms thus played a crucial role in shoring up the credibility of City Hall and the participatory budgeting process. However, just as important was the community movement's insistence on making participation meaningful, especially in the face of the administration's continuing desire to direct the decision-making process.

In the 1990 budget assemblies, community leaders reiterated their complaints that the administration had failed to implement the projects they had prioritized the year before. They demanded that the 1991 investment plan reflect their decisions and that the plan be respected. On the other side, city officials again called for concentrating investments in a few areas.[17] Specifically, the administration proposed allocating 70 percent of the investments to the five poorest districts and dividing the remainder among the other eleven districts. In addition, GAPLAN wanted the right to determine which neighborhoods within the districts would receive the investments, such that it could focus spending on a few neighborhoods in order to transform them completely. The administration could then point to visible results. Budget councilors protested, arguing that the participants themselves should have the power to determine which neighborhoods should receive priority and insisting that the investments be divided among the districts according to their own criteria.

City officials and budget councilors eventually reached a compromise. The budget councilors were adamant that investments be dispersed across neighborhoods within each district, but agreed that 65 percent of investments could be concentrated in five districts. The five districts would be selected according to four criteria: (1) the level of community mobilization, measured by participation in the budget assemblies; (2) the level of need for infrastructure and services, measured as a percentage of houses lacking the service; (3) the size of the population in the neediest areas; and (4) the importance of the district for the development of the city. The same criteria also determined the allocation of the remaining 35 percent of investment spending among the other districts. These criteria largely mirrored the standards developed by community activists to prioritize demands within their districts, though the administration's hand is evident as well, particularly in the last criterion.

Most importantly, the budget councilors' insistence on the participants' right to choose which neighborhoods should receive public works projects meant that the 1991 investment plan did reflect the participants' decisions. And while the previous year's plan had been an unfulfillable and unsystematic wish list, the 1991 plan was based on jointly agreed criteria and was more realistic in that each district would only be guaranteed to receive investments in its top three priorities. With the city's finances returned to order, the municipal departments under new coordination by GAPLAN,

---

17. The following discussion is based on Fedozzi (1992, 13–14).

and realistic investment goals, the administration succeeded in carrying out the 1991 investment plan almost in its entirety (Augustin 1994, 54). The upshot was that as public works projects began to appear across the city, PB participants could point out to their neighbors and friends the very projects they had prioritized the year before. This direct connection between participation and results not only galvanized prior participants to continue in PB, but stimulated large numbers of new participants who had doubted the process at first. Compared to 1990, participation in the 1991 budget assemblies more than tripled.

In addition, rather than the budget delegates meeting annually in a city-wide assembly, district-level budget forums began to meet once or twice a month throughout the year, further enhancing participation. In the district forums, the delegates prioritized their local needs, monitored the administration's implementation of the investment plan, and met with city officials to learn more about the budget process. Each district elected four budget councilors (two titular and two substitute) to sit on the municipal budget council and to coordinate the district forum.

Despite the improvements in PB, many community leaders remained unsatisfied with the methods used to distribute investments, especially leaders from the eleven districts considered low priority. Thus, in 1991 the budget councilors decided to abandon the focusing of investments in five districts and to allocate investments by type or sector instead. City officials, pleased with the rise in participation, did not contest the changes made by the budget councilors. Participants could prioritize among eight types of investments: street paving, sewage and water, housing, health care, education, transportation, social assistance, and city organization (including parks, sports and cultural facilities, public lighting, and economic development initiatives such as cooperatives). In addition, most budget councilors considered two of the criteria for investment distribution—the level of participation and importance for the city's development—to be subjective.[18] They replaced these criteria with two new measures—population size and the district's prioritization of the particular type of investment—while keeping level of need and population size in the neediest areas. In later years, the budget councilors also dropped the criterion of population size in the neediest areas because it overlapped with population size and level of need, leaving

18. The second of these is obviously subjective. Participants considered the first subjective because certain community leaders had been accused of engaging in unfair and artificial "swelling" (*inchaço*) of participation in the budget assemblies by renting buses to bring residents to vote for them in the elections for the budget council.

three general criteria. Together with GAPLAN, the budget councilors agreed on a mathematical formula using these criteria to determine what percentage of each type of sectoral investment each district would receive (see the appendix to this chapter for the formula and a description of how the process works).[19] This formula privileges those areas with the largest numbers of people who lack public services, and thus, as in Montevideo, Porto Alegre's participatory process is redistributive.[20]

By 1991, the community activists' persistent demands for power within PB had transformed what had been a faltering government-initiated participation program into a fairly effective tool for citizen decision making. Although limits existed on the amount of money and the parts of the budget under community discussion, participatory budgeting had evolved into a process that allowed city residents to decide both which types of investments were most necessary and which neighborhoods needed them most, and that also provided the government with clear, objective criteria for allocating investments among city districts.

The Weakly Institutionalized Opposition Fails to Resist

While community activists and PT city officials debated and shaped the design of participatory budgeting, opposition party leaders remained largely absent. Although the opposition harshly criticized the PT administration in the press on numerous occasions, its attacks focused almost entirely on issues other than participatory budgeting. In any case, the poorly institutionalized opposition lacked the connections and coherence—seen in Caracas and Montevideo—to affect the participation program and the daily workings of the administration. As chapter 2 illustrates, the PT's opponents had negligible organizational existence and no history of cooperation amongst themselves,

---

19. Some debate exists as to the exact origins of this formula. Eunice Araujo (interview 4/26/99) claims that she and PB delegates and councilors in Leste developed the idea for the method in Leste first and suggested it to GAPLAN, while members of GAPLAN maintain that they proposed the formula to the budget councilors. Fedozzi (1997, 231n141) reports that the formula was a joint creation of a few budget councilors and city officials, and was approved by the budget council.

20. I conducted various tests of the relationship between poverty or lack of public services and municipal government investment spending using data from the annual budgets and government agency documents, and regardless of the measures used, the relationship was always strong. For example, in a correlational analysis of the percentage of households not linked to the city's sewage system and without a septic tank (1991) and investment spending per capita (1996), the Pearson correlation coefficient was .89, and was highly statistically significant (at $p < .001$).

and for the most part were only weakly embedded in social life, with minimal ties to voters, business associations, unions, and community groups. Because of the divisions both among rival parties and within the parties internally, no single, uniform reaction to PB characterized the opposition as a whole. In general, the PT's rivals failed to act quickly and decisively against PB, and the individual attempts they did make lacked support from other parties and social groups. The opposition's tepid response to PB was important for its success because it permitted the administration and community organizations to negotiate the design of the new program freely. Compared to its counterparts in Caracas and Montevideo, then, the opposition in Porto Alegre was the dog that never barked.

Evidence from interviews with opposition party leaders, PT officials, PB participants, the business elite, and from newspaper reports all points to the lack of a strong, united opposition. The bluntest assessment of the opposition comes from João Dib, mayor of Porto Alegre from 1983 to 1985 and veteran city councilor for the conservative PPB (Partido Progressista Brasileiro or, ironically, the Brazilian Progressive Party). Dib was appointed mayor toward the end of the dictatorship, and his party (now the PP) was formed by ex-members of ARENA, the progovernment party during military rule. According to Dib (interview 4/20/99), his party was the only one to react against participatory budgeting. For Dib, participatory budgeting as practiced by the PT removed power from city councilors—who were democratically elected by all city residents—and hindered efficient city planning by professionals in the municipal executive. Yet his party's response was tempered because Dib usually acted alone and almost solely within the City Council: "The party reacted because I reacted. . . . Sometimes I lost, including times that even my party colleagues did not vote with me." Dib complained that his party and indeed all the parties in Porto Alegre, except the PT, lack discipline and a program, which mirrors the situation at the federal level in Brazil. As Dib told me, "The other parties are groups of people who meet but do not think together."

While Dib and his colleagues were (and remain) ideologically opposed to participatory budgeting, the PT's other rivals had divided opinions. The president of the municipal PMDB, Sebastião Mello (interview 5/4/99), admits that his party never discussed participatory budgeting when it first began in Porto Alegre and never took a clear position. Rather, he says, "there was an accommodation of the forces in my party, which in the beginning was neither against nor did it work in favor [of PB] in the sense of going within the process, of participating, of influencing." Mello claims his party did not discuss PB because the budget is a competency of the executive branch, and thus the mayor can formulate the budget however he wants. Now, however, the PMDB regrets its absence in the early stages of participatory budgeting because the process consolidated and became "the most powerful arm of City Hall [and] of the PT." In fact, like Dib, Mello argues that the "lack of a systematic, articulated opposition in the city" is the main reason for the PT's success in Porto Alegre.

The PT's opponent with the best chance of organizing a coherent opposition was the PDT, given its plurality in the City Council and relatively strong ties to neighborhood associations in the late 1980s. However, the PDT also faced internal divisions. Some PDT city councilors criticized participatory budgeting, and PDT leaders close to former mayor Collares did try to convince party members not to participate in the budget assemblies, particularly through their neighborhood association allies in UAMPA. Yet attacking PB was not a priority, and the lower echelons of the party did not always follow the Collares party line. Even members of UAMPA-affiliated neighborhood associations ignored the instructions from the PDT and UAMPA not to participate. All of my interviewees, including current and former PDT members, concurred that PDT activists and UAMPA affiliates participated in PB from the beginning, as did members of other parties to a lesser extent. And according to former UAMPA president Bohn Gass (interview 3/15/99), "The neighborhood associations left UAMPA to the side. UAMPA was unable to impose its decision [not to participate in PB] on the associations." Former mayor Dib (interview 4/20/99) claims that the opposition party most responsible for accommodating the implementation of PB was the PDT: "The PDT let the thing [PB] happen, it let things happen in the City Council and only later did they realize." In fact, several of the original budget councilors were allied with opposition parties, particularly the PDT, and they defended participatory budgeting actively. For example, one of Leste's first budget councilors recalled that in budget council meetings he frequently worked with PDT members because the more leftist factions in the PT did not believe in participatory budgeting ("João," interview 4/29/99).

Thus, one cannot detect a united stance toward participatory budgeting, given the divisions within the opposition. In fact, the general pattern noted by PT city and party officials was that, other than occasionally denouncing PB in the City Council, most opposition leaders ignored PB at first. Interviewees gave two reasons for the opposition's timid reaction. One was that participatory budgeting started without much publicity and did not appear to be a threat. As described above, many sectors of the PT itself doubted participatory budgeting at first; thus it began with little fanfare. In addition, much of the opposition had focused on attacking the administration's bus company intervention, leaving PB "almost hidden in a corner," as one former city planner put it (interview with Nuñez 4/12/99). Another former city official, Fedozzi (interview 5/12/99), shared a similar view:

In the beginning of the Popular Administration, no one had any idea of the power PB would end up having. So it was being built almost imperceptibly. The opposition itself had no notion of what it was going to mean for the immediate political history of the city. So what happened? For one thing, the traditional parties did not believe in PB and did not take part in it. They did not take it very seriously. Some gave opinions against it. But they did not have a concrete practice of either inserting themselves in the process or trying to block it.

Indeed, in Porto Alegre's major daily newspaper, *Zero Hora,* only five articles mentioned participatory budgeting between the end of 1988 and January 1992.[21] Several PT leaders claim that conservative forces dominate the media and that the media ignored PB as a strategy to keep the party's successes out of the public eye.

The other reason given by PT officials for the tepid opposition they faced coincided more with the views of their rivals: their opponents lacked the organization necessary to derail the new budget process. The city employee with the longest experience of working with PB, Marlene Steffen (interview 4/7/99), argues that if the opposition parties wanted to cause problems in the PB, they "would have to be more organized at the base. That might even be their objective, but the problem is that they do not have a consistent enough membership to overthrow the process. They do not have that much organization." This notion was echoed by the ex-president of UAMPA, Bohn Gass (interview 3/15/99), and by Mello, the PMDB leader, who suggested that because his party was created from the top down, it did not have the local structure that would have been necessary to combat PB. According to Mello (interview 5/4/99), the PMDB "never had an organic life as a party. It always had the popular vote but never an organic life. And any party that lacks an

---

21. A computer search of *Zero Hora*'s archives I conducted on December 8, 1998, showed that in later years PB was mentioned much more frequently. From 1992 to 1996 there were 172 mentions, and from 1997 to December 1998 there were 214 mentions.

organic life has a lot of trouble mobilizing, influencing the day-to-day life of society."

In a few city districts where particular opposition parties had strongholds, resistance to PB was greater, but usually in isolated occurrences of short duration and limited impact. In one poor area of Leste, for example, two neighborhood association leaders allied with the opposition arrived at a budget meeting armed with pistols and tried to break it up. They had led their associations for decades, and to maintain their control of neighborhood politics they wanted to prevent PB from taking root. However, by the following year, new leaders had been elected to preside over the associations and the budget meetings continued unimpeded.[22] Several city councilors also attempted to discredit PB at the neighborhood level by claiming either that it was manipulative and would not work or, when the public works projects began to appear, that they themselves had pushed for those projects in the City Council.

By the time opposition leaders realized PB had started gaining popularity (in late 1991), they attempted little other than derision to combat it. As Nuñez (interview 4/12/99) recalled, "There was no resistance but there was a policy to discredit PB. They went from ignoring it to mocking it, you could say, to making jokes of PB." Even when the municipal workers' union went on a sixteen-day strike in May 1991, the opposition parties did not capitalize on this opening. At that time a coalition of leaders from across the political spectrum led the union, including some on the extreme Left who belonged to a PT faction but opposed Dutra. The administration, however, outmaneuvered this potential opposition coalition by holding a joint meeting of the municipal workers' union and the budget council. With this meeting, city officials intended to convince union leaders that their salary demands were too high and that if the administration complied with their demands, few of the public works projects decided in PB could be implemented.[23] It would not be until the late 1990s that any of the PT's opponents mounted a serious, city-wide—though ultimately unsuccessful—campaign to discredit participatory budgeting.[24]

22. Interviews with "João" (4/29/99), who called this episode part of the "folklore" of PB in Leste, and with Renato Guimarães (4/28/99), a veteran PB participant and later city councilor for the PT.

23. See Harnecker (1993, 16–19) for a detailed discussion of the strike and Schabbach (1995) for an analysis of the relationship between the union and the administration during the PT's first term in office.

24. In 1999, in view of the 2000 mayor's race, the PMDB attacked the PT's participatory budgeting program in the press and distributed a seventy-page booklet criticizing PB to community

PB After 1991: Minor Changes and Rapid Growth

Following its turnaround in 1991, participatory budgeting continued to evolve mostly in response to community groups and the administration rather than to the opposition, and participation in PB continued to grow. In 1992, the number of people participating in the budget assemblies more than doubled from the year before. With some justification, PT leaders claimed that the popularity of participatory budgeting (and the wave of public works projects that it unleashed) was one of the keys to their victory in the 1992 mayor's race. Tarso Genro, Dutra's vice-mayor and the PT's unanimous candidate, promised to maintain and expand PB, and he won the election easily.[25] During Genro's term (1993–96), PB participants and particularly budget councilors gained greater influence over more aspects of the budget process while the administration worked to attract new segments of the population and enhance PB's technical efficiency.

In Genro's first year as mayor, he recommitted the PT administration to participatory budgeting by calling on municipal department heads to dedicate themselves to attending directly to the demands of PB participants and by introducing new elements to the process to increase its scope. An early memo from Genro and his vice-mayor, Raul Pont, directed cabinet members to meet with community groups personally and warned against allowing a "bureaucratic spirit" to take over (Genro and Pont 1993). The memo appears to have been a response to complaints from PB participants that the highest-ranking administration officials did not attend the budget assemblies and failed to establish a direct relationship with the community. Genro also launched a new project alongside the budget assemblies in 1993 called the "Constituent City" (Cidade Constituinte), which consisted of a series of working groups and assemblies to discuss city-wide urban development goals and guidelines. The second round of budget assemblies

---

leaders (PMDB 1999). The attempt to discredit the process failed in that the number of participants in PB continued to grow and in that the PT won its fourth consecutive municipal election in 2000.

25. Genro received 48 percent of the valid vote, nearly 30 percentage points more than his closest rival, but not quite enough to avoid a second round of voting (runoffs were introduced in cities with over two hundred thousand voters after 1988). In the runoff election, Genro's total was 61 percent of the valid vote (calculated from Passos and Noll 1996, 51, 56, 61). How much PB contributed to Genro's success is not clear. In a 1993 survey conducted by city officials (and thus of questionable validity), only 19 percent of Porto-Alegrenses interviewed had heard of PB. Nonetheless, 66 percent considered that the PT administration "invested in poor areas" of the city, where PB had begun to direct resources (see PMPA 1993, 19, 5). Election laws, which would be changed in 1997, prohibited Dutra from running for reelection.

that year was dedicated to debating these goals. Simultaneously, city offi-cials held meetings with dozens of unions and NGOs to sound out ways of expanding PB's role in long-term strategic planning.

Two ideas guided Genro's initiatives: encouraging a wider variety of public interests to participate and encouraging PB participants to think beyond the neighborhood or district level.[26] Budget participants in the first few years largely came from neighborhood associations and other community-based groups that tended to focus on immediate local concerns, while profes-sionals, union members, and NGO activists—who presumably have wider interests—had mostly stayed away. Genro's initiatives culminated in a proposal to introduce five thematic forums parallel to the sixteen district forums already operating in PB. The five themes were Economic Development and Taxes, Circulation and Transportation, Health and Social Assistance, City Organi-zation and Urban Planning, and Education, Culture, and Sports. Like the district forums, the thematic forums would be composed of delegates selected in two rounds of open budget assemblies, and they would send four repre-sentatives to the city budget council. The emphasis of the thematic forums, however, would be on developing guidelines and long-term plans and policies for the whole city rather than on short-term projects involving individual districts. The budget council approved the administration's proposal in time for the 1994 budget assemblies, and the number of participants in PB grew with the addition of the thematic assemblies.

Further changes in PB came as a result of pressure from community leaders for greater power over the organization of participatory budgeting and over more areas of municipal spending. With the administration's consent, the budget council created two new commissions: a coordinating commis-sion (comissão paritária), composed of budget councilors and city officials, to direct the PB process in terms of setting the agenda and conducting the meetings; and a tripartite commission including a third group—represen-tatives of the municipal workers' union—to discuss city hiring of new per-sonnel. Budget delegates and councilors also demanded more training so that they could challenge the administration more effectively when their project proposals were rejected on technical grounds.

While Dutra's administration had accepted nearly all proposals decided on by PB participants regardless of their technical feasibility, under Genro city officials gradually began to deny certain proposals they deemed technically

26. Abers (2000, 84–85) seems to suggest that Genro's efforts were also at least partially in response to the opposition's claims during the 1992 election campaign that the PT admin-istration had only introduced small changes and neglected larger projects.

flawed. City housing officials would not, for instance, construct new housing on the banks of rivers or on hills with a more than 30 percent grade (see Abers 2000, 86–87; 204–9; Fedozzi 1997, 158–59). Participants chafed at these new limits on their decision-making power, and participants and city planners constantly debated the technical viability of the prioritized projects. At many budget meetings, I observed budget councilors and delegates strongly arguing with city officials who tried to defend their technical reasons for denying one or another project, and sometimes threatening officials that they would denounce the city government to *Zero Hora* if the officials did not comply with their demands. Several budget councilors and city officials I interviewed described the often intense debates. Assis Brasil (interview 12/10/98), the coordinator of the Community Relations Office in the late 1990s told me that planning officials facing PB meetings felt "like they were being thrown into a snake pit," given the ferocity with which the participants defended their demands.

Partly in response to the participants' demands for technical training and partly in response to planning officials' complaints of verbal abuse, the administration agreed to publish a set of rules (*regimento interno*) for PB that specified the technical criteria each municipal department would use to determine the viability of demands. The rulebook—first printed and distributed in the budget assemblies in 1994—also laid out the rights and responsibilities of the budget delegates and councilors as well as the formula for allocating the investments to the different districts. Since then, the budget delegates and councilors have redebated these rules every year and made significant changes, even to the technical criteria. In the 1999 debates over the rules, participants remained active in trying to push the scope of their decision-making power. One group of councilors from the Centro district planned to argue for PB influence in the city's finance committee (*junta financeira*), which estimates budget receipts and decides the timing of government spending ("Humberto," interview 12/3/98). Another group, from Leste, advocated that the administration move beyond paying for teachers at existing community day care centers and begin building new centers ("Paulo," interview 5/13/99).

In the mid-1990s, PB continued to expand despite the national trend toward recentralization and the opposition's heightened attacks. Brazil's fiscal difficulties led Fernando Henrique Cardoso, first as Itamar Franco's finance minister and then as president, to begin to reverse the decentralizing tendencies of the 1988 constitution. Cardoso's policies included a series of measures that increased federal receipts and reduced municipal receipts, such as the creation of an Emergency Social Fund (later called the Fiscal Stabilization Fund) in 1994 out of money formerly allocated for municipal transfers and the elimination of a municipal fuel tax in 1996. Despite these losses for Porto Alegre's finances, however, the city's own receipts continued to expand, which allowed the administration to maintain a relatively high rate of investment in public works projects (Augustin 1997, 91–100).

After the PT's reelection in 1992, the expansion of participation in PB, the UN Habitat award, and then the third consecutive PT victory in the 1996 municipal elections, with Raul Pont besting his nearest competitor by over 30 percentage points, opposition parties began to see a link between PB and the PT's success.[27] They were not alone. By 1996, approximately 75 percent of Porto Alegre's population had heard of participatory budgeting and over 15 percent had attended a PB meeting. Two-thirds of those who had heard of it had a positive opinion of the process, and more than four-fifths of them believed that it had contributed to the PT's victory.[28] The city government had already begun to publicize the participatory budget process more under Genro, and Pont's administration increased its exposure by advertising the annual budget assemblies on the city's bus fleet. With the growing popularity and visibility of participatory budgeting, opposition members of the City Council began to step up their attacks on the process.

Members of both the PDT and the PTB have gone as far as likening participatory budgeting to politics under Hitler and Stalin, in which the masses were manipulated to participate in large rallies. On several occasions, City Council members have attempted to introduce legislation to regulate participatory budgeting so as to reduce the percentage of the budget under PB control and increase the City Council's role. At one City Council meeting I attended (4/29/99), a PDT councilman made just such a proposal, prompting dozens of budget councilors to pressure the City Council to vote against the bill. A few budget councilors held a sign with the words "Whoever alters PB is the enemy of the people." In response, PTB Councilman Luiz Braz called the budget councilors lackeys of the administration and referred to the budget process in the following terms: "Unfortunately, the Executive uses this system so that its Nazi, fascist will . . . can grow, can be put into practice."[29] Animosity

27. Pont won the election in the first round with 55 percent of the valid vote; his closest rival received just 22 percent. (Results calculated from absolute figures provided by the Tribunal Regional Eleitoral.)

28. These estimates come from a survey of 1200 Porto-Alegrenses by Amostra (1996, 22, 27, 29–30), a locally based company that periodically conducts opinion polls for the city government.

29. City Council staff provided me with a transcript of Braz's exact words.

between opposition city councilors on the one hand, and the budget councilors and the PT administration on the other, has grown steadily since the introduction of PB. Nonetheless, despite the fact that the PT has always held a minority of seats in the City Council, the opposition never achieved enough coordination to regulate the participatory budget process and increase its own budgetary influence.

To summarize, intransigent community leaders, aided by a capable city administration and a weakly institutionalized and divided opposition, shaped PB, after its inauspicious beginning, into a powerful public program with an open design. This open design, in turn, helped PB attract tens of thousands of citizens to continue participating each year.

PB's Open Design: Sustaining and Expanding Participation

In 1990, only a few hundred people attended Porto Alegre's two rounds of district budget assemblies. Ten years later, nearly twenty thousand people attended. If one also includes the dozens of neighborhood and subdistrict assemblies held between the two district assemblies, an estimated forty thousand people participated. Key to explaining the success of PB in sustaining and expanding the number of participants is its open design, which provided citizens with a direct, accessible structure through which to make real decisions over a wide range of important issues. The open design facilitated the continuation and expansion of participation by helping community leaders overcome collective action problems. The informal structure reduces the impediments to participating and prevents the encrustation of an elite leadership. Participatory budgeting's wide range helps engage people with different needs and interests. The informal and broad nature of PB helps ensure that a diverse, representative group of citizens remains active, thus preventing it from being captured by a few organizations or distorted by partisan interests. Just as importantly, the significant decision-making power granted to participants shows them that their voices matter. Participants realize that their input can directly enhance local living conditions, and that without their participation these improvements might be lost.

Structure

The structure of participatory budgeting is based on the fundamental premises that anyone can participate in the annual rounds of budget assemblies and that everyone who does participate has the same rights to voice, to vote, and to be elected delegate to the district or thematic budget forums and subsequently to the municipal budget council.[30] Delegates to the district forums may serve repeated terms if elected, while councilors may serve two consecutive terms and may be elected again after a one-term absence. The terms last one year-long cycle of the budget process, and delegates may recall councilors with a two-thirds supermajority vote. All of the meetings at each level are open to the public. This kind of structure privileges accessibility, equality, and informality and helps build in accountability of the budget delegates and councilors to their local communities. This informal structure contrasts notably with the structure of participation in Montevideo and Caracas, in which political party members had formally guaranteed long-term positions at the highest levels and public access was somewhat limited. A description of Porto Alegre's annual participatory budget cycle will provide a clearer picture of the structure of participation and the differences with the other cities.[31]

The first round of public assemblies begins in March. In the sixteen district assemblies and five thematic assemblies, city officials distribute the current year's investment plan, provide a written accounting of implementation of the previous year's plan, and briefly present estimates of the following year's revenues and investment capability. Community participants who volunteer to speak then have three minutes each to evaluate how well the government complied with the previous year's investment plan—alternating between denunciations, complaints, and praise—and to lobby their fellow participants to prioritize specific types of investments for the next year. Typically, the previous year's most-voted-for councilor either begins or concludes the list of between ten and twenty community speakers and exhorts the attendees to continue participating throughout the year. In the last part of the assembly, members of the mayor's cabinet may respond to questions and the mayor closes with a short speech of five to ten minutes. Finally, city officials announce how many delegates each neighborhood association or other community group is entitled to, based on the level of attendance.

---

30. The major exceptions are elected officials and party-designated municipal workers (see PMPA 1999, 7).

31. The following description is based on the PB cycle existing from 1990 to 2000. Giacomoni (1993, 126–29) provides a quite similar account of PB assemblies in 1992 and throughout his text notes the informality of PB. Since 2000, some modifications have been made, including the introduction of demand making through the Internet and the elimination of the second round of assemblies. For a description of the current process, see http://www2.portoalegre.rs.gov.br/op/.

Organizations that mobilize more people to attend earn greater numbers of delegates. The rulebook lays out a declining proportional system, beginning with one delegate for every ten attendees up to the first one hundred partici-pants, and ending with one for every forty after four hundred (PMPA 1999, 6). In 1999, attendance at the first-round assemblies averaged 712 people per district/theme, with a minimum of 326, in the Sul district, and a maximum of 1,885, in Lomba do Pinheiro (Pont 2000, 27, table IV). Once they know how many delegates they have earned, community groups choose their delegates either by voting—if there are few slots and many applicants—or by accepting whoever volunteers. In my experience attending neighborhood-level meetings, the latter pattern always prevailed; convincing residents to participate on a regular basis never appeared easy. For example, in a neigh-borhood association meeting in the Cruzeiro district (4/21/99), the associ-ation's president announced that given their participation at the district assembly, their members had the right to five delegates. He then asked, "Who wants to be a delegate?" When only one person volunteered, the president had to persuade four other members to volunteer by telling them, "Come on, I know you have time to come to meetings on Wednesday nights." As many participants told me, PB is time consuming and completely voluntary; delegates and councilors do not receive a salary, bus fare, nor even a little cup of coffee (*nem um cafezinho*).

Importantly, individuals without associational ties can also become dele-gates. Before the assemblies, residents from the same street or neighborhood frequently form ad hoc committees, usually for the purpose of pursuing a specific demand and sometimes with the help of the district coordinators or workers from the CARs. If enough neighbors come together, they can select a delegate to represent them in the district budget forum. Thus, PB's informal structure tends to encourage the formation of new organizations among the previously unorganized (see chapter 6). In the first round of assemblies in 1998, approximately a third of the participants, and 10 percent of the delegates, were not members of preexisting associations (CIDADE 1999, 68, 81).

Following the first round of assemblies, each district holds an intermediate round of meetings in which the prioritizing of local investment needs takes place. These intermediate assemblies are held at the neighborhood level, and in about half the districts again at the subdistrict level, before a final district-wide assembly. An intermediate round of thematic assemblies is also held, organized by subtheme or by association. The prior year's budget councilors organize and run these meetings, often helped by the district or thematic PB coordinator from the Community Relations Office. The exact manner in which the intermediate meetings are conducted varies across the city, but in each case participants rank their sectoral needs—street paving versus education versus health care—and determine which precise projects within these sectors should be prioritized, thus creating a comprehensive list of local demands.[32] Attendance at these meetings is also used to allocate an additional number of delegates to the district budget forum. The final assembly of the intermediate round is, in most districts, reserved for delegates, and its purpose is to aggregate the neighborhood or subdistrict lists to create a single set of prioritized demands for the entire district.

In May and June, the second round of assemblies is held, in which all participants in each district and theme present their list of demands to the mayor and his cabinet and then elect representatives to the municipal budget council. In many districts, usually only one slate (*chapa*) of candidates runs in these elections, which again highlights the difficulty of recruiting volunteers to participate on a more permanent basis. Where two slates run, a proportional system determines the distribution of the four seats between the slates. To obtain one seat, a slate needs at least 25 percent of the vote (PMPA 1999, 6). After the second round concludes, the budget delegates and councilors continue meeting regularly throughout the fiscal year, with a summer break. The budget council meets twice weekly, and its sessions cover nearly all aspects of the municipal budget, including the annual budget law (*Lei de Diretrizes Orçamentárias*) and investment plan, the execution of the current year's budget, tax policy, the application of extrabudgetary funds, and the hiring of new personnel. In the monthly or biweekly meetings of the district and thematic forums, the delegates' major topics are defending demands against any challenges from city officials that they do not meet the technical criteria laid out in the rulebook and questions concerning why specific demands from the current year's investment plan have not yet been carried out or have been executed poorly. In a little over half the district and thematic forums, the delegates have also created at least one separate commission dedicated to a specific issue, and most of these have several, such as Restinga, with one commission for each of the five major themes. After

---

32. The differences among the meetings involve whether to prioritize the sectors or the projects first, whether each sector is discussed or only the most urgent sectors, and the degree to which more experienced community leaders direct the meeting. This last issue ranges from situations in which a neighborhood activist will present his or her own preferred ranking and then ask participants to vote, to completely open debates with multiple viewpoints on how to prioritize the projects and sectors. Most meetings I attended in 1999 ran more closely to this second scenario.

Structure of participatory budgeting since 1995

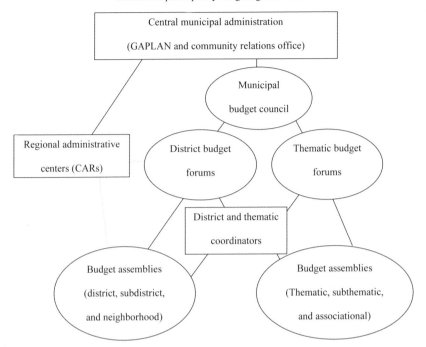

*Rectangular shapes indicate that the structure is part of the executive branch; circular shapes indicate that the structure is independent. Dashed lines indicate less consistent interaction than whole lines.

Fig. 5.1 Structure of participatory budgeting

the final budget documents have been approved in November, the municipal budget council and each of the district and thematic forums discuss the rules governing PB and sometimes propose and vote on changes.

Overall, the structure of participatory budgeting provides citizens with a direct, informal channel through which to pursue their demands on the city government. Rather than a formal, party-selected set of leaders being imposed at the top of the structure as in Caracas and Montevideo, the delegates and municipal budget councilors directly represent and are accountable to the participants at the structure's lower level.

Range

The wide range of significant issues the public debates within Porto Alegre's PB also distinguishes it from the participatory programs in the other cities.

Because of the greater degree of national decentralization in Brazil, Porto Alegre's city government provides more services than its counterparts in Montevideo and especially Caracas, and thus can potentially welcome citizen input on a broader range of issues. Community leaders within PB have continually attempted to ensure that the city government made use of this potential. The types of demands that can be made through PB have thus grown over the years, although during the first decade participants nearly always ranked the same three municipal services as their top priorities: sewage, street paving, and housing.

The range of participation is also broader in Porto Alegre's budget process compared to the other cities in the sense that PB encompasses several decisional areas: expenditure decisions, policy making, and operational practices (Burns, Hambleton, and Hoggett 1994, 160). The priorities established in the district assemblies determine the expenditures made in each district. The aggregated lists of priorities from the different districts shape the city government's resource allocation across the districts and among the different sectors, and the deliberations of the municipal budget council affect government policy making on other issues as well, including tax policy and the level of investment. The thematic forums contribute to the policy-making and operational practices of specific municipal departments. For example, in 1998 the thematic forum for Education, Sports, and Culture debated with the municipal education and social assistance departments over the community day care center policy in general and the specific rules concerning which centers qualify for government support and how the centers should be managed. Overall, PB's wide range of issues and decisional areas makes it attractive to citizens with diverse needs and interests.

Decision-Making Power

The last element of PB's design is the high degree of decision-making power it offers participants. Porto Alegre stands out in comparison to the other cities in terms of how much power is granted and to which types of participants. As is true of the programs in Caracas and Montevideo, PB assigns an array of roles to those who participate, from receiving and providing information to providing opinions and proposals. Participatory budgeting differs in allowing participants more opportunities to go beyond proposing to making real decisions.

Some of these decisions are binding on the city government, most importantly the lists of prioritized projects from the district assemblies. Assembly participants select and rank these projects, the delegates vote on the final list, and neither the government nor the budget council may make alterations to these spending priorities. Certain specific projects contained in the lists may of course violate the technical criteria laid out in the rulebook. When this occurs, the city agency responsible may veto the project, but usually proposes changes in the project to the district delegates in order to meet the criteria (Abers 2000, 203–4). Other decisions, particularly those of the budget council concerning broader policy issues, are subject to the mayor's veto. The budget council may overturn the veto with a two-thirds majority, but the final decision rests with the mayor (PMPA 1999, 10). In practice, the mayor almost never uses the veto; instead, city officials usually negotiate with the budget councilors until some agreement can be reached. As Abers (2000, 199–203) observes, for many city-wide policy issues the budget council approves the executive's proposals without lengthy debate, but on occasion challenges the government and demands—and often wins—changes.

Thus, citizens at all levels of PB—from assembly participants to delegates and councilors—play deliberative roles, discussing, debating, proposing, and most importantly, deciding on significant issues. Volunteer participants make the key decisions about neighborhood spending, rather than party members and city officials as in Caracas and Montevideo.

The notion that participatory budgeting is an avenue for effective decision making is supported by results from a variety of surveys of PB participants and of the public in general. In 1995 and again in 1998, surveys carried out by a local NGO asked participants in the district and thematic assemblies whether "the people who participate in PB really decide concerning the projects and services."[33] In each year, over 60 percent of the respondents circled "always" or "almost always." A quarter of the respondents answered that the participants decide "sometimes," a tenth did not know, and fewer than 3 percent answered "never." Another question the surveys asked was "Do the community's representatives in PB (delegates and councilors) respect the demands defined by the community and work towards achieving them?" The results in both years were again similar: over two-thirds of the participants surveyed answered "always" or "almost always," around 15 percent circled "sometimes," about a tenth did not know, and between 1 and 4 percent answered "never." A large majority of those who participate in the assemblies thus agree that their decisions count.

33. The results of the surveys can be found in CIDADE (1995; 1999). My calculations from these sources do not include those who did not respond to the question.

Table 5.1   Opinion of participatory budgeting

	1994	1995	2000
PB . . .			
Respects the decisions taken by the participants		44%	64%
Does not respect the decisions taken by			
the participants		27%	26%
(Didn't know / didn't respond)		29%	10%
PB . . .			
Contributes to a better distribution of public resources	71%	68%	
Does not contribute to a better distribution of			
public resources	6%	11%	
(Didn't know / didn't respond)	24%	21%	
N	555	745	600

The questions in these polls were asked only of those respondents who had heard of participatory budgeting: in 1994, 555 of 1200 respondents knew of PB (46 percent); in 1996, 745 of 1229 (61 percent); and in 2000, apparently it was assumed that all of the respondents knew of PB. The full results are reported in Ethos (1994; 1995) and Meta (2000a).

The results of opinion polls show that the majority of Porto-Alegrenses also see participatory budgeting as an arena in which the participants' decisions are respected and important. Table 5.1 illustrates a sample of these surveys. Other surveys, asking related but differently worded questions, reveal similar results (Amostra 1993, 35; 1996, 25; 1997, 29).

Finally, in a series of interviews with budget councilors, I asked an open-ended question: "What criticisms do you have of PB, or how could it be improved?" Of the twenty-nine responses, not one complained of lacking power or called for greater power for PB. This is in marked contrast with the responses to a similar question by the local councilors in Montevideo, for whom lack of power was one of the two most frequent complaints. The other major criticism in Montevideo was the lack of participation (tied for lack of power with 28 percent of local councilors), while just 10 percent of Porto Alegre's budget councilors mentioned a need for greater participation. For the budget councilors, the main problems with PB were not lack of decision-making power or lack of participation, but rather the overly bureaucratized and technical nature of the process and the slowness with which the government implemented the prioritized projects (see figure 5.2).

Overcoming Collective Action Problems

How and why does PB's open design stimulate widespread participation? My central argument is that the open design makes clearly apparent the

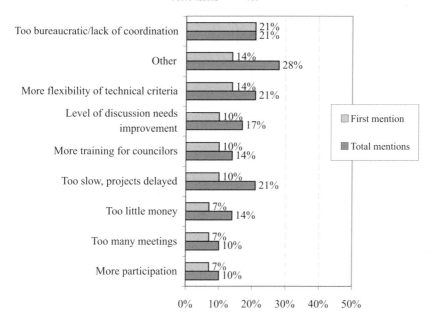

Too bureaucratic/lack of coordination 21% 21%

Other 14% 28%

More flexibility of technical criteria 14% 21%

Level of discussion needs improvement 10% 17%

More training for councilors 10% 14%

Too slow, projects delayed 10% 21%

Too little money 7% 14%

Too many meetings 7% 10%

More participation 7% 10%

First mention

Total mentions

0% 10% 20% 30% 40% 50%

Fig. 5.2 How could the PB be improved?

link between an individual's participation and the realization of public works projects that he or she demands. By reinforcing this link, PB's open design avoided two common collective action problems that plagued the programs in the other cities: lack of participation because residents doubt its effectiveness and lack of participation because residents think others will participate for them. The wide range of issues open for discussion within PB and the high degree of decision-making power it allows show residents that participation is effective, and the informal structure, in which all participants have equal chances to make neighborhood- and district-level decisions without privileging some interests over others, makes clear that each voice counts. The results of a series of surveys of PB participants by local NGOs—as well as of my own observations of meetings and interviews— suggest that these features helped to encourage an ever-growing number of broadly representative participants.

For instance, given PB's wide range of issues, citizens with interests that vary extensively—whether related to one or another specific municipal service, to a particular neighborhood demand, or to more general city government policies—may be drawn to participate. At the annual public assemblies, people and groups from all walks of local life show up. The variety of groups that participate is enormous and includes, among dozens of others, samba schools, fishing cooperatives, mothers' clubs, homeless rights advocates, the Gaúcho traditionalist movement, local business associations, Catholic educators, soccer clubs, the organization for the physically handicapped, *capoeira* instructors, recyclers, the taxi drivers' union, and a punk movement (which was seeking funding for community-operated radio stations). In 1998, 67 percent of those surveyed at PB assemblies participated in a civil society organization of some kind, which compares to about 38 percent of Porto Alegre's population in general (CIDADE 1999, 67; Santos Junior 2000). The most popular type of organizations included neighborhood associations (41 percent), religious or cultural groups (9 percent), unions (5 percent), popular councils (4 percent), and community centers (3 percent) (CIDADE 1999, 68). When asked in which organization they participated most, respondents provided quite similar answers. For example, 48 percent of participants, 56 percent of delegates, and 55 percent of councilors selected neighborhood associations (my calculations from CIDADE 1999, 68, 83).

At the same time, the informal structure of PB has helped ensure that participants at all levels of the participatory budgeting process not only represent a variety of civil society organizations, but also reflect Porto Alegre's population in terms of class, race, gender, and party affiliation fairly well, albeit with some degree of overrepresentation of people from lower income brackets (see below). The accessibility of public assemblies and meetings, which are widely advertised and scheduled on nights or weekends in locations around the city—and at the larger assemblies often include some form of entertainment and child care as well as a sign language interpreter—encourages participation by a broad spectrum of people. The informal process through which delegates are selected, as described above, makes it relatively easy for anyone to become a delegate if she or he wishes to do so, and thus facilitates the maintenance of diversity in the district and thematic forums. And the short terms, recall mechanism, term limits, proportional electoral method, and public nature of all meetings each help ensure that PB councilors continue to represent the diversity of their communities, as delegates and participants can use these measures to hold councilors accountable. Indeed, turnover in budget council seats is fairly high. From 1991 to 2002, each year new councilors obtained an average of 66 percent of the seats (my calculations from CIDADE 2007b, 4). In turn, this high replacement rate, combined with the short terms and lack of privileges for budget councilors, may help to dissuade political parties from investing much energy in encouraging their activists to participate. Since the early years of PB, the unwritten rule has been that discussing party politics in any budget meeting is prohibited (Giacomoni 1993, 127–28). In my interviews with budget councilors, they overwhelmingly agreed (82 percent) that party politics did not enter into the discussion.

The results of surveys of budget assembly participants show that the lower and lower-middle classes are generally overrepresented in PB. Nonetheless, though most participants still come from lower income and education brackets, the percentage of participants with higher socioeconomic status has increased over the years. The addition of the thematic budget forums in 1994 seems to have worked to attract the middle classes, as the education and income levels of participants in the thematic assemblies are substantially higher than those in the district assemblies (CIDADE 2003, 16–17). Comparing the surveys across the years, one can see a general progression from the clear overrepresentation of the lower classes to a situation somewhat closer to equal representation across classes. In 1993, 15 percent of the population but 38 percent of PB participants lived in households earning up to one minimum salary; on the other side, 28 percent of the population but only 16 percent of PB participants came from households earning more than five minimum salaries (Fedozzi and Nuñez 1993). In the late 1990s and early 2000s, there was greater parity in participation rates across income brackets, though the top bracket always participated at lower rates (see Fedozzi 2007, 20). In 2002, the vast majority of participants—69 percent—had a family income of less than four minimum salaries, which compared to an average family income for Porto Alegre "estimated around 6 minimum salaries" (CIDADE 2003, 27). Budget delegates and councilors tend to have incomes that more closely match those of Porto Alegre residents. In 2002, 57 percent of Porto Alegre's population, 55 percent of PB delegates, and 50 percent of PB councilors had a family income of less than four minimum salaries (CIDADE 2003, 26; Fedozzi 2007, 20).

As with income levels, education levels have risen slightly over time and across degrees of participation. For example, the percentage of participants with education beyond high school increased from 8 percent in 1993 to 16 percent in 1998, while the percentage with up to a primary education dropped from 69 to 61 percent (see Fedozzi and Nuñez 1993; CIDADE 2003, 23). According to the 2000 census, about 54 percent of Porto Alegre's population had up to a primary education (Fedozzi 2007, 17). Budget delegates and councilors generally possess higher levels of education than do assembly participants. In 2002, 28 percent of participants, 31 percent of delegates, and 48 percent of councilors had at least a high school degree, compared to 37 percent of the population (CIDADE 2003, 23; Fedozzi 2007, 17).

Survey results also indicate that Afro-Brazilians are well represented in participatory budgeting. While the 2000 census indicates that 17 percent of the population in Porto Alegre self-identifies as black (*negro* or *pardo*), in 2002 23 percent of participants, 26 percent of delegates, and 24 percent of councilors did the same (Fedozzi 2007, 18–19). This figure has not changed much over time (see CIDADE 1995, 6). The relatively high percentage of participants who are Afro-Brazilian does not reflect a strategy by black leaders or a particular policy initiative on the local government's part (Tális Rosa interview, 11/10/98). Rather, figures for participation broken down by income bracket presented by CIDADE (2003, 19) suggest that it is class more than race that drives the higher participation rates of Afro-Brazilians in participatory budgeting.

With regard to gender, survey results show that the role of women has increased at all levels of PB over the years. Women made up roughly 47 percent of PB assembly participants in 1993 and 1995, 51 percent in 1998, and 56 percent in 2000 and again 2002, compared to the 2000 census figure of 53 percent (Fedozzi 2007, 16). In 1995, about 41 percent of delegates were women, and this figure grew to 45 percent in 1998 and to 61 percent in 2002 (CIDADE 1995, 31; 1999, 73; 2003, 18). A separate study of all budget councilors since 1990 (CIDADE 2007a, 9) shows that throughout the 1990s women generally garnered between one-fifth and one-third of council seats, reaching parity (49 percent) only in 2002. Thus, while women have become predominant as assembly participants and delegates, they have been underrepresented on the budget council until recently. Nonetheless, almost exactly equal percentages of women and men report that they regularly speak at PB meetings, from the large public assemblies to the municipal budget council (my calculations from CIDADE 2003, 18, 51). Furthermore, women have achieved much greater representation on the budget council than they have on the city council or in state and national governments. In 1988, only 3 percent of Porto Alegre's city councilors were women, and this figure rose to only 18 percent in 2000 (Moritz 2001, 4). And even by 2002, despite gender quotas for party candidates, only one in ten representatives in state legislative assemblies and the national congress were women (Nogueira and Lopes 2008, 6548).

In terms of partisanship, between 1995 and 2002, the percentage of PB assembly participants who belonged to a party ranged from 4 to 8 percent, roughly similar to the 6 percent for the general population of Porto Alegre according to the 1996 census (CIDADE 2003, 54; Carlos and Zorzal 2006, 173). Party membership was higher among budget delegates and councilors; in 2000, approximately 22 percent of delegates and 33 percent of councilors belonged to a political party, though in 2002 these percentages dropped to 13 and 20, respectively (Baierle 2002, 9).[34] And unlike in Montevideo, where local councilors (roughly equivalent to district delegates) overwhelmingly preferred the incumbent party, in Porto Alegre about 50 percent of delegates and councilors preferred the PT in 2000 (CIDADE 2003, 55). This is not much different from assembly participants, of whom 39 percent preferred the PT, and from Porto Alegre's population, of whom about 37 percent preferred the PT (CIDADE 2003, 55; my calculations from Rodrigues 2000). On the whole, then, participatory budgeting attracted a more or less representative group of Porto-Alegrenses. But how did it succeed in making the number of participants grow?

A particularly important feature of PB's design, one that helped community leaders overcome their neighbors' initial inertia, is that the locus of key decision making is in the neighborhood- and subdistrict-level budget assemblies. Participants in these assemblies prioritize the types of investments needed and select delegates who will decide on the distribution of public works projects throughout the district's neighborhoods. Delegates take into account neighborhood size and level of poverty, and they often try to make decisions by consensus. Yet most decisions come down to a vote. What this means is that the more residents a neighborhood leader mobilizes for the budget assemblies, the more delegates the neighborhood (or association) will have and the more likely they will be to secure public works projects. And because many meetings take place in relatively small subdistricts or neighborhoods, a minor increment in the number of participants can mean the difference between winning and losing a particular project. Therefore, once PB's basic design had been agreed upon and the city government had the capacity to invest in public works, activists could convince their neighbors that if they participated in budget assemblies in large numbers, they could obtain paved streets or underground sewage connections, or a new school or health clinic; and if they did not participate, these projects would go to a different neighborhood in the district. In other words, activists could persuasively claim that individual participation is both effective and nontransferable.

---

34. One of CIDADE's principal researchers, Sérgio Baierle, provided me with the figures for 2002.

Methodologically, it would be impossible to directly test this open design argument within Porto Alegre, as all sixteen PB districts shared the same design. Yet one can examine corollaries. If it is correct to argue that PB's open design stimulated participation by clearly linking individual participation to concrete results, three corollary claims should hold. First, participants in budget assemblies should be driven more by needs (or desires) for tangible public works projects and less by abstract ideas, such as beliefs in radical democracy or community empowerment. Second, the delivery of these tangible projects should engender greater levels of participation. And third, in more populous districts or neighborhoods, where each individual's involvement is less consequential, participation rates should be lower than in smaller districts, where each individual has a greater chance of affecting the outcome. Surveys, interviews, and statistical analysis of budgetary and demographic data provide confirmatory evidence for these three claims.

> 1. *In general, those involved in PB tend to be from districts*
> *that are underserved by public services, and they*
> *participate because they want to achieve specific demands.*

When I asked budget councilors who participates most in their districts' assemblies, nearly uniformly they responded that it was the poor, the lower-middle class, and the people with the most needs. The survey results reported above bear out their answers regarding income. And my own analysis of Porto Alegre's sixteen PB districts illustrates that higher participation rates are also correlated with low levels of public services. That is, in districts lacking services, the percentage of the district population participating in budget assemblies increases, as figures 5.3 and 5.4 show. The Pearson correlation coefficient between the percentage of streets unpaved and the rate of participation was .72 and between the percentage of domiciles without a sewage connection and the rate of participation was .84, and both were highly statistically significant at $p < .001$.[35] Generally, higher percentages of

---

35. I calculated the participation rates from the participation figures provided in Pont (2000, 27, table IV) and population figures in GAPLAN (1993; 1998). For calculations in all the statistical analyses presented in this chapter, I took the higher number of participants from the two rounds of district budget assemblies. This is a conservative estimate of the number of participants. It avoids double counting those people who participate in both rounds of assemblies, but it also ignores those who participate in only the smaller of the two assemblies and it obviously does not count all those who participate in the intermediate rounds of subdistrict assemblies. The percentage of miles of streets not paved comes from GAPLAN (1993). The figure for domiciles without adequate sewerage (not connected to the city sewage system and lacking a septic tank) comes from FESC (1997, table 23). This indicator was only available in 1991 and calculated for the districts as of the 1996 district boundaries.

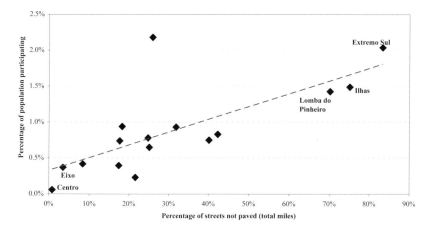

Fig. 5.3 Underserved population and budget assembly participation (1993)

residents participate in underserved districts, such as Extremo Sul, Nordeste, Lomba do Pinheiro, and Ilhas (which merged into another district in 1995), than in districts where needs for infrastructure are not so great, such as Centro, Eixo da Baltazar, and Noroeste (which was created in 1995 out of parts of Centro and Eixo).

The fact that members of the lower classes from underserved districts participate in higher numbers underscores the responses from participants to the question of why they participate in the budget assemblies. The most frequent answer is "to make a demand," whether for the participant's neighborhood, district, or association, or for himself. Although many respondents cite several reasons for participating, including a desire to serve the community or improve local democracy, most respondents say they participate in order to demand specific public works projects or improvements in particular public services. Figure 5.5 compares results of CIDADE's 1995 and 1998 budget assembly surveys with those from my interviews with budget councilors of the 1998–99 PB cycle.[36] In each case, multiple responses were allowed, so the percentages do not add to 100.

36. For the 1995 and 1998 survey results, see CIDADE (1995; 1999, 44, 100–101). I made minor changes in the grouping of answers. In figure 5.5, "Make a demand" includes demands or references to projects for the city, a district, a neighborhood, a street, or for a specific service, as well as "participate to get something" and "personal demand." (In 1995 and 1998, CIDADE considered the last two of these as separate categories.) "Democratic ideals" includes references to participation, democracy, citizenship, rights, struggle, unity, and solidarity. (In 1995 and 1998, CIDADE considered generic references to participation a separate category.) "Serve the community" includes references to serving the neighborhood, district,

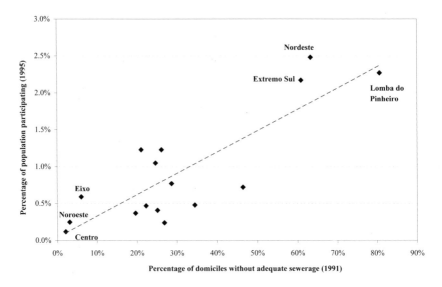

Fig. 5.4 Underserved population and budget assembly participation, by district (1995)

"Participating for demands" was always the most common response. This consistency across the three surveys is impressive, given that they were taken in different years and had different sample sizes. The less impressive differences in the three survey results may be attributed to slight differences in the exact questions asked and, most likely, to the timing of the surveys. The 1995 survey was carried out during the second round of district and thematic assemblies, when participants elect budget councilors, while the 1998 survey took place during the first round of assemblies, when participants begin debating their investment priorities, and my 1998/1999 interviews with budget councilors asked why they first participated in the participatory budget process, rather than why they attended the budget assembly on a particular day or why they participate in general. The difference in the timing probably explains the higher percentage of respondents in 1995 who answered that they participated in order to vote (14 percent), since the main purpose of the second round of assemblies is to elect budget councilors. This difference may also explain why fewer respondents in 1995 said they were participating in order to make a demand, although this answer remained the

_____

or association, and references to being in a position of leadership or being a member of an association. (In 1995 and 1998, CIDADE considered the last two as a separate category from serving the community.) The other categories in figure 5.5 contain each of the responses in the label.

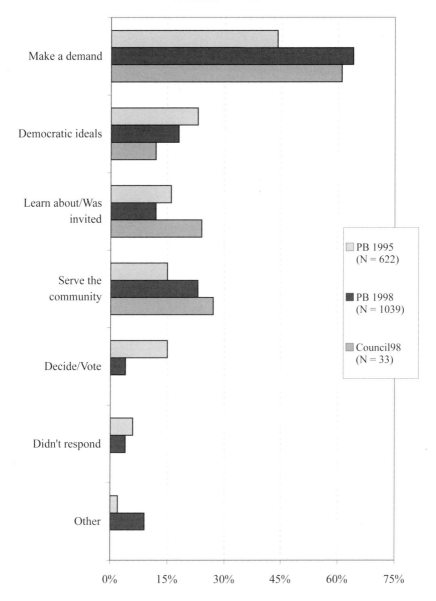

Fig. 5.5 Why do you participate in PB assemblies?

most common. In general, while both assembly participants and budget councilors give many reasons for participating, the pursuit of objective results stands out as the primary motivation.

The first claim within my argument thus appears to be substantiated: participation is mostly driven by need or desire for concrete improvements.

If participation were motivated mostly by other forces, it would not make sense to argue that PB's open design stimulated participation by linking individual participation to material outcomes.

2. *As investments in city services and public works projects increase, overall participation grows over time, and districts where investments are greater experience higher rates of participation.*

As the early history of PB shows, Porto Alegre's community activists initially faced collective action problems, just as their counterparts in Montevideo and Caracas would later on. Porto-Alegrenses did not mobilize in great numbers for the budget assemblies at the beginning, but had to be convinced to participate over several years, as nearly all my interviewees reported. Several longtime PB activists told me that motivating community members to participate was the principal challenge in the first several years. One veteran from a lower-class neighborhood in the Leste district reported,

> The [PB] meetings are farther away from the *vila* [neighborhood] and more frequent for the delegates, and it was difficult for my *vila* to get the delegates to go to the meetings. The *vila* only really started to participate after a big effort to make the community conscious of the necessity of their participating in those meetings. And that effort took four years. . . . We tried to convince them that if we have needs, we have to participate in order to improve the quality of life in the *vila,* and if we participate, we can win some demands. And gradually the people started going. ("Paulo," interview 5/13/99)

Large numbers of residents only began to participate after new paved streets, sewage pipes, and housing projects began to appear in different neighborhoods across the city. As "Gloria" (interview 11/26/98), a budget councilor from Partenon, told me, "It's where the benefits appear that people are stimulated to participate more, because people really like to see the things happen first before they get involved." It was not until around the beginning of 1991 that many public works projects began to be completed. In that year, the number of participants jumped tremendously, and participation continued growing in the following decade as city residents saw the transformation of adjacent neighborhoods and districts. The recollections of "Regina" (interview 12/7/98), a multiterm budget councilor from Humaitá/Navegantes/Ilhas who had participated in each of her district's budget assemblies since 1989, were typical. She told me, "My *vila* didn't have water, didn't have electricity, it didn't have anything. And I went to participate and I got all those things and then the other *vilas* started participating."

Like the correlation between residents' needs and PB participation, the connection between increases in city investments in public works projects and growth of participation in the participatory budget process that PB veterans report can also be tested using statistical analysis. I examined the relationship between the annual planned total city spending on investments (measured in current U.S. dollars) with the number of participants in the annual district and thematic budget assemblies, taking 1989 as the starting point for investment spending and 1999 as the end point (the number of cases was thus 11). The logic is that investments planned the previous year (in 1991 for example) are carried out in the following year (1992), stimulating the first year's participants to participate again to make sure what they demanded was implemented, and encouraging new participants among residents who saw public-works projects completed in other city neighborhoods.[37] The results of this analysis showed that investment spending and participation in budget assemblies are highly correlated: the Pearson correlation coefficient between the two is .87, and this result is statistically significant at $p < .001$.[38] Because each year many projects are not completed until after June (when the second round of budget assemblies takes place), I also tested the relationship between spending planned for Time 1 (1991, for example) and participation at Time 2 (in the example, 1992). The results were similar to the original analysis, but slightly stronger: the Pearson correlation coefficient was .91 and the relationship was again highly statistically significant.

The findings from the two correlational analyses suggest that both the hope that one's planned project from the previous year will be completed

---

37. For this analysis, I took planned spending on investments from the city government's annual investments plans from 1991 to 1999 (PMPA, 1991–99). Unlike many Brazilian cities, where much of the money planned for investments is not spent, in Porto Alegre, nearly 100 percent of planned projects are completed, if not in the year planned, then in later years (see http://www2.portoalegre.rs.gov.br/op/, click on Prestação de Contas and Acompanhamento de Obras, where one can find every project planned since 1990, along with information about the current stage of the project [such as completed, underway, in the bidding process, or under study]). For 1989 and 1990, I estimated the investments using the figures listed in the city government's Statistical Yearbook (PMPA, 1997, 191, 121) for central administration investments and a percentage of the revenues for the indirect administration's individual departments (water and sewage, housing, garbage collection, and social assistance) based on an average of the percentage of revenues planned for investments in the following three years.

38. To be sure the relationship was robust, I ran the correlation analysis using just the figures from 1991 through 1999 (eliminating the two estimated data points), and the results were essentially identical to the full 1989–99 analysis (the correlation coefficient was .90).

and the actual completion of projects stimulated city residents to participate in the budget assemblies. This corresponds to the facts that many budget assembly participants return frequently and that PB also attracts thousands of new participants each year. Generally, between 50 and 60 percent of budget assembly participants each year have participated in prior years, and between 10 and 15 percent have participated in at least six of the previous years (Fedozzi and Nuñez 1993, 13; CIDADE 1995, 8–9; 1999, 69).

Figure 5.6 displays the data from the correlational analyses and illustrates that when investments grew from one year to the next, in most cases the number of participants grew in the following year. For example, while the dollars planned for investments grew from $33 million in 1990 to $60 million in 1991, the number of participants jumped from 3,086 in 1991 to 6,168 in 1992. The figure also suggests that the correlation between spending and participation is not merely a function of time; that is, that both simply grew over time. The drop in investment spending from 1998 to 1999 (from $130 million to $121 million), for example, corresponds to the falling off in participation from 1999 to 2000 (down 575 participants). And the similar drop in spending from 1994 to 1995 corresponds to the decrease in participation from 1995 to 1996.

Another method of testing the relationship between investment spending and participation is to compare across city districts. For this analysis, I divided the cases into pre- and post-1995, the year the districts were reorganized. The analysis tested the relationship across the districts between the average amount of investment spending planned per capita between 1991 and 1994 and the average percentage of the population participating in the district budget assemblies during the same years.[39] I repeated this analysis for the years between 1995 and 2000. The Pearson correlation coefficients were again quite high: .83 for the 1991–94 period and .75 for the 1995–2000 period. Figures 5.7 and 5.8 present the data for these analyses, and show that, by and large, in districts where per capita spending on investments is greater, the rate of participation is also higher.

The evidence suggests that the expectation and delivery of public works projects are strongly related to the level of participation, and this can be seen both over time and across city districts.

39. The analysis did not include the years 1989 and 1990 because the investments for 1989 were planned prior to the initiation of participatory budgeting, and the only 1990 investment plan available (the one on the city government Web site) does not include the monetary value of the projects listed.

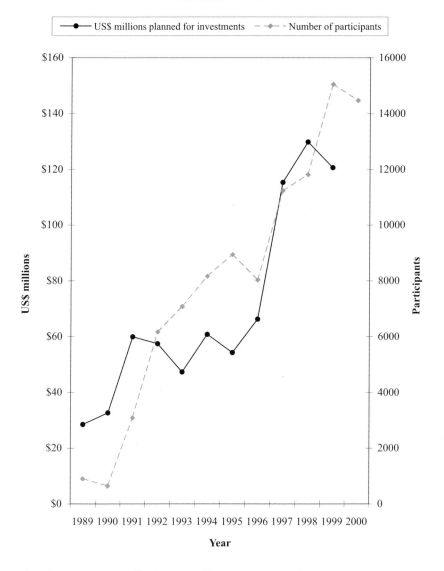

Fig. 5.6   Investments and budget assembly participation, 1989–2000

3. The rate of participation in heavily populated districts is lower than the rate of participation in districts with smaller numbers of inhabitants.

A final set of correlational analyses tested the relationship between the size of each district's population and the rate of participation in the annual budget assemblies. I analyzed the data for each year between 1992 and 2000. The

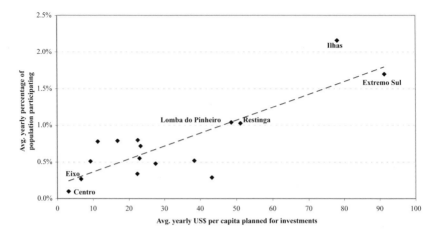

Fig. 5.7 Investments planned and budet assembly participation, by district (1991–1994)

results indicated that districts with larger populations tend to have lower rates of participation, though the Pearson correlation coefficients for population size were not as high as for the other variables tested earlier (level of need and investments). The correlation between district population size and the percentage of the population participating in budget assemblies ranged from -.52 to -.65, and the correlation was always statistically significant at p < .01. Figures 5.9 and 5.10 present the data for two years (1993, when the correlation was -.55 and 1998, when it was -.53), showing that participation rates were usually higher in districts with smaller populations.

The interview, survey, and correlational data analyses thus all provide evidence for the three claims: participation is driven by need for infrastructure and public services, delivery of the projects demanded engenders further participation, and participation rates are higher where the connection between individual involvement and results is most clear (in the less populous city districts). These findings support the central argument, that PB's ability to sustain and expand the number of participants derives from its direct linking of individual involvement to the provision of public works projects. This interpretation also corresponds to what several PB veterans reiterated to me in interviews. A founder of the Popular Council of Partenon and long-time PB activist told me, "The key to success is that the people can say 'I discussed that project in my neighborhood. The money I paid in taxes is being invested in a project that I helped discuss'" ("Edilson," interview 3/23/99). And a budget councilor from the Centro district argued similarly: "The key is the completion of the public works projects. . . . What is important to

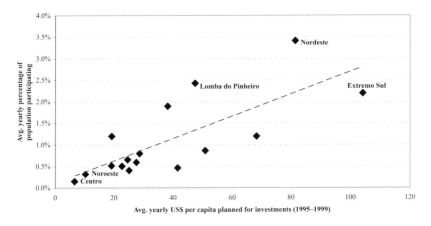

Fig. 5.8 Investments planned and budget assembly participation (1995–2000)

highlight is this: those who participate get something; those who don't, do not" ("Humberto," interview 12/3/98).

A question that remains after viewing the correlational evidence from the city districts is whether each of the three "variables"—degree of need, concrete results, and district population size—actually contributes to higher participation rates, or if any of the correlations are spurious. In other words, if one controls for the size of the district population, will the relationship between lack of public services and the participation rate disappear? Or, why do Nordeste, Extremo Sul, and Lomba do Pinheiro have higher participation rates than the other districts? Is it because their lack of public services is greater, because they receive more or bigger and more expensive public works projects, or because they have smaller populations?

To answer these questions, I used ordinary least squares regression analysis of data from the sixteen city districts. The dependent variable was the percentage of the district population participating in the annual district budget assemblies. The independent variables were also taken from the correlational analyses presented above. I measured level of need by percentage of total miles of streets not paved because this was the only indicator available on an annual basis (from 1993 forward) and because it was highly correlated with other less frequently measured indicators (such as percentage of domiciles without adequate sewage services).[40] Investment spending from

---

40. The correlation coefficient between unpaved streets (1995) and lack of sewage connections (1991) was .86, which is highly statistically significant.

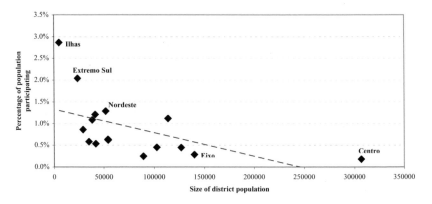

Fig. 5.9   Population size and budget assembly participation (1993)

the current and the previous year were tested separately and then jointly, such that there were three different models. Each district-year was considered a separate case, and, using the data available from the period between 1989 and 2000, the total number of cases was either 110 or 111, depending on the variables in the model. Table 5.2 presents the regression coefficients and standard errors for the three models, and it shows that the relationships found in the correlational analyses presented above were not spurious. Each of the independent variables is statistically significant in each model (except for population size in model 3). On the whole, residents of districts with greater levels of need, higher amounts of investment spending, and relatively small populations participate in budget assemblies at higher rates.

The level of need variable shows that for every 10-percentage-point increase in the number of miles of streets not paved, participation increases by a little less than 0.2 percent. Given that on average, there are around 81,000 residents in each district, in an average district this would represent 163 more participants at an annual budget assembly. As for current investment spending, every $100 per capita in the current year's investment plan yields nearly a 1-percentage-point increase in the participation rate. As of 2001, the highest participation rate in any year was 6 percent, when 1,446 residents attended the second-round budget assembly in the Nordeste district in the year 2000. The previous year's investment spending also has a substantive effect on participation: every $100 per capita in the previous year's investment plan generates about two-thirds of a percentage point in the participation rate. Perhaps surprisingly, the positive relationship between investment spending (both current and previous) and participation remains substantively meaningful and statistically significant even in the third model,

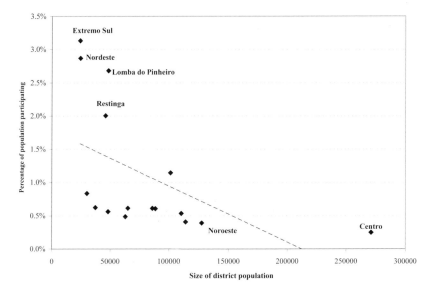

Fig. 5.10 Population size and budget assembly participation (1998)

when both spending variables are entered into the equation. The robustness of this relationship reconfirms the notion that residents are encouraged to participate both by the completion of projects in the past year and by the wish to follow up on the projects they prioritized for the current year. Last, the regression coefficients for population size indicate that for every ten thousand more inhabitants in a district, the participation rate declines by between one-fifth and one-third of a percentage point. In the third model, however, the effect loses statistical significance.[41]

Conclusion

This chapter has made two separate but related arguments. The first was that the design of the participatory budget process differed from the design of the participation programs in Caracas and Montevideo primarily because of the different political party context in Porto Alegre and the greater degree

41. As a final check on the robustness of the results, I ran the third model using time-series, cross-sectional GLS regression, which corrects for possible auto-correlation. The R-squared was again .52 and the regression coefficients for investments in the previous year and investments in the current year remained the same, with the statistical significance improving to $p < .01$ for investments in the previous year. Population size was again statistically insignificant. And with

Table 5.2   Need, spending, population size, and participation (district-years)

Variable	Model 1	Model 2	Model 3
Level of need	.015***	.016***	.012**
	(.003)	(.004)	(.004)
Current investment spending	.009***		.008***
	(.002)		(.002)
Previous investment spending		.007**	.006**
		(.003)	(.002)
Population size	-.000002*	-.000003**	-.000002
	(.000001)	(.000001)	(.000001)
Constant	.53***	.65***	.35*
	(.18)	(.19)	(.19)
R^2	.50	.45	.52
N	111	110	110

*Significant at p < .10; **significant at p < .05; ***significant at p < .01.

NOTE: Standard errors are in parentheses below coefficients.

of decentralization in Brazil. The weakly institutionalized opposition parties, in combination with the resources and responsibilities granted to the municipal government, allowed for the creation of an open design for PB. Moreover, the autonomy of the community movement vis-à-vis opposition parties and the incumbent administration freed neighborhood activists to push for this open design, and they helped invent some of the most innovative features of PB, such as the annual investment plan and the formula for allocating investments across city districts. Participants thus gained real decision-making power over a wide range of issues and were unfettered by a formal structure with party-appointed leaders. The second argument was that this open design facilitated the maintenance and expansion of participation by avoiding the reproduction of hierarchy, by making the process accessible to citizens with a variety of interests, and by making palpable the link between each individual's attendance at budget assemblies and the delivery of public works projects.

While new investments in public works and government programs continued through the 1990s, participation was sustained and even increased, more and more city services reached an ever greater portion of the population

---

these specifications, the level of need also lost statistical significance, and its coefficient dropped to .007. It makes sense that level of need, as measured by percentage of miles of street paved, should lose significance when controlling for auto-correlation. In each district, the percentage of street miles unpaved has decreased over the years, while the percentage of the population participating in budget assemblies has increased. Thus, level of need should only account for some of the cross-district differences in participation, not for over-time differences within individual districts.

Table 5.3   Distributional formula

Criterion 1: District need for service or infrastructure	Weight: 4
From 0.01% to 20.99%	Score: 1
From 21% to 40.99%	Score: 2
From 41% to 60.99%	Score: 3
From 61% to 79.99%	Score: 4
80% and above	Score: 5
Criterion 2: Total district population	Weight: 2
Up to 30,999 residents	Score: 1
From 31,000 to 60,999 residents	Score: 2
From 61,000 to 119,999 residents	Score: 3
More than 120,000 residents	Score: 4
Criterion 3: Sectoral priority of the district	Weight: 4
Fifth priority	Score: 1
Fourth priority	Score: 2
Third priority	Score: 3
Second priority	Score: 4
First priority	Score: 5

Source: PMPA (1999, 19).

(see the next chapter), PB gained greater national and international notoriety, and voters continued to elect the PT. In 1998, Olívio Dutra was elected governor of Rio Grande do Sul, and in 2000, Tarso Genro was elected mayor of Porto Alegre again. However, in the twenty-first century, for reasons explained in the final chapter, the PT lost the mayor's office and the new mayor deemphasized the participatory budget process.

Appendix: Distributional Formula in 1999 (for the 2000 Investment Plan)

After each of the sixteen districts has voted on sectoral priorities, GAPLAN adds their scores and uses them to determine how to allocate investments by sector. Following that, the three criteria are used to allocate investments by district. For example, if street paving had the highest number of points overall, it should receive the largest share of the budget for investments. Suppose this budget share allows for twenty miles of streets to be paved. City officials then use the formula to determine what percentage of these twenty miles will go to each district. If District X had 50 percent of its streets paved and seventy thousand residents, and elected street paving as its second priority, its total score for street paving would be $(4 \times 3) + (2 \times 3) + (4 \times 4) = 34$.

If all the sixteen districts combined had a street-paving score of 340, District X would receive 10 percent of the twenty miles of street paving, or two miles. Participants in the budget assemblies decide which of the district's unpaved streets will benefit from those two miles of pavement.

6

Stronger Citizens, Stronger State?

Implementing a participation program that actually sustains ongoing citizen interest is not easy, even when political leaders have an ideological commitment to radical democracy. The Causa Radical's parish government program in Caracas failed almost completely to keep city residents actively involved. In Montevideo, the Frente Amplio fared better, yet its program was still mired in a "crisis of participation" by the end of 1990s. Only the participatory budget program in Porto Alegre continued to attract an ever-growing and diversifying number of participants throughout the decade. The preceding chapters argued that these differences were most immediately related to the different design of the participation programs in each city, and that the variation in the designs, in turn, was ultimately due to (1) the greater degree of national decentralization in Uruguay and Brazil, which allowed the FA and the PT more flexibility than LCR, and to (2) the strongly institutionalized opposition parties in Montevideo and Caracas, which forced the FA and LCR to compromise on their original programs while the PT negotiated its program not with opponents but with independent community organizations (see table 6.1).

This chapter provides evidence for the changes—or lack of changes—in the quality of democracy across the three cities following the introduction of the new participatory institutions. It thus completes the argument, showing that the Left incumbents' ability to reach the ultimate goal of deepening democracy primarily varied according to the different designs of the new programs. In Porto Alegre, the open design of participatory budgeting helped create a virtuous cycle of strengthening citizenship and democratizing the state. When citizens realized that their participation yielded concrete results in a more responsive government, they accentuated their participation, joining or forming new organizations in order to gain greater influence. Moreover, they demanded more transparency and decision-making power from the government over an expanding range of issues and even backed the government's taxation efforts in order to improve local capacity to provide infrastructure and services, which helped continue the cycle. The success of participatory budgeting in deepening democracy in Porto Alegre has garnered widespread attention from scholars, government officials, and social movement activists, giving PB status as an "international benchmark" for participation programs (Kliksberg 2000, 164).

The parish government program in Caracas provides a sharp contrast. The program's restrictive design contributed to a short and vicious cycle that prevented deepening democracy. The fact that real decision-making power over important issues lay in the hands of political party representatives discouraged sustained citizen participation as well as the revitalization of community organizations. At the same time, the Causa Radical's administration lacked the jurisdictional authority and the resources to attend to the citizens' most urgent needs, and the sabotage by municipal unions tied to Acción Democrática only made its efforts more difficult. In Caracas, therefore, LCR found itself largely unable to deepen democracy.

The FA's participatory decentralization program in Montevideo aided in improving responsiveness and transparency but fared poorly in strengthening citizenship because of its regulated design. In Montevideo one finds neither a virtuous cycle of deepening democracy nor a vicious cycle to destroy its potential, but rather a disconnect. While Uruguay's relatively high degree of decentralization afforded the local administration the capacity to respond to citizen demands in general, the specific participation of individual volunteers in public assemblies and local councils was mostly unrelated to policy outcomes, as genuine decision-making power lay elsewhere. Nonetheless, the FA succeeded in establishing effective democracy in Montevideo and in winning popular support.

Democratizing the Local State

As presented in chapter 1, democratizing the state has two elements: transparency and responsiveness. Transparency was the only element for which each case showed improvement over the previous administrations. Under

Table 6.1   Summary

Case	National decentralization	Opposition party institutionalization	Program design
Porto Alegre	High	Weak	Open
Montevideo	High	Strong	Regulated
Caracas	Low	Strong	Restrictive

prior administrations, clientelism and personalism had prevailed, but with the implementation of the participation programs, channels of influence became public rather than private. The new administrations in each city provided participants with detailed information about the budget and particularly how much money was available for investment in public-works projects. City officials also provided printed records disclosing the implementation of the previous year's budget. In Caracas, the level of detail and the breadth of information were not so great as in Montevideo and Porto Alegre, but still represented an improvement over the past. In each city, the increase in the number of citizens monitoring the budget process and public works projects reduced the space for corruption and government waste of resources. As for indicators of responsiveness, Montevideo and Porto Alegre saw substantial if not massive extension of essential public services to meet the demands emanating from the new participation programs, while Caracas did not. This section demonstrates changes in transparency and responsiveness in as much detail as the data allow for each city.

Caracas

When Aristóbulo Istúriz sought reelection in 1995 to continue LCR's parish government program in Caracas, he did not campaign on a record of extending services, nor did he promise to do so in the future. In his first campaign speech, he declared, "Don't fool yourselves, I am not Father Christmas who goes around distributing gifts. The era of the problem solvers is over, and whoever thinks that era continues is stupid" (*El Universal* 10/8/95, 13). Indeed, given the inability of his administration to make significant advances in the provision of infrastructure and services, it would have been difficult for Istúriz to run as a "problem solver."

Newspaper reports, public opinion polls, and interviews, even with LCR supporters and activists, all indicate that no dramatic expansion of services occurred during Istúriz's term. According to several newspaper articles in the 1990s, Caracas remained "ungovernable" and "full of problems: dirty, unlit, with deteriorated streets, and increasing marginality."[1] The three largest and poorest city parishes, La Vega, Antímano, and Sucre, were often highlighted as sinking further into disrepair, chaos, and accumulation of garbage. Neighborhood leaders complained to reporters that the municipal government invested too little in public works projects to improve their communities, and that those projects that had started had suffered repeated delays or were never fully completed (*El Diario de Caracas* 4/3/95; *El Universal* 2/7/95, 14; 10/10/94, 26). Results of a survey of the Caracas metropolitan area by Gallup in 1994 showed that none of the public services had an approval rating above 50 percent except electricity, which was not a municipal competency. Eighty percent of the respondents were unsatisfied with the government of the city (*El Globo* 3/17/94, 45). These results correspond to the generally negative ratings that residents gave the Istúriz administration (see chapter 3).

Members of LCR's administration also acknowledged the failure to respond effectively to citizen demands for services.[2] Istúriz started dozens of plans and small pilot projects in various parts of the city, but made few permanent, large-scale contributions. The largest public works projects included the aqueducts and water plant for Antímano, yet they were postponed for months, and not inaugurated until after the 1995 elections. Similarly, the repairs on the highway leading to El Junquito parish faced delays until the end of Istúriz's term and never were completed. The administration did succeed in making relatively minor improvements in some areas, like the installation of trash ducts and regular garbage collection for the public housing blocks in the 23 de Enero parish, the extension of public lighting in Santa Teresa, and the small increase in the number of children attending municipal preschools.

In general, the narrow scope of jurisdiction and the limited resources of the Caracas city government combined with the constant sabotage from Acción Democrática and its municipal union allies made it exceedingly difficult

---

1. See *El Universal* (10/14/95, 7). The issue of the governability of Caracas appeared frequently in newspapers during the 1990s. I found only one article claiming that Caracas could be governable if its problems were studied and sufficient resources were allocated to solving them (see *El Globo* 1/26/96, 10).

2. Interviews with Alirio Martínez, the former budget director (1/18/99); Raúl Pinto, technical cabinet member in Macarao (10/28/99); Gisela Aybar, local board president in San José 12/13/99); Jesús Jiménez, technical cabinet member in La Vega (2/4/99); and Carlos Castillo, LCR activist in El Junquito (2/10/99), among others (see chapter 3).

for LCR to expand service provision significantly, thereby diminishing the potential for improving responsiveness. On the other hand, most observers recognize that transparency was enhanced considerably during Istúriz's term. Newspaper and magazine articles frequently cited the honesty of the Istúriz administration, a sentiment echoed to me by independent leaders of civil society organizations (interviews with Father Armando Jansen, head of CESAP, 10/7/99, and with Elías Santana, former president of FACUR, 12/23/99).

Claudio Fermín, the previous mayor of Caracas, had been jailed briefly on corruption charges, including "suspicious payments" for unfinished public works projects (see *El Universal* 3/7/98; 5/13/98). In their study of municipal governments in the Caracas metropolitan area, Vallmitjana et al. (1993, 147–49) emphasize that under Fermín the Caracas municipal government's finances showed irregularities in comparison with the others they examined, particularly in the extraordinarily high percentage of spending, 43 percent in 1990, under the "miscellaneous" rubric. The Istúriz administration, by contrast, was championed by journalists for its cleaning up of city finances and its fight against corruption and clientelism. In his first year in office, the amount of spending under the miscellaneous rubric fell to 14 percent, and consisted of emergency expenses related to Hurricane Brett; in the following two years, there were no miscellaneous expenditures (IESA 1998, 283–87; Alcaldía 1994a). Istúriz also took on the "political mafias" that controlled the municipal bank, the city cemetery, and the wholesale market in Coche (Hoag 1995, 31–32; Helms 1994, 24; Timmons 1995, 19).

Perhaps most significant among the efforts to improve transparency was the discussion of the parish public works budget, which for the first time in Caracas allowed citizens to find out how much money could be spent in each parish and for what purposes. According to Santiago Arconada, cited in Harnecker (1995d, 31),

> For the first time, administration directors went to the parish government and said, "Here is the money." The people's reaction was stupor. I had never seen anything like this and I saw that the *adecos* [members of AD] were realizing that this was happening for the first time. Before nobody knew how many millions were available. I remember that when the *adecos* snapped out of their stupor they said, "This is very little money, nothing can be solved with this." And we said, "It's very little, right? But it's more than when we didn't know how much there was."

In the end, despite the greater transparency achieved under LCR, the Istúriz administration failed to transform Caracas in the way that the FA and PT administrations did in Montevideo and Porto Alegre. Istúriz's term as mayor was aptly summarized by Timmons (1995, 19) shortly before the December 1995 elections: "Instead of concentrating on new problems and solving them well, he seems to be juggling myriad tasks, holding down the fort but not necessarily making major improvements."

Montevideo

In 1990, the Frente Amplio inherited a city that by all accounts was "full of potholes, dirty and dark, with problems regarding transportation, sanitation, the environment, and housing among the most cited" (Rubino 1991a, 6). Even the mayoral candidate for the incumbent Colorado Party in 1989 admitted that Montevideo faced an emergency situation. By all accounts, the Colorado administration (1985–89) after the fall of military rule had proved unable to make substantial improvements in the major services the city government provided—street paving, sanitation, trash collection, and public lighting—nor in offering citizens politically neutral channels of participation (Rubino 1991a; Filgueira 1991; Martínez and Ubila 1989; Aguirre 1990; 1993; and Canel 1992). In fact, the Colorado administration saw a succession of accidents and failures: the Colorados' popular candidate elected in 1984 died a few months after taking office; his first replacement faced accusations of corruption and his party forced him to resign; and the third Colorado mayor in the five-year term proved unable to reverse the image of incapable management left by his predecessors. Opinion polls from the period reflect these negative assessments. More respondents disapproved of the Colorado mayors than approved throughout the period.[3] In a 1988 survey, 52 percent of the respondents reported that the Colorado administration was "bad," 35 percent called it "fair," and only 10 percent called it "good." Two years later, results from another survey showed that 48 percent of respondents considered the Colorado administration to have been similar to the previous (military) administrations, 42 percent thought it was worse, and only 9 percent judged it better (Rubino 1991b, 95).

By the late 1990s, Montevideo looked dramatically different, and public opinion of the municipal government had completely turned around. The

---

3. The first Colorado mayor, Aquiles Lanza, had a 29 percent disapproval rating vs. 23 percent approval; the second and third mayors, Jorge Elizade and Julio Iglesias, received 62 percent vs. 8 percent and 36 percent vs. 16 percent, respectively. See *El Observador* (9/29/00).

extension of local infrastructure and services showed evident progress. After eight years of municipal government under the Frente Amplio, a survey in December 1997 reported that 73 percent of those asked considered Montevideo to be better or much better than it was ten years before, and a wide majority of respondents consistently approved of the job done by FA mayors.[4] City records and surveys of city residents provide evidence of the advances in service provision corresponding to the municipal administration's increased responsiveness.

Examination of the FA's performance in Montevideo may start with the services that citizens consider most important. A survey of adult residents carried out shortly before the 1989 elections asked respondents which services the municipality should provide. The top four answers were (1) trash collection, 47 percent; (2) public lighting, 13 percent; (3) basic sanitation (sewerage), 5 percent; and (4) street paving, 4 percent (Rubino 1991b, 81).

(1) With regard to disposal of municipal waste, the city increased the amount of waste disposed by trash collectors and street sweepers from 231,245 tons per year to 331,700 tons in the period from 1992 to 2000, an increase of 43 percent.[5] In addition, while at the beginning of the first FA administration in 1990 there had been 1,700 illegal garbage dumps, by 1994 there were only 150. These collection efforts were accompanied by the renewal of the fleet of garbage trucks, the installation of more than two thousand new trash cans, several education campaigns around maintaining a clean city (with the slogan "Montevideo, Your Home"—which is emblazoned on all the trash cans), and the implementation of recycling programs in several parts of the city, including the building of two recycling plants and the creation of an innovative plastic-recycling program focused on schoolchildren (IMM 1994, 16–19; Unidad 2002, 94).

(2) It is perhaps surprising that public lighting should be so important to residents, but two considerations suggest why this should be the case. First, adequate lighting theoretically improves safety by deterring crime, which has been a chief concern of Montevideans in the 1990s. Second, the city's light fixtures during the Colorado administration in the late 1980s operated sporadically. The number of public lights working declined over the period from 67 percent in 1985 to 55 percent in 1989. Nearly half the

---

4. For the 1997 survey, see *Posdata* (1/23/98, 32). Frente mayors Tabaré Vázquez and Mariano Arana always had approval ratings hovering around 50 percent, with disapproval ratings below 30 percent. Arana's approval ratings hit 65 percent in September 1999 (see *El Observador* 9/29/00 and 11/12/00).

5. See Unidad (2002, 88). Figures prior to 1992 are not available.

public lights were out in 1989 when the FA was elected. By 1992, 80 percent were functioning, and 90 percent functioned by 1997 (IMM 1998a, 17). At the same time, the number of light fixtures increased: the 45,000 light fixtures existing in 1990 had increased to 52,000 in 1993 and to 64,000 by 1999 (IMM 1994, 51; Habitat 2000).

(3) In the last two decades of the twentieth century, Montevideo's city government launched three major sanitation projects, all with loans from the Inter-American Development Bank, in 1985, 1990, and 1996 (and at the end of 2002, the IADB agreed to finance a fourth project). From 1985 to 2002, the percentage of the population living in domiciles connected to the municipal sewage system increased from 74 percent to approximately 92 percent, with most of the increase coming after 1992, when 76 percent of the population was connected to the system.[6] In other words, the number of residents lacking complete sewage services dropped by two-thirds since the FA took office.[7]

(4) Also striking is the enormous change in the amount of street paving done by the city government under the Frente Amplio. Whereas during the Colorado administration (1985–89) an average of 430,000 square meters of pavement was poured per year to maintain old and construct new roads, during Vázquez's administration (1990–94) the average was 755,345 m²/yr. During Arana's first few years (1995–97), the average jumped even higher, to 826,383 m²/yr (IMM 1998a, 106). This nearly doubles the average during the Colorado years, and compares favorably to the entire period from 1934 to 1955, when the maximum constructed was 420,000 m² in 1934 (Rial 1986, 10).[8] In addition to the increase in the amount of pavement poured, the quality of the materials used improved as well: the amount of "economical pavement" (poor quality) decreased from about 60 percent of the total poured in 1985 to below 30 percent in 1997, while the percentage of asphalt rose from less than 20 percent to nearly 70 percent (IMM 1998a, 106).

The improvements in service delivery in these four crucial areas were accompanied by important advances in many other domains as well. For instance, succesive FA administrations have implemented several new housing policies, including basic home construction, regularization of land

---

6. For the earliest figure, see Bluth (1988, 43); for the latest, see *La República* (10/14/02, 7); and see IMM (1998a, 114) for the 1992 figure.

7. The sanitation projects had other effects as well. Prior to the project started in 1990, hazardous water conditions at the city's beaches had prevented their use by the public, but by the mid-1990s all but two beaches were safe for swimming (see Unidad 2002, 80–81).

8. Figures for the 1955 to 1985 period are not available.

ownership, and the creation of a municipal housing fund and a construction materials bank.[9] The Vázquez administration built more than one thousand "basic housing units" for low-income families. By 1998, approximately five thousand families in irregular housing settlements had received titles to their property and improvements in infrastructure. During the decade of the 1990s, the FA government donated 220 hectares of municipal land for housing cooperatives to build their own homes collectively, benefiting over eight thousand more families. The construction materials bank has achieved less success than the other housing policies, yet still helped several hundred families to make improvements and repairs. Overall, the percentage of inadequate homes decreased from 38 percent in 1991 to 27 percent in 2000.[10]

With regard to primary health care, the number of municipal health clinics nearly tripled during the FA administrations, from seven to twenty, providing access for 280,000 residents (Habitat 2000). It is most likely not coincidental that the increased access to health care and the expansion of the sewage system coincided with a drop in infant mortality, which decreased in the ten-year period starting in 1990 from 20.3 per thousand births to 14.4 per thousand (Unidad 2002, 124). In fact, the municipal government gave special attention to programs for women and children, creating seven women's centers, a domestic violence program with a twenty-four-hour hotline, eighteen preschools, a system of scholarships for sixteen already existing preschools, and donating 1.5 million liters of milk each year to local schools and day care centers (Habitat 2000; IMM 1998a, 175). The municipal government also transformed the public transportation system in the 1990s, introducing discount and free passes for students and the elderly, completely renovating the fleet of buses, and implementing new services such as express routes to peripheral areas of the city and special routes for low-density areas that had lacked public transit options in the past (IMM 1994, 43–46; IMM 1998a, 13–14; Portillo 1996, 67–70).

A comparison of the results of the surveys conducted in 1992 and 1999 (described in chapter 4) demonstrates that city residents have noticed the improvements in municipal service provision. The first survey took place in early 1992, before the FA's decentralized participation program was fully in place and before many services had been deconcentrated, thus providing a good contrast to the later survey. One pair of questions asked people to

9. For information on the housing policies, including the figures presented here, see IMM (1994, 27–30; 1998a, 181–82; 1998b, 10–11), Portillo (1996, 76–80), and Habitat (2000).

10. The percentage of the population living in inadequate housing fell to 35 percent from 44 percent (Unidad 2002, 134).

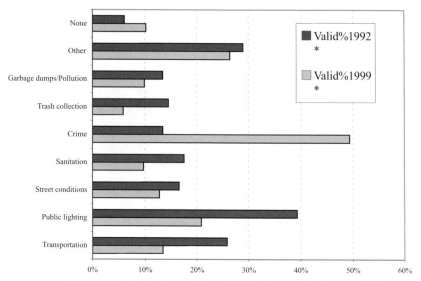

*Valid% is total number of mentions over the number of those who answered, so does not total 100%

Fig. 6.1   Principal problems of the neighborhood

name the two biggest problems in their neighborhood. Figure 6.1 shows a decrease in mentions of all types of problems except for crime.

Large differences appear in terms of trash collection, public lighting, sanitation, and transportation. About half as many people mentioned these as problems in 1999 compared to 1992. Only one problem, crime, caused concern among more respondents in the later survey. There are two likely reasons for this result. One is that certain types of violent crime became more frequent.[11] However, because the national government is responsible for the police, the increased crime rate has not damaged public opinion regarding the city administration. The other reason is that the remaining municipal services received higher ratings from Montevideans at the end of the decade than they did at the beginning.

A series of questions in the 1992 and 1999 surveys asked residents their opinions of specific services. Table 6.2 presents the results for both years, separating out each zone.[12] The zones represent the different types of city

11. While the number of homicides and armed robberies increased substantially in the late 1990s, crimes such as property damage and assault and battery decreased in the same period (Goldfrank 2002, 76, app. B).

12. Unfortunately, the authors of the 1992 study did not report their complete findings regarding these questions. Thus, one is forced to compare only the favorable responses, which I

Table 6.2   Favorable ratings of city services (in percentages)

Service	1992 Zone 3	1999 Zone 3	1992 Zone 7	1999 Zone 7	1992 Zone 9	1999 Zone 9	1992 Total	1999 Total
Transportation	65	68	53	68	36	51	51	59
Public lighting	40	59	38	66	29	44	35	53
Street conditions	34	40	45	66	32	28	36	39
Trash collection	67	82	62	85	37	64	55	74
Sanitation	86	81	80	93	32	42	65	65
Street sweeping	39	45	38	59	9	17	28	35

Note: Percentages are of those saying the service is very good or good over those who responded.

areas: Zone 3 represents the mostly middle-class central urban areas, Zone 7 represents the wealthier areas along the eastern coast, and Zone 9 represents the peripheral areas with significant numbers of poor households.

The total results show that residents rated nearly all city services more favorably in 1999 than they did in 1992, and especially public lighting and trash collection, which were the top two services citizens believed the city should provide in 1989. If one compares across the three zones, it is clear that the aggregate picture actually masks some other improvements in ratings of city services.[13] For instance, satisfaction with transportation seems to have improved considerably in zones 7 and 9, which are zones farther from the center of the city that historically had had fewer transportation options. In fact, the respondents in Zone 7, the wealthiest area, note large improvements in each of the six services they were asked about. It is also clear that while the residents of the poorer area (Zone 9) do evaluate most services more favorably than they did before, their degree of satisfaction is still much lower than that of their counterparts in the other two zones. Finally, it should be noted that other recent surveys of the general population (not limited to the three zones studied here) also show mostly high degrees of satisfaction

---

assumed here to be those that were "very good" and "good" rather than including "fair" as well. If one adds the "fair" answers to the favorable category for 1999, the differences in the responses in 1992 and 1999 show enormous increases in the favorable rating of city services. Thus, I did not include "fair" answers in the favorable category, making this a stronger test. I also assumed here that the percentages reported in 1992 were of those who responded, excluding "Didn't answer," given that in many other sections of the 1992 report, the percentages are reported in that fashion (see Aguirre et al. 1992; Aguirre, Sierra, and Iens 1993).

13. The large improvements in certain services in certain zones get averaged out in the totals. The 1992 survey had a much higher proportion of respondents from Zone 3 and Zone 7 than did the 1999 survey The 1992 survey had 303 respondents in Zone 3, 221 in Zone 7, and 300 in Zone 9. The 1999 survey had 130 respondents in Zone 3, 86 in Zone 7, and 218 in Zone 9.

with municipal services consistent with the results here, attesting to the validity of our survey.[14]

In general, then, city records and public opinion polls both demonstrate that the FA administration has improved service provision over the previous years, bringing services up to a high level of approval by the majority of residents.[15] The administration seems to have responded to residents' concerns by making extra efforts to deliver the very services that residents found most important in 1989, as reflected in the output of these services and in the increased number of residents giving these services positive ratings. Indeed, the FA administration achieved some measure of success in ameliorating each of the problems listed by residents (except for crime) in 1992 and 1999.

The evidence suggests that the improved responsiveness of the municipal government during the 1990s was not simply due to the increased size of the city budget and the FA's use of budget deficits to finance extra spending most of its years in office, which is the explanation opposition leaders often provide. They point to the fact that total expenditures on investments in constant Uruguayan *pesos* doubled from 1989 to 1998. However, if one looks comparatively, it is clear that increased spending is not the whole story. In the Colorado administration from 1985 to 1989, prior to the participatory decentralization program, investments rose 47 percent and the government ran deficits in most years, yet government service delivery stayed the same or even declined. From 1989 to 1993, investments increased at the same rate (48 percent), but there was a marked improvement in services, corresponding with the initiation of the FA's participation program.[16] It follows that the increased investments and budget deficits alone cannot explain the improvement in services, and they certainly cannot explain which services the administration prioritized. Thus, one has to look beyond greater availability of resources to include how the new participatory institutions provided the administration with information about citizen preferences and, as I argued in chapter 4, how the presence of decentralized municipal workers in the CCZs facilitated a more efficient response.

---

14. See, for example, the 1998 survey results and discussion of previous surveys by FACTUM at http://www.factum.com.uy/encuepol/opipub/1998/opp98029a.html. See also the 2001 survey by IDES (2001, 33), which shows further improvements in certain services since 1999.

15. Taking the 1999 results from the question of how is your neighborhood in terms of specific services, fewer than 25 percent of respondents rate five of the six services as "bad" or "very bad," and for the remaining service, street sweeping, less than 50 percent rate it as "bad" or "very bad."

16. All calculations are made from IMM Budget and Planning Division (no date).

Regarding transparency, the very creation of the participation program forced the FA administration to open its decision-making processes to public scrutiny, as was true for LCR and the PT in the other cities. In Montevideo, the commitment to transparency was evident in several policies, including the weekly public cabinet meetings held by Vázquez in the first FA term and the yearly "administrative commitments" document invented by the Arana administration, which lists all the proposed public works projects and social policies for the annual budget in detail (providing precise locations and *peso* amounts). The succession of city-wide public conferences regarding the decentralization participation program, as well as other public forums on other municipal subjects, showed a similar commitment to openness. Finally, in contrast to the previous Colorado period in Montevideo and to the series of major corruption scandals involving the mayors of the neighboring department of Canelones, there have been virtually no such accusations during the FA's reign in Montevideo.[17]

Porto Alegre

Responsiveness and transparency have also improved since the creation of participatory budgeting in Porto Alegre. As many observers of the city have noted, the expansion of basic services has been impressive under the succession of PT administrations (see, among others, Navarro 1997; Santos 1998; and Baiocchi 2001). Even leaders of opposition parties and the business elite acknowledge the transformation of the city's poor neighborhoods.[18] Sebastião Mello, the president of the municipal branch of the PMDB, told me that given the amount of street paving in the city's peripheral areas, the municipal government should be called the "asphalt administration" rather than the "popular administration" (the name adopted by PT city officials). The participatory budget councilors and delegates I interviewed all could name

---

17. The former three-term Colorado mayor of Canelones, Tabaré Hackenbruch, was investigated for but never convicted of the numerous charges of corruption against him.

18. Interviews with Antônio Hohlfelt, city councilor for the Partido da Social Democracia Brasileira (Brazilian Social Democratic Party, PSDB) (5/11/99); João Dib, former mayor and leader of the PPB (4/20/99); Sebastião Mello, municipal president of the PMDB (5/4/99); Stephan Wendzel, exporter (10/26/98); João Klee, restaurant chain owner and leader of several business associations (11/14/98); Ricardo Guimarães, superintendent of FEDERASUL, the state-wide business association (11/10/98); Joel Iuchno, president of the chamber of commerce (11/9/98); and Mario Espindola, commercial real estate agent and vice president of FEDERASUL (11/11/98).

various public works projects that they and their neighbors had demanded. Several residents walked around their neighborhoods with me, pointing out new schools, housing projects, and, often with particular emphasis, areas that had once been open-air gutters with raw sewage but were now paved streets and sidewalks.

In the 1980s, Porto Alegre's community movement leaders had ranked sewage systems, paved streets, and housing as their highest priorities, and throughout PB's first decade, participants ranked these three issues at the top. Education, health care, and transportation have usually been next on the list of priorities, although in surveys of the general population, these issues often are ranked higher in terms of importance. Provision of all of these services improved and expanded in the 1990s.

In 1988, Porto Alegre's network of sewage pipes extended a total of 768 kilometers, and only 2 percent of the sewage was treated before passing on to the Guaíba River. By the year 2000, the network's extension reached 1,399 kilometers, thus nearly doubling what had been built in more than six decades in just twelve years.[19] And, with the building of four new treatment plants in the same period, 27 percent of the waste was being treated (Dutra 2000, 203–5). Some analysts and some government documents report that the percentage of domiciles with sewage connections jumped from 46 percent to 85 percent between 1989 and 1997.[20] However, based on figures in the city's statistical yearbooks, my estimate is that the number for 1989 is actually closer to 73 percent.[21] Whatever the true figure, there has been an evident increase in the extension of sewage hook-ups.

Street paving registered similar advances. Since 1990, approximately twenty kilometers of new streets have been paved each year, primarily in the peripheral areas of the city (Knijnik 2000, 93). Table 6.3 displays the average yearly amount of asphalt used in building and repairing streets, showing a steady increase throughout the 1990s. As in Montevideo, the use of poorer quality materials diminished, while asphalt usage increased (PMPA 1997, 129–30).

In terms of housing, the municipal administration has provided improvements for thousands of families through a series of policies. These range from regularization and urbanization of existing lots, construction of new

19. Porto Alegre has two types of sewage collection, one through *esgoto misto* (mixed sewage, which takes both rainwater and sewage) and one through *esgoto cloacal* (which takes only sewage).

20. See Navarro (1997, 215) and PMPA (1998, 62, table 6.2).

21. Marquetti (2001, 12) makes a similar estimate. One reason for the difficulty in determining the exact figure is that until 1990 the city's statistical yearbooks did not record the number of domiciles connected to the mixed system separately.

Table 6.3   Increased street paving

Average yearly asphalt (in m²)			
1986–1988	1989–1992	1993–1996	1997–1999
240,137	308,090	576,579	813,475

SOURCES: My calculations from Marquetti (2001, 13, table 3) and from PMPA (1997, 130).

Table 6.4   Municipal government housing construction from 1950 to 2000 (total housing units)

1950–1963	1964–1985	1986–1988	1989–2000
7,021	9,278	901	11,513

SOURCE: Data derived from Da Silva 2000, 161.

housing projects, and aid for housing cooperatives, to the creation of a "negotiating commission" that helps resolve disputes between squatters and private landowners. Each of these programs was new to Porto Alegre except for the construction of houses. Rather than pushing for the removal of squatters and ignoring their demands for infrastructure as had occurred in the past, the new programs aided squatters in legalizing their claims to occupied land and in improving their living conditions. Over 27,000 families living in irregular areas benefited from these new programs from 1989 to 1996 (my calculations from Pozzobon 1998, 38). Moreover, the city government simultaneously accelerated the construction of new houses in the 1990s, producing more housing units in twelve years than during the twenty-one years of dictatorship (see table 6.4).

Education, health care, and public transportation advanced as well. In 1988, Porto Alegre's municipal school district included twenty primary schools, two middle schools, and seven kindergartens, for a total of twenty-nine schools. By 2000, the number of municipal schools had more than tripled, while the number of state schools remained relatively stable. In addition to the municipality's ninety schools (almost entirely primary and preschools), the city government began funding community-run day care centers, reaching a total of 114 centers by 2000. The municipality also created a specialized education program for working adults (Azevedo 2000, 118; Pozzobon 1998, 27–29).

Health care too was a shared responsibility with other levels of government in the early 1990s, with the municipality playing a minor part, operating one emergency hospital and twelve primary health posts. However, the city government advocated for and gradually took on a larger role. By 1996, health care had been completely "municipalized" in terms of regulating the city's twenty-two hospitals and two hundred or more specialty clinics and operating more than eighty primary health posts and six polyclinics. Since 1996, approximately one quarter of the municipal government's budget comes earmarked for health care from the federal Unified Health System, and the municipality always spends more than 13 percent of its own revenues on health care as well (something the city's own organic law requires). The city has invested in building twenty new health posts since the transfer of responsibility. While there has been some controversy over the municipalization of health care, the overall results seem positive. Porto Alegre's infant mortality rate fell from 18.7 per thousand births in 1992 to 12.2 per thousand between 1996 and 1999 (Barcelos 2000, 131–36; Pozzobon 1998, 31–34).

Finally, after the PT administration's disastrous attempt to take over the public transportation system in 1989, the system gradually improved over the next decade. When the PT took office, the municipal bus company, Carris, had large outstanding debts, operated at a loss, and had outmoded buses. Since 1995, Carris has turned a profit every year, reduced the average age of the buses, and increased the number of routes, buses, passengers, market share, and on-time percentage. Carris also receives consistently high ratings in public opinion polls, above those received by private bus companies, and has won several service awards (Piovesan 2000, 101–9). The transportation system in general has seen similar expansion, with more bus routes, greater frequency, and a larger number of passengers. Indeed, the number of passengers increased by about 17 percent between 1988 and 1997, after remaining roughly the same throughout the prior decade and a half (my calculations from PMPA 1989, 140; 1997, 165). This pattern suggests that steady population increase does not explain the rise in passengers, especially given that the population grew more slowly in the 1990s than in previous decades.

While municipal investments have been concentrated on these six areas, other public services provided by the municipality were by no means neglected. The total amount of garbage collected tripled between 1988 and 1997, from 403 tons per day to 1297 tons per day, and several recycling programs were implemented as well, which earned national and international recognition.[22]

---

22. My calculations from PMPA (1997, 269). For a description of the recycling programs (including an innovative use of pig farming) and the various awards given the municipal government, see Campani and Mello (2000, 207–10).

And the annual average number of public lights installed increased from about 927 per year in the 1980–88 period to 2,339 per year in the 1989–96 period (my calculations from PMPA 1989, 125; 1997, 132).

The expansion and quality of service provision has met with widespread approval, as evidenced in public opinion poll results.[23] Initially, the PT government received extremely low ratings in surveys, with most respondents judging Olívio Dutra's administration "bad" or "terrible," and a larger majority considering that Dutra was worse or the same as the previous mayor, Alceu Collares. However, positive ratings increased in 1991, and in all surveys from 1992 forward, more than 50 percent of respondents have rated the PT administrations as "good" or "excellent."[24] Most municipal services achieve similar ratings, with trash collection, public lighting, transportation, and water provision regularly receiving scores of "good" or "excellent" from over 70 percent of survey respondents. Sewage and street paving generally obtained approval from slightly lower percentages of respondents, though the trend was upward throughout the 1990s. In general, when asked, the majority of respondents affirmed that services had improved. A recent survey asked if residents knew of any municipal public works had benefited their neighborhood or district: 86 percent named a specific project, with 26 percent citing paved streets and avenues, 8 percent citing public transportation improvements, and sewage extension, schools and health posts each mentioned by 6 percent of respondents (Meta 2000b, sec. 4).

The same surveys also indicate that most city residents considered the PT's municipal administration to be honest, democratic, innovative, and competent, as opposed to corrupt, authoritarian, traditional, and incompetent. In fact, prior to a corruption scandal in the PT's national administration in 2005, honesty in government had been one of the PT's hallmarks (Goldfrank and Wampler 2008). Even the relatively conservative national weekly magazine *Veja* published an extremely laudatory article on the PT administration in Porto Alegre after the party's fourth consecutive local victory in October 2000. The article cited a study by the Federal University

23. The following paragraph is based on the results of a series of surveys conducted semi-annually throughout the 1990s by local private polling firms hired by the municipal government (see, for example, Amostra 1993, 1996, 1997; and Meta 2000a, 2000b). Given that similar approval ratings for the PT mayors have been presented by national polling firms like Datafolha and that the PT won reelection three times successively, the survey results from these local firms seem reliable, even if the government paid for them.

24. In an August 1999 and a January 2000 survey, this percentage slipped to 47 and 48, respectively, but was back up above 65 percent by November 2000 (see Meta 2000b, sec. 1).

of Rio Grande do Sul showing that "98%—that's right, 98%—of Porto-Alegrenses think that the PT municipal government is honest" (*Veja* 11/8/00, 49). The tone of astonishment is not surprising given the general distrust of politicians in Brazil and the stream of corruption scandals in the late 1990s involving all levels of government, with the forced resignations of senators and the attempt to impeach the mayor of São Paulo in 2000 after revelations of an extensive kickback scheme. In Rio Grande do Sul, nearly 25 percent of the state's 467 mayors were expelled from office over corruption allegations in the 1993–96 period (Downie 2000, A10–14).

The Porto Alegre survey results coincide with what budget councilors and neighborhood leaders told me in interviews: that in the 1990s, incidents of corruption were extremely rare, obtaining information from the city government had become easier, and that clientelist exchanges had virtually disappeared at the municipal level. While accusations of vote-buying remained common, after the consolidation of participatory budgeting politicians had a harder time convincing residents with promises of future public works projects or with claims that existing projects were their doing. Neighborhood leaders know that the only way to get a street paved in Porto Alegre, for example, is to attend a budget assembly and convince the other participants that the street should be a priority. They also can find out whether a particular project was achieved through political favor or was demanded through the participatory budget by looking in the annual budget plan. In the new context of greater government openness and availability of information, politicians' promises have less currency. At the same time, with PB, a larger number of citizens are aware of city-funded public works projects and monitor their progress to ensure that city workers or contractors implement the projects well. In many budget meetings and assemblies I attended, participants often questioned municipal officials about specific projects across the city, and used their sometimes new technical knowledge from the rulebook in doing so, asking, for example, why contractors were using a thinner layer of asphalt than was required and demanding that city inspectors investigate.

Other analysts of Porto Alegre also affirm the rise of transparency and accountability in the municipal government, and a corresponding decline of clientelism and corruption, as results of the participatory budget program (Navarro 1997, 215, 212; Fedozzi 1997, 167–69; Abers 2000, chap. 8; Santos 1998). Even one of the PT's harshest critics in Porto Alegre, Antônio Hohlfelt, claims that clientelism was reduced dramatically in the 1990s. Hohlfelt, a PSDB city councilor, has a different interpretation, however, of the decline in clientelism. He told me that Porto Alegre's City Council had been marked by "populism," with each councilor politically controlling specific city neighborhoods, but that this pattern had changed not because of participatory budgeting, but because Brazil had changed: "This trend away from populism in the City Council is a general tendency of all the major cities, except São Paulo" (interview 5/11/99). A comparative study by Setzler (2000, 12–18, 21) suggests that this is not the case. Setzler demonstrates that Porto Alegre is different from Salvador and Belo Horizonte in at least three telling ways: it has a higher rate of voters selecting parties rather individual candidates in the open-list city council elections, the votes for winning candidates are less concentrated in a few precincts, and the number of requests for executive action from city councilors is dramatically lower. Clientelism remained alive in Belo Horizonte and particularly so in Salvador, according to Setzler, but not in Porto Alegre.

Strengthening Citizenship

Prior to the participatory experiments, Caracas, Montevideo, and Porto Alegre had all experienced a similar pattern of a proliferation of community and civic associations in the late 1970s and early 1980s, followed by their partial decline toward the end of the latter decade. Only in Porto Alegre did the experiment in participation contribute to a reversal of this downward trend. The PT's budget program not only encouraged tens of thousands of citizens to participate in the annual rounds of public assemblies, but also stimulated the creation and political activation of hundreds of new civic associations. The participation programs in Caracas and Montevideo did neither of these things. The number of citizens and civic associations regularly and directly involved in municipal government decision making was much larger in Porto Alegre than in the other cities, and it continued to increase throughout the PT's multiple terms in office. In Montevideo, after the implementation of a regulated program design, participation in the FA's decentralized participation program stagnated and associational life failed to rebound. LCR's parish government program in Caracas attracted fewer and fewer participants over the course of its three-year existence and had very little lasting effect on local community organizations. More detailed accounts of the programs' effects on strengthening citizenship in each city confirm that this goal was achieved in Porto Alegre, but not in Caracas or Montevideo.

Caracas

The Istúriz administration's inability to sustain participation in its parish government program was accompanied by its failure to stimulate new organizational endeavors or strengthen the existing neighborhood associations, and for largely the same reasons. Essentially, because of its restrictive design, the program did not offer an effective channel for achieving solutions to local problems. Thus it provided little incentive for residents to create new organizations in order to act collectively within the program. The opposition parties' penetration of neighborhood associations made it even more difficult for LCR to encourage a revitalization of local organizing, despite its concerted efforts to do so.

In contrast to city officials in Montevideo and Porto Alegre, who assumed that the creation of participation programs alone would automatically promote associational activity, Istúriz implemented special policies aimed specifically at building new organizations and democratizing the existing neighborhood associations. These "Citizen Formation" and "Community Democracy" policies were carried out by municipal social workers sent to the parishes to meet with association leaders, hold training workshops, and help the associations hold elections and achieve legal status (Alcaldía 1995a, 8–9). By and large, the policies did not succeed.

In several city parishes, not a single neighborhood association held new elections to replace the ensconced presidents.[25] Most parishes saw elections in only a small minority of the neighborhood associations. For example, toward the end of LCR's administration, one of the city's social promoters reported that "ninety-five percent of the neighborhood associations in Caricuao remain in the hands of the same people that have been there for years and that have not wanted to hold elections" (Harnecker 1995d, 23). In La Vega, eleven or twelve of the thirty-eight associations held elections (Jiménez, interview 2/4/99). In Altagracia, the figure was five of twelve (Rubén Oropeza, former local board president, interview 1/27/99). According to Francke (1997, 98), four new associations were created in El Valle, but the attempts to hold elections in existing associations were unsuccessful. Macarao was the one parish in which the democratization policy achieved substantial results. There, the number of associations holding regular elections and weekly meetings jumped

25. Interviews with Carlos Contreras, technical cabinet member in La Candelaria (1/11/99), Aida Henríquez, technical cabinet member in El Recreo (11/18/99), and Aybar (12/13/99).

from four out of thirty-five existing associations to twenty-six (Pinto, interview 10/28/99; also Harnecker 1995d, 24–26).

Generally, the neighborhood associations in Caracas did not break away from the traditional pattern of excessive presidentialism, in which the president not only dominated the association, but often was the lone active member. In 1994, about 14 percent of the neighborhood associations in Caracas held biannual elections, which were required to maintain legal status; three years later, fewer than 10 percent met this requirement (Wikander 1994, 82; Francke 1997, 118). For most associations, then, entrenched presidents remained the norm. Not surprisingly, Francke's (1997, 116–18) study of the parish government program's effects on community organizing reports that corruption and clientelist relations persisted in the neighborhood associations. She argues that because of this pattern as well as the avoidance of regular elections, residents became increasingly distant from the associations. Francke reports that the city government's attempts to organize cultural groups, such as theater and dance troupes and groups providing popular education, mostly failed as well. In the parishes she analyzed (La Vega, El Valle, and La Pastora), "the majority of the cultural groups came out of the experience weakened" (Francke 1997, 126).

Even after a promising start for the Istúriz administration, with thousands of participants in the first year's assemblies and the creation of the parish governments, LCR did not achieve its often-stated goal of strengthening citizenship. As Father Jansen told me (interview 10/7/99), "Evidently, a large mobilization was achieved in Aristóbulo's era, but they did not transform it into something permanent, into a new mentality."

Montevideo

The stagnation or even deterioration of civic associations in Montevideo occurred after the redesign of the FA's program, as did the decline of participation in the budget assemblies and local councils (analyzed in chapter 4). Before the design changed, it appeared that the vibrant associational life of the early 1980s might be rekindled. And the eventual regulated design of the FA's program did offer greater opportunities for effective participation than the parish governments in Caracas, but only marginally. What was missing in both Montevideo and Caracas—but present in Porto Alegre—was the sense that, by organizing a group to participate in the municipal government's program, one could obtain concrete benefits for one's community. Because

Table 6.5   Participation in civic organizations (in percentages)

Type of organization	1989	1992	1999
Parish or religious organization	18	18	12
Social or sports club	14	17	10
Parents' association	11	12	7
Neighborhood association	5	8	4
Party or political club	16	5	3
Nursery or soup kitchen	6	5	1
Women's organization	4	3	3
Neighborhood health clinic	5	5	1
Local council or CCZ commission	N/A	5	3

NOTE: Columns do not add to 100 percent because membership may be more than one organization and because the organizations with the fewest participants are not listed here.

N/A = not applicable.

it was unclear whether participation at all would be productive and whether organizing to participate would increase the chances of obtaining results, the FA's participation program failed to stimulate the renaissance in community organizing that the party sought. Over-time comparison of the rate of participation in local civic organizations and of the number and functioning of neighborhood associations provides more evidence of withering citizenship than of its blossoming.

Leaders of the Frente Amplio expected that the opening of new channels of participation by the municipal government would encourage the creation of local organizations and stimulate activism in them because organized groups could gain a larger voice than individuals. Skeptics might assume the opposite, that opening new mechanisms of participation would decrease other forms of civic activity by drawing people from them. A comparison of survey results from 1989, 1992, and 1999 shows that neither of these scenarios accurately captures what occurred.[26] Table 6.5 displays selected results of a question that listed a series of organizations and asked respondents in which organizations they participated, if any.

The results from 1989 to 1992 are mixed. There appears to be little change, except for small increases in the percentage of respondents participating in social or sports clubs and in neighborhood associations, and a steep decline in the percentage of respondents active in political parties and clubs. This latter finding is explained partially by the crisis in the Uruguayan Communist Party,

26. Respondents for the 1989 survey were drawn from across Montevideo; respondents for the 1992 and 1999 surveys were selected from three representative zones (as described above). For the results of the 1989 survey, see Canzani (1989, 33, Cuadro 16); and for 1992, see Aguirre, Sierra, and Iens (1993, 120, Cuadro 6). For details on the 1999 survey, see chapter 4, app. 4A.

which had a large and active membership in the 1980s but descended into disarray with the demise of the Soviet Union in 1990 and lost thousands of members. While the implementation of the FA's decentralized participation program in 1990 may have had some effect on associationalism in the first phase, when one compares the 1992 and 1999 results, the program appears to have done nothing to stop the decline in participation across the entire spectrum of civic organizations. This decline cannot be attributed to the replacement of other organizations by the FA's program, because participation also declined in the local council and CCZ activities.

The neighborhood associations had been the primary targets of the FA's participation program, and the waxing and waning of membership in the 1990s was also reflected in the evolution of these associations. Two excellent studies by an Uruguayan expert, Mariana González (1992; 1995), show that in the pre-1993 period the profile of the associations changed. Her initial study was a census of associations carried out in 1988 and 1989. González compared associations based on the date of their formation and found that those formed during the dictatorship or earlier were qualitatively different from those formed during the Colorado administration from 1985 to 1988. These later associations were distinguished from the earlier ones by several traits: "higher relative percentage of organizations that did not hold meetings or held them with less frequency, the majority did so in family houses, more than half had never elected leaders, the majority lacked legal status [*personería jurídica*], a low level of coordination both with other neighborhood associations and other types of organizations in the area, an important rate of dissolution, greater dependency on the Municipal Executive to resolve their demands, and it was also in this group that a greater percentage showed the existence of political affinity among the membership" (González 1995, 197–98).

González conducted her second census at the end of 1991 and made several interesting discoveries. In addition to the spurt of new associations—136 had formed since mid-1989—and the demise of 257 associations that had formed in the 1985–88 period, the profile of the associations changed.[27] Higher percentages of associations held regular meetings, elected their leaders, held meetings in public places, applied for legal status, and had regular contact with other organizations in their area (González 1995, 199). The character of the associations thus became more democratic and active in the early 1990s, corresponding to the beginning of the FA's decentralized participation program.

27. My calculations from González (1992, 103; 1995, 39, 113).

Although in-depth studies like the ones by González have not been done since 1991, the general sense in Montevideo is one of decline in the neighborhood associations. The notion of waning citizenship appears in city government documents describing the "crisis of participation" (IMM 1997, 9–10), in academic studies lamenting the "weakening network of neighborhood organizations" (IDES 2001, 70), and in the FA's own worrying over the declining motivation to participate "that threatens to disappear" (Zabalza 1998, 37–38). It is perhaps most clearly evident in the diminishing number of associations.

At the end of 1988, there were 436 functioning neighborhood associations; in 1991, their number had declined to 371. The most recent tabulation of neighborhood associations available is from an incomplete series of reports from the CCZs in 1998 and suggests that there were at least 224 neighborhood associations in that year.[28] Even assuming that the actual number of associations was 300 (by imputing that the missing zones each had the average number of associations), there was still a sharp decline from 1991. Indeed, in several zones, CCZ workers told me that the number of active associations had initially increased in the early 1990s, but began to dwindle after the institutionalization of the local councils and boards at the end of 1993. In at least two zones (1 and 7), not a single neighborhood association functioned by 1999.[29] Even in historically combative zones like 9 and 14, the number of neighborhood associations fell by half between 1991 and 1997.[30]

In sum, after ten years of the decentralized participation program in Montevideo, there was little indication of strengthened citizenship.

Porto Alegre

While Caracas and Montevideo witnessed the stagnation of citizenship, Porto Alegre saw, according to various authors, an "explosion of experience," a "revitalization of civic life," and a "synergized civil society" (Baierle 1998; Abers 2000; Baiocchi 2002). Indeed, throughout the 1990s, the direct participation

---

28. My calculations from official reports by fourteen of the eighteen CCZs provided to me by CCZ workers. Assuming that the four zones for which the reports were missing (2, 6, 7, 17) had the average number of associations (nineteen), the total would be three hundred.

29. Interviews with "Rosa" in Zone 1 (7/23/99), "Dinora" in Zone 7 (7/21/99), and "Malena" in Zone 5 (6/8/99), where the number of associations fell from thirteen to four.

30. In Zone 9, the number of associations fell from eighty-four in the early 1990s (CIDC 1997, 28) to thirty-nine in 1997. In Zone 14, the number of associations dropped from sixty to thirty-one according to the CCZ's official reports. Zone 14 includes the well-known neighborhood of La Teja, where Vázquez worked in a health clinic prior to becoming mayor.

of city residents in shaping the municipal budget increased from fewer than a thousand to upwards of forty thousand, and community activism flourished, with the number of neighborhood associations nearly doubling from 1988 to 1998 and the creation of several new district-wide organizations as well. Porto Alegre's distinctive pattern is largely due to the open design of its participatory budget program. The open design gave PB two unique attributes that made it stand out compared to the programs in Caracas and Montevideo: it offered residents confidence that their participation would be rewarded, and it made acting collectively not only beneficial but virtually imperative.

In contrast to the tales of declining interest in neighborhood organizing that I heard in the other cities, 85 percent of the budget councilors I interviewed in Porto Alegre told me that residents in their neighborhood began participating more in community organizations since the start of the budget program. The veteran councilors, who had participated in the early years, told me that the initial challenge was convincing neighbors to trust in the PB. A former councilor from Leste, "Luiz," told me that after years of authoritarian rule and broken promises, his neighbors "were surprised that they were being given the right to talk, the right to criticize, to choose what they wanted, and with the assurance that it would actually get carried out" (interview 5/2/99). Crucially, this assurance only existed if the project the resident demanded was ranked highly enough in the public assemblies to make it into the annual budget plan for public works projects. While each district would elaborate long lists of priorities, the municipal government could only afford to give the top priorities an assured spot in the investment plan. In the early 1990s, approximately 25 percent of the demands listed in the district assemblies gained a place in the plan (Fedozzi 1997, 230, En 135). As all the neighborhood activists told me, in order to place a desired public works project at the top of the list, it became necessary to organize one's neighbors to participate en masse in the budget assemblies.

A leader of the União de Vilas (Neighborhood Confederation) in Cruzeiro, "Margarete," explained the process in detail (interview 4/11/99):

> There are neighborhood associations in almost all the *vilas* in Cruzeiro, because when residents ask us how to make demands for water or sanitation, what do we say? "Look, the first thing you have to do is organize an association. Because it won't work for you to sign a petition and take it to City Hall, because they'll say that that kind of demand goes through the PB. And a group of disorganized people won't get

anywhere in the PB." You need to go with an organized association, with elections, because that is what makes people realize the need to be together, to be organized. Because we know that's the only way for people to grow as citizens, to go from being people without a name to citizens who belong to a certain *vila*, to a certain association. It's only then that they're going to participate in the process, a process that usually requires arguing and even fighting: "Why can't my *vila* get such and such a project?" Hence the necessity of bringing as many people as possible from the *vila* to the assembly, to win delegates and strengthen the *vila*. Because the *vila* only strengthens with participation.

Gradually, district-wide neighborhood confederations like Cruzeiro's União de Vilas became the norm in Porto Alegre, with presence in eleven of the sixteen districts by 1998. Even where such confederations did not exist to encourage organization, a similar logic stimulating organization operated through example rather than exhortation. For instance, "Humberto," a housing rights lawyer and activist in the Centro district, told me (interview 12/3/98), "Each year new associations, new communities appear in the budget process. Principally in the Centro district, we see that there has been a change in the people participating. When one community achieves its goals, the other says: 'Hey, they went to the PB and they succeeded. Let's see if we can do it.' New associations are also created because they know that individually they can't win. You have to unite in order to make demands." Many councilors told me similar stories. Abers (2000, 142–47) reports the same pattern of associational growth in the Extremo Sul and Glória districts.

Baiocchi's in-depth studies of neighborhood associations in Porto Alegre confirm the stories told to me by PB participants. The number of active neighborhood associations grew from approximately 300 in 1988 to about 540 in 1998 (Baiocchi 2002, table 3). Baiocchi calls the latter figure a conservative estimate. One of the leaders of UAMPA, "Nelson," told me that UAMPA alone had 420 member associations and that his organization estimated that 1,000 neighborhood associations existed in Porto Alegre as of 1998 (interview 12/15/98). This estimate seems high. According to municipal government records, there were 664 neighborhood associations registered with the Community Relations Office as of May 2001. Still, a clear upward trend in neighborhood organizing is evident. And tellingly, Baiocchi shows that associational density grew most in the poorest districts (2001, 56–58), which were also the districts where the rate of participation in the budget process was highest.

The studies by Baiocchi and Abers also demonstrate a change in the character of Porto Alegre's neighborhood associations, from a more presidentialist, top-down style to a more participatory, bottom-up style, as a result of the PB. Abers (2000, 161–66) reports an increase in the holding of elections and regular meetings in the associations in Glória and Extremo Sul; Baiocchi (2001, 55; 2002, 49, 83) reports the same in the three districts he studied closely: Partenon, Nordeste, and Norte. My interviews with budget councilors similarly suggest that the PB had a direct effect on the democratization of neighborhood associations. A number of the councilors had never been socially or politically active in their neighborhoods but had been motivated by the PB to begin organizing precisely for the reasons described above. Councilors from Restinga and Sul related very similar stories about their entrance into community activism. They told me that when they asked municipal division directors for public works projects, they were told to go to the PB. When they went to the PB, they were asked if they belonged to a community organization. They then discovered that their local neighborhood associations were not participating in the PB and had not held elections for several years. After organizing new elections, they brought their associations into the PB process and succeeded in prioritizing their original demands—for street paving in Restinga and a sewage project in Sul.[31]

Finally, a survey of Brazil's six largest state capitals in 1996 shows that the surge in associationalism in Porto Alegre is not part of a larger trend, but an exception. While the rate of membership in community organizations of various types had fallen in Brazil in general since 1988, it increased in Porto Alegre, which had the highest percentage of residents belonging to community organizations, at 38 percent.[32]

Conclusion

Only in Porto Alegre did the participation program succeed on each component of deepening democracy. The program implemented in Caracas by LCR was an almost complete failure, lacking advances in nearly every aspect. And the FA's program in Montevideo achieved partial success, improving

---

31. Interviews with "Claudio" (12/9/98) and "Nelson" (12/15/98), who later joined UAMPA and became UAMPA's designated budget councilor.

32. See the analysis of associationalism in Brazil's state capitals by Santos Junior (2000) and a report of the survey on the IBGE Web site: http://www.ibge.gov.br.

Table 6.6   Quality of local democracy

Case	Transparency	Responsiveness: service extension	Direct participation	Civic associations
Porto Alegre: Deeper democracy	Very high	Massive	Increasing	Activation
Montevideo: Effective democracy	High	Massive	Decreasing	Stagnation
Caracas: Shallow democracy	Medium	Minimal	Rapidly decreasing	Stagnation

transparency and responsiveness but falling short in terms of strengthening citizenship (see table 6.6).

While Porto Alegre's successful experiment with participatory democracy engendered broad national and even international political repercussions, including the adoption of PB in hundreds of cities in Brazil and beyond, the identification of Porto Alegre with the World Social Forum, and, arguably, assistance in the rise of the Workers' Party to national power, the experiences in Montevideo and Caracas had important implications as well. The popularity of successive Frente Amplio administrations helped their first mayor, Tabaré Vázquez, win the presidency in Uruguay, ending over a century of traditional party dominance. And the failure of LCR in Caracas helped seal the party's fate and opened the way for a more radical challenger on the Left in Venezuela, Hugo Chávez, who has taken up the mantle of participatory democracy. I explore the issues of the international diffusion of PB and whether Porto Alegre's success can be replicated as well as the future of participatory democracy under Latin America's new Left governments in the conclusion.

Conclusion: The Diffusion of Participatory Democracy and the Rise of the Left

As Latin American leaders of both old and new democracies in the 1980s and 1990s began the transition away from the centralized and often authoritarian regimes of previous decades, the general notions that the region's governments required more citizen participation and greater decentralization found support from an uncommonly wide swath of the ideological spectrum. Mainstream international development organizations like the World Bank and the United Nations Development Program encouraged adoption of these policies as part of a larger reform of the state. They viewed decentralization and participation as methods of expanding and improving public services, which in turn would help governments gain legitimacy in the eyes of citizens and thus promote the stability of democracy. Social movements and political parties on the Left, meanwhile, pushed the two policies as part of a general call for deepening democracy. Parties like the PT, the FA, and LCR led the way in implementing new participation programs in cities such as Porto Alegre, Montevideo, and Caracas. Ultimately, it was the PT's participatory budgeting program in Porto Alegre that achieved the most acclaim, both from the Latin American Left, which has attempted to replicate the model in hundreds of cities throughout the region, and from international development organizations, which began to promote participatory budgeting not only in Latin America but throughout the world.

In this concluding chapter, I reflect on three questions: What have we learned about the attempts to deepen democracy in Porto Alegre, Montevideo, and Caracas? Can those lessons help us understand the success or failure of participatory budgeting in other Latin American cities as it spreads? And what future for participatory democracy does the region hold now that political forces on the Left have attained national office? I suggest that several clear lessons emerge and that they do indeed provide insight into similar experiments in citizen participation elsewhere in the region. Nonetheless, the current era presents some paradoxical results regarding both the diffusion of participatory budgeting to other cities and the fate of participatory democracy more generally under the Left's new national administrations.

Lessons Learned

The first and most promising lesson is that deepening local democracy is possible. Under certain conditions, the combination of decentralization and participation can lead to more democratic city government, even in the relatively short term. Robert Putnam's (1993) pessimistic suggestion that making democracy work takes centuries seems exaggerated. Although a history of community organizing is helpful, deepening democracy does not require an ancient stock of social capital. In fact, many supposed stumbling blocks to effective participation programs, such as social inequality, bureaucratic venality and resistance, and party factionalism, can be overcome. As in Caracas and Montevideo, society in Porto Alegre is highly unequal, and many municipal government employees opposed new channels of citizen participation. Factional rivalry plagued not only the FA and LCR, but the PT as well.[1] The success of Porto Alegre's participatory budgeting program despite these obstacles thus justifiably has raised the hopes of decentralized participation's advocates that they are not expecting pears from elm trees. It should also give pause to adversaries like Samuel Huntington and Fareed Zakaria, who argue that expanding direct citizen participation in government leads to "tyranny or chaos" (Zakaria 2003, 255).

Second, although deepening democracy is possible, not just any participation program guarantees it. For an effective program that will consistently attract a large and diverse group of citizens, the right institutional design is vital. Designs that focus narrowly, offer insufficient decision-making power, and are overly formal, privileging party officials and elected representatives rather than ordinary citizens, tend to discourage participation, as the cases of Caracas and Montevideo show. By contrast, the key features of participatory budgeting's open design in Porto Alegre were its wide range of issues under debate, its informal structure, which allowed all citizens access without

---

1. Of course, exceptionally high levels of intraparty rivalry can be fatal, as Couto (1995, 153–55) argues for several of the PT's first experiences in local government.

favoring party loyalists, and its deliberative decision-making process, which gave citizens a real taste of power. This lesson underscores and extends earlier arguments that participatory budgeting's success in Porto Alegre is related to its ability to attract unorganized sectors of the population through its open format (Baiocchi 2004).

Third, even mayors with an ideological commitment to deepening democracy through designing open participation programs are constrained by national and local political contexts. Where resources and authority remain mostly centralized at the national level, as in Venezuela, the capacity of municipal reformers to design meaningful participatory institutions is severely undermined. Still, decentralization alone is not sufficient. In cities with strongly institutionalized parties, decentralization will likely result in elite capture and exclusionary politics; even where a new progressive party wins office, as in Montevideo, the old established parties can debilitate participatory reforms. In cities with weakly institutionalized parties, however, decentralization's democracy-enhancing benefits are more likely to filter through. Contrary to the frequently negative assessments of the democratic prospects of Brazil's weakly institutionalized parties and weakly institutionalized party system (Mainwaring 1999; Power 2000; Ames 2001), it was this political context that allowed the PT to establish a genuinely effective channel of citizen participation and indeed deepen democracy in Porto Alegre.

These findings echo some of the work on posttransition democracies that argues that overinstitutionalized party systems often prevent new ideas from being implemented (Mettenheim and Malloy 1998; O'Dwyer and Kovalčík 2007). They also help explain why other attempts by Left parties to implement participation programs in some Latin American cities have met with such difficulties. The participatory initiatives under the United Left in Lima in the mid-1980s, for example, were hampered both by the lack of decentralization in Peru and by the attacks from APRA, one of the country's oldest and strongest parties (Schönwälder 2002). And the original efforts to create new participation channels in Mexico City by the Party of the Democratic Revolution faced significant obstacles created by the very strongly institutionalized Institutional Revolutionary Party (Alvarado and Davis 2004). Even in Brazil, the PT fared much better with participatory budgeting in Porto Alegre than in São Paulo, for example, partially because in the latter city the party faced fierce legislative and bureaucratic resistance from the political machines set up by traditional politicians Jânio Quadros, Orestes Quércia, and Paulo Maluf (Keck 1992, 234–35; Couto 1995; Harnecker 1993b, 18–21, 117–20, 125). Moreover, as dozens of countries, especially in Asia,

Africa, and Latin America, continue to engage in experiments with decentralization that yield different outcomes (Manor 2006), this lesson regarding strongly institutionalized parties may help answer one of the major questions posed by scholars of decentralization: "why some subnational governments become successful innovators in democratic governance while others reinforce authoritarian patterns" (Selee and Tulchin 2004, 314).

A fourth lesson becomes clear when looking back from the present era, one in which the Left has risen to national power in Venezuela, Uruguay, and Brazil, and to prominence virtually throughout the region, and one in which the notions of participatory democracy and the practice of participatory budgeting have become widespread: attempts to open up government to foster citizen participation can have important political consequences whether they succeed or not. Take the case of LCR in Caracas, which had at least two major impacts on Venezuelan politics. On one hand, LCR's failure to make participation work in Caracas, and generally poor performance in this key city, prevented Mayor Aristóbulo Istúriz from winning reelection in 1995. Had Istúriz succeeded in implementing an effective participation program and won reelection, he and LCR would have been well poised for the 1998 presidential race. Instead, their loss in Caracas contributed to the party's division in early 1997 and its inability to maintain its status as the leading contender against the traditionally dominant parties. Rather than breaking the hold of Punto Fijo – era politicians on Venezuelan politics, LCR virtually disappeared, making space for Hugo Chávez.

On the other hand, Chávez became the leading proponent of participatory democracy in the region, and LCR's parish government program became one of the main models for citizen participation in Venezuela's new "Bolivarian" constitution. When LCR divided, Istúriz and other leaders founded the PPT and, along with other political parties on the Left, supported Chávez in the 1998 election. The PPT received important positions in the Chávez administration, and after the PPT won nearly 10 percent of the seats in the Constituent Assembly in 1999, Istúriz was named the body's second vice president. It is not surprising that several of the participatory initiatives under Chávez were based on those promoted by Istúriz and LCR (López Maya 2008, 7). The most important of these, until recently, were the Local Public Planning Councils. These councils first appeared in the 1999 constitution and were later legally mandated in all Venezuelan municipalities in 2002. They closely resembled the parish governments, especially as envisioned in the Municipal Ordinance of November 1995 (Concejo 1995). More recently, an internal struggle within the forces supporting Chávez seems to have pushed the LCR/PPT version of participation aside, and the Local Public Planning Councils have been essentially superseded by a newer participatory endeavor, the Communal Councils (see below).

The long-term political effects of the FA's participatory efforts in Montevideo are more straightforward. There, despite the fact that participation did not reach the levels achieved in Porto Alegre, the improvements in government responsiveness and transparency helped the FA attract more and more voters. Unlike LCR in Caracas, the FA succeeded in expanding from its initial base of unionized workers and part of the middle-class intelligentsia to capture poorer voters and continue to win municipal elections and eventually the presidency with Tabaré Vázquez, its first mayor of Montevideo (Luna 2007, 4–8). Vázquez maintained the FA's participatory discourse during his three runs for the presidency in 1994, 1999, and the victorious 2004 campaign. In his inaugural speech in March 2005, he promised to "deepen, expand, and broaden democracy and citizen participation in the exercise of government" (Vázquez 2005). Indeed, the Vázquez administration has opened several new channels of participation in Uruguay. Furthermore, the FA's continued success in Montevideo's municipal government, along with the weakening of Uruguay's traditional parties—the Blancos and Colorados—has allowed recent FA mayors to experiment with new forms of participation. Although the rate of participation in the local councils and thematic commissions is still very low (Zibechi 2008), in 2005 Montevideo adopted its own version of "participatory budgeting" under Mayor Ricardo Ehrlich. This differs from Porto Alegre's in that it is more of an electoral process, but it may be breathing new life into the city's participatory institutions; nearly seventy-five thousand Montevideanos voted in the 2007/2008 budget cycle (CIGU 2008, 4). In addition, with its majority in the national congress, the FA passed a law in 2009 that will make all local boards elective bodies (rather than appointed) in the future, which was what it tried to do in Montevideo in the early 1990s. Thus, participatory institutions in Montevideo have begun to be modified so as to make them more open and direct, a trend which may continue as the FA won at the national level again in 2010.

The political repercussions of the PT's participatory budgeting experiment in Porto Alegre have been numerous and varied. For the PT, participatory budgeting became one of its signature municipal programs, which it has adopted in more than one hundred cities throughout Brazil. Participatory budgeting's success also helped launch former mayor Olívio Dutra to the governor's seat in Rio Grande do Sul, where he implemented a statewide PB process, and even helped give Lula and the PT credibility in the 2002 national election, as they could point to Porto Alegre and other well-governed cities as evidence of their honesty and competence. Lula's platform in 2002 called for implementing some form of PB at the national level, but although his administration has essayed a number of new forms of participation, PB is not one of them. And while participatory budgeting helped the PT win several municipal elections in Porto Alegre, the party finally lost in 2004 after sixteen consecutive years in office. What happened?

While the PT remained the single most popular party, winning a plurality of the votes, it lost in the second-round runoff to a coalition of twelve parties ranging from Center-Left to Right. The opposition ran a smart campaign, in which its leading mayoral candidate, ex-senator José Fogaça, accepted that the PT administrations had realized certain achievements. Specifically, Fogaça recognized the importance of participatory budgeting and repeatedly promised to maintain it under a non-PT government. Fogaça's slogan was to "keep what's working, change what's not." The opposition also capitalized on the notions of "ending one-party rule" and allowing "democratic alternation" after the PT's consecutive prior victories (Baiocchi 2006). At the same time, the PT suffered from leadership battles that hurt its standing with voters.

The key battle involved former mayors Dutra and Tarso Genro. After Dutra beat Genro to be the PT's gubernatorial candidate in a bitter 1998 primary, Genro decided to run for mayor of Porto Alegre in 2000, which upset the then vice-mayor, who had expected to head the ticket and ended up leaving the party. Genro promised in the 2000 campaign that he would serve his full four-year term. However, just fifteen months into his term, he again faced Dutra in the party's gubernatorial primary in 2002, and left the mayor's office to be the PT's (losing) candidate. Genro's broken promise was bad enough on its own for the PT's chances with Porto Alegre voters, but it also meant that his uncharismatic vice-mayor finished out the term. In addition, Dutra's term as state governor proved controversial, and Lula's first two years as president had been underwhelming; economic growth was slow and municipal tax revenues and federal transfers decreased throughout Brazil (Teixeira and Albuquerque 2006, 218). With the threat of losing participatory budgeting removed by the opposition, the PT's internal problems, and the PT administration's weakening capacity for public investments, the party's hold on Porto Alegre slipped. Under the current coalition government, Fogaça kept his promise to maintain PB, but it has lost much of its former vitality as the municipal administration has downplayed its importance and participation rates have declined (CAMP 2007; Baierle 2008).

While participatory budgeting is in danger of "pasteurization" in Porto Alegre (Chavez 2008), its influence has continued, with thousands of other cities worldwide implementing PB in some form or another. Especially after the UN Habitat award for PB in 1996, observers from around the world began arriving in Porto Alegre to study and advocate it. Since then, political parties and social movements on the Left as well as international development organizations have taken up PB, either adopting it or pushing for its adoption throughout Latin America and the world. With varying degrees of faithfulness to the Porto Alegre model, Left parties have now implemented PB in dozens of cities stretching from Mexico to Argentina, while international organizations like the World Bank have made PB part of the mainstream development agenda for governments globally (similar to the mainstreaming of gender and environmental concerns).[2] At present, two countries in Latin America explicitly require PB. With encouragement from international donors in 2003 and 2007, respectively, Peru and the Dominican Republic passed national laws mandating PB in all local governments, which in the case of Peru includes municipal, district, and regional governments. Several other countries in the region also have laws requiring some form of citizen consultation and oversight in the municipal budget process, including Guatemala, Nicaragua, and Bolivia, though they do not all use the term "participatory budgeting." Many cities in Africa, Asia, and Europe have adopted PB as well, and in 2007 the Labour Party government announced its intention that all local governments in Great Britain would use PB by 2012 (Communities 2008).

In the first decade of the twenty-first century, then, participatory democracy has become a key element in the national governments of the Latin American Left, and participatory budgeting, in particular, has spread to cities throughout the region, adopted by governments from Left to Right. Can the lessons from the study of participation in Caracas, Montevideo, and Porto Alegre help us understand PB's successes and failures in these new contexts and help us speculate about the future of participatory democracy at the national level?

Replicating Participatory Budgeting: Porto Alegre Is Not Unique

Budget councilors in Porto Alegre told me that their success with participatory budgeting could be replicated in any city, with some qualifications:

---

2. For the argument that international financial institutions have attempted to co-opt counterhegemonic participatory institutions in order to shore up neoliberal hegemony, see Ruckert (2009, 142–43).

"All you need is an organized community and a politician with the will to do it. And of course money. You need money. It's not enough to have the will if you don't have money."[3] With PB becoming an international buzzword in recent years, it seems that many outsiders would agree that successful PB can be duplicated. On the other hand, some studies of participatory budgeting suggest that its emergence in Porto Alegre strongly reflects the unique histories of the city and the state of Rio Grande do Sul, arguing that the *gaúchos* had a more participatory, egalitarian culture dating back to, and because of, the wars of secession in the mid-nineteenth century; the Brazilian South's lesser dependence on slavery; and the greater numbers of immigrants and small farmers (Avritzer 2006a, 624–25). Others have gone further, suggesting that successfully replicating PB in other cities would be exceedingly difficult. The fact that Left administrations independently and simultaneously implemented very similar participatory institutions else-where in Latin America, including in Montevideo and Caracas, however, indicates that the reasons for the emergence of PB-like institutions can be better found in the specific political conjuncture of the early 1990s (as argued in the Overview) than in deeply engrained cultural values. But the other question still remains: can PB help deepen democracy outside its famed original home?

If successful PB is strictly culturally determined and Porto Alegre is unique, then the arguments I have made in this book, about the importance of national decentralization, weak opposition party institutionalization, and an open design for the participation program, would be invalidated. If PB can be successfully replicated in any and every city, my arguments would be invalidated as well. Because the diffusion of PB is fairly recent, research on PB outside of Brazil remains scarce, which makes testing the validity of these arguments somewhat difficult. Still, comparisons of PB in other Latin American countries suggest that participatory budgeting is being successfully replicated and is improving the quality of democracy in some cities but not others. They also suggest that while decentralization, opposi-tion, and especially institutional design matter, other factors—some of which my study of Caracas, Montevideo, and Porto Alegre controlled for—count as well. Perhaps most significant is the ideology of the incumbent party. When parties in the Center or on the Right adopt PB, the design tends to differ from PB designed by parties on the Left, and the results for the quality of democracy tend to be less promising. In addition, while weak

3. Interview with "Humberto," budget councilor from the Centro district (12/3/98).

traditions of local social organization do not appear to prevent successful PB, particularly strong traditions of local organizing can sometimes help overcome other obstacles.

Evidence for these claims comes from comparing locally implemented PB in Brazil to nationally mandated citizen participation in the municipal budget process in four other Latin American countries—Bolivia, Guatemala, Nicaragua, and Peru—during the early 2000s.[4] By and large, while analyses of Brazilian PB portray many more cases of improvements in the quality of local democracy, observers of non-Brazilian experiences are less sanguine. Of course, not all cases of Brazilian PB have uniformly positive results (Baiocchi, Heller, and Silva 2008; Wampler 2007a). Still, econometric analyses of Brazilian cities show that in those with PB, per capita social spending tends to be higher and more redistributive (Marquetti and Bêrni 2006) and access to public services like water and sewerage tends to increase while poverty tends to decrease, especially in cities where PB remains in place for a longer period (Banco Mundial 2008). Brazilian PB also often encourages solidarity among citizens, stimulating the adoption of pluralist rather than clientelist or personalist strategies for obtaining public services (Wampler 2007b). On the whole, the outcomes in Bolivia, Guatemala, Nicaragua, and Peru tend to be less heartening. In these countries, the new participatory bodies have suffered from a number of ills. In many cases, mayors refused to implement the national laws, created phantom bodies, or only allowed participation of political allies; generally, citizen participation in local budgeting processes has been neither extensive nor sustained, and government responsiveness and transparency have not seen much improvement.[5]

The major reason that Brazilian PB has tended to be more successful than its counterparts in the Andes and Central America is that political actors with different ideologies designed and employed the new institutions. In Bolivia, Guatemala, Nicaragua, and Peru, radical democratic ideology was not a major motivation. Rather, international financial institutions hoping mostly to reduce corruption pressured Centrist or Rightist presidents to create and/or implement laws requiring citizen participation in municipal

---

4. For a fuller treatment of participatory budgeting in these four countries, see Goldfrank (2007).

5. For Bolivia, see Altman (2003) and Krekeler, Quezada, and Rey (2003); for Guatemala, Puente and Linares (2004) and World Bank Institute (2004a); for Nicaragua, Ortega (2003) and Pineda (2003); for Peru, Chirinos (2004) and López and Bravo (2004); and for a comparison, Goldfrank (2007).

budget processes, especially with the start of the Heavily Indebted Poor Countries relief initiative in 2000. While the names of the new participatory bodies varied, in each country national laws mandated the creation of local councils charged with contributing to municipal planning, budgeting, and oversight.[6] A large majority of municipal governments in these countries were controlled by political parties in the Center or on the Right, with no tradition of promoting citizen participation. On the other hand, because Brazil does *not* have a national law requiring PB of all municipalities, the mayors who implement it there tend to be more committed to participatory democracy. In the 2001–4 period, nearly half of the 170 Brazilian cities with PB were governed by the PT, and many of the others were governed by other Left-leaning parties (Avritzer 2006b, 40–41).

Thus, the institutional design of PB in Brazil generally contrasts with the designs in the other countries. Brazilian PB tends to follow Porto Alegre's open design, while PB elsewhere is regulated or restrictive. While PB in Brazil is usually much more deliberative, offering citizens the opportunity to debate and decide upon investment priorities in public assemblies, the participation laws in the other countries give mostly consultative powers to the local development councils. The structure of Brazilian PB is also less formal; it is open to individual participants regardless of their organizational affiliation. In the Andean and Central American cases, participation is often restricted to representatives of government-selected preexisting civil society organizations. And in Guatemala, Nicaragua, and Peru, government officials receive half of the council seats or more. In Brazil, few cities beyond the lone case of Santo André use such a formalized structure for PB, and in Santo André, where government officials held half the seats, PB's effects on the quality of democracy have been mixed at best (Wampler 2007, chap. 6).

Other advantages also aided the more generalized success of Brazilian PB. Brazil's greater degree of decentralization and greater wealth meant that its local governments benefitted from larger budgets, on average, compared to those in the other countries. Bolivia was nearly as administratively and fiscally decentralized as Brazil, but was (and still is) much poorer. Brazil, along with Peru, was also more politically decentralized, with elected officials at both the municipal and regional levels. By contrast, regional officials

---

6. In Bolivia, the councils are called oversight committees; in Peru, coordination councils; and in Nicaragua and Guatemala, there are neighborhood or community development councils as well as municipal development councils.

were appointed in Nicaragua, Guatemala, and Bolivia (until 2005), and the national governments often decentralized resources to the regional rather than municipal governments so as to privilege their allies and punish the opposition. Finally, because of their relatively recent civil wars, many communities in Nicaragua, Guatemala, and Peru remained polarized to different degrees, and local civil society organizations thus often had shorter-lived and weaker traditions of cooperation with one another and were sometimes wary of government-led collaborative initiatives. In Brazil, as well as in Bolivia, insurgencies and counterinsurgencies had been much less relevant and much further in the past, and they did not impose any additional stress on already existing class and ethnic divides among civil society organizations.

The preceding comparison might suggest that PB can only be successfully replicated in Brazil. However, despite the generally poor results of participatory budgeting institutions in the Andean and Central American contexts, several stories of deepening democracy exist, some of them relatively predictable and some quite surprising. In a comparison of fourteen studies of participatory budgeting in Bolivia, Guatemala, Nicaragua, and Peru, the most unexpected cases of genuinely effective PB that I found were in Huaccana and Limatambo, Peru, and Curahuara de Carangas, Bolivia (Goldfrank 2007). All three are very poor, rural, and mostly indigenous small towns (with a population of around ten thousand inhabitants) with severe deficiencies in public services and scarce local resources. Both Huaccana and Limatambo suffered from Peru's civil war in the 1980s. Limatambo, in addition, faced long-standing, violent, and deep divisions between the majority Quechua-speakers and the richer minority Ladinos, or *mistis,* who had controlled politics for generations. And Curahuara de Carangas is among the poorest towns of Bolivia's harsh highlands, with well over half the residents living in extreme poverty; prior to the mid-1990s it never had a municipal government and was ignored by regional governments. Though each town overcame these obstacles in different ways, they shared in common an indigenous mayor who could draw on prior local customs of participation and an institutional design that made PB more open than the national laws suggested.

Crucially, as in the other more successful cases of Peruvian PB, in Huaccana participatory budgeting started prior to the 2003 national law requiring it. The year before, the Catholic charity organization CARE-Peru chose Huaccana for a PB pilot project, and the mayor agreed to implement it. Because political parties were largely absent, no strongly institutionalized opposition with clientelist ties to local social organizations existed, which facilitated the creation of a relatively open process. Even after the national law passed and a new mayor took office, Huaccana's PB remained open. The new mayor did not follow the law's requirement that only legally registered social organizations with at least three years of proven existence could participate, but continued to allow all citizens the right to voice and vote in submunicipal public assemblies that established the community's investment priorities and elected representatives to the municipal assembly. In addition to the absence of opposition to PB, also helpful were the technical and financial aid provided by CARE-Peru, Oxfam, and the British Department for International Development, as well as the strong bonds among peasant communities created by collective landholding. Overall, in PB's first two years, about 20 percent of voting-age citizens participated, previously excluded sectors of civil society (including women's and peasant organizations) gained access to public policy decision making and began building networks of cooperation with other organizations and with government institutions, and municipal spending became more equitable, as the poorest and most previously neglected zones in Huaccana received the most resources (Ventura 2004a).

Curahuara de Carangas provides a similar story, in that external aid helped overcome the lack of local resources, and the formalization of participation by national laws was circumvented thanks to local indigenous participatory traditions and the absence of strongly institutionalized political parties.[7] Foreign aid (including HIPC II funds) made up over half of the municipal budget from 2001 to 2003, primarily from the German Agency for Technical Cooperation. The trade union NGO Swiss Workers Aid played a leading role through its Program to Support Democracy, which provided information on the participation laws to the newly endowed municipal authorities. Curahuara de Carangas had been virtually untouched by the national government for decades, which meant that political parties had been mostly absent and that the town had been self-governed using the Aymara practice of reciprocal, rotating volunteer labor (cargos) through kinship-based communities (ayllus) on collectively owned land. Unlike much of the rest of Bolivia, where political parties in power tried to structure the new budget oversight committees in their favor and those out of power tried to obstruct participation, in Curahuara de Carangas all the municipal candidates signed an agreement to remain autonomous of their respective political parties and to avoid party interference in municipal affairs. Subsequently, citizens from each of the ten

---

7. This section is based on case studies by the World Bank Institute (2004b) and Hofmann (2002).

ayllus as well as the one existing neighborhood association participated in the election of members to the budget oversight committee as well as in workshops to decide upon the municipal government's annual budget and five-year development plan and in an annual municipal assembly to evaluate implementation. Because everyone in the town is a member of an *ayllu* (or, in the town seat, of the neighborhood association), no one is excluded.

As in Huaccana, Curahuara de Carangas saw significant advances in the quality of local democracy after the adoption of PB reforms. While mayors in many other Bolivian towns have been censured for corruption and had their mandates revoked by the city council (Altman 2003), municipal government in Curahuara de Carangas has been characterized by a high degree of transparency and the continuity in office of the mayor. Local infrastructure has also improved considerably, especially with regard to schools, roads, and electricity, which was the primary demand of the participants in budget discussions. The participation reforms also revitalized and helped change the nature of existing social organizations, particularly the *ayllus*. Perhaps most significantly, after a long tradition of political exclusion had reduced their interest in participating, women's involvement in the *ayllu* system (and in local government) increased and became more important. Female holders of the highest *cargo*, Mama t'alla, report that "now they are listened to and respected as traditional authorities within their *ayllus* and also by the municipal government" (World Bank Institute 2004b, 14).

Whereas the success of PB in Huaccana and Curahuara de Carangas seems at least partly determined by the strong presence of international NGOs and the absence of an institutionalized opposition, the mayor of Limatambo faced the opposite situation.[8] Yet Wilber Rozas, Limatambo's mayor for three consecutive terms from 1993 to 2002, still managed to invent and implement a sophisticated and open participatory budgeting process prior to Peru's national PB law. Drawing on Quechua customs of working for the community (*minka*) or the government (*mita*) and Limatambo's more recent history of peasant organizing, as well from his own experience as a rural development worker, Rozas created a Communal and Neighborhood Council with six delegates (three women and three men) elected in public assemblies in each of the thirty-three indigenous communities and the mostly Ladino city center. This new Council was charged with drawing up a municipal development plan, prioritizing annual investments, and overseeing government implementation. Despite opposition from the traditionally most

---

8. This section is based on case studies by Ventura (2004b) and Llona and Soria (2005).

powerful political parties—APRA and Acción Popular—and the history of Ladino paternalistic and clientelistic control of the indigenous population, the new PB system stimulated widespread participation, with assemblies in each community to prioritize public works projects and elect delegates. Because indigenous communities are exempt from property taxes and the municipal government had a small budget, in order for public works projects to be feasible, participation also included volunteer labor and resources such as wood, tools, and adobe. Following years of neglect, participatory budgeting in Limatambo succeeded in bringing much-needed improvements to infrastructure in all thirty-three communities, including potable water, irrigation pipes, and reservoirs, as well as roads linking the communities to one another and to the town center. And after being excluded from politics and living under essentially feudal relations with Ladino landowners for centuries, the Quechua-speaking population of Limatambo became the primary decision makers but without excluding the Ladinos, whom they specifically called on to participate in assemblies of the town center. Rozas, moreover, went on to be elected mayor of the Province of Anta (in which Limatambo is located), where he adopted PB as well.

Many of the other more well-regarded and well-known cases of PB in Peru, including those of Ilo and Villa El Salvador, are less unexpected. For example, PB in Ilo and Villa El Salvador was implemented by a political party on the Left with a commitment to participation (the United Left); both had strong civil society support from either unions or popular associations, and both faced weak opposition. Villa El Salvador, one of the larger (over three hundred thousand residents) and poorer municipalities within metropolitan Lima, made up for its weaker resource base compared to the relatively developed port city of Ilo with the strong presence of national and international NGOs. As in most of Peru's other successful cases, in both Ilo and Villa El Salvador, PB began before the national law passed and was thus more open than the national law suggested, allowing for direct citizen participation in public assemblies to determine investment priorities and democratic election of delegates to the city-wide decision-making bodies. Not surprisingly, PB in Ilo and Villa El Salvador has achieved high rates of participation and has helped revitalize neighborhood organizations, increase transparency, and improve municipal government responsiveness.

Examining additional cases makes it clear that neither Porto Alegre nor Brazil is uniquely capable of successfully deepening democracy through participatory budgeting. Rather, the propitious conditions and open design of PB in Porto Alegre can be found elsewhere, although clearly not everywhere.

The continuing rise of Left and indigenous politicians in the region's local governments should bode well for the future of PB in Latin America, whether it is nationally mandated or locally driven. Also promising is the discovery that even under adverse conditions PB can occasionally succeed if participatory reformers find facilitating local or external resources. In the face of strongly institutionalized opposition, reformers may try invoking older community norms of participation, if available, and inviting rivals to participate (as Rozas did in Limatambo). In the face of centralized national government, reformers may call on donor organizations for technical and financial support. And, at the national level, reformers might continue to push for decentralizing measures that provide local governments with resources that better match their responsibilities. In all cases, reformers should strive to ensure an open design of participatory budgeting.

The Latin American Left and the Future of Participatory Democracy

Since the inauguration of Hugo Chávez in Venezuela in 1999, Latin America has witnessed a decade-long progression of Left-leaning candidates ascend to the presidency, including not only Lula in Brazil and Vázquez in Uruguay, but also those in Bolivia, Ecuador, El Salvador, Paraguay, and, perhaps more questionably, Argentina, Chile (before 2010), and Nicaragua. Even in countries presently governed by the Right, such as Mexico and Colombia, the Left controls the capital city. Does this unparalleled political shift toward the Left signify the spread of participatory democracy as well? Will the Left somehow scale up its local participatory institutions to the national level, extend them throughout the national territory, and/or invent new institutions, or will it scale back participatory endeavors? Do the chances for developing participatory institutions capable of deepening democracy increase or decrease with the Left in national power? While these questions are ripe for future research, some conjectures about the current patterns of and prospects for participatory democracy in the region are possible at present.

Though a great deal of uncertainty exists about the future, one can divide the recent national participatory experiences of the Left into four groups. For the first group, citizen participation plays a role in national discourse but remains a primarily local-level phenomenon in practice. This is the case not only for those places where the Left has obtained local but not national power, such as in Mexico City and Bogotá, but also for countries with Left-leaning presidents, including those in Argentina and, until recently, Chile.

While Argentine and Chilean presidents have spoken of the importance of expanding citizen participation, none has created important new channels of participation. The Peronist and Socialist parties, however, have implemented participatory budgeting locally, in a dozen cities in Chile and several in Argentina, where the most enduring and well-known case of PB is under the Socialists of Rosario. Given the absence of a strong commitment to participatory democracy within the ruling parties, it appears unlikely that national or nationwide participatory institutions are on the horizon in Chile and Argentina. On the other hand, it is not inconceivable that the Left will eventually win national power in Mexico or Colombia, where Left mayors have won consecutive victories in the capital city and have recently introduced or reinforced participatory budgeting.

For the second group, comprising Ecuador, Bolivia, and perhaps Paraguay, participatory democracy plays a stronger role in discourse than in the first group. More importantly, new channels of citizen participation have been written into the proposed constitutions of Ecuador and Bolivia. Article 95 of Ecuador's new constitution, for example, states that "citizens [male and female], individually and collectively, will participate as protagonists in decision making, planning, and management of public affairs and in the popular control of the institutions of State and society, and of their representatives, in a permanent process of building citizen power." Articles 100 and 267 mention participatory budgeting, but it is unclear from the phrasing whether PB will be mandated for all local governments.[9] Bolivia's new constitution suggests perhaps an even stronger and wider role for citizen participation, in everything from public planning, education, health care, and the environment to management of state-owned businesses. Article 321.II seems to suggest that PB-like institutions will continue to be required in Bolivia: "The determination of public spending and investment will take place through citizen participation mechanisms and state technical and executive planning."[10] In Paraguay, the new president announced that he would attempt to reform the constitution, too, and it will likely include new participatory avenues as well. This second group, however, is also characterized by uncertainty. It is not clear how the new participatory institutions will operate or even if they will be implemented. In all three countries, the president faces strong opposition from previously entrenched elites who opposed modifying the constitution and multiplying the spaces for participation. Thus, while it is

---

9. See http://pdba.georgetown.edu/Constitutions/Ecuador/ecuador08.html.
10. See http://pdba.georgetown.edu/Constitutions/Bolivia/bolivia09.html.

relatively likely that attempts at expanding participation will be forthcoming, it is equally likely that they will be accompanied by significant conflict.

Such has been the case for the third group, comprising Chávez in Venezuela and Ortega in Nicaragua. In the nearly ten years under Chávez, the Venezuelan government has experimented with dozens of new avenues for citizen participation that have been resisted by opposition political parties and civil society organizations who charge that they are clientelist or even totalitarian tools for undermining representative democracy rather than advances toward participatory democracy. Notably, the efforts to expand participation under Chávez occurred simultaneously with recentralization of resources and responsibilities, not decentralization. One of the most important participatory initiatives was the attempt to create Local Public Planning Councils in all municipalities, which essentially entailed spreading LCR's "parish government" idea throughout Venezuela. This attempt failed due to tensions between pro- and anti-Chávez forces and to opposition from mayors and city councilors who were reluctant to share power with citizens. Currently, Venezuela is undergoing the largest experiment in direct citizen participation in the region (and perhaps the world), with roughly a third of its total population, over eight million people, participating in 33,549 Communal Councils (Goldfrank 2008, 24). An invention of the Chávez administration, the Communal Councils can be formed by between two hundred and four hundred families in urban areas, a minimum of twenty families in rural areas, and a minimum of ten indigenous families. Their role is to act as microgovernments, selecting, planning, implementing, and monitoring community projects. The primary decision-making body is the citizens' assembly, in which all those fifteen years or older may participate, and 10 percent of the adults in the community must participate for the decisions to be legitimate.

The number of participants in the Communal Councils is impressive, and the percentage of the population involved is much higher than that of most cases of participatory budgeting. However, thus far many scholars and activists have strongly questioned the quality of participation within the Communal Councils. Specifically, they have criticized the Communal Councils for the lack of transparency and clear rules governing the allocation of funds to them, the multiplication and overlapping of their roles with those of more technically qualified municipal governments and already existing participatory bodies, their lack of autonomy vis-à-vis the central government, and the excessively micro-level focus, which hinders effective urban planning and tends to create social and political homogeneity among participants, thus contributing to continued polarization as minority, anti-Chávez voices fear exclusion (Goldfrank 2008, 29). Nonetheless, the multiplication of spaces for participation under Chávez, combined most likely with expanded social spending and the general approval of the Chávez presidency, have led large majorities of Venezuelans to view their democracy favorably. Venezuelans' "satisfaction with the functioning of democracy" has generally been higher than the Latin American average during the Chávez presidency and invariably higher than it was before Chávez, when Venezuelans usually ranked lower on satisfaction with democracy.[11]

The Citizen Power Councils in Nicaragua are quite similar to the Communal Councils but have been in place for less time and are under the personal direction of the first lady. The Citizen Power Councils have received many of the same criticisms as the Communal Councils. However, compared to Venezuela's Communal Councils, the Citizen Power Councils seem to be much less successful in attracting participants, more directly linked to the ruling party, and more controversial, as they were held up in court for nearly a year before being authorized. Even advocates of participation view them as clientelist vehicles (Cuadra and Ruiz 2008; *Revista Envío* 2008). The Citizen Power Councils are unlikely to help pacify Nicaraguan politics or help the government improve its democratic qualifications or popularity.

The administrations of Lula in Brazil and Vázquez in Uruguay make up the last grouping, one also characterized by multiple participatory endeavors, as in Venezuela, but of a much more social-democratic, corporatist type that relies less on direct participation and that has not encountered nearly as much opposition (Goldfrank 2008). Each administration created a council bringing together representatives of business associations, unions, and nongovernmental organizations: Brazil's Council for Economic and Social Development and Uruguay's National Economic Council. In Brazil the representatives are handpicked by the government and do not have a mandate from their own organizations, while in Uruguay the organizations choose their representatives. Each administration has also convened several (and in Brazil, dozens of) consultative public policy conferences, in which thousands (and in Brazil, millions) of citizens participated. In addition, Lula's first administration implemented an NGO-driven consultation process for

11. From 1995 to 1998, the percentage of Venezuelans surveyed who were very satisfied or satisfied with democracy averaged 34 percent, compared to 36 percent for all of Latin America, and compared to 48 percent for Venezuela and 32 percent for Latin America in the 1999–2007 period when Chávez was president (my calculations from Latinobarómetro 2006, 74, 2007, 88).

the multiyear budget and Vázquez reinitiated the system of tripartite salary councils that had been a part of Uruguayan labor relations from the 1940s to the 1970s, expanding it to include rural as well as urban unions in collective bargaining with business and government representatives.

On the whole, participatory initiatives under Vázquez received better reviews from analysts and activists than those under Lula. The PT's social movement allies, in particular, criticized not only the Lula administration's corruption scandals, but even more, its failure to recreate the kinds of open participatory institutions the PT was known for at the local level. Their expectations perhaps exceeded those of their Uruguayan counterparts, but while they roundly criticize the lack of impact citizen participation has had on public policy in Lula's Brazil, in Uruguay the perception is that participation efforts have been structured more democratically and have yielded more positive results, especially with regard to wages, working conditions, and economic policy. In addition, at the local level, the FA has renewed its participatory budgeting efforts in Montevideo and expanded it to five other departments where they hold power, meaning that well over half of Uruguay's population can now use local-level PB. In Brazil, while the PT has expanded the number of municipal governments under its control, the percentage of the population under a PT mayor declined as the party lost in many large state capitals, including Porto Alegre, where participatory budgeting remains in place albeit in a weakened form, and São Paulo, where the new administration abandoned PB. Given the record of the Lula administration and the changes within the PT, serious doubts have arisen over the party's commitment to participatory democracy.

The current era is thus characterized by two paradoxes of participation. On the one hand, the Latin American Left's most famous local government innovation, participatory budgeting, has been taken up by parties from across the political spectrum as well as by international development organizations intent on encouraging PB throughout the region and the globe. On the other hand, for the most part, the Left's national governments have *not* adopted participatory budgeting either as a model for national participatory initiatives or as a requirement for municipal governments. Both paradoxes invite future research. It remains to be seen whether or not political forces that do not have an ideological commitment to deepening democracy through expanding citizen participation can make PB work, and do so in contexts for which it was not initially designed. My expectation is that PB will not successfully serve as a politically neutral "tool" for democracy and development, as many international donors are advertising. My fear is that as it spreads, participatory budgeting will continue in many cases to be designed in such a way as to restrict its potential. My hope, however, is that in countries where PB is nationally mandated, such as Peru, local movements will continue to push for a more open design. It is promising that the Dominican Republic's national PB law requires an accessible, informal structure of participation reminiscent of the Porto Alegre model, yet it is too early to predict how well the law will be implemented.

It is also unclear whether the Left's national governments can succeed in deepening democracy with the participation mechanisms they currently employ. My expectation is that because few, if any, of the new institutions are simultaneously broad-based, inclusive, transparent, and deliberative, any improvements in the quality of democracy will be relatively small. Those that are more broad-based and transparent lack decision-making power, and those that have some degree of decision-making power are either not broad-based, not transparent, or not inclusive. My fear is that the attempts to design and implement participatory institutions that combine these features will lead to violent reactions from previously entrenched political forces who are willing to save representative democracy from too much citizen participation by destroying democracy altogether.[12] Finally, my hope is that participatory reformers of all political stripes might learn from the lessons of the local experiences so as to avoid weakening or destroying democracy and instead find ways to create institutions that deepen democracy.

---

12. Arguably, this is what occurred in Honduras in 2009 when President Manuel Zelaya was overthrown in a military coup.

Bibliography

Abers, Rebecca. 1996. "From Ideas to Practice: The Partido dos Trabalhadores and Participatory Governance in Brazil." *Latin American Perspectives* 23 (4): 35–53.
———. 1998. "From Clientelism to Cooperation: Local Government, Participatory Policy, and Civic Organizing in Porto Alegre, Brazil." *Politics and Society* 26 (4): 511–37.
———. 2000. *Inventing Local Democracy: Grassroots Politics in Brazil.* Boulder: Lynne Rienner.
Ackerman, John. 2004. "Co-governance for Accountability: Beyond 'Exit' and 'Voice.'" *World Development* 32 (3): 447–63.
Aguirre, Rosario. 1990. "Carencias urbanas, organizaciones barriales, y gestión municipal en Montevideo (1980–1990)." Serie Seminários y Talleres 32. Montevideo: CIEDUR.
———. 1993. "Relación entre organizaciones barriales y la gestión municipal: El caso de Montevideo." *Medio Ambiente y Urbanización* 10 (43–44): 91–99.
Aguirre, Rosario, Gerónimo de Sierra, and Inés Iens. 1993. "Descentralización, participación y los Centros Comunales Zonales vistos por los vecinos." In *Participación ciudadana y relaciones de gobierno,* edited by CIEDUR, CIESU, ICP, and FESUR. Montevideo: Trilce.
Aguirre, Rosario, Gerónimo de Sierra, Inés Iens, and Blanca Charbonnier. 1992. "Informe de una encuesta a vecinos sobre descentralización, participación y Centros Comunales Zonales." Serie Investigaciones 99. Montevideo: CIEDUR.
Alcaldía del Municipio Libertador. 1994a. *Memoria y cuenta: 1993.* Caracas.
———. 1994b. "Anotaciones sobre la democracia." *Carta del Despacho* 2.
———. 1995a. *Gestión municipal: 1993–1995.* Caracas.
———. 1995b. *Memoria y cuenta: 1994.* Caracas.
Altman, David, with Rickard Lalander. 2003. "Bolivia's Popular Participation Law: An Undemocratic Democratisation Process?" In *Decentralisation and Democratic Governance: Experiences from India, Bolivia and South Africa,* edited by Axel Hadenius. Stockholm: Expert Group on Development Issues.
Alvarado, Arturo, and Diane Davis. 2004. "Citizen Participation, Democratic Governance, and the PRD in Mexico City: The Challenge of Political Transition." In *The Left in the City: Participatory Local Governments in Latin America,* edited by Daniel Chavez and Benjamin Goldfrank. London: Latin American Bureau and Transnational Institute.
Alvarez, Angel. 1998. "Venezuelan Local and National Elections, 1958–1995." In *Urban Elections in Democratic Latin America,* edited by Henry Dietz and Gil Shidlo. Wilmington: Scholarly Resources.
Alvarez, Rosangel. 1997. "Redefinición del ambito de 'Lo Público' en el marco del proceso de descentralización adelantado en Venezuela: El caso del Municipio Libertador (1993–1995)." Master's thesis, Universidad Central de Venezuela.

Alvarez, Sonia. 1990. *Engendering Democracy in Brazil: Women's Movements in Transition Politics*. Princeton: Princeton University Press.

————. 1993. "'Deepening' Democracy: Popular Movement Networks, Constitutional Reform, and Radical Urban Regimes in Contemporary Brazil." In *Mobilizing the Community*, edited by Robert Fisher and Joseph Kling. London: SAGE.

————. 1999. "Advocating Feminism: The Latin American Feminist NGO 'Boom.'" *International Feminist Journal of Politics* 1 (2): 181–209.

Ames, Barry. 2001. *The Deadlock of Democracy in Brazil*. Ann Arbor: University of Michigan Press.

Amostra. 1993. "Avaliação da atual administração: Prefeitura Municipal de Porto Alegre." Mimeograph. December.

————. 1996. "Avaliação da administração municipal de Porto Alegre." Mimeograph. December.

————. 1997. "Relatório de pesquisa: Avaliação da administração municipal de Porto Alegre." Mimeograph. September.

Andreatta, Humberto. 1997. *Orçamento Participativo, Porto Alegre: Você é quem faz uma cidade de verdade*. Porto Alegre: Prefeitura Municipal de Porto Alegre.

Angell, Alan. 1996. "Incorporating the Left into Democratic Politics." In *Constructing Democratic Governance: Latin America and the Caribbean in the 1990s*, edited by Jorge Dominguez and Abraham Lowenthal. Baltimore: Johns Hopkins University Press.

Angotti, Thomas. 1996. "Latin American Urbanization and Planning: Inequality and Unsustainability in North and South." *Latin American Perspectives* 23 (4): 12–34.

Arana, Mariano, and Fernando Giordano. 1992. "Montevideo: Between Participation and Authoritarianism." In *Rethinking the Latin American City*, edited by Richard Morse and Jorge Hardoy. Washington, D.C.: Woodrow Wilson Center Press; Baltimore: Johns Hopkins University Press. [Originally published in Spanish in 1988.]

Arconada, Santiago. 1995. "Ordenanza municipal de los gobiernos parroquiales." *Revista SIC* 578:347–48.

————. 1996. "La experiencia de Antímano. Reflexiones sobre algunos aspectos de la lucha por la constitución de los Gobiernos Parroquiales en el Municipio Libertador de la ciudad de Caracas." *Revista Venezolana de Economía y Ciencias Sociales* 2 (4): 155–68.

Arnstein, Sherry. 1971. "A Ladder of Participation in the USA." *Journal of the Royal Town Planning Institute* 57:176–82.

Assies, Willem. 1997. "Social Movements, Democracy, and Political Culture in Brazil." *European Review of Latin American and Caribbean Studies* 63:111–19.

Augustin Filho, Arno. 1994. "A experiência do Orçamento Participativo na Administração Popular da Prefeitura Municipal de Porto Alegre." In *Porto Alegre: O desafio da mudança*, edited by Carlos Henrique Horn. Porto Alegre: Editora Ortiz.

————. 1997. "Finanças Públicas." In *Porto da cidadania: A esquerda no governo de Porto Alegre*, edited by Tarso Genro. Porto Alegre: Artes e Ofícios.

Avritzer, Leonardo. 2002. *Democracy and the Public Space in Latin America*. Princeton: Princeton University Press.

————. 2006a. "New Public Spheres in Brazil: Local Democracy and Deliberative Politics." *International Journal of Urban and Regional Research* 30 (3): 623–37.

————. 2006b. "Reforma política e participação no Brasil." In *Reforma política no Brasil*, edited by Leonardo Avritzer and Fátima Anastasia. Belo Horizonte: Editora UFMG.

Azevedo, José Clóvis de. 2000. "A Escola Cidadã: Políticas e práticas." In *Porto Alegre: Uma cidade que conquista*, edited by Raul Pont and Adair Barcelos. Porto Alegre: Artes e Ofícios.

Azevedo, Ricardo de. 1988. "Conselhos Populares: Uma varinha de condão?" *Teoria e Debate* 4:46–49.

Baierle, Sérgio Gregório. 1992. "Um Novo Princípio Ético-Político: Prática Social e Sujeito nos Movimentos Populares Urbanos em Porto Alegre nos Anos 80." Master's thesis, Universidade Estadual de Campinas.

————. 1998. "The Explosion of Experience: The Emergence of a New Political Ethical Principle in Popular Movements in Porto Alegre, Brazil." In *Cultures of Politics, Politics of Cultures: Revisioning Latin American Social Movements*, edited by Sonia Alvarez, Evelina Dagnino, and Arturo Escobar. Boulder: Westview.

————. 2002. "Transformation and Empowerment Through the Participatory Budget." Paper presented at the LogoLink International Workshop on Participatory Planning: Approaches for Local Governance. Bandung, Indonesia, January 20–27.

————. 2008. "Whittling Down the Potential of Participatory Budgeting?" *The Governance Link*. Action Aid. Issue 4.

Baiocchi, Gianpaolo. 2001. "Participation, Activism, and Politics: The Porto Alegre Experiment and Deliberative Democratic Theory." *Politics and Society* 29 (1): 43–72.

————. 2002. "Synergizing Civil Society: State-Civil Society Regimes in Porto Alegre, Brazil." *Political Power and Social Theory* 15:3–86.

————, ed. 2003. *Radicals in Power: The Workers' Party (PT) and Experiments in Urban Democracy in Brazil*. London: Zed Books.

————. 2004. "Porto Alegre: The Dynamism of the Unorganized." In *The Left in the City: Participatory Local Governments in Latin America*, edited by Daniel Chavez and Benjamin Goldfrank. London: Latin American Bureau and Transnational Institute.

————. 2005. *Militants and Citizens: The Politics of Participatory Democracy in Porto Alegre*. Stanford: Stanford University Press.

————. 2006. "The Citizens of Porto Alegre: In Which Marco Borrows Bus Fare and Enters Politics." *Boston Review* 31 (2).

Baiocchi, Gianpaolo, Patrick Heller, and Marcelo Kunrath Silva. 2008. "Making Space for Civil Society: Institutional Reforms and Local Democracy in Brazil." *Social Forces* 86 (3): 911–36.

Balarine, Oscar Fernando Osório. 1995. "Determinação do impacto de fatores sócio-econômicos na formação do estoque habitacional em Porto Alegre." Ph.D. diss., Universidade Federal de Santa Catarina.

Banco Interamericano de Desarrollo (BID) and Programa de las Naciones Unidas para el Desarrollo (PNUD). 1993. *Reforma social y pobreza: Hacia una agenda integrada de desarrollo*. Washington, D.C.: BID and PNUD.

Banco Mundial. 2008. "Rumo a um Orçamento Participativo mais inclusivo e efetivo em Porto Alegre." Washington, D.C. February.

Barber, Benjamin. 1984. *Strong Democracy: Participatory Politics for a New Age*. Berkeley and Los Angeles: University of California Press.

————. 1998. *A Place for Us: How to Make Society Civil and Democracy Strong.* New York: Hill and Wang.

Barcelos, Lúcio. 2000. "A construção de um sistema público de saúde em Porto Alegre: Um objetivo vitorioso." In *Porto Alegre: Uma cidade que conquista*, edited by Raul Pont and Adair Barcelos. Porto Alegre: Artes e Ofícios.

Barinas Uribe, Marcos. 1999. "Condominio: El Caribe y la vivienda pública." Periferia: Architecture and Urban Design in the Caribbean, Architectural Resources Network, http://www.periferia.org/3000/condominio.html.

Bava, Silvio Caccia. 1995. "Dilemas da gestão municipal democrática." In *Governabilidade e pobreza no Brasil*, edited by Licia Valladares and Magda Prates Coelho. Rio de Janeiro: Civilização Brasileira.

————. 1996. "Desenvolvimento local: Uma alternativa para a crise social?" *São Paulo em Perspectiva* 10 (3): 53–59.

Benton, Lauren. 1986. "Reshaping the Urban Core: The Politics of Housing in Authoritarian Uruguay." *Latin American Research Review* 21 (2): 33–52.

Berman, Serri. 1997. "Civil Society and the Collapse of the Weimar Republic." *World Politics* 49 (3): 401–29.

Berry, Jeffrey, Kent Portney, and Ken Thomson. 1993. *The Rebirth of Urban Democracy.* Washington, D.C.: Brookings Institution.

Biles, Robert. 1978. "Political Participation in Urban Uruguay: Mixing Public and Private Ends." In *Political Participation in Latin America*, vol. 1, *Citizen and State*, edited by John Booth and Mitchell Seligson. New York: Holmes and Meier.

Blair, Harry. 2000. "Participation and Accountability at the Periphery: Democratic Local Governance in Six Countries." *World Development* 28 (1): 21–39.

Bluth, Alejandro, ed. 1988. *Desarrollo urbano y políticas comunales.* Montevideo: PNUD and IMM.

Booth, John, and Mitchell Seligson. 1978. "Images of Political Participation in Latin America." In *Political Participation in Latin America*, vol. 1, *Citizen and State*, edited by John Booth and Mitchell Seligson. New York: Holmes and Meier.

Borja, Jordi, ed. 1989. *Estado, descentralización y democracia.* Bogotá: Foro Nacional por Colombia.

————. 1992. "Past, Present, and Future of Local Government in Latin America." In *Rethinking the Latin American City*, edited by Richard Morse and Jorge Hardoy. Washington, D.C.: Woodrow Wilson Center Press; Baltimore: Johns Hopkins University Press.

————. 1996. "The City, Democracy and Governability: The Case of Barcelona." *International Social Science Journal* 48 (147): 85–93.

Borja, Jordi, and Manuel Castells. 1997. *Local and Global: Management of Cities in the Information Age.* London: UN Centre for Human Settlements and Earthscan Publications.

Bradford, Colin, Jr., ed. 1994. *Redefining the State in Latin America.* Washington, D.C.: OECD Publications and Information Centre.

Branford, Sue, and Bernardo Kucinski. 1995. *Brazil: Carnival of the Oppressed.* London: Latin American Bureau.

Braselli, Selva. 1994. "Dificultades y soluciones para desconcentrar y descentralizar servicios." In *Descentralización y participación ciudadana*, edited by IMM, AECI, and CAM. Montevideo: Trilce.

Bruera, Silvana. 1993. "Apuntes para una evaluación del proceso de descentralización desde las Comisiones Vecinales." In *Participación ciudadana y relaciones de gobierno*, edited by CIEDUR, CIESU, ICP, and FESUR. Montevideo: Trilce.

Bryan, Frank. 1999. "Direct Democracy and Civic Competence: The Case of Town Meeting." In *Citizen Competence and Democratic Institutions*, edited by Stephen Elkin and Karol Soltan. University Park: Pennsylvania State University Press.

Buchabqui, Jorge Santos. 1994. "Reforma administrativa e mudança no modelo de gestão." In *Porto Alegre: O desafio da mudança*, edited by Carlos Henrique Horn. Porto Alegre: Editora Ortiz.

Bucheli, Marisa, and Máximo Rossi. 2001. "Poverty Status in Montevideo (Uruguay) in the 1980s." *Revista de Economía y Administración*. Universidad de Concepción, Chile, 38 (56).

Burki, Javed, and Sebastian Edwards. 1996. *Dismantling the Populist State: The Unfinished Revolution in Latin America and the Caribbean*. Washington, D.C.: World Bank.

Burns, Danny, Robin Hambleton and Paul Hoggett. 1994. *The Politics of Decentralisation: Revitalising Local Democracy*. London: Macmillan.

Buxton, Julia. 2001. *The Failure of Political Reform in Venezuela*. Aldershot, U.K.: Ashgate.

Cabannes, Yves. 2004. "Participatory Budgeting: A Significant Contribution to Participatory Democracy." *Environment and Urbanization* 16 (1): 27–46.

Cabrera San Martín, Laura. 1994. *La descentralización en Montevideo: Reflexiones de los protagonistas*. Colonia: Fin del Siglo.

Calvetti, Jaqueline, Pablo Gorritti, Graciela Otonelli, Adriana Pizzolanti, Pilar Varela, and Silvia Zapata. 1998. "Análisis sobre los Concejos Vecinales." Montevideo: IMM.

CAMP. 2007. "Orçamento Participativo perde espaço na Prefeitura de Porto Alegre." *Vento Sul* 13:14–15.

Campani, Darci, and Rosalino Mello. 2000. "Da limpeza pública à gestão ambiental de resíduos sólidos." In *Porto Alegre: Uma cidade que conquista*, edited by Raul Pont and Adair Barcelos. Porto Alegre: Artes e Ofícios.

Campbell, Tim. 2003. *The Quiet Revolution: Decentralization and the Rise of Political Participation in Latin American Cities*. Pittsburgh: University of Pittsburgh Press.

Canache, Damarys. 2002. *Venezuela: Public Opinion and Protest in a Fragile Democracy*. Miami: North-South Center Press, University of Miami.

Canel, Eduardo. 1992. "Democratization and the Decline of Urban Social Movements in Uruguay: A Political-Institutional Account." In *The Making of Social Movements in Latin America: Identity, Strategy, and Democracy*, edited by Arturo Escobar and Sonia Alvarez. Boulder: Westview.

———. 1998. "Political Opportunities and Local Agency: Municipal Decentralization and Community Participation in Montevideo." Paper presented at the International Congress of the Latin American Studies Association, Chicago, September 24–26.

Canzani, Augustín. 1989. "La sociedad montevideana: Problemas y desafíos." Serie Uruguay hoy 5. Montevideo: CIEDUR.

Carlos, Euzinia, and Marta Zorzal e Silva. 2006. "Associativismo, participação e políticas públicas." *Política e Sociedade* 5 (9): 163–94.

Carr, Barry, and Steve Ellner, eds. 1993. *The Latin American Left: From the Fall of Allende to Perestroika*. Boulder: Westview.

Cassel, Guilherme, and João Verle. 1994. "A política tributária e de saneamento financeiro da Administração Popular." In *Porto Alegre: O desafio da mudança*, edited by Carlos Henrique Horn. Porto Alegre: Editora Ortiz.

Castañeda, Jorge. 1994. *Utopia Unarmed: The Latin American Left After the Cold War*. New York: Random House.

Castells, Manuel, Mireia Belil, and Jordi Borja. 1989. "Urbanización y democracia local en América Latina." In *Estado, descentralización y democracia*, edited by Jordi Borja. Bogotá: Foro Nacional por Colombia.

Celiberti, Liliana, and Solana Quesada. 2004. *Ciudadanía de las mujeres desde los espacios locales de Montevideo: La Comuna Mujer del CCZ 12*. Montevideo: Comisión Nacional de Seguimiento Mujeres por Democracia, Equidad y Ciudadanía.

Centro de Participación Popular. 1989. "Descentralización Municipal y Participación Popular." Transcript of Seminar, Montevideo, September 29–October 4.

CEPAL. 2000. "De la urbanización acelerada a la consolidación de los asentamientos humanos en América Latina y el Caribe: El espacio regional." http://www.eclac.cl/publicaciones MedioAmbiente/6/LCG2116/G-2116-e.pdf. Santiago, Chile: United Nations Economic Commission for Latin America and the Caribbean.

Chambers, Robert. 1998. Foreword to *Who Changes? Institutionalizing Participation in Development*, edited by James Blackburn with Jeremy Holland. London: Intermediate Technology.

Charbonnier, Blanca. 1992. "Análisis de entrevistas en profundidad a siete coordinadores de los Centros Comunales Zonales." Serie Investigaciones 97. Montevideo: CIEDUR.

Chasquetti, Daniel. 1995. "Entre la complicidad y el lamento: La relación IMM-ADEOM (1985–1993)." *Cuadernos del CLAEH* 72:97–111.

Chavez, Daniel. 2008. "Hacia la participación pasteurizada: La transición del presupuesto participativo a la gobernanza solidaria local en Porto Alegre, Brasil." In *Presupuestos participativos: Nuevos territorios*, edited by Joaquín Recio and Andrés Falck. Málaga: Atrapasueños.

Chavez, Daniel, and Benjamin Goldfrank, eds. 2004. *The Left in the City: Participatory Local Governments in Latin America*. London: Latin American Bureau and Transnational Institute.

Chirinos Segura, Luis. 2004. "Participación ciudadana en gobiernos regionales: El caso de los Consejos de Coordinación Regional." In *La participación ciudadana y la construcción de la democracia en América Latina*, edited by Grupo Propuesta Ciudadana. Lima: Ser, Consode, Oxfam, Grupo Propuesta Ciudadana, Participa Peru, DFID, EED, and USAID-Peru.

CIDADE. 1995. "Pesquisa sobre a população que participa da discussão do orçamento público junto à Prefeitura Municipal de Porto Alegre." Porto Alegre: CIDADE.

———. 1999. *Quem é o público do Orçamento Participativo: Seu perfil, por que participa e o que pensa do processo*. Porto Alegre: CIDADE and PMPA.

———. 2003. *Who Is the Public of the Participatory Budgeting? 2002*. Porto Alegre: CIDADE.

———. 2007a. *Olhar de mulher: A fala das conselheiras do Orçamento Participativo de Porto Alegre*. 2nd ed. Porto Alegre: CIDADE.

———. 2007b. "Renovação de lideranças e democracia, uma reflexão necessária." *Boletim CIDADE* 6 (39): 4.

CIDC. 1997. *Descentralización, una experiencia en proceso: Elección y conformación del Concejo Vecinal de Zona 9, 1993–1995*. Montevideo: Ediciones IDEAS.

CIGU. 2008. "News Briefs." *Breves de Reforzar: Reinforcing Participatory Budgeting in Latin America* 8, International Center for Urban Management, March.

CLAEH. 1996. *Montevideo en cifras.* Montevideo: CLAEH and IMM.

Collier, David. 1993. "The Comparative Method." In *Political Science: The State of the Discipline II,* edited by Ada Finifter. Washington, D.C.: American Political Science Association.

Collier, David, and Steven Levitsky. 1997. "Democracy with Adjectives: Conceptual Innovation in Comparative Research." *World Politics* 49:430–51.

Comisión Permanente de Participación Ciudadana. 1994. *Experienca de Gobiernos Parroquiales en el Municipio Libertador (Primer Encuentro).* August 26–27. Caracas: Alcaldía de Caracas.

Communities and Local Government. 2008. "Participatory Budgeting: A Draft National Strategy." Department for Communities and Local Government, United Kingdom. March.

Concejo del Municipio Libertador. 1994. *Cabildo Abierto.* Caracas. September–October.

———. 1995. "Ordenanza sobre la creación y funcionamento del Gobierno Parroquial." *Gaceta Municipal del Distrito Municipal* 1549-A. Caracas. November 23.

———. 1996a. "Ordenanza sobre la organización y funcionamiento de las Juntas Parroquiales y Comunales." *Gaceta Municipal del Distrito Municipal* 1608-A. Caracas. August 5.

———. 1996b. "Reglamento interior y de debates para las Juntas Parroquiales del Municipio Libertador." *Gaceta Municipal del Distrito Municipal* 1639-A. Caracas. December 27.

Contreras, Carlos, and Lucmila Martínez. 1996. "La experiencia participatoria en el Municipio Libertador en la Gestión del Alcalde Aristóbulo Istúriz (1993–1995): El Gobierno Parroquial de Antímano." Master's thesis, Universidad Central de Venezuela.

Cooke, Bill, and Uma Kothari. 2001. "The Case for Participation as Tyranny." In *Participation: The New Tyranny?* edited by Bill Cooke and Uma Kothar. London: Zed Books.

Coppedge, Michael. 1994. *Strong Parties and Lame Ducks: Presidential Partyarchy and Factionalism in Venezuela.* Stanford: Stanford University Press.

Coraggio, José Luis. 1991. *Ciudades sin rumbo: Investigación urbana y proyecto popular.* Quito: CIUDAD and SIAP.

———. 1999. *Descentralización, el día después . . .* Buenos Aires: Universidad de Buenos Aires.

Cornwall, Andrea. 2006. "Historical Perspectives on Participation in Development." *Commonwealth and Comparative Politics* 44 (1): 49–65.

Costa Bonino, Luis. 1995. *La crisis del sistema político uruguayo: Partidos políticos y democracracia hasta 1973.* Montevideo: Fundación de Cultura Universitaria.

Couto, Cláudio Gonçalves. 1995. *O desafio de ser governo: O PT na prefeitura de São Paulo (1989–1992).* Rio de Janeiro: Paz e Terra.

Crook, Richard, and James Manor. 1998. *Democracy and Decentralisation in South Asia and West Africa: Participation, Accountability, and Performance.* Cambridge: Cambridge University Press.

Cuadra, Rosario, and Damaris Ruiz. 2008. "Por todo el país los CPC están esperando 'orientaciones' de arriba." *Revista Envío* 312:22–27.

Cunill, Nuria. 1991. *Participación ciudadana: Dilemas y perspectivas para la democratización de los estados latinoamericanos.* Caracas: CLAD.

Cunill Grau, Nuria. 1997. *Repensando lo público a través de la sociedad: Nuevas formas de gestión pública y representación social*. Caracas: CLAD and Nueva Sociedad.

Dagnino, Evelina, Alberto Olvera, and Aldo Panfichi. 2006. "Para uma outra leitura da disputa pela construção democrática na América Latina." In *A disputa pela construção democrática na América Latina,* edited by Evelina Dagnino, Alberto Olvera, and Aldo Panfichi. São Paulo: Paz e Terra; Campinas: Unicamp.

Dahl, Robert. 1989. *Democracy and Its Critics*. New Haven: Yale University Press.

———. 1990. *After the Revolution? Authority in a Good Society*. Rev. ed. New Haven: Yale University Press.

Da Silva, Flávio. 2000. "A política habitacional no 3° mandato da Administração Popular." In *Porto Alegre: Uma cidade que conquista,* edited by Raul Pont and Adair Barcelos. Porto Alegre: Artes e Ofícios.

Daudelin, Jean, and W. E. Hewitt. 1995. "Churches and politics in Latin America: Catholicism at the crossroads." *Third World Quarterly* 16 (2): 221–36.

DEMHAB. 1999. *Mapa da irregularidade fundiária de Porto Alegre*. Porto Alegre: Departamento Municipal de Habitação, Prefeitura Municipal de Porto Alegre.

Dienel, Peter. 1999. "Planning Cells: The German Experience." In *Participation Beyond the Ballot Box: European Case Studies in State-Citizen Political Dialogue,* edited by Usman Khan. London: UCL Press.

Dietz, Henry, and Gil Shidlo, eds. 1998. *Urban Elections in Democratic Latin America*. Wilmington: Scholarly Resources.

Dillinger, William. 1994. *Decentralization and Its Implications for Service Delivery*. Washington, D.C.: World Bank.

Dirección General de Personal. 1993. "La Alcaldía de Caracas rinde cuentas." Pamphlet. Caracas.

Division of Decentralization, Coordination Unit. 1997. "Guía para el trabajo de definición de los Compromisos de Gestión, Año 1997." IMM document. March 14.

Doimo, Ana Maria. 1995. *A vez e a voz do popular: Movimentos sociais e participaçãao política no Brasil pós-70*. Rio de Janeiro: Relume-Dumará and ANPOCS.

Dowbor, Ladislau. 1998. "Decentralization and Governance." *Latin American Perspectives* 98 (2): 28–44.

Downie, Andrew. 2000. "Clean Sweep in Brazil." *San Francisco Chronicle,* August 31, A10, A14.

Dutra, Arnaldo Luis. 2000. "O DMAE e a qualificação do saneamento ambiental." In *Porto Alegre: Uma cidade que conquista,* edited by Raul Pont and Adair Barcelos. Porto Alegre: Artes e Ofícios.

Dutra, Olívio. 1990. "A hora das definições estratégicas: Um roteiro para orientar as mudanças políticas, institucionais e administrativas na Prefeitura Municipal de Porto Alegre." Administração Popular, Porto Alegre. April.

———. 1994. "A Experiência na Cidade de Porto Alegre." In *Descentralización y participación ciudadana,* edited by IMM, AECI, and CAM. Montevideo: Trilce.

Eaton, Kent. 2004. "The Link Between Political and Fiscal Decentralization in South America." In *Decentralization and Democracy in Latin America,* edited by Alfred Montero and David Samuels. Notre Dame: University of Notre Dame Press.

Eckstein, Susan, ed. 1989. *Power and Popular Protest: Latin American Social Movements*. Berkeley and Los Angeles: University of California Press.

———. 2006. "Urban Resistance to Neoliberal Democracy Across Latin America." Paper presented at the International Congress of the Latin American Studies Association. San Juan, Puerto Rico, March 15–18.

Elkin, Stephen, and Karol Soltan, eds. 1999. *Citizen Competence and Democratic Institutions.* University Park: Pennsylvania State University Press.

Ellner, Steve. 1999. "Obstacles to the Consolidation of the Venezuelan Neighborhood Movement: National and Local Cleavages." *Journal of Latin American Studies* 31 (1): 75–94.

Ellner, Steve, and David Myers. 2002. "Caracas: Incomplete Empowerment amid Geopolitical Feudalism." In *Capital City Politics in Latin America: Democratization and Empowerment,* edited by David Myers and Henry Dietz. Boulder: Lynne Rienner.

Escobar, Arturo, and Sonia Alvarez, eds. 1992. *The Making of Social Movements in Latin America: Identity, Strategy, and Democracy.* Boulder: Westview.

Ethos. 1994. "Pesquisa: Avaliação da administração municipal." Mimeograph. June.

———. 1995. "Pesquisa de avaliação da administração municipal." Mimeograph. September.

Evans, Peter. 1996a. "Introduction: Development Strategies across the Public-Private Divide." *World Development* 24 (6): 1033–37.

———. 1996b. "Government Action, Social Capital and Development: Reviewing the Evidence on Synergy." *World Development* 24 (6): 1119–32.

———. 1997. "The Eclipse of the State? Reflections on Stateness in an Era of Globalization." *World Politics* 50 (1): 62–87.

———. 2001. "Looking for Agents of Urban Livability in a Globalized Political Economy." In *Livable Cities? Urban Struggles for Livelihood and Sustainability,* edited by Peter Evans. Berkeley and Los Angeles: University of California Press.

———. 2004. "Development as Institutional Change: The Pitfalls of Monocropping and the Potentials of Deliberation." *Studies in Comparative International Development* 38 (4): 30–52.

Facultad de Arquitectura. 1994. *Montevideo: Una aproximación a su conocimiento.* Montevideo: Nordan-Comunidad and Instituto de Teoría de la Arquitectura y Urbanismo.

FASE. 1989. "Uma avaliação inicial do processo de discussão do orçamento." Mimeograph. Porto Alegre. September.

———. 1990. "Porto Alegre—em discussão o orçamento municipal." Mimeograph. Porto Alegre.

Fedozzi, Luciano. 1992. "Avaliação dos quatro anos de Administração Popular: Planejamento de governo e Orçamento Participativo." Internal memo. GAPLAN. PMPA.

———. 1997. *Orçamento Participativo: Reflexões sobre a experiência de Porto Alegre.* Porto Alegre: Tomo Editorial; Rio de Janeiro: FASE and IPPUR.

———. 2007. *Observando o Orçamento Participativo de Porto Alegre. Análise histórica de dados: Perfil social e associativo, avaliação e expectativas.* Porto Alegre: Tomo Editorial.

Fedozzi, Luciano, and Tarson Nuñez. 1993. "Quem é quem no Orçamento Participativo." Mimeograph. Porto Alegre.

Felicissimo, José Roberto. 1994. "A descentralização do estado frente às novas práticas e formas de ação coletiva." *São Paulo em Perspectiva* 8 (2): 45–52.

Fernandes, Sujatha. 2007. "Barrio Women and Popular Politics in Chávez's Venezuela." *Latin American Politics and Society* 49 (3): 97–127.

Ferretti, Rosemary Brum. 1984. "Uma casa nas costas: Análise do Movimento Social Urbano em Porto Alegre, 1975–1982." Master's thesis, Universidade Federal do Rio Grande do Sul.

FESC. 1997. "Porto Alegre e as regiões do Orçamento Participtativo: Alguns indicadores sociais." Mimeograph. Porto Alegre: PMPA. April.

Fialho Alonso, José Antonio. 1994. "Descentralização e participação cidadã: O caso de Porto Alegre." In *Descentralización y participación ciudadana*, edited by IMM, AECI, and CAM. Montevideo: Trilce.

Figuera, Dinorah. 1996. "El Gobierno Parroquial." In *Foro Taller: El Gobierno Parroquial*. Mimeograph. Caracas. July 28.

Filgueira, Fernando. 1991. "La Intendencia Municipal de Montevideo: Dinámica interna y relación con actores privados." In *Gobierno y política en Montevideo*, edited by Carina Perelli, Fernando Filgueira, and Silvana Rubino. Montevideo: PEITHO.

Filgueira, Fernando, Herman Kamil, Fernando Lorenzo, Juan Andrés Moraes, and Andrés Rius. 1999. "Decentralization and Fiscal Discipline in Subnational Governments: The Bailout Problem: The Case of Uruguay." Paper prepared for the project "Fiscal Decentralization in Latin America: The Bailout Problem." Interamerican Development Bank. Montevideo: CIESU-CINVE.

Fiorina, Morris. 1999. "Extreme Voices: A Dark Side of Civic Engagement." In *Civic Engagement in American Democracy*, edited by Theda Skocpol and Morris Fiorina. Washington, D.C.: Brookings Institution; New York: Russell Sage Foundation.

Fishkin, James S. 1992. *The Dialogue of Justice: Toward a Self-Reflective Society*. New Haven: Yale University Press.

———. 1995. *The Voice of the People: Public Opinion and Democracy*. New Haven: Yale University Press.

Font, Núria. 1998. *New Instruments of Citizen Participation*. Barcelona: Institut de Ciències Polítiques i Socials.

Fox, Jonathan. 1995. "The Crucible of Local Politics." *NACLA: Report on the Americas* 29 (1): 15–19.

Francke, Marfil. 1997. "Los caminos de la ciudadanía popular: Un estudio exploratorio en tres parroquias de Caracas." Master's thesis, Universidad Central de Venezuela.

Frente Amplio. 1989. *Bases programáticas para el gobierno departamental*. Documentos 6. Montevideo: Comisión Nacional de Propaganda.

Fullinwider, Robert, ed. 1999. *Civil Society, Democracy, and Civic Renewal*. Lanham, Md.: Rowman and Littlefield.

Fundacomún. 1993. *III Inventario Nacional de Barrios*. Pamphlet.

Fung, Archon. 2007. "Democratic Theory and Political Science: A Pragmatic Method of Constructive Engagement." *American Political Science Review* 101 (3): 443–58.

Fung, Archon, and Erik Olin Wright. 2001. "Deepening Democracy: Innovations in Empowered Participatory Governance." *Politics and Society* 29 (1): 5–41.

———, eds. 2003. *Deepening Democracy: Institutional Innovations in Empowered Participatory Governance*. London: Verso.

GAPLAN. 1991. "Democracia e participação popular." Porto Alegre: PMPA.

———. 1993. "Orçamento Participativo 1994: Critérios e notas." Mimeograph. PMPA.

———. 1995. "Prioridades temáticas OP 1996." Mimeograph. PMPA.

———. 1998. "Plano de Investimentos 1999: Critérios gerais, distribuição de recursos." Mimeograph. PMPA.

García-Guadilla, María Pilar. 1994. "Configuración espacial y movimientos ciu-dadanos: Caracas en cuatro tiempos." In *Las ciudades hablan. Identidades y movimientos sociales en seis metrópolis latinoamericanas*, edited by Tomás Villasante. Caracas: Nueva Sociedad.

Geddes, Barbara. 1990. "How the Cases You Choose Affect the Answers You Get." In *Political Analysis*, vol. 2, edited by James Stimson. Ann Arbor: University of Michigan Press.

Genro, Tarso. 1997. "21 teses para a criação de uma política democrática e socialista." In *Porto da Cidadania: A esquerda no governo de Porto Alegre*, edited by Tarso Genro. Porto Alegre: Artes e Ofícios.

Genro, Tarso, and Raul Pont. 1993. "A presença do governo na comunidade." Internal memo. September.

Genro, Tarso, and Ubiratan de Souza. 1997. *Orçamento Participativo: A experiência de Porto Alegre*. 2nd ed. São Paulo: Fundaçao Perseu Abramo.

Giacomoni, James. 1993. "A comunidade como instância executora do planejamento: O caso do 'Orçamento Participativo' de Porto Alegre." Master's thesis, Universidade Federal do Rio Grande do Sul.

Gillespie, Charles, and Luis Gonzalez. 1989. "Uruguay: The Survival of Old and Autonomous Institutions." In *Democracy in Developing Countries*, vol. 4, *Latin America*, edited by Larry Diamond, Juan Linz, and Seymour Martin Lipset. Boulder: Lynne Rienner.

Goldfrank, Benjamin. 2002. "The Fragile Flower of Local Democracy: A Case Study of Decentralization/Participation in Montevideo." *Politics and Society* 30 (1): 51–83.

———. 2007. "Lessons from Latin American Experience in Participatory Budgeting." In *Participatory Budgeting*, edited by Anwar Shah. Washington, D.C.: World Bank Institute.

———. 2008. "The Left and Participatory Democracy: Scaling Up or Scaling Back?" Paper presented at the conference Latin America's Left Turn: Causes and Implications. Weatherhead Center for International Affairs, Harvard University, April 4–5.

Goldfrank, Benjamin, and Brian Wampler. 2008. "Como o modo petista ficou fora da moda." *Revista Debates* 2 (2): 245–71.

Gómez Calcaño, Luis. 1990. "Movimientos Sociales y Reforma Institucional: El Caso de Venezuela." In *Movimientos sociales y política: El desafío de la democracia en América Latina*, edited by Grupo de Trabajo CLACSO Movimientos Sociales y Participación Popular. Santiago: CES Ediciones and CLACSO.

———. 1998. "Civic Organizations and Reconstruction of Democratic Legitimacy in Venezuela." In *Reinventing Legitimacy: Democracy and Political Change in Venezuela*, edited by Damarys Canache and Michael Kulisheck. Westport, Conn.: Greenwood.

González, Mariana. 1992. *Las redes invisibles de la ciudad: Las Comisiones Vecinales de Montevideo, 1985–1988*. Montevideo: CIESU.

———. 1995. "¿Sencillamente vecinos? Las Comisiones Vecinales de Montevideo: Impactos del gobierno municipal sobre formas tradicionales de asociación." Master's thesis, Instituto Universitario de Pesquisas de Rio de Janeiro.

González de Pacheco, Rosa Amelia. 1998. "Las finanzas municipales." In *Descentralización en perspectiva: Federación y finanzas públicas*, edited by Rafael de la Cruz and Juan Carlos Navarro. Caracas: IESA.

Goodwin, Jeff. 2001. *No Other Way Out: States and Revolutionary Movements, 1945–1991.* Cambridge: Cambridge University Press.

Gott, Richard. 2001. *In the Shadow of the Liberator: Hugo Chávez and the Transformation of Venezuela.* London: Verso.

Grespan Muñoz, Marizandra. 1994. "Un caso atípico de campaña electoral: Alcaldía de Caracas 1992." Master's thesis, Universidad Simón Bolívar.

Grohmann, Peter. 1996. *Macarao y su gente: Movimiento popular y autogestión en los barrios de Caracas.* Caracas: ILDIS, Nueva Sociedad, and UNESCO.

Guerón, Gabrielle, and Giorgio Manchisi. 1996. "La descentralización en Venezuela: Balance de un proceso inconcluso." In *El sistema político venezolano: Crisis y transformaciones,* edited by Angel Alvarez. Caracas: Universidad Central de Venezuela.

Habitat. 2000. "Descentralización en Montevideo: Intendencia Municipal de Montevideo." Best Practices Dubai 2000. http://habitat.aq.upm.es/bpal/onu00/bp096.html.

Hagedorn, John M. 1995. *Forsaking Our Children: Bureaucracy and Reform in the Child Welfare System.* Chicago: Lakeview.

Handler, Joel. 1996. *Down from Bureaucracy: The Ambiguity of Privatization and Empowerment.* Princeton: Princeton University Press.

Hanes de Acevedo, Rexene. 1993. "Los vecinos: La movilización de los recursos del municipio." In *Gerencia municipal,* edited by Janet Kelly. Caracas: IESA.

Harnecker, Marta. 1991. *Frente Amplio: Los desafíos de una izquierda legal. Segunda parte: Los hitos más importantes de su historia.* Montevideo: La República.

———. 1993a. *Alcaldía de Porto Alegre: Aprendiendo a gobernar.* Durango, Mexico: MEPLA and Alcaldía de Durango.

———. 1993b. *Brasil—São Paulo: Una alcaldía asediada.* Havana: MEPLA.

———. 1995a. *Forjando la esperanza.* Santiago: LOM; Havana: MEPLA.

———. 1995b. *Intendencia de Montevideo: Un pueblo que se constituye en gobierno.* Havana: MEPLA; Caracas: Fundarte.

———. 1995c. *Haciendo camino al andar.* Santiago: FLACSO.

———. 1995d. *Caracas: La alcaldía donde se juega la esperanza.* Havana: MEPLA; Caracas: Fundarte.

Hellinger, Daniel. 1996. "The Causa R and the *Nuevo Sindicalismo* in Venezuela." *Latin American Perspectives* 23 (3): 110–31.

Helms, Paxton. 1994. "Descentralización: Cosechando frutos, pero lentamente." *VenEconomía* 11 (4).

Herzer, Hilda, and Pedro Pirez. 1991. "Municipal Government and Popular Participation in Latin America." *Environment and Urbanization* 3 (1): 79–95.

Hoag, Christina. 1995. "Rompiendo la cadena alimentaria." *VenEconomía* 12 (12).

Hochstetler, Kathryn. 2000. "Democratizing Pressures from Below? Social Movements in the New Brazilian Democracy." In *Democratic Brazil: Actors, Institutions, and Processes,* edited by Peter Kingstone and Timothy Power. Pittsburgh: University of Pittsburgh Press.

Hofmann, Renata. 2002. "Estudio de caso en los Municipios de Curahuara de Carangas y Tarabuco sobre 'Empoderamiento y Lucha Contra la Pobraza.'" Progama de Apoyo a la Democracia, Ayuda Obrera Suiza. La Paz: PADEM.

Horn, Carlos Henrique, ed. 1994. *Porto Alegre: O desafio da mudança. As políticas financeira, administrativa e de recursos humanos no Governo Olívio Dutra, 1989–92.* Porto Alegre: Editora Ortiz.

Horn, Carlos, Hélio Henkin, Júlio Brunet, Luiz Viapiana, and C. Malinski. 1988. "Diagnóstico sócio-econômico comparativo e atuação do poder público municipal: Porto Alegre, Belo Horizonte, Curitiba, e Campinas." Porto Alegre: Federação das Industriais do Rio Grande do Sul.

Huntington, Samuel. 1968. *Political Order in Changing Societies.* New Haven: Yale University Press.

———. 1975. "The United States." In *The Crisis of Democracy: Report on the Governability of Democracies to the Trilateral Commission,* edited by Michel Crozier, Samuel Huntington, and Joji Watanuki. New York: New York University Press.

Huntington, Samuel, and Joan M. Nelson. 1976. *No Easy Choice: Political Participation in Developing Countries.* Cambridge, Mass.: Harvard University Press.

IBGE. 1991. *Censo Demográfico 1991. N. 24, Rio Grande do Sul.* Rio de Janeiro: Instituto Brasileiro de Geografia e Estatística.

Icochea, Olympia. 1996. "Decentralization, Politics and Development: How Are They Interrelated? The Cases of Chile and Colombia." Master's thesis, University of California, Berkeley.

IDES. 2001. "10 años de descentralización." Mimeograph. Montevideo: IDES and IMM.

IESA. 1998. *Descentralización en perspective.* Caracas: IESA.

IMM. n.d. "Qué está haciendo la Intendencia de Montevideo por los asentamientos." Mimeograph. Montevideo: IMM.

———. 1990. *Primer Foro de Descentralización y Participación Ciudadana Realizado el 5 de Mayo de 1990.* Montevideo: IMM.

———. 1994. "Montevideo en tu barrio: Balance de Gestión, Guía del CCZ 8." Pamphlet. Montevideo: IMM.

———. 1997. *Construyendo ciudadanías: Montevideo en Foro II.* Montevideo: IMM.

———. 1998a. *Montevideo, Capital.* Montevideo: IMM.

———. 1998b. *Aquí va el dinero de los vecinos: Presupuesto 1998.* Montevideo: IMM.

IMM, AECI, and CAM, eds. 1994. *Descentralización y participación ciudadana.* Montevideo: Trilce.

IMM Budget and Planning Division. n.d. "Evolución de los ingresos y egresos." Mimeograph. Montevideo.

INE. 1996. *VII Censo General de Población, III de Hogares y V de Vividiendas: Montevideo.* Montevideo: Instituto Nacional de Estadística, República Oriental del Uruguay.

InfoAmericas. 1999. "Mining for Opportunities in Latin America: After the Goldrush." February. http://www.infoamericas.com/onlinelibrary/studies_guides/After_Goldrush.pdf.

Inter-American Development Bank. 2001. "Making Decentralization Work in Latin America and the Caribbean." Washington, D.C.: IADB. May.

Istúriz, Aristóbulo. 1996. "Fundamentos filosóficos del Gobierno Parroquial." In *Foro Taller: El Gobierno Parroquial.* Mimeograph. Caracas. July 28.

———. 1997. "Cultura, política y servicios públicos." In *Servicios públicos: Clave para el bienestar,* edited by Janet Kelly. Caracas: IESA.

Jacobi, Pedro. 1994. "Alcances y limites de governos locais progressistas no Brasil: As prefeituras petistas." *Cadernos de CEAS* 152:11–31.

Junta Departamental de Montevideo. 1994. *Comisión Mixta para la Descentralización Política del Departamento de Montevideo: Descentralización y participación vecinal en Montevideo.* Montevideo: Junta Departamental de Montevideo.

———. 1999. *Digesto Municipal.* Vol. 2. Montevideo: Junta Departmental de Montevideo.

Junta Parroquial San Juan. 1994. "Experiencia, reflexión, y evaluación del Gobierno Parroquial durante su gestión." Memo. July 18.

Karl, Terry Lynn. 1997. *The Paradox of Plenty: Oil Booms and Petro-States.* Berkeley and Los Angeles: University of California Press.

Keck, Margaret. 1992. *The Workers' Party and Democratization in Brazil.* New Haven: Yale University Press.

King, Gary, Robert Keohane, and Sidney Verba. 1994. *Designing Social Inquiry: Scientific Inference in Qualitative Research.* Princeton: Princeton University Press.

Klein, Darío, and Fabián Lazovski. 1993. "Tabaré Vázquez: Un líder bien imaginado." *Cuadernos del CLAEH* 67.

Kliksberg, Bernardo. 2000. "Six Unconventional Theses About Participation." *International Review of Administrative Sciences* 66 (1): 161–74.

Knijnik, Celso. 2000. "A SMOV e a modernização urbana de Porto Alegre." In *Porto Alegre: Uma cidade que conquista,* edited by Raul Pont and Adair Barcelos. Porto Alegre: Artes e Ofícios.

Krekeler, Jorge, David Quezada, and Oscar Rea. 2003. "Planificación participativa municipal: Apuntes sobre el contexto boliviano." In *Memoria del Seminario Internacional "Presupuestos Participativos en el contexto boliviano,"* edited by Red Nacional de Participación Ciudadana y Control Social. Quito: UN-Habitat.

Kreuzer, Marcus, and Vello Pettai. 2004. "Political Parties and the Study of Political Development: New Insights from the Postcommunist Democracies." *World Politics* 56 (4): 608–33.

Kugelmas, Eduardo, and Lourdes Sola. 2000. "Recentralização/Descentralização: Dinâmica do regime federativo no Brasil dos anos 90." *Tempo Social* 11 (2): 63–83.

Kweit, Mary Grisez, and Robert W. Kweit. 1981. *Implementing Citizen Participation in a Bureaucratic Society: A Contingency Approach.* New York: Praeger.

Lander, Edgardo. 1995. "Movimientos sociales urbanos, sociedad civil, y nuevas formas de ciudadania en Venezuela." *Revista Venezolana de Economia y Ciencias Sociales* 2–3:165–87.

Langton, Stuart. 1978. "What Is Citizen Participation?" In *Citizen Participation in America: Essays on the State of the Art,* edited by Stuart Langton. Lexington, Mass.: Lexington Books.

Latinobarómetro. 2006. *Informe Latinobarómetro 2006.* Santiago: Corporación Latinobarómetro.

———. 2007. *Informe Latinobarómetro 2007.* Santiago: Corporación Latinobarómetro.

Leonard, David. 1982. "Analyzing the Organizational Requirements for Serving the Rural Poor." In *Institutions of Rural Development for the Poor,* edited by David Leonard and Dale Rogers Marshall. Berkeley: Institute of International Studies.

Levine, Daniel. 1989. "Venezuela: The Nature, Sources, and Future Prospects of Democracy." In *Democracy in Developing Countries,* vol. 4, *Latin America,* edited by Larry Diamond, Juan Linz, and Seymour Martin Lipset. Boulder: Lynne Rienner.

———. 1998. "Beyond the Exhaustion of the Model: Survival and Transformation of Democracy in Venezuela." In *Reinventing Legitimacy: Democracy and Political Change in Venezuela,* edited by Damarys Canache and Michael Kulisheck. Westport, Conn.: Greenwood.

Levitsky, Steven. 2003. *Transforming Labor-Based Parties in Latin America: Argentine Peronism in Comparative Perspective.* Cambridge: Cambridge University Press.

Lijphart, Arend. 1975. "The Comparable-Cases Strategy in Comparative Research." *Comparative Political Studies* 8 (2): 158–77.

Listre, Julio. 1999. "Descentralización participativa: Aprendiendo desde los conflictos." In *Democracia, ciudadanía y poder: Una mirada desde el proceso de descentralización y participación popular,* edited by José Luis Rebellato and Pilar Ubilla. Montevideo: Nordan Comunidad.

Llona, Mariana, and Laura Soria. 2005. "Presupuesto Participativo: Alcances y límites de una política pública." *Revista Actualidad Económica.* July. http://www.actualidadeconomica-peru.com/anteriores/ae_2005/julio/art_04_jul_2005.pdf.

Lombardi, Mario, Andrea di Candia, Mora Podestá, Cristina Rodríguez, and Rosa Barreix. n.d. "Estudio empírico sobre niños y adolescentes en los asentamientos irregulares de Montevideo." Unpublished paper, Montevideo.

López Maya, Margarita. 1995. "El ascenso en Venezuela de La Causa R." *Revista Venezolana de Economía y Ciencias Sociales* 2–3:205–39.

———. 1997. "El repertorio de la protesta popular venezolana entre 1989 y 1993." *Cuadernos del CENDES* 14 (36): 109–30.

———, ed. 1999a. *Lucha popular, democracia, neoliberalismo: Protesta popular en América Latina en los años de ajuste.* Caracas: Nueva Sociedad.

———. 1999b. "Alcaldías de izquierda en Venezuela: Gestiones locales de La Causa Radical (1989–1996)." In *Gobiernos de izquierda en América Latina: El desafío del cambio,* edited by Beatriz Stolowicz. Mexico City: Plaza y Valdés Editores and Universidad Autónoma Metropolitana-Xochimilco.

———. 2008. "Caracas: The State, Popular Participation and How to Make Things Work." Paper presented at the conference The Popular Sectors and the State in Chávez's Venezuela, Yale University, January.

López Ricci, José, and Elisa Wiener Bravo. 2004. "Planeamiento y el presupuesto participativo regional 2003–2004: Enfoque de desarrollo, prioridades de inversión y roles de los 'Agentes participantes.'" *Cuadernos Descentralistas* 11:17–57. Lima: Grupo Propuesta Ciudadana.

Luna, Juan Pablo. 2007. "Frente Amplio and the Crafting of a Social Democratic Alternative in Uruguay." *Latin American Politics and Society* 49 (4): 1–30.

Magallanes, Rodolfo. 1995. "Patrones de organización de la sociedad civil en Venezuela (cambios recientes)." *Politeia* 18:233–65.

Mainwaring, Scott. 1989. "Grass Roots Popular Movements and the Struggle for Democracy: Nova Iguaçu, 1974–1985." In *Democratizing Brazil: Problems of Transition and Consolidation,* edited by Alfred Stepan. New York: Oxford University Press.

———. 1998. "Party Systems in the Third Wave." *Journal of Democracy* 9 (3): 67–81.

———. 1999. *Rethinking Party Systems in the Third Wave of Democratization: The Case of Brazil.* Stanford: Stanford University Press.

Mainwaring, Scott, and Timothy Scully, eds. 1995. *Building Democratic Institutions: Party Systems in Latin America.* Stanford: Stanford University Press.

Mammarella, Rosetta. 1998. "Espacialização da economia e da exclusão social metropolitana." Paper presented at the Annual Meeting of ANPOCS, Caxambu, Minas Gerais, October 27–31.

Manor, James. 2006. "Renewing the Debate on Decentralization." *Commonwealth and Comparative Politics* 44 (3): 283–88.

Mansbridge, Jane. 1983. *Beyond Adversary Democracy.* Chicago: University of Chicago Press.

————. 1999. "On the Idea that Participation Makes Better Citizens." In *Citizen Competence and Democratic Institutions*, edited by Stephen Elkin and Karol Soltan. University Park: Pennsylvania State University Press.

Marcano, Esther Elena. 1993. "De la crisis al colapso de los servicios públicos en la metropoli." *Urbana* 13:57–68.

Marquetti, Adalmir. 2001. "Democracia, eqüidade e eficiência: O caso do Orçamento Participativo em Porto Alegre." Paper presented at the "O Orçamento Participativo no Olhar do Mundo" Seminar, Porto Alegre, Brazil, May 31–June 2.

Marquetti, Adalmir, and Duilio Bêrni. 2006. "Democracia participativa, performance fiscal e distribuição: A evidência dos municípios gauchos." Terceiro Encontro de Economia Gaúcha. Porto Alegre. 2006.

Martínez, Ember, and Pilar Ubila, eds. 1989. *Políticas municipales y participación popular: Seminario-Taller Mayo 15 al 21, 1989 Montevideo*. Montevideo: Túpac Amaru Editorial.

Martins, Clitia, and Amilcar Loureiro. 1997. "Porto Alegre Anos 90: Características sócio-econômicos da metrópole gaúcha." In *Dinámica da urbanização no RS: Temas e tendências*, edited by Naia Oliveira, Tanya de Barcellos, Aurea Breitbach, Clitia Martins, Amilcar Loureiro, and Sheila Borba. Porto Alegre: Fundação de Economia e Estatística.

Martins Filho, João Roberto. 1998. "Critical Sociology or Social Engineering? Commentary on Ladislau Dowbor's 'Decentralization and Governance.'" *Latin American Perspectives* 98 (2): 45–48.

Martinussen, John. 1997. *Society, State and Market: A Guide to Competing Theories of Development*. London: Zed Books.

Mascareño, Carlos. 2000. *Balance de la descentralización en Venezuela: Logros, limitaciones, y perspectivas*. Caracas: PNUD, ILDIS, and Nueva Sociedad.

Mattos, Carlos A. de. 1989. "La descentralización, ¿una nueva panacea para impulsar el desarrollo local?" *Cuadernos del CLAEH* 51:60–62.

McCarney, Patricia. 1996. "New Considerations on the Notion of 'Governance'—New Directions for Cities in the Developing World." In *Cities and Governance: New Directions in Latin America, Asia, and Africa*, edited by Patricia McCarney. Toronto: Centre for Urban and Community Studies.

McConnell, Grant. 1966. *Private Power and American Democracy*. New York: Knopf.

Medina, Pablo. 1999. *Rebeliones*. Caracas: The Author.

Melo, Marcus André. 1996. "Crise federativa, guerra fiscal e 'Hobbesianismo Municipal': Perverse Effects of Decentralization?" *São Paulo em Perspectiva* 10 (3): 11–20.

Meta. 2000a. "Prefeitura Municipal de Porto Alegre: Resultados da pesquisa quantitativa." Mimeograph. Porto Alegre. July.

————. 2000b. "Prefeitura Municipal de Porto Alegre: Resultados da pesquisa quantitativa." Mimeograph. Porto Alegre. November.

Mettenheim, Kurt von, and James Malloy. 1998. Introduction to *Deepening Democracy in Latin America*, edited by Kurt von Mettenheim and James Malloy. Pittsburgh: University of Pittsburgh Press.

Mieres, Pablo. 1994. *Desobediencia y lealtad: El voto en el Uruguay de fin de siglo*. Montevideo: Fin de Siglo.

Migdal, Joel, Atul Kohli, and Vivienne Shue, eds. 1994. *State Power and Social Forces: Domination and Transformation in the Third World*. Cambridge: Cambridge University Press.

Ministerio de la Familia, Venezuela. n.d. "Estadísticas." http://www.platino.gov.ve/minfamilia/estadist.htm.

Mirza, Christian Adel. 1996. "El proceso de descentralización municipal en Montevideo." In *Desarrollo local, democracia y ciudadanía*, Various Authors. Montevideo: IMM, Comisión de la Unión Europea, Comité Catholique contre la Faim et pour le Developpement.

Mitchell, Jeffrey. 1998. "Political Decentralization: A New Tool for the Segregation of Urban Space? The Case of Chacao in Caracas, Venezuela." Paper presented at the International Congress of the Latin American Studies Association, Chicago, September 24–26.

Molina, José. 1999. "Partidos y sistemas de partidos en la evolución política venezolana: La desinstitucionalización y sus consecuencias." In *Los partidos políticos venezolanos en el siglo XXI*, edited by José Molina and Ángel Álvarez. Caracas: Vadell Hermanos.

Montalvo, Daniel. 2008. "Citizen Participation in Municipal Meetings." *AmericasBarometer Insights* 4:1–6.

Montero, Alfred. 2000. "Devolving Democracy? Political Decentralization and the New Brazilian Federalism." In *Democratic Brazil: Actors, Institutions, and Processes*, edited by Peter Kingstone and Timothy Power. Pittsburgh: University of Pittsburgh Press.

Moreira, Constanza. 1993. "Cohabitación y lógica de gobierno: Un análisis de la experiencia municipal de Montevideo (1990–1992) de cara a sus relaciones con el gobierno nacional." In *Participación ciudadana y relaciones de gobierno*, edited by CIEDUR, CIESU, ICP, and FESUR. Montevideo: Trilce.

Moritz, Maria Lúcia Rodrigues de Freitas. 2001. "Participação política da mulher e a experiência do sistema de cotas no Brasil." Unpublished paper, Political Science Department, Universidade Federal do Rio Grande do Sul. www.nupergs.ifch. ufrgs.br/deptpolitica/num3/malu.pdf.

Moura, Maria Suzana de Souza. 1989. "Limites á participação popular na gestão da cidade: O projeto dos Conselhos Populares em Porto Alegre." Master's thesis, Universidade Federal do Rio Grande do Sul.

———. 1993. "Governo local e participação popular. Ideário e prática." In *Estudos urbanos: Porto Alegre e seu planejamento*, edited by Wrana Panizzi and João Rovatti. Porto Alegre: PMPA and Editora da Universidade.

Moynihan, Daniel. 1969. *Maximum Feasible Misunderstanding: Community Action in the War on Poverty*. New York: Free Press.

Muñoz, Agustín Blanco. 1998. *Habla el Comandante Hugo Chávez Frias*. Caracas: Universidad Central de Venezuela.

Myers, David. 1978. "Caracas: The Politics of Intensifying Primacy." In *Latin American Urban Reseach*, vol. 6, edited by Wayne Cornelius and Robert Kemper. London: SAGE.

Myers, David, and Henry Dietz, eds. 2002. *Capital City Politics in Latin America: Democratization and Empowerment*. Boulder: Lynne Rienner.

NACLA: Report on the Americas. 1995. 29 (1).

Navarro, Zander. 1997. "Uma análise do Orçamento Participativo: Sua implantação e desenvolvimento." In *Porto da Cidadania: A esquerda no governo de Porto Alegre*, edited by Tarso Genro. Porto Alegre: Artes e Ofícios.

Nickson, Andrew. 1995. *Local Government in Latin America*. Boulder: Lynne Rienner.

Nogueira, Luciana, and Ana Maria D'Avila Lopes. 2008. "Democratizando a democracia: A participação política das mulheres no Brasil e a reforma do sistema político." In *XVI Congresso Nacional do CONPEDI, 2008, Belo Horizonte*. Florianópolis: Fundação Boiteux.

Noll, Maria Izabel, and Hélgio Trindade. 1996. *Estatísticas eleitorais comparativas do Rio Grande do Sul, 1945–1994.* Porto Alegre: UFRGS and Estado do Rio Grande do Sul Assembléia Legislativa.

Nunes, Edison. 1996. "Poder local, descentralização e democratização: Um encontro difícil." *São Paulo em Perspectiva* 10 (3): 32–39.

Nylen, William. 1995. "The Workers' Party in Rural Brazil." *NACLA: Report on the Americas* 29 (1): 27–32.

———. 1996. "Popular Participation in Brazil's Workers' Party: 'Democratizing Democracy' in Municipal Politics." *Political Chronicle* 8 (2): 1–9.

———. 2000. "Contributions of the Workers' Party to the Consolidation of Democracy in Brazil." In *Democratic Brazil: Actors, Institutions, and Processes,* edited by Peter Kingstone and Timothy Power. Pittsburgh: University of Pittsburgh Press.

———. 2002. "Testing the Empowerment Thesis: The Participatory Budget in Belo Horizonte and Betim, Brazil." *Comparative Politics* 34 (2): 127–45.

———. 2003. *Participatory Democracy Versus Elitist Democracy: Lessons from Brazil.* New York: Palgrave Macmillan.

OCEI. 1993. *El Censo 90 en el Distrito Federal.* Caracas: República de Venezuela.

OCEI, PNUD, and FNUAP. 1997. *Informe sobre índice y entorno del desarrollo humano en Venezuela.* Caracas: OCEI.

O'Donnell, Guillermo. 1997. "Polyarchies and the (Un)Rule of Law in Latin America." Paper presented at the Annual Meeting of the American Political Science Association, Washington, D.C., August 28–31.

O'Dwyer, Conor, and Branislave Kovalčík. 2007. "And the Last Shall Be First: Party System Institutionalization and Second-Generation Economic Reform in Postcommunist Europe." *Studies in Comparative International Development* 41 (4): 3–26.

O'Dwyer, Conor, and Daniel Ziblatt. 2006. "Does Decentralisation Make Government More Efficient and Effective?" *Commonwealth and Comparative Politics* 44 (3): 326–43.

Oholeguy, Christina. 1999. "Lo que aprendimos de la descentralización." In *Democracia, ciudadanía y poder: Una mirada desde el proceso de descentralización y participación popular,* edited by José Luis Rebellato and Pilar Ubilla. Montevideo: Nordan Comunidad.

Oliver, J. Eric. 2000. "City Size and Civic Involvement in Metropolitan America." *American Political Science Review* 94 (2): 361–73.

Olson, Mancur. 1971. *The Logic of Collective Action: Public Goods and the Theory of Groups.* Cambridge, Mass.: Harvard University Press.

Ortega Hegg, Manuel. 2003. "La conversión de un 'canal formal' en un 'espacio real' de participación social." In *Participación ciudadana y desarollo local en Centroamérica,* edited by Ricardo Córdova and Leslie Quiñónez. San Salvador: FUNDAUNGO.

Ostrom, Elinor. 1996. "Crossing the Great Divide: Co-Production, Synergy, and Development." *World Development* 24 (6): 1073–87.

Panizza, Francisco. 1990. *Uruguay: Batllismo y después. Pacheco, militares, y tupamaros en la crisis del Uruguay Batllista.* Montevideo: Ediciones de la Banda Oriental.

Passos, Manoel and Maria Izabel Noll. 1996. "Eleições municipais em Porto Alegre (1947–1992)." *Cadernos de Ciência Política,* Série: Relatos de Pesquisa 4. Porto Alegre: Universidade Federal do Rio Grande do Sul.

Pateman, Carole. 1970. *Participation and Democratic Theory.* Cambridge: Cambridge University Press.

Pereira, Simone, and Suzana Moura. 1988. "Pesquisa entre os delegados do III Congresso da UAMPA: 15, 16 e 17 de Julho de 1988." Porto Alegre: FASE.

Perelli, Carina, Fernando Filgueira and Silvana Rubino, eds. 1991. *Gobierno y política en Montevideo: La Intendencia Municipal de Montevideo y la formación de un nuevo liderazgo a comienzos de los años 90.* Montevideo: PEITHO.

Pérez Novella, María Jesús, and Blanca Charbonnier. 1992. "Encuesta a dirigentes de organizaciones barriales sobre la experiencia de Descentralización-Participación y los Centros Comunales Zonales." Serie Investigaciones 96. Montevideo: CIEDUR.

Peterson, George. 1997. *Decentralization in Latin America: Learning Through Experience.* Washington, D.C.: World Bank.

Petras, James. 1997. "Latin America: The Resurgence of the Left." *New Left Review* 223:27–47.

Petras, James, and Henry Veltmeyer. 2005. *Social Movements and State Power: Argentina, Brazil, Bolivia, Ecuador.* London: Pluto Press.

Pineda Gadea, Claudia. 2003. "Condiciones del marco nacional para los procesos de preparación participativa de presupuestos municipales en Nicaragua." Managua: World Bank Institute.

Piovesan, Maria Cristina. 2000. "Carris: Uma empresa pública qualificada." In *Porto Alegre: Uma cidade que conquista,* edited by Raul Pont and Adair Barcelos. Porto Alegre: Artes e Ofícios.

PMDB. 1999. *Orçamento Participativo 98. A manipulação da vontade popular.* Porto Alegre: Partido do Movimento Democrático Brasileiro.

PMPA. 1993. "Relatório de pesquisa. Avaliação da Administração Municipal de Porto Alegre, Maio 1993." Mimeograph. Porto Alegre: PMPA.

———. 1997. *Anuário estatístico 1997.* Porto Alegre: PMPA.

———. 1998. *Relatório de indicadores sociais de Porto Alegre.* Gabinete do Prefeito, Assessoria de Economia, 2nd Edition. Porto Alegre: PMPA.

———. 1999. "Regimento interno: Critérios gerais, técnicos e regionais." Porto Alegre: PMPA.

Pont, Raul. 2000. "Porto Alegre e a luta pela democracia, igualdade e qualidade de vida." In *Porto Alegre: Uma cidade que conquista,* edited by Raul Pont and Adair Barcelos. Porto Alegre: Artes e Ofícios.

Portes, Alejandro. 1989. "Latin American Urbanization During the Years of the Crisis." *Latin American Research Review* 24 (3): 7–44.

Portillo, Alvaro. 1991. "Montevideo: La primera experiencia del Frente Amplio." In *Ciudades y gobiernos locales en la América Latina de los noventa,* edited by Alicia Ziccardi. Mexico: FLACSO, Instituto Mora, and Grupo Editorial M.A. Porrua.

———. 1996. *Montevideo: La ciudad de la gente.* Montevideo: Facultad de Arquitectura and Nordan-Comunidad.

———. 1999. "Innovación política y transformaciones en Montevideo luego de ocho años de gobierno de izquierda." In *Gobiernos de izquierda en América Latina: El desafío del cambio,* edited by Beatriz Stolowicz. Mexico City: Plaza y Valdés Editores and Universidad Autónoma Metropolitana-Xochimilco.

Power, Timothy. 2000. "Political Institutions in Democratic Brazil: Politics as a Permanent Constitutional Convention." In *Democratic Brazil: Actors, Institutions, and Processes,* edited by Peter Kingstone and Timothy Power. Pittsburgh: University of Pittsburgh Press.

———. 2000. *The Political Right in Postauthoritarian Brazil: Elites, Institutions, and Democratization.* University Park: Pennsylvania State University Press.

Pozzobon, Regina. 1998. *Os desafíos da gestão municipal democrática: Porto Alegre, 1993–1996*. São Paulo and Recife: Instituto Pólis and Centro Josué de Castro.

Pretty, Jules and Robert Chambers. 1993. "Towards a Learning Paradigm: New Professionalism and Institutions for Agriculture." IDS Discussion Paper 334. Brighton: IDS/IIED.

Prodasen. 1982. *Sistema de informações eleitorais*. Porto Alegre.

Prud'homme, Rémy. 1995. "The Dangers of Decentralization." *World Bank Research Observer* 10 (2): 201–20.

Przeworski, Adam, and Henry Teune. 1970. *The Logic of Comparative Social Inquiry*. New York: John Wiley and Sons.

Puente Alcaraz, Jesús, and Luis Felipe Linares López. 2004. "A General View of the Institutional State of Decentralization in Guatemala." In *Decentralization and Democratic Governance in Latin America*, edited by Joseph Tulchin and Andrew Selee. Washington, D.C.: Woodrow Wilson Center Press.

Putnam, Robert, with Robert Leonardi and Raffaella Y. Nanetti. 1993. *Making Democracy Work: Civic Traditions in Modern Italy*. Princeton: Princeton University Press.

———. 1995. "Bowling Alone: America's Declining Social Capital." *Journal of Democracy* 6 (1): 65–78.

———. 2000. *Bowling Alone: The Collapse and Revival of American Community*. New York: Simon and Schuster.

Rama, Germán. 1971. *El club político*. Montevideo: ARCA.

Ramos Rollon, Maria Luisa. 1995. *De las protestas a las propuestas: Identidad, acción y relevancia política del movimiento vecinal en Venezuela*. Caracas: Instituto de Estudios de Iberoamérica y Portugal and Nueva Sociedad.

Randall, Vicky, and Lars Svåsand. 2002. "Party Institutionalization in New Democracies." *Party Politics* 8 (1): 5–29.

Rankin, Aidan. 1998. "Why Are There No Local Politics in Uruguay?" In *Urban Elections in Democratic Latin America*, edited by Henry Dietz and Gil Shidlo. Wilmington: Scholarly Resources.

Rebellato, José Luis, and Pilar Ubilla. 1999. "Un recorrido por el processo." In *Democracia, ciudadanía y poder: Una mirada desde el proceso de descentralización y participación popular*, edited by José Luis Rebellato and Pilar Ubilla. Montevideo: Nordan Comunidad.

Regent, Susana. 1999. "Descentralización participativa . . . ¿Construyendo la utopia o el hijo no deseado?" In *Democracia, ciudadanía y poder: Una mirada desde el proceso de descentralización y participación popular*, edited by José Luis Rebellato and Pilar Ubilla. Montevideo: Nordan Comunidad.

Reilly, Charles, ed. 1995. *New Paths to Democratic Development in Latin America: The Rise of NGO-Municipal Collaboration*. Boulder: Lynne Rienner.

———. 1995. "Public Policy and Citizenship." In *New Paths to Democratic Development in Latin America: The Rise of NGO-Municipal Collaboration*, edited by Charles Reilly. Boulder: Lynne Rienner.

REPPOL/IMM (Red de Poder Local del Centro para la Educación de Adultos de América Latina / Intendencia Municipal de Montevideo). 2003. "Gobernabilidad participativa para el acceso a los servicios urbanos y el desarrollo local. Descentralización y Servicios Públicos, Montevideo, Uruguay." Cuaderno de Trabajo 70. Quito: Programa de Gestión Urbana and UN-Habitat.

República Oriental del Uruguay, Instituto Nacional de Estadística. Various years. *Uruguay: Anuario estadístico*. Montevideo: INE.

Revello, María del Rosario. 1999. "Descentralizacón y participación: La experiencia montevideana." Paper presented at the II Taller de Gestión Local Para Iberoamericanos, Stetson University, Florida, May 29–June 5.

Revista Envío. 2008. "Nicaragua Briefs: Murillo Acquires Even More Power." *Revista Envío* 324. http://www.envio.org.ni/articulo/3835.

Rial, Juan. 1986. "El municipio: Instancia paralela o base de participación?" CIESU Working Paper 126. Montevideo: CIESU.

Ribot, Jesse. 1998. "Decentralization and Participation in Sahelian Forestry: Legal Instruments of Central Political-Administrative Control?" Paper presented in the Environmental Politics Seminar, Institute of International Studies, UC Berkeley, February 6.

Roberts, Kenneth. 1998. *Deepening Democracy? The Modern Left and Social Movements in Chile and Peru.* Stanford: Stanford University Press.

Robinson, William. 1992. "The São Paulo Forum: Is There a New Latin American Left?" *Monthly Review* 44 (7): 1–12.

Rodrigues, Fernando. 2000. Pesquisas eleitorais—1ero Turno 2000, Porto Alegre-RS. http://www1.uol.com.br/fernandorodrigues/arquivos/pesquisas/cidades/pe-portoalegre.shl.

Rodríguez, Alfredo, and Lucy Winchester. 1996. "Cities, Democracy, and Governance in Latin America." *International Social Science Journal* 48 (147): 73–83.

Rodríguez Villasante, Tomás. 1993. "¿Descentralización administrativa o ciudadanía popular?" *América Latina Hoy* 6:7–13.

Rondinelli, Dennis A., James S. McCullough, and Ronald W. Johnson. 1989. "Analyzing Decentralization Policies in Developing Countries: A Political-Economy Framework." *Development and Change* 20 (1): 57–87.

Rosenblatt, David, and Gil Shidlo. 1996. "Quem tem mais recursos para governar? Uma comparação das receitas *per capita* dos estados e municípios brasileiros." *Revista de Economia Política* 16 (1): 101–6.

Rubino, Silvana. 1991a. "Una realidad 'tétrica': La Intendencia Municipal de Montevideo." In *Gobierno y política en Montevideo,* edited by Carina Perelli, Fernando Filgueira, and Silvana Rubino. Montevideo: PEITHO.

———. 1991b. "Los habitantes de Montevideo: Visión de la Intendencia en una coyuntura de cambio." In *Gobierno y política en Montevideo,* edited by Carina Perelli, Fernando Filgueira, and Silvana Rubino. Montevideo: PEITHO.

Ruckert, Arne. 2009. "The World Bank and the Poverty Reduction Strategy of Nicaragua: Towards a Post-Neoliberal World Development Order?" In *Post-Neoliberalism in the Americas,* edited by Laura MacDonald and Arne Ruckert. New York: Palgrave Macmillan.

Salmen, Lawrence. 1994. "Listening to the Poor." *Finance and Development* 31 (4): 45–48.

Samuels, David. 2000. "Reinventing Local Government? Municipalities and Intergovernmental Relations in Democratic Brazil." In *Democratic Brazil: Actors, Institutions, and Processes,* edited by Peter Kingstone and Timothy Power. Pittsburgh: University of Pittsburgh Press.

Sanders, Lynn. 1997. "Against Deliberation." *Political Theory* 25 (3): 347–76.

Santos, Boaventura de Sousa. 1998. "Participatory Budgeting in Porto Alegre: Toward a Redistributive Democracy." *Politics and Society* 26 (4): 461–510.

Santos Junior, Orlando Alves dos. 2000. "Gestão urbana, associativismo e participação nas metrópoles brasileiras." In *O futuro dos metrópoles: Desigualdades e governabilidade,* edited by Luiz Cesar de Queiroz Ribeiro. Rio de Janeiro: Revan-FASE.

Schabbach, Letícia Maria. 1995. "Práticas e representações de funcionários públicos: Prefeitura Municipal de Porto Alegre (1989–1992)." Master's thesis, Universidade Federal do Rio Grande do Sul.

Schmidt, Carlos, and Ronaldo Herrlein Jr. 2001. "Desenvolvimento do Rio Grande do Sul: Dois projetos." Discussion Paper 2001/9, Programa de Pos-Graduação em Economia, Universidade Federal do Rio Grande do Sul. http://www8. ufrgs.br/ppge/pcientifica/pdf/vs2-paraSEP.pdf.

Schmidt, David Luiz. 1994. "A 'desidiotização' da cidadania: A formação do cidadão para a coisa pública, através da sua participação no processo do Orçamento Participativo de Porto Alegre, entre 1989 e 1992." Master's thesis, Universidade Federal do Rio Grande do Sul.

Schneider, Aaron. 2003. "Decentralization: Conceptualization and Measurement." *Studies in Comparative International Development* 38 (3): 32–56.

Schneider, Aaron, and Marcelo Baquero. 2006. "Get What You Want, Give What You Can: Embedded Public Finance in Porto Alegre." IDS Working Paper 266. Brighton: Institute of Development Studies, University of Sussex.

Schneider, Aaron, and Benjamin Goldfrank. 2002. "Budgets and Ballots in Brazil: Participatory Budgeting from the City to the State." IDS Working Paper 149. Brighton: IDS.

Schönleitner, Günther. 2006. "Between Liberal and Participatory Democracy: Tensions and Dilemmas of Leftist Politics in Brazil." *Journal of Latin American Studies* 38 (1): 35–63.

Schönwälder, Gerd. 1997. "New Democratic Spaces at the Grassroots? Popular Participation in Latin American Local Governments." *Development and Change* 28 (4): 753–70.

———. 1998. "Local Politics and the Peruvian Left: The Case of El Agustino." *Latin American Research Review* 33 (2): 73–102.

———. 2002. *Linking Civil Society and the State: Urban Popular Movements, the Left, and Local Government in Peru, 1980–1992.* University Park: Pennsylvania State University Press.

Selee, Andrew, and Joseph Tulchin. 2004. "Decentralization and Democratic Governance: Lessons and Challenges." In *Decentralization, Democratic Governance, and Civil Society in Comparative Perspective: Africa, Asia, and Latin America,* edited by Philip Oxhorn, Joseph Tulchin, and Andrew Selee. Washington, D.C.: Woodrow Wilson Center Press; Baltimore: Johns Hopkins University Press.

Serna, Miguel. 2000. "Democracias nuevas y nuevas izquierdas, un vínculo incompleto: Argentina, Brasil y Uruguay en perspectiva comparada." In *La larga espera: Itinerarios de las izquierdas en Argentina, Brasil y Uruguay,* edited by Susana Mallo and Constanza Moreira. Montevideo: Ediciones de la Banda Oriental.

Setzler, Mark. 2000. "Democratizing Urban Brazil: Institutional Legacies and Determinants of Accountability in Local Elections and Legislatures." Paper presented at the International Congress of the Latin American Studies Association, Miami, March 15–18.

Shidlo, Gil. 1998. "Local Urban Elections in Democratic Brazil." In *Urban Elections in Democratic Latin America,* edited by Henry Dietz and Gil Shidlo. Wilmington: Scholarly Resources.

Sierra, Gerónimo de and Blanca Charbonnier. 1993. "Descentralización y participación: Los partidos y los actores directamente implicados en la experiencia de los Centros Comunales Zonales (1990–1992)." In *Participación ciudadana y relaciones de gobierno,* edited by CIEDUR, CIESU, ICP, and FESUR. Montevideo: Trilce.

Silberberg, Mina Ruth. 1992. "Community Organizations and Outside Linkage: Strategies for Participation Among Venezuela's Urban Poor." Ph.D. diss., University of California, Berkeley.

Silva, Marcelo Kunrath. 2001. "Construção da 'Participação Popular': Análise comparativa de processos de participação social na discussão pública do orçamento em municípios da Região Metropolitana de Porto Alegre/RS." Ph.D. diss., Universidade Federal do Rio Grande do Sul.

Sintomer, Yves, Carsten Herzberg, and Anja Röcke. 2008. "Participatory Budgeting in Europe: Potentials and Challenges." *International Journal of Urban and Regional Research* 32 (1): 164–78.

Skocpol, Theda. 2004. "Voice and Inequality: The Transformation of American Civic Democracy." *Perspectives on Politics* 2 (1): 3–20.

Skocpol, Theda, and Morris P. Fiorina, eds. 1999. *Civic Engagement in American Democracy.* Washington, D.C.: Brookings Institution; New York: Russell Sage Foundation.

Slater, David. 1989. "Territorial Power and the Peripheral State: The Issue of Decentralization." *Development and Change* 20 (3): 501–31.

Snyder, Richard. 2001. "Scaling Down: The Subnational Comparative Method." *Studies in Comparative International Development* 36 (1): 93–110.

Sotelo Rico, Mariana. 1999. "La longevidad de los partidos tradicionales uruguayos desde una perspectiva comparada." In *Los partidos políticos uruguayos en tiempos de cambio,* edited by Luis Eduardo González, Felipe Monestier, Rosario Queirolo, and Mariana Sotelo Rico. Montevideo: Fundación Cultura Universitaria.

Souza, Celina. 1996. "Reinventando o Poder Local: Limites e Possibilidades do Federalismo e da Descentralização." *São Paulo em Perspectiva* 10 (3): 38–52.

———. 2007. "Local Democratization in Brazil: Strengths and Dilemmas of Deliberative Democracy." *Development* 50 (1): 90–95.

Stepan, Alfred. 1997. "Democratic Opposition and Democratization Theory." *Government and Opposition* 32 (4): 167–80.

Stolowicz, Beatriz, ed. 1999. *Gobiernos de izquierda en América Latina: El desafío del cambio.* Mexico City: Plaza y Valdés Editores and Universidad Autónoma Metropolitana-Xochimilco.

Tarrow, Sidney. 1994. *Power in Movement: Social Movements, Collective Action and Politics.* Cambridge: Cambridge University Press.

Teixeira, Ana Claudia Chaves, and Maria do Carmo Albuquerque. 2006. "Orçamentos Participativos: Projetos políticos, partilha de poder e alcance democrático." In *A disputa pela construção democrática na América Latina,* edited by Evelina Dagnino, Alberto Olvera, and Aldo Panfichi. São Paulo: Paz e Terra; Campinas: Unicamp.

Tendler, Judith. 1997. *Good Government in the Tropics.* Baltimore: Johns Hopkins University Press.

Timmons, Jeff. 1995. "Gobernar a Caracas no es coser y cantar." *VenEconomía* 12 (11).

Tocqueville, Alexis de. 1988 [1848]. *Democracy in America.* New York: Perennial Library.

Treisman, Daniel. 2007. *The Architecture of Government: Rethinking Political Decentralization.* New York: Cambridge University Press.

UAMPA. 1989. "Participação na elaboração do orçamento municipal." Mimeograph.

UNDP. 1996. *Índice y entorno del desarrollo humano en Venezuela, 1996.* http://www. pnud.org.ve/IDH96/index.html.

Unidad de Estadística Municipal. 2002. *Montevideo en cifras 2000.* Montevideo: IMM.

Valladares, Licia and Magda Prates Coelho, eds. 1995. *Governabilidade e pobreza no Brasil.* Rio de Janeiro: Civilização Brasileira.

Vallmitjana, Marta, ed. 1993. *Caracas: Nuevos escenarios para el poder local.* Caracas: COPRE, UNDP, and Nueva Sociedad.

Vallmitjana, Marta, Victor Fossi, Carmelita Brandt, Gustavo Urdaneta, Rosa Amelia González, Laura González, Hugo Manzanilla, Mélida de Brewer, and Elizabeth Beracasa. 1993. "Diagnóstico del ámbito metropolitano: Funciones urbanas y participación ciudadana." In *Caracas: Nuevos escenarios para el poder local,* edited by Marta Vallmitjana. Caracas: COPRE, UNDP, and Nueva Sociedad.

Varela Petito, Gonzalo. 1996. "Una experiencia de desburocratización: El municipio de Montevideo durante la transición a la democracia." *Cuadernos del CLAEH* 76:93–106.

Vázquez, Tabaré. 2005. "Discurso íntegro del presidente Tabaré Vázquez en el acto realizado en el Palacio Legislativo." March 2. http://www.observa.com.uy/ Obuscar/notaarchivo.aspx ?id=29432.

Veiga, Danilo. 1989. "Segregación socioeconómica y crisis urbana en Montevideo." In *Las ciudades en conflicto: Una perspectiva latinoamericana,* edited by Mario Lombardi and Danilo Veiga. Montevideo: CIESU and Ediciones de la Banda Oriental.

Ventura Egoávil, José. 2004a. "Estudio de caso: Huaccana-Chincheros, Perú." Lima: World Bank Institute.

———. 2004b. "Estudio de caso: Limatambo-Cuzco, Perú." Lima: World Bank Institute.

Verba, Sidney, Kay Lehman Schlozman, and Henry Brady. 1995. *Voice and Equality: Civic Voluntarism in American Politics.* Cambridge: Harvard University Press.

Verle, João, and Paulo Müzell. 1994. "Receita e capacidade de investimento da Prefeitura Municipal de Porto Alegre, 1973–92." In *Porto Alegre: O desafio da mudança,* edited by Carlos Henrique Horn. Porto Alegre: Editora Ortiz.

Villa, Miguel, and Jorge Rodríguez. 1996. "Demographic Trends in Latin America's Metropolises, 1950–1990." In *The Mega-City in Latin America,* edited by Alan Gilbert. New York: United Nations University Press.

Violich, Francis, with Robert Daughters. 1987. *Urban Planning for Latin America: The Challenge of Metropolitan Growth.* Boston: Oelgeschlager, Gunn and Hain.

Walton, John. 1989. "Debt, Protest, and the State in Latin America." In *Power and Popular Protest: Latin American Social Movements,* edited by Susan Eckstein. Berkeley and Los Angeles: University of California Press.

Wampler, Brian. 2007a. *Participatory Budgeting in Brazil: Contestation, Cooperation, and Accountability.* University Park: Pennsylvania State University Press.

———. 2007b. "Can Participatory Institutions Promote Pluralism? Mobilizing Low-Income Citizens in Brazil." *Studies in Comparative International Development* 41 (4): 57–78.

Wampler, Brian, and Leonardo Avritzer. 2004. "Participatory Publics: Civil Society and New Institutions in Democratic Brazil." *Comparative Politics* 36 (3): 291–312.

Waylen, Georgina. 1994. "Women and Democratization: Conceptualizing Gender Relations in Transition Politics." *World Politics* 46 (3): 327–54.

Weffort, Francisco. 1989. "Why Democracy?" In *Democratizing Brazil: Problems of Transition and Consolidation,* edited by Alfred Stepan. New York: Oxford University Press.

Weissberg, Robert. 2006. "Politicized Pseudo Science." *PS: Political Science and Politics* 39 (1): 33–37.

Wikander, Cynthia. 1994. "Participación ciudadana: Análisis de dos experiencias en los Municipios Libertador y Baruta." Mimeograph. Fundación Escuela de Gerencia Social. Caracas. June.

Willis, Eliza, Christopher Garman, and Stephan Haggard. 1999. "The Politics of Decentralization in Latin America." *Latin American Research Review* 34 (1): 7–56.

Winn, Peter. 1995. "Frente Amplio in Montevideo." *NACLA: Report on the Americas* 29 (1): 20–26.

Woolcock, Michael. 1998. "Social Capital and Economic Development: Toward a Theoretical Synthesis and Policy Framework." *Theory and Society* 27 (2): 151–208.

World Bank. 1997. *Venezuela: Decentralized Provision of Urban Services: Finding the Right Incentives.* Washington, D.C.: World Bank.

World Bank Institute. 2004a. "Condiciones del marco nacional para los procesos de preparación de presupuestos subnacionales en Guatemala." Guatemala: World Bank Institute.

———. 2004b. "Experiencias de participación cívica en políticas y procesos de preparación de presupuestos municipales en Curahuara de Carangas." La Paz: World Bank Institute.

Zabalza, Jorge. 1998. *La estaca.* Montevideo: Ediciones del Cerro.

Zakaria, Fareed. 2003. *The Future of Freedom: Illiberal Democracy at Home and Abroad.* New York: W. W. Norton.

Zibechi, Raúl. 2008. "La 'descentralización participativa' cumple 15 años." *Brecha.* August 13.

Ziccardi, Alicia, ed. 1991. *Ciudades y gobiernos locales en la América Latina de los noventa.* Mexico City: FLACSO, Instituto Mora, and Grupo Editorial M. A. Porrúa.

Zimmerman, Joseph. 1986. *Participatory Democracy: Populism Revived.* New York: Praeger.

Index

Abers, Rebecca, 32 n. 14, 39 n. 10, 61 n.
  50, 64 n. 54, 69 n. 58, 188 n. 26, 197,
  244–45
Acción Democrática (AD), 43, 64, 76–77,
  77 n. 68, 82, 84, 92–98, 101, 108–20,
  222–23
Acción Popular, 260
accountability, 1, 18, 24, 80, 192, 195, 200,
  236
activists and activism, 10, 32, 38, 62, 83, 116,
  130 n. 9
  Catholic, 55, 55 n. 39, 115
  La Causa Radical, 221, 222 n. 2
  neighborhood, 55, 61, 75–76, 92, 108–9,
  126, 137–39, 151, 158, 167–82, 194 n.
  32, 243, 245
  NGO, 188
Advisory Unit for Special Projects.
  See Unidad Asesora de Proyectos
  Especiales (UAPE)
Afro-Brazilians, 49, 202
Afro-Uruguayans, 49, 154 n. 36
Afro-Venezuelans, 50, 109, 109 n. 27
Alianza Popular Revolucionaria Americana
  (APRA), 249, 260
Alvarez, Ana, 112 n. 31, 113
American Popular Revolutionary Alliance.
  See Alianza Popular Revolucionaria
  Americana (APRA)
anti-neoliberal, 9, 44 n. 22
Arana, Mariano, 60, 132 n. 11, 137 n. 17,
  139, 152 n. 32, 163, 163 n. 43, 225 n. 4,
  226, 231
Argentina, 3, 35, 253, 261–62
Asamblea Uruguay, 41 n. 16, 163 n. 43
Asociación de Empleados y Obreros
  Municipales (ADEOM), 131, 131 n. 10
Association of Municipal Employees and
  Workers. *See* Asociación de Empleados
  y Obreros Municipales (ADEOM)
Augustin, Arno, 173, 178
authoritarian regime, 4, 4 n. 3, 28, 28 n. 12,
  38, 41, 43, 49–52, 55, 57, 60, 67–68,

68 n. 56, 76–80, 111, 154 n. 36, 183,
  233, 241, 243, 247
authority, 7–8, 15–16, 19, 26–27, 66, 70,
  72, 82, 92, 97–102, 105, 107, 111, 128,
  136, 141, 144, 220, 249
Avritzer, Leonardo, 24
ayllu, 258–59

Baierle, Sérgio, 60 n. 48, 64, 203 n. 34
Baiocchi, Gianpaolo, 24, 36 n. 5, 244–45
Baraibar, Carlos, 129–30
Barber, Benjamin, 12–14
barrio, 43 n. 21, 50, 57–58, 85, 89 n. 8, 94,
  103–7, 110–15
Barrio Sur (Montevideo), 49, 154 n. 36
black populations, 49–50, 109, 109 n. 27,
  154 n. 36, 202
Blanco, Carlos, 97
Blancos. *See* National Party (Blancos)
Bohn Gass, Waldir, 172, 184–85
Bolivarian Revolution, 9, 43 n. 21, 118, 250
Bolivia, 253, 255–59, 261–62
Borja, Jordi, 15, 32
Braselli, Selva, 133
Braz, Luiz, 190, 190 n. 29
Brazilian Democratic Movement. *See* Movi-
  mento Democrático Brasileiro (MDB)
Brazilian Labor Party. *See* Partido Trabalhista
  Brasileiro (PTB)
Brazilian Progressive Party. *See* Partido
  Progressista Brasileiro (PPB)
Brazilian Social Democratic Party. *See* Partido
  da Social Democracia Brasileira (PSDB)
Brizola, Leonel, 51, 80–81
Broad Front. *See* Frente Amplio, FA

cabildos abiertos, 85–86
Caldera, Rafael, 117 n. 41
Canel, Eduardo, 56, n. 40, 59
Canelones, 231
Caracas, 2, 6–10, 23, 34–36, 36 n. 6,
  43–50, 52–59, 61–68, 71–77, 82–122,
  138 n. 21, 219–24, 237–39, 245–54

Caracazo (riots), 4, 44, 55, 59, 111, 115
Caraqueños, 72, 98
Cárdenas, Francisco Arias, 117 n. 40
Cardoso, Fernando Henrique, 189–90
CARE-Peru, 257–58
cargos, 258–59
Carris (municipal bus company), 234
Castañeda, Jorge, 5
Catholic Church, 38, 55, 55 n. 39, 58–62, 88,
    125, 200, 257
Catuche Consortium, 89, 89 n. 8, 94, 105
Causa Radical. See La Causa Radical (LCR)
Center for Information and Study of
    Uruguay. See Centro de Informaciones
    y Estudios del Uruguay (CIESU)
Center for Research and Cultural Develop-
    ment. See Centro de Investigaciones y
    Desarrollo Cultural (CIDC)
Center in Service of Popular Action. See
    Centro al Servicio de al Acción Popular
    (CESAP)
Centro Administrativo Regional (CARs),
    179, 193, 195
Centro al Servicio de al Acción Popular
    (CESAP), 58, 85 n. 1, 88, 105, 223
Centro Assessoria Multi Profissional
    (CAMP), 61
Centro de Informaciones y Estudios del
    Uruguay (CIESU), 59
Centro de Investigaciones y Desarrollo
    Cultural (CIDC), 59
Centro Gumilla, 58
Centros Comunales Zonales (CCZs), 123–26,
    127 n. 7, 129–30, 130 n. 8, 134–36,
    138 n. 21, 139–43, 149–52, 154, 230,
    240–42
Charão, Iria, 168 n. 3
Chavez, Daniel, 36 n. 5, 148 nn. 29, 31, 158
    n. 39
Chávez, Hugo, 9, 30, 43 n. 21, 44, 46, 95
    n. 19, 118, 118 n. 43, 246, 250, 261,
    263–64, 264 n. 11
Chile, 3, 18 n. 9, 261–62
Christian Democrats (Uruguay), 41, 41 n.
    15–16
Christian Democrats (Venezuela), 52. See
    also Comité de Organización Politica
    Electroral Independiente (Copei)
Citizen Power Councils, 264
citizenship, strengthening, 13, 23–24, 36 n.
    3, 219–20, 237–46
Ciudad Guayana, 35, 44 n. 23
Ciudad Vieja (Montevideo), 49
civic engagement, 12, 24

civic associations, 2, 8–9, 23, 27–28, 237–46
class, social, 4, 6, 37, 52, 52 n. 34, 57–58, 78,
    92 n. 16, 94, 103, 107–11, 118, 145 n.
    26, 167, 200–205, 208, 229, 251, 257
clientelism, 7, 13, 21, 30, 62–65, 78, 90,
    108, 236–37, 239, 255, 257, 260,
    263–64
Collares, Alceu, 64, 81, 81 n. 75–76, 167,
    184, 235
collective action, 27, 30, 191, 198–215
Collor, Fernando, 80
Colombia, 1, 3, 18 n. 9, 35, 261–62
Colorado Party, 41–42, 69, 77–79, 82,
    127–133, 132 n. 11, 135–37, 139, 162,
    224–26, 230–31, 241, 251
Comité de Organización Política Electoral
    Independiente (Copei), 43, 64, 76–77,
    92, 96–97, 113, 115
Communal Councils, 251, 263–64
Communist Party (Uruguay), 41, 131, 240–41
Communist Party (Venezuela), 43
Communist Party of Brazil. See Partido
    Comunista da Brasil (PC do B)
community movement, 37, 43, 55–56,
    59–61, 115 n. 36, 122, 137, 163, 169–73,
    176–79, 216, 232
Compañía Anónima Nacional Teléfonos de
    Venezuela (CANTV), 68, 101
Comunidade Eclesial de Base (CEB), 59
conservatives, 32 n. 14, 78, 80 n. 73, 131, 135,
    183, 185, 235
Constitution of 1988 (Brazil), 66, 68–69,
    69 n. 58, 166, 189
Contreras, Carlos, 94–95, 110–11, 111 n. 30
Contreras, Juan, 108
Convergencia Socialista, 38 n. 8
Convergencia, 96
Coppedge, Michael, 76–77
Coraggio, José Luis, 18
Corporation for Municipal Services, 90, 90
    n. 11
corruption, 1, 13, 18, 21, 62–65, 221, 223–24,
    231, 231 n. 17, 235–36, 239, 255, 259,
    265
Council for Economic and Social Develop-
    ment (Brazil), 264
crime, 71–72, 86, 89 n. 8, 90, 101, 110, 143,
    225, 228, 228 n. 11, 230
Curahuara de Carangas, 257–59

da Silva, Luiz Inácio Lula, 9, 251–52, 261,
    264–65
Dahl, Robert, 14
de Soto, Hernando, 15

decentralization
   administrative, 15
   adversaries of, 19–20
   degree of national, 66–73
   economic, 15
   FA and, 42
   indicators, 74
   LCR and, 45, 45 n. 24
   and participation, 16–23
   political, 2, 15
   pragmatic advocates for, 17–18
   PT and, 40
   radical advocates for, 18–19
   skeptics of, 21–22
   types of, 15–16
   stages of, 16
   See also participatory decentralization
      (Montevideo)
deconcentration, 15–16, 42, 227
Democracia Socialista (DS), 168, 170
democracy
   deepening of, 1–2, 5–6, 11–16, 19, 21,
      39–40, 42, 45, 219–20, 245–49, 251,
      254, 257, 260 61, 265–66
   democratization, 23, 39–40, 42, 68
   See also participatory democracy
Democratic Action. See Acción Democrática
   (AD)
Democratic Labor Party. See Partido
   Democrático Trabalhista (PDT)
deprivatization, 40
devolution, 15–16, 25, 139
Dib, João, 183–84, 231 n. 18
dictatorship. See authoritarian regime
Doimo, Ana Maria, 28
Domínguez, Ricardo, 129, 137
Dominican Republic, 253, 266
double simultaneous vote, 70 n. 62
dual power strategy, 19
Dutra, Olívio, 9, 38–40, 166–70, 177–79,
   186–88, 217, 235, 251–52

Ecclesial/Christian Base Community. See
   Comunidade Eclesial de Base (CEB)
economic crisis, 3, 51, 59, 60, 155, 167
Ecuador, 261–62
education, 4, 17, 19, 52, 59, 61–63, 71, 86,
   101, 143, 154, 159 n. 40, 163–64, 174,
   181, 196, 200–201, 225, 227, 232–33,
   239
Ehrlich, Ricardo, 251
El Salvador, 1, 261
elections, 3, 5–6, 13–15, 38–45, 61–62
   in Brazil, 3, 38–39, 61, 68, 79–81, 251–52

FA and, 3, 40–42, 122, 130, 139, 161, 163,
   251
   LCR and, 43–45, 77, 87, 91, 96, 116–19,
      221, 224, 250
   PT and, 38–39, 168, 187, 190, 217,
      251–52
   in Uruguay, 3, 41–42, 69–70, 78, 128,
      139, 152–53, 163, 251
   in Venezuela, 3, 57–59, 58 n. 45, 67,
      76–77, 87, 96, 116–19, 250
electricity, 52–54, 78, 90, 208, 222, 259
elites, 14, 21–22, 167, 183, 191, 231, 262
empowerment, 15, 24, 29, 204
Encuentro Progresista, 41 n. 16
Escuela de Vecinos, 57–58, 76 n. 67
Estado Novo, 51, 68
Evans, Peter, 24–27, 29, 31

favela, 50
Federação de Orgãos para Assistência Social
   e Educacional (FASE), 61, 172 n. 10,
   176 n. 14
Federação Riograndense de Associações
   Comunitárias e de Amigos de Bairros
   (FRACAB), 60–61, 82
Federación de Asociaciones de
   Comunidades Urbanas (FACUR),
   56–58, 76 n. 67, 77, 223
Federación Uruguaya de Cooperativas de
   Vivienda de Ayuda Mútua (FUCVAM),
   59–60, 79
federal government. See national government
Federal of Social and Education Assistance
   Organizations. See Federação de Orgãos
   para Assistência Social e Educacional
   (FASE)
federalism, 45, 66–68
Federation of Community and
   Neighborhood Associations of
   Rio Grande do Sul. See Federação
   Riograndense de Associações
   Comunitárias e de Amigos de Bairros
   (FRACAB)
Federation of Urban Community
   Associations. See Federación de
   Asociaciones de Comunidades Urbanas
   (FACUR)
Fedozzi, Luciano, 64, 180 n. 17, 182 n. 19,
   185
Fermín, Claudio, 76, 118, 223
Fernandez, Miguel, 134
Fishkin, James, 12
Fogaça, José, 252
Francke, Marfil, 101, 238–39

Frente Amplio (FA), 2, 6, 8, 32, 35, 35 n. 2,
    37–38, 74, 74 n. 66, 79, 121–23, 129–30,
    132–39, 152–53, 155, 158, 160, 162–63,
    219–20, 224–31, 248, 251, 265
  history of, 40–42
  See also participatory decentralization
    (Montevideo); Vázquez, Tabaré
Fung, Archon, 12, 24, 24 n. 11

Gabinete de Planejamento (GAPLAN), 168
    n. 3, 179–82, 182 n. 19, 195, 204 n.
    35, 217
garbage collection, 53, 72, 112, 124, 143, 222,
    224–25, 228, 229, 234–35
"gaúcho model," 51, 200
gaúchos, 51 n. 33, 254
gender, 6, 55, 60, 108–9, 109 n. 27, 154, 163,
    200, 202, 204, 253. See also women
Genro, Tarso, 39, 174, 187–90, 217, 252
Gómez, Juan Vicente, 57, 67
González, Mariana, 241–42
Guatemala, 253, 255–57

Hackenbruch, Tabaré, 231 n. 17
Harnecker, Marta, 34 n. 1, 35 n. 2, 41 n. 13,
    131 n. 10, 186 n. 23, 223
health care, 4, 35, 71, 101, 115, 115 n. 35,
    143–44, 172, 174, 227, 232–34
Hidrocapital, 53, 53 n. 35, 68, 101, 114, 116
Highly Indebted Poor Countries (HIPC),
    256, 258
Hohlfelt, Antônio, 231 n. 18, 236–37
Homeland for All. See Patria Para Todos (PPT)
housing, 35, 38, 48, 51–52, 60, 122, 125,
    143–44, 173, 173 n. 11, 181, 189, 196,
    209 n. 37, 224
  cooperatives, 41, 56, 59, 126, 145 n. 26, 227
  irregular, 53–54, 54 n. 37, 227
  homeless, 200
  laws and policies, 49, 226–27, 227 n. 9
  public, 50, 50 n. 30, 71, 111–12, 159–60 n.
    40, 208, 222, 227, 232–33
Huaccana, 257–59
Huntington, Samuel, 14 n. 3, 19–20, 23,
    73, 248

ideology, 3–6, 9–10, 15, 22, 37–38, 41–44,
    51, 62, 107, 219, 247, 249, 254–55, 265
Iglesias, Maria Cristina, 35 n. 2, 93 n. 17
Ilo, 260
import-substitution industrialization (ISI)
    model, 3
income, 3, 53, 64–65, 92 n. 16, 154, 167,
    200–202, 204, 227

Independent Organizational Committee
    for Electoral Politics. See Comité
    de Organización Politica Electroral
    Independiente (Copei)
indigenous, 257–61, 263
inequality, 3, 12, 14, 18, 20–21, 51, 53, 248
inflation, 3, 39, 60, 167
Inter-American Development Bank (IADB),
    226
international development organizations
    and donors, 1, 17, 20, 247, 253, 265
Istúriz, Aristóbulo
  Acción Democrática and, 92–97, 117–18
  Chávez and, 9, 43 n. 21, 44
  condemnation of Pérez administration,
    117 n. 41
  elected mayor of Caracas, 44–45, 85
  failed reelection bid of, 116–18, 250
  parish government program of, 86, 88–89,
    100–103, 107, 109, 111–12, 114–16,
    238–39
  reforms and, 89–92
  transparency and, 221–24
investment spending, 51–52, 88 n. 4, 103–7,
    145, 173–82, 189–96, 208–17, 230,
    234, 243, 252, 256–62
Izquierda Unida, 19 n. 10, 32, 249, 260

Jansen, Armando, 85–86 n. 1, 223, 239
Jefferson, Thomas, 17
juntas parroquiales, 86. See also parish
    government program

Karl, Terry Lynn, 91
Keck, Margaret, 38 n. 7
KGB, 130

La Calle es de los Niños, 89, 89 n. 8
La Casa del Agua Mansa, 43
La Causa Radical (LCR), 2, 6, 8, 32, 35, 35
    n. 2, 37–38, 74, 74 n. 66, 77, 85–87,
    91–92, 96, 108–9, 112, 116–19, 118 n.
    42, 138 n. 21, 219, 246, 248, 250
  history of, 43–45
  See also Istúriz, Aristóbulo; parish
    government program (Caracas)
La Teja (Montevideo), 59, 242 n. 30
Lacalle, Luis Alberto, 128, 130–31
Ladinos, 257, 259–60
Lanza, Aquiles, 224 n. 3
Latin America, 3, 5, 9–13, 18, 21, 23, 25, 32,
    46–48, 51, 54, 62, 65–66, 78, 247–255,
    261, 264
Ledezma, António, 117, 119

Left, political parties of
  in Brazil, 256
  factionalism and, 32, 168, 170, 186, 248,
    250–51
  ideology of, 4–6, 19, 37, 247, 261–66
  local elections and, 1–4, 261
  national governments of, 9–10, 247–48,
    250, 253, 261–66
  participatory programs and, 1–6, 11,
    28–30, 32, 247–52, 254, 256, 260–66
  in Uruguay, 40–41s
  in Venezuela, 111, 250
  See also individual parties
Liberal Front Party. See Partido da Frente
    Liberal (PFL)
liberation theology, 55, 55 n. 39, 60, 115
Lima, 26, 32, 35, 249, 260
Limatambo, 257, 259–61
Listre, Julio, 126, 151
López Maya, Margarita, 43 n. 20, 56 n. 40,
    58 n. 44, 96 n. 22

Macarao y Su Gente, 95, 95 n. 20, 115
Maluf, Paulo, 249
Maneiro, Alfredo, 43, 43 n. 21, 45
Manor, James, 14 n. 3, 22
Mansbridge, Jane, 21
Martínez, Alirio, 89–91, 92 n. 16, 102, 107
Matancero (union movement), 43
Mattos, Carlos, 21
Medina, Pablo, 43 n. 21, 44, 44 n. 22, 118
    n. 42
Mello, Sebastião, 80 n. 74, 183–84, 231, 231
    n. 18
Mexico, 1, 3, 47, 58, 249, 253, 261–62
Mexico City, 47, 58, 249, 261
middle class, 4, 57–58, 92 n. 16, 94, 110–11,
    118, 201, 204, 229, 251
Mill, John Stuart, 17
mistis, 257
Mixed Commission (Montevideo), 132–39
Montero, Alfred, 69
Montes, Julio, 90, 107
Montevideo, 2, 6–10, 23, 34–36, 36 n.
    6, 41–42, 46–56, 59–66, 69–79,
    82–83, 121–64, 219–21, 224–31,
    237, 239–42, 245–46, 248–49, 251,
    265
Montevideo in Forum, 132–37
Montevideo in Forum II, 146, 150, 155
Montevideo Neighborhood Movement. See
    Movimiento de Vecinos de Montevideo
    (MOVEMO)
Morales, Reinaldo, 97

Movement for Decent Housing. See
    Movimiento Pro–Vivienda Decorosa
    (MOVIDE)
Movement for Popular Participation. See
    Movimiento de Participación Popular
    (MPP)
Movimiento Democrático Brasileiro (MDB),
    68 n. 56, 79
Movimiento al Socialismo (MAS), 117 n. 40
Movimiento Bolivariano Revolucionario, 118
Movimiento de Participación Popular
    (MPP), 41 n. 15, 138 n. 20, 163
Movimiento de Vecinos de Montevideo
    (MOVEMO), 59–60
Movimiento Pro–Vivienda Decorosa
    (MOVIDE), 59–60
Movimiento Revolucionario Oriental, 41
    n. 15
Moynihan, Daniel, 19–20, 23
Multiprofessional Consulting Center. See
    Centro Assessoria Multi Profissional
    (CAMP)
Myers, David, 52

National Economic Council (Uruguay), 264
national government, 9, 27, 84, 228, 253,
    257–58, 261, 265–66
  in Brazil, 66, 68, 178, 202
  decentralization and, 15, 57, 66–67
  in Peru, 19 n. 10
  in Uruguay, 69, 130–32, 132 n. 12, 144,
    148–49, 162
  in Venezuela, 68, 112
National Party (Blancos), 41–42, 69, 77–79,
    127–28, 130 n. 9, 131–33, 135–36, 138 n.
    20, 139, 162, 251
Neighborhood Confederation. See União de
    Vilas
neighborhood associations, 32, 36–37, 53 n.
    35, 54–62, 60 n. 49, 75–82, 87–88,
    93–95, 110–14, 115 n. 35, 120, 125 n.
    3–4, 128, 130, 130 n. 9, 131, 141, 155, 171,
    184, 186, 192–93, 200, 237–45, 259
neoliberalism, 3, 18, 42, 253 n. 2
Nicaragua, 253, 255–57, 261, 263–64
Nickson, Andrew, 62, 64–65, 72 n. 63
Nieto, Josefina, 97
Nuevo Espacio, 41 n. 15, 42 n. 17
Nuñez, Tarson, 168 n. 3, 170 nn. 6–7, 186
Nylen, William, 12, 24, 32, 39 n. 9

O'Donnell, Guillermo, 23
opposition parties, 7–8, 10, 30, 32, 32 n. 14,
    34, 36, 36–37 n. 6, 62, 66, 73–82, 84,

87, 92–93, 95 n. 21, 97, 108, 112–13,
    118, 120–22, 127–39, 152, 162, 165–67,
    177, 182–86, 189–91, 216, 219, 221,
    231, 238, 252, 254, 257–64
orçamento participativo, 169, 169 n. 5. *See
    also* participatory budgeting
Organic Law of the Municipal Regime, 87
    n. 3
Ortuño, Edgardo, 154 n. 36
OXFAM, 258

Pact of Punto Fijo, 96, 250
Panizza, Francisco, 78
Paraguay, 261–62
parish government program (Caracas)
    Acción Democrática and, 82, 84, 92–98,
        101, 108–20
    beginnings of, 85–89
    decision-making power and, 102–5
    design of, 98–105
    participation and, 105–20
    range and, 101–2
    structure of, 98–101
Parteli, Carlos, 55 n. 39, 59
participation
    debates over, 16–23, 168–70
    design of, 8, 25, 30–31
    implementing and sustaining, 26–33
    politics of, 2, 25, 29–33, 37, 251
    rates of, 7–10, 31, 84–85, 105–16, 121–22,
        125–26, 150–56, 161–62, 176–77,
        187–91, 198–217, 240, 246, 251–52,
        255, 258–60, 263
    types of, 12, 14–15, 24–25
    See also decentralization and, participatory
        budgeting, participatory decentraliza-
        tion, parish government program
participatory budgeting (PB, Porto Alegre),
    2, 7, 9–10, 25, 35 n. 2, 36 n. 3, 82,
    165–210, 219–20, 231, 236–37, 243,
    247–66
    collective action problems and, 198–215
    decision-making power and, 196–98
    open design and, 8, 166, 191, 198–99,
        204, 208, 216, 219, 243, 248, 254, 246,
        260–61
    opinion polls on, 197–98
    participation and, 168–91
    range of, 195–96
    structure of, 195
participatory budgeting
    in Bolivia, 255–59, 262
    in Brazil, 249, 255–57, 265
    in the Dominican Republic, 253, 266

in Ecuador, 262
in Latin America, 10, 247, 253–61,
    265–66
in Peru, 253, 255–60, 266
in Uruguay, 251, 265
participatory decentralization (Montevideo),
    121–22, 162–63, 220, 230
    crisis of participation, 150–62
    decision–making power and, 145–50
    original design of, 122–27
    range and, 142–44
    regulated design and, 139–50
    structure of, 140–42
participatory democracy, 2, 9–11, 20–21, 30,
    35, 45, 58, 246–53, 261–66
Partido Comunista da Brasil (PC do B), 172,
    172 n. 9
Partido da Frente Liberal (PFL), 39, 80 n. 73
Partido da Reconstrução Nacional, 80
Partido da Social Democracia Brasileira
    (PSDB), 231 n. 18, 237
Partido Democrático Trabalhista (PDT),
    80–81, 167, 172, 184, 190
Partido do Movimento Democrático
    Brasileiro (PMDB), 39, 80–81, 183–85,
    196–97 n. 24, 231
Partido dos Trabalhadores (PT), 2, 5–9, 5
    n. 4, 19 n. 10, 32, 35, 35 n. 2, 37–40,
    74–75, 74 n. 66, 82, 138 n. 21, 165–72,
    177, 183–87, 190–91, 203, 217, 219,
    231, 235, 248–49, 251–52, 256, 265
    history of, 38–40
    institutionalization of, 74–75
Partido Progressista Brasileiro (PPB), 183,
    231 n. 18
Partido Republicano Riograndense (PRR),
    51
Partido Trabalhista Brasileiro (PTB), 81, 190
party institutionalization, 7–10, 14, 33–35,
    36–37 n. 6, 66, 73–84, 121–22,
    126–27, 132–33, 162, 165–67, 182,
    191, 216, 219–21, 249–50, 154,
    257–61
Party for the Government of the People
    (PGP), 41 nn. 15–16
Party of the Brazilian Democratic
    Movement. *See* Partido do Movimento
    Democrático Brasileiro (PMDB)
Patria Para Todos (PPT), 44 n. 22, 118 n. 42,
    250–51
peasants, 38, 258–59
Percovich, Margarita, 55 n. 39
Pérez Jiménez, Marcos, 43, 50, 50 n. 30, 57,
    76, 111

Pérez, Carlos Andrés, 44, 56, 56 n. 40, 58, 77, 117 n. 41
Peronists, 262
Peru, 1, 3, 19 n. 10, 249, 253, 255–60, 266
Pinto, Raúl, 95 n. 20, 108
Planning Cabinet. *See* Gabinete de Planejamento (GAPLAN)
Plato, 19
Plenario de Mujeres del Uruguay (PLEMUU), 55 n. 39, 60
police, 71, 90, 101, 113, 228
political parties, 8, 26, 29–32, 35, 55, 62, 65, 68 n. 56, 76–86, 92, 107, 128–30, 142, 200, 240, 247, 250, 253, 256–60, 263. *See also individual political parties*; Left, political parties of; Right, political parties of
Pont, Raul, 187, 190, 190 n. 27
poor
  people, 3–4, 18 n. 8, 21–22, 37, 39, 51, 92 n. 16, 126, 153–54, 161, 163, 204
  neighborhoods, 13, 78, 111, 118–19, 174–75, 186, 229, 231, 257
  See also poverty
Popular Participation Movement. *See* Movimiento de Participación Popular (MPP)
populism and populists, 3, 6, 51, 81, 237
Portillo, Alvaro, 63, 136, 140
Porto Alegre, 2, 6–10, 23, 25, 34–36, 36 n. 6, 38–40, 46–56, 60–66, 68–76, 80–83, 165–217, 219–21, 231–37, 242–49, 251–54, 260, 265–66
Porto Alegrenses, 81, 187 n. 25, 190 n. 28, 198, 203, 208, 236
positivism, 51
poverty, 3–4, 18 n. 8, 21–22, 46, 51, 53–54, 104 n. 25, 145 n. 26, 154, 159–63, 175, 182 n. 20, 203–4, 255, 257
Prag (student movement), 43
privatization, 15–18, 21, 44 n. 22. *See also* deprivatization
Pro-Catia (community movement), 43, 58, 58 n. 44
progressives, 6–7, 33, 38, 51, 55 n. 39, 58–59, 62–63, 120, 183, 249
protests, cycles of, 54–56
public assemblies, 6, 14, 32 n. 13, 36, 43, 46, 85–90, 95, 95 n. 21, 98–100, 103, 110–13, 117 n. 38, 120 n. 45, 121–25, 132 n. 11, 142, 146–47, 152–58, 161–63, 169–73, 176, 179–81, 184–92, 195, 199–218, 220, 236–37, 243, 256, 258–60

public transportation, 233–34
Putnam, Robert, 12, 23–24, 27, 248

Quadros, Jânio, 249
Quércia, Orestes, 249

race, 6, 49–50, 109, 109 n. 27, 154 n. 36, 202
Radical Cause. *See* La Causa Radical (LCR)
redistribution, 5, 24, 104, 161, 182, 255
Regent, Susana, 128, 141
regional administrative centers. *See* Centro Administrativo Regional (CARs)
regression analyses, 160, 160 n. 41, 161, 213
responsiveness, 2, 12–13, 22–24, 220–25, 230–31, 246, 251, 255
Revello, Rosario, 141 n. 23, 152, 157 n. 38
revolution, 6, 19, 19 n. 10, 38, 95 n. 19, 167–68, 170
Right, political parties of, 39, 81 n. 67, 252–61
Rio Grande do Sul, 9, 38, 46, 51, 60, 80, 217, 236, 251, 254
riots. *See* Caracazo
Roberts, Kenneth, 13, 13 n. 2
Rondinelli, Dennis, 17
Rosario, 262
Rousseau, Jean-Jacques, 17
Rozas, Wilber, 259–261
rural areas and population, 3, 38, 47–48, 69, 78, 123 n. 2, 134 n. 14, 257, 259, 263, 265

Santana, Elías, 76 n. 67, 93–94, 223
Santos, Boaventura de Sousa, 24
São Paulo (city), 35, 39, 61, 236, 237, 249, 265
São Paulo Forum, 5, 5 n. 5, 35 n. 2
Schneider, Aaron, 46, 46 n. 25
Schönwalder, Gerd, 26, 28, 32
School for Neighbors. *See* Escuela de Vecinos
Schumpeter, Joseph, 19
Seregni, Líber, 41–42, 42 n. 17
sewage, 51–53, 71–72, 109, 114, 159, 159 n. 40, 159–60 n. 41, 173 n. 11, 182 n. 20, 204, 204 n. 35, 206, 213, 225–27, 232, 232 n. 19, 235, 255
shantytowns, 3, 40, 49, 59
Sindicato dos Municipários de Porto Alegre (SIMPA), 81
social capital, 23–24, 27–29, 248
social movements, 4–6, 27–29, 37–38, 43, 55–61, 82, 115 n. 36, 122, 137, 167–79, 222, 247, 253, 265

socialism, 5, 38, 41, 79, 167–69, 170 n. 7, 262
Socialist Democracy. *See* Democracia Socialista (DS)
Socialist Party (Chile), 262
Socialist Party (Uruguay), 41, 79, 79 n. 71, 163 n. 43
soup kitchens, 41, 56, 59–60, 154, 159–60 n. 40, 240
Soviet Union, 19 n. 10, 130, 241
Soviet model, 5–6, 168–70
state-society forums, 15–16, 19, 28–29
Steffen, Marlene, 185
strategy, 2, 19, 21, 25, 29–33, 43 n. 21, 45, 86, 132, 138, 168, 179, 188, 255
Street Is for the Children, The. *See* La Calle es de los Niños
student groups, 38, 41, 43, 58, 169
synergy, 24, 27, 29

Tocqueville, Alexis de, 17
Toromaina Coordinator, 112–13
transparency, 2, 12–13, 23, 39, 45, 64, 220–38, 246, 251, 255, 259–60, 263, 266
trash collection. *See* garbage collection
Treisman, Daniel, 22
tugúrio, 51, 54
Tupamaros, 41, 41 n. 15, 135 n. 15
tyranny, 11, 20, 30–31, 248

unemployment, 3, 46, 50, 53–54, 60
União de Associações de Moradores de Porto Alegre (UAMPA), 61, 81–82, 171–73, 184–85, 244, 245 n. 31
União de Vilas, 243–44
Unidad Asesora de Proyectos Especiales (UAPE), 78–79
Union of Municipal Workers of Porto Alegre. *See* Sindicato dos Municipários de Porto Alegre (SIMPA)
Union of Residents Associations of Porto Alegre. *See* União de Associações de Moradores de Porto Alegre (UAMPA)
unions, 3–6, 32, 37–38, 41–44, 61, 65, 76–78, 88, 93–94, 120, 167–72, 186–88, 200, 220, 222, 251, 260, 264–65. *See also* individual unions
United Left. *See* Izquierda Unida
United Nations, 17, 36 n. 3, 165, 190, 247, 253
United States, 12, 15, 20–21, 24, 46
urban economic crises, 3–4, 6, 50–54
urban growth patterns, 46–54

urban involution, 51, 63
Uruguayan Federation of Mutual Aid Housing Cooperatives. *See* Federación Uruguaya de Cooperativas de Viviendas por Ayuda Mutua (FUCVAM)
Uruguayan Women's Assembly. *See* Plenario de Mujeres del Uruguay (PLEMUU)
USAID, 17
Uzcátegui, Rafael, 58 n. 44, 89 n. 8

Vargas, Getúlio, 51, 81
Vázquez, Tabaré, 9, 41–42, 79 n. 71, 122–24, 126–33, 137 n. 17, 139, 163, 225 n. 4, 226–27, 231, 242 n. 30, 246, 251, 261, 264–65
Frente Amplio and, 122–24
Velázquez, Andrés, 43–44, 44 n. 22, 118 n. 42
Venezuelan National Telephone Company. *See* Compañía Anónima Nacional Teléfonos de Venezuela (CANTV)
Verle, João, 167
Vertiente Artiguista, 41 n. 16, 163 n. 43
vila, 50, 82, 175, 208–9, 243–44
Villa El Salvador, 260

Wampler, Brian, 25, 27, 29–30, 235, 255–56
water, 52–53, 53 n. 35, 71–72, 101, 104 n. 25, 114–16, 159 n. 40, 222, 226 n. 7, 260
women, 38, 55, 55, n. 39, 58–62, 108–9, 109 n. 27, 154–55, 164, 202, 227, 240, 258–59
workers, 3, 31–33, 37–38, 42–43, 62–65, 75–76, 93–95, 122–24, 167–68, 170–72, 186–88, 230, 236, 251
CCZ, 124–26, 138, 146, 151, 242
factory, 115
preretired, 89, 89 n. 9
social, 87–89, 100, 109–10, 124, 126, 142, 157, 238
technical cabinet, 87, 94, 94 n. 18, 98, 106–8, 111, 116
See also individual unions; unions
Workers' Party. *See* Partido dos Trabalhadores (PT)
World Bank, 18 n. 8, 247, 253
World Social Forum, 9, 246
Wright, Olin, 24

Zakaria, Fareed, 20, 248
Zelaya, Manuel, 266 n. 12
Zero Hora (newspaper), 185, 189
Zonal Community Centers. *See* Centros Comunales Zonales (CCZs)